AUTOMOBILE SPORT

82 83

FOREWORD

Having won at Le Mans in 1981, DEREK BELL wrote the Foreword for the very first edition of AUTOMOBILE SPORT. When he won the 24-Hour classic for the third time we were pleased to invite him back to introduce this 82 83 edition.

ANOTHER racing year has passed and once again it is my pleasure to write the foreword to Automobile Sport. I was delighted to see the success the first issue had and I am sure it bodes well for future years. It was refreshing to see that motor racing became the topic of the media in 1982, and not the politics we had been inflicted with previously.

As a sportscar driver I was pleasantly surprised to see so many Group C cars at Le Mans, perhaps a little disappointed that the grids were not so full elsewhere, although for a first season with a new formula it could be said that Group C has well and truly arrived. With alterations to the regs plus more cars to fill the grids, I can visualise stability entering the series in 1983.

After some tragic events, the Formula One Championship saw some exciting races as the title wasn't determined until the last race. In spite of the upsurge in turbo engine competitiveness, we all know what remarkable power plant the World Champion and runner up used — but what next year? Whatever changes are introduced into the regulations for next year, I do hope the accent is put on driver safety.

In rallying, the four-wheel-drive cars took some beating and no doubt this will lead to other manufacturers following the trend. Racing throughout the world seems to have achieved higher audience ratings than ever before. Here's hoping plenty of them will find Automobile Sport an inevitable purchase!

AUTOMOBILE SPORT

EDITOR
IAN BAMSEY

EUROPEAN EDITOR
PHILLIP BINGHAM

AMERICAN EDITOR
STEVE POTTER

PRODUCTION EDITOR
BRIAN LABAN

CHIEF PHOTOGRAPHER
KEITH SUTTON

As readers will be aware, motorsport at the highest level continues to face grave problems, particularly in the Grand Prix arena where political and safety problems seem ever worsening. Indeed, we have now reached a situation where a repeat of the 1955 Le Mans disaster could realistically occur at any of a number of Grand Prix circuits. Worryingly, so many vested interests influence the muddled political arena that effective regulation changes are long overdue. Ironically, perhaps there are so many of those vested interests *because* the sport is so well supported at the Grand Prix level. Worldwide interest in motorsport at all levels is as strong as ever it has been, even if the recession has cut grids and attendances at certain types of event. Worldwide recession or not, people around the globe remain enthusiastic about motorsport — there were even some in Russia who welcomed the thought of a Moscow Grand Prix! This continuing international interest meant that the first issue of Automobile Sport Yearbook was very well received, and it is pleasing to be able to report that from this edition onwards, the annual will be published by the Haynes Publishing Group of Somerset, England, and Los Angeles, California. I sincerely hope that the sport can quickly resolve the problems which threaten it and that automobile sport and Automobile Sport continue to prosper.

Ian Bamsey
Chiselborough, Somerset
October 1982

"Reading is to the mind is to the body."

Sir Richard Steele

On your marks......

GRAND PRIX
RACING

WORLD CHAMPIONSHIP OF DRIVERS

1950-1982

1950	Giuseppe Farina	Italy	Alfa Romeo
1951	Juan-Manuel Fangio	Argentina	Alfa Romeo
1952	Alberto Ascari	Italy	Ferrari
1953	Alberto Ascari	Italy	Ferrari
1954	Juan-Manuel Fangio	Argentina	Mercedes/Maserati
1955	Juan-Manuel Fangio	Argentina	Mercedes
1956	Juan-Manuel Fangio	Argentina	Lancia/Ferrari
1957	Juan-Manuel Fangio	Argentina	Maserati
1958	Mike Hawthorn	Great Britain	Ferrari
1959	Jack Brabham	Australia	Cooper-Climax
1960	Jack Brabham	Australia	Cooper-Climax
1961	Phil Hill	United States	Ferrari
1962	Graham Hill	Great Britain	BRM
1963	Jim Clark	Great Britain	Lotus-Climax
1964	John Surtees	Great Britain	Ferrari
1965	Jim Clark	Great Britain	Lotus-Climax
1966	Jack Brabham	Australia	Brabham-Repco
1967	Denny Hulme	New Zealand	Brabham-Repco
1968	Graham Hill	Great Britain	Lotus-Ford
1969	Jackie Stewart	Great Britain	Matra-Ford
1970	Jochen Rindt	Austria	Lotus-Ford
1971	Jackie Stewart	Great Britain	Tyrrell-Ford
1972	Emerson Fittipaldi	Brazil	Lotus-Ford
1973	Jackie Stewart	Great Britain	Tyrrell-Ford
1974	Emerson Fittipaldi	Brazil	McLaren-Ford
1975	Niki Lauda	Austria	Ferrari
1976	James Hunt	Great Britain	McLaren-Ford
1977	Niki Lauda	Austria	Ferrari
1978	Mario Andretti	United States	Lotus-Ford
1979	Jody Scheckter	South Africa	Ferrari
1980	Alan Jones	Australia	Williams-Ford
1981	Nelson Piquet	Brazil	Brabham-Ford
1982	Keke Rosberg	Finland	Williams-Ford

1982 World Champion, Keke Rosberg (above left) had to fight for his title right up to the last GP of the season while Ferrari (below left) salvaged the Constructors' title from a disastrous year. In 1966, Jack Brabham (below) won both championships.

Fangio (top) winning for Mercedes at Zandvoort in 1955. Cosworth (above) have now powered ten Constructors Champions.

WORLD CHAMPIONSHIP FOR FORMULA ONE CONSTRUCTORS

1958-1982

1958	Vanwall
1959	Cooper-Climax
1960	Cooper-Climax
1961	Ferrari
1962	BRM
1963	Lotus-Climax
1964	Ferrari
1965	Lotus-Climax
1966	Brabham-Repco
1967	Brabham-Repco
1968	Lotus-Ford
1969	Matra-Ford
1970	Lotus-Ford
1971	Tyrrell-Ford
1972	Lotus-Ford
1973	Lotus-Ford
1974	McLaren-Ford
1975	Ferrari
1976	Ferrari
1977	Ferrari
1978	Lotus-Ford
1979	Ferrari
1980	Williams-Ford
1981	Williams-Ford
1982	Ferrari

1982
GRAND PRIX DIARY

Paris, December '81: new FISA rules have reduced F1 weight limit, legalised 'fixed' skirts — but without hydropneumatic suspensions — and increased maximum number of cars to start in each GP. Frank Williams has described changes as 'a step in the right direction'.

Maranello, 8 January: first fruits of Harvey Postlethwaite's work at Ferrari have been unveiled as 126C2 was announced as successor to evil handling 126C. Two cars should be ready for Kyalami.

Kyalami, 23 January: season has opened in chaos following a drivers' strike over 'Super Licence' regs. Niki Lauda, back from retirement with a bang, led the action. Team managers' attitudes range from sympathy to extreme acrimony.

Buenos Aires, 3 February: the Argentine GP — scheduled for 7 March — has been cancelled. Rampant inflation is taking the blame!

Paris, 7 February: the Grand Prix Drivers Association has been disbanded and the Professional Racing Drivers Association formed — with membership open outside F1. Pironi is President and looks to have a thorny problem in dealing with FISA and M. Balestre.

Didcot, 1 March: the Williams team has announced that 1981 British F3 Champion Jonathan Palmer has been signed as a F1 test driver. Palmer has impressed mightily in driving a McLaren as part of his F3 prize and he is also to run the works Ralt-Honda in F2.

Marseilles, 4 March: Didier Pironi has survived unscathed in a massive testing accident at Paul Ricard. His 126C2 ended a 180mph flight in an unoccupied spectator area. People will watch from there at the Grand Prix and the implications are terrifying. The latest generation cars are causing concern even at such 'safe' circuits; as Pironi says, 'if nothing is done immediately on the cars and circuits, the 1982 season could turn out to be a very black one . . .'.

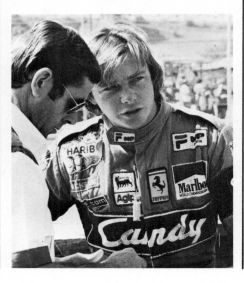

Rio de Janeiro, 21 March: most of the cars in today's Brazilian GP ran with 'water cooled' brakes. Does a loophole in the rules allow cars to run below the weight limit during the face but pass scrutineering once the water tanks have been replenished with 'permitted' coolant after the race? M. Balestre has stated his own views on the future with generalities such as 'reduction of cornering speeds' and 'give back a balance to engine power . . .'.

Didcot, 26 March: Carlos Reutemann has again informed Frank Williams that he is retiring forthwith and this time it looks as though he means it. He has driven in 146 GPs and won a dozen but as many suspected at Las Vegas his heart isn't in it any more.

Paris, 11 April: M. Balestre has announced his own proposals for F1 rule changes; they include weight reductions, a limit on tyre sizes, aerodynamic restrictions and a ban on qualifying tyres.

Poole: Basil Tye, President of the FIA Safety Commission, head of the RAC Motor Sports Association and recently defeated candidate for the FISA Presidency, has died of a heart attack.

Imola, 25 April: ten FOCA teams have boycotted the San Marino GP in protest at the Brazilian GP disqualifications. The 'Grandee' teams intend to resist changes which could ultimately ban turbocharging. Balestre says such threats will not weaken his resolve for change.

Casablanca, 6 May: Sponsors have collectively expressed their concern over their future involvement in GP racing in light of

13

the continuing disputes and the inevitable damage to the sport's public image.

Zolder, 8 May: Gilles Villeneuve's death following a needless practice accident has underlined the farcical qualifying tyre situation. With a limited number of sticky tyres allowed, many drivers are forced into kamikaze practice laps with the same potential outcome as in Villeneuve's case.

West Drayton, 14 May: Avon have withdrawn from GP racing, leaving Ensign and Theodore in the cold. Avon came into F1 through Bernie Ecclestone's International Race Tire Services in the wake of Goodyear's 1981 withdrawal. Avon will now concentrate on F2 and the World Endurance Championship.

Monte Carlo, 21 May: the FISA Enquiry Commission investigating Villeneuve's fatal accident has concluded that 'the cause of the accident was attributed to driver error on the part of Gilles Villeneuve. No blame is attached to Jochen Mass'. The Commission also 'called for immediate action to reduce the risks posed by qualifying tyres'.

Monte Carlo, 23 May: Many FISA officials have dissociated themselves from Balestre's latest proposals, emphasising that

they are his ideas and not FISA's. His proposals include very narrow cars with narrow, grooved tyres. Meanwhile it was also announced here that the 'on-off' Spanish GP is finally off but the Dutch GP is on, for 3 July! According to Balestre, new rules on tyres will be in force by then, with availability limited to six sets per car per GP allocated by a ridiculously complicated ballot system ...

Maranello, 1 June: Patrick Tambay, who left GP racing in disgust after the South African 'Super Licence' fiasco, has been tempted back as Pironi's new team mate at Ferrari — giving the team its first ever all-French driver combination.

Paris, 25 June: Jean-Marie Balestre has resigned as Executive President of the FIA, although he remains a Vice President! The latest statement on future F1 rules from the FISA Executive Committee includes a demand for treaded tyres from 1983, reduced weight limits, fuel capacities and wing dimensions and the total prohibition of skirts from 1983. The Technical Commission has been replaced by 'a group of technicians ... under the authority of ... the FISA engineer'. Having also advocated deletion of the 'unanimous agreement' clause on safety matters in the Concorde Agreement, the Executive Committee has put the onus for acceptance of the rules on the constructors.

Zandvoort, 3 July: the constructors strike back! Predictably, the non-FOCA teams have rejected deletion of the 'unanimous agreement' clause of the Concorde, but they are surprisingly amenable to many of FISA's other suggestions — other than the complete ban on skirts and the introduction of grooved tyres.

Brands Hatch, 17 July: the Professional Racing Drivers Association has proposed changes in qualifying procedures, aimed at resolving the safety problems. The changes are based on splitting the field into two halves, each with its own, separate qualifying sessions.

Meanwhile, representatives of the major tyre manufacturers have also met at Brands

Hatch and have replied to the FISA edict that treaded tyres will be mandatory in all international racing from 1983. Their reaction questions the lack of time allowed for the changeover, increased costs to both manufacturers and competitors, methods for policing the new rules and potential susceptibility of the grooved tyres to punctures. In a nutshell, the manufacturers are not wholeheartedly in support of the FISA proposals and conclude by suggesting that FISA looks elsewhere to reduce car speeds. Only Pirelli and Michelin declined to append their names to the document.

Paul Ricard, 25 July: the unthinkable almost happened in today's French GP, when Jochen Mass's March flew into a spectator area after touching Mauro Baldi's Arrows in the extremely fast Courbe des Signes — nowadays approached at almost 200mph. Mass and several spectators were injured and it is little short of miraculous that none was killed but agreement on how to restore some margin of safety seems as far off as ever.

Zeltweg, 15 August: Elio de Angelis's dramatic, surprise victory for Lotus in today's Austrian GP marks the 150th GP win from 218 races for the remarkable Cosworth DFV engine. Jim Clark and Lotus scored the first win for the DFV, on its debut, at Zandvoort in 1967 and Jody Scheckter notched up the century for Walter Wolf at Monaco in 1977. The DFV was already being written off then in favour of the V12s and more recently the turbos were supposed to sound its death-knell but the good old Cossie goes on and on. Ironically, Lotus announced a couple of days ago that they will be using Renault turbos next year . . .

Dijon, 29 August: FOCA are apparently thinking in terms of a 2-litre formula with fuel flow restrictions for the next F1, alongside their already known thoughts on weight, skirts *et al.* The Professional Racing Drivers Association also has ideas on the next formula and they too are talking in terms of smaller cars with less downforce and improved crash protection, although they are less than specific on how all this might be achieved.

This week, Patrick Tambay, for one, understands only too well the strains of driving the current, suspensionless cars, having missed the Swiss GP because of a stress induced back injury.

Como, 5 September: René Arnoux is spending the night in hospital, having hurt his back slipping on the deck of a powerboat before a race for GP drivers. Eddie Cheever won the race.

Monza, 12 September: the turbo revolution goes on; Frank Williams' long-time and ever enthusiastic sponsor *Techniques d'Avant Garde* have announced the formation of TAG Turbo Engines, whose first project will be the Porsche F1 turbo engine, a V6 and

Porsche's first ever racing 'V'. Surprisingly, the engine is a joint venture with McLaren rather than with Williams and, initially at least, it appears that McLaren will have exclusive use of the new motor.

Under pressure from no less a luminary than President Mitterand, Renault will now apparently supply *their* V6 turbo to Guy Ligier as well as to Lotus — albeit somewhat reluctantly it seems.

Paris, 20 September: it seems that Keke Rosberg will still have to race for his apparent title in Las Vegas next Saturday, the Paris Court of Appeal having delayed judgement on Frank Williams' appeal against the Brazilian disqualification until 11 October. The FIA Court which had previously rejected Williams' case is also considering Niki Lauda's forfeited Belgian GP points and if Lauda is awarded those points he too would have an outside chance of taking the title in Vegas!

Las Vegas, 26 September: whatever the outcome of the forthcoming tribunal decisions on various forfeited points, Keke has won the title. He finished a careful fifth here in this strange arena today but John Watson was beaten into second place anyway (after another brilliant drive) — by Michele Alboreto! Alboreto's win is Ken Tyrrell's first nine-pointer for over four years, since Depailler won for him at Monaco in 1978. It has been a strange and often sad season but Rosberg has worked hard for his title and Alboreto has clearly marked himself the man of the future.

Paris, 5 October: McLaren's appeal over Lauda's disputed Belgian GP points has finally been rejected and McLaren, although naturally disappointed and not a little confused over the logic of the decision, intend to pursue it no further. So now the season proper is well and truly closed — but the 'who goes where' season has begun! René Arnoux has already signed for Ferrari, Laffite is heading back to his old boss, Frank Williams, and there will be some anxious moments for many drivers between now and contract time. Alfa Romeo look to be about to shut up shop, while more and more teams turn to turbo power. Maybe next season the politics and the in-fighting will take a back seat and maybe the turbos really *will* outrun the Cosworths.

Provisional dates for 1983 have been announced as follows:

13 March	Brazil
27 March	Long Beach
17 April	France
1 May	San Marino
15 May	Monaco
22 May	Belgium
5 June	Detroit
12 June	Canada
10 July	Switzerland
17 July	Great Britain
7 August	Germany
14 August	Austria
28 August	Holland
11 September	Italy
25 September	New York
9 October	Las Vegas
29 October	South Africa

New York? That should be interesting . . .

THE TEAM MANAGERS' `TOP 10´ DRIVERS

THE key decision makers so often responsible for determining the overnight success or continuing struggle of the world's top racing drivers have reiterated their joint opinion. Last year, *Automobile Sport's* authoritative poll of Grand Prix Team Managers voted Alan Jones as Formula One's top candidate, with 1981 World Champion Nelson Piquet placed second — and, in the absence of AJ, Piquet has duly moved to the top of the list.

More so than last year, the TM's opinions bear little resemblance to the final championship standings of the drivers. Piquet won only one Grand Prix this season, for instance, while both Lauda and John Watson scored two wins apiece in identical cars — and yet Lauda is rated second highest, and Watson appears nowhere! Interesting too, is the meteoric rise of Las Vegas GP winner Michele Alboreto, while both Patrese and Jacques Laffite slip down the list, and World Champion Keke Rosberg is considered only fourth best.

1	NELSON PIQUET	87	6	MICHELE ALBORETO	20
2	NIKI LAUDA	73½	7	RENÉ ARNOUX	17
3	ALAIN PROST	56	9	JACQUES LAFFITE	9
4	KEKE ROSBERG	42	9	ELIO DE ANGELIS	8
5	DIDIER PIRONI	41	10	RICCARDO PATRESE	7½

Piquet

Lauda

Prost

Rosberg

Pironi

Alboreto

Arnoux

Laffite

de Angelis

Patrese

THE *Automobile Sport 82 83 Team Managers' Top Ten Drivers' Survey was conducted by* BOB CONSTANDUROS *towards the end of the 1982 season. Each Team Manager was asked to list his own personal top six drivers and for each list points were awarded on the race scoring system of 9-6-4-3-2-1 — tied places receiving split points.*

The Team Managers polled were: Jo Ramirez and Julian Randles (Theodore Racing); Frank Williams (TAG Williams Team); Alex Hawkridge (Toleman Motor Sport); John MacDonald (March Grand Prix); Gerard Larousse (Equipe Renault-Elf); Carlo Chiti (Autodelta); Mo Nunn (Ensign Racing); Ron Dennis (Marlboro Team McLaren); Jack Oliver (Team Ragno-Arrows); Ken Tyrrell (Team Tyrrell); Emerson Fittipaldi (Fittipaldi Automotive); Enzo Osella (Osella Automobili); Guy Ligier (Equipe Talbot-Gitanes); Marco Piccinnini (Spa Ferrari SEFAC); Alastair Caldwell (ATS Wheels). Bernie Ecclestone (Parmalat Racing Team) and Colin Chapman (John Player Team Lotus) were also polled but declined to present a list of nominations.

ANOTHER BEGINNING

In a super competitive Grand Prix season in which no driver scored more than two Grands Prix wins, Keke Rosberg took the World Championship with a mixture of aggressive speed and mature restraint. JEFF HUTCHINSON, Grand Prix writer and close friend of the new champion, looks at what makes him tick.

"KEKE who?". One could hear the questioning rumble in the crowd when Keke Rosberg, arms raised high over his head in triumph, acknowledged the 1982 World Drivers Championship title — his title now, whether or not his team found success in pending courtroom appeals. A fifth-place finish in the Caesar's Palace Grand Prix which had ended moments before, and the two points an unruffled, mistake-free performance brought with it, capped the end of a gruelling 16-race Formula 1 season. For the newly crowned World Champion, another fresh beginning . . .

Minutes later a crowd of 30 or 40 journalists queued outside the TAG Williams Team motorhome which cosied up to the tennis courts outside the mammoth Casino Hotel. The newsmen elbowing

for a few words with the new World Champion were a diverse lot, many awaiting "Rosberg Gospel" for the first time and many as ignorant about the man as the paying crowd in the stands for whom they would soon be writing.

Not until the Finn, Rosberg, had won his first Grand Prix a month earlier did many of the writers assigned the F1 beat deign to interview him at all. In fact, some had spent most of the past several years studiously ignoring him, an also-ran, a backmarker. Through the second half of the 1981 season Keke had been lucky to earn a berth on the starting grid at all, but after the Swiss GP at Dijon, with the World Championship more than a strong possibility, the world's press were ready to talk to Keke Rosberg — only he wasn't necessarily ready to talk to them . . .

"They all want a few words with me now, as if the Championship is already decided," Keke barked as we boarded a London to Los Angeles Pan-Am flight, a full eight days before the crucial final race in Las Vegas. "I am not a superstitious person, but it would be wrong to talk about it as though it was already over. That's a silly attitude to take on the eve of the most important race of my life. Wrong because if I don't win I will look stupid."

He was tense from the previous weekend's debacle at Monza, where a rear wing mount failure had kept him out of the points for only the fourth time this year. It was a scary reminder of his own philosophy that nothing is won until it's over, and the fact that only John Watson of his Championship rivals came away from Monza with a chance was but small consolation.

That interminable pressure, which has cracked many another superb driver on the eve of The Big One, was eating at him.

"The 'phone has not stopped ringing and I have hardly slept thinking about all the things that could go wrong in Las Vegas. My head is starting to spin," said Keke, who chose to get away from England early and "clean out" his mind. Next to him on that Pan-Am flight was his beautiful and long-suffering girl friend, Yvonne Rosenlew, who was on the receiving end of his sharp tongue and short temper, living his anguish with him.

I knew exactly how she felt. Two years earlier Keke decided he wanted to learn about flying and as his friend — and freshly qualified flight instructor — I offered to teach him. He accepted bravely and the long weeks which followed were rewarding for both of us. I really came to understand the man who would become the 1982 World Champion. In the three months we shared a Southern California apartment, just minutes from the Long Beach airport, we uncovered many of our own faults and foibles — as well as each other's — and both of us went back to work on the '81 GP season changed men.

For Keke the concentrated hard work, the studying, exams, frustrations, tension, anger, thrills and even fear which come with learning to fly, made him analyse himself more deeply than he had ever done in the past. The sky and the control of it was a completely new environment, just as challenging and with less room for mistakes than the similarly cramped "other kind of cockpit" he'd grown used to.

"It was a period in my life that really changed me," Keke says now. "For the first time I had to become serious, less impulsive and more analytical about the world around me. I suppose you could say I grew up. It's less fun now," he adds with a grin, "but I suppose everybody has to do it sometime . . ." Keke will be 34 years old in December.

Peter Warr, Keke's Fittipaldi team manager in 1981, was one of the first to note the change in his driver. "I don't know what it was the two of you were doing all winter, but whatever, it was fantastic for Keke," he told me at the Brazilian GP.

Unfortunately, only another keen and experienced observer could have noticed that Rosberg's driving had matured greatly, that impulse had given way to logic — such were his difficulties in the financially troubled Fittipaldi team. Qualifying was suddenly the goal and few onlookers could wrench their eyes away from the Piquets and Joneses and Reutemanns and Villeneuves to notice the dozen or more drivers behind, scratching to beat their own path into the superstar category.

Yet there it was. The wild, aggressive, tail-out style so well remembered from his Formula Atlantic and Can-Am years, mellowed into a business like skill cut from the same mould as another man who'd adopted flying as a second passion: Niki Lauda.

But at the end of the '81 season all Keke had was a string of DNQs and a mailbox empty of offers from more competitive teams. He decided to stay on in the USA after the Caesar's Palace finale to add an instrument rating to his private single and multi-engine flying licenses. "I was considering another season of Can-Am, for I enjoyed doing that," says Keke. "Better that than another season of F1 with an uncompetitive team."

By then he had an expensive life style to support, although the season had brought little in the way of results, he had an advantage over most of his colleagues in the same position: he had been well paid.

He has seemingly always been well paid. Before Fittipaldi he spent a season in Paul Newman's Budweiser Can-Am team, had resided for almost a year in Walter Wolf's Equipe (after James Hunt quit at the start of the '79 season) and before that had driven the odd F1 race for Theodore and ATS. He rose to prominence in North America at the wheel of a Fred Opert Chevron in Formula Atlantic and in Europe in the German TOJ F2 team. Rosberg had even been paid to race in the German and European Super Vee championships after graduating from the Vee in which he began his career.

But at the end of the '81 season he was worried about his career and about his future in Grand Prix racing. And then both concerns evaporated in November with a 'phone call from Frank Williams: Alan Jones' retirement was now definite, would Keke like to test the Williams?

Needless to say, Keke dropped everything and was on the next plane to England. It came as no surprise to learn that a suitably impressed Frank had offered Keke the drive after some sterling fast lappery at Paul Ricard.

Confident that his talent had always been there, even if it had

never before been strapped into a competitive F1 chassis, Rosberg hit it off at Williams right from the word go. He was one of the fastest Cosworth runners in the GP season-opening South African GP and carried that mantle with him through the season. In fact, he was the only Cosworth-engined driver to earn a pole position in 1982, the reward for a staggering all-out effort at Brands Hatch.

At Monaco, Keke crashed trying to pass Andrea de Cesaris' "wide" Alfa Romeo, but otherwise his drives have been the model of consistency, with nary a spin to blot his copybook. But for the luckless Italian GP and the controversial Brazilian race (where he finished a moral second to Nelson Piquet, even if the FIA does not agree), Rosberg has scored points in every race he has finished (mechanical problems sidelined him in Canada and Great Britain).

"When I started the season I was confident I could win a couple of races, but I never thought about the championship. That came later," Keke explains. "Except for my Monaco mistake, I have been pleased with my driving of a car that has not always been the easiest. I could have won in Austria if I had not had to wait so long for the tyre pressures to come up — which cost me all that time on de Angelis in the opening laps. In Belgium I almost made it, too, but we went too soft on the tyres. That's two races I could have added to the Swiss GP victory if things had gone right, but that's the way it goes," adds a man who holds a very fatalistic view about his racing.

There are those who will say Rosberg's title came only by virtue of Didier Pironi's accident, or even of Gilles Villeneuve's fatal crash at the start of the European season. But to Keke, that's all part of the sport. "Like everyone else, I thought that either Renault or Ferrari would take the title and that, with luck, maybe Williams or McLaren would win a couple of races. In the end, Renault didn't win because their cars were unreliable and Ferrari didn't win because both their drivers made mistakes and crashed. I hate to see any of my colleagues hurt, of course, but to win the championship a driver must avoid making mistakes and a team must build a car that will finish. I haven't made any mistakes yet," said Keke as we relaxed in Southern California on the weekend before Las Vegas, "so if I win the title, I deserve it and the team deserves it."

Keke was saying the same thing two years ago, when F1 success still eluded him. What has changed? "Nothing really," he retorts. "Just the amount of work you have to do. Up to now I have had plenty of time to lie on the beach and play between races, but this year has been incredibly hard. Every week between races we have tested. I have only spent three days at my house on Ibiza this year, and now I really need a holiday. That's another reason why I needed this break (before the race at Caesar's), away from all the people trying to write stories and take pictures, a chance to lie in the sun by a swimming pool where no one knows me."

At this point Keke lit up another cigarette and drank up the last of his wine, visibly starting to relax after several hours of light conversation and the reading of some flying magazines. Rosberg's smoking and drinking habits have never bothered him, but they do bother others, especially teetotaller and non-smoker Frank Williams. After trying to get Keke to stop at the start of the season, he gave up, realizing it was fruitless. "I guess Frank has gotten used to the idea now," Keke says innocently. "I never have a problem in a race car. Sure, it's physically hard, but some other drivers seem to have a lot more trouble than I do — even those who don't drink and smoke," he adds with a wide grin.

"My big problem is that I have had to buy all new shirts — my neck had grown two sizes since the start of the season. No, I don't do any special exercises. The amount of time I spend in the car, that's all the exercise I need to keep fit."

Since the start of the season, Keke calculates he has spent something like 90 days driving the Williams, either on race weekends or in private testing. That translates to something on the order of 16,000 miles, four worn-out helmets, 10 pairs of shoes, 20 pairs of gloves and six sets of overalls.

"Some days, after a long testing session, my backside is so sore I cannot sit down for more than a couple of minutes — which makes it pretty uncomfortable flying home."

His back has a permanently open sore where the curve of his spine has hammered against the back of the driving seat, while an inflamed tendon in his right hand often hurts badly after the race. Even worse is a painful nerve on the ball of his foot which comes from pushing so hard on a vibrating bare metal brake pedal, but to Keke that's all part of the job. "Sure, the cars are tough to drive, but that's what we are paid for. We are professional sportsmen and that's tough. I am sure athletes or tennis players hurt just as much after a match as I do after a race. If a driver cannot take it, he should do something else and not complain all the time," says the straight-talking Finn who left the GPDA (PRDA) because he was not prepared to have his own beliefs compromised. His thoughts on car safety are just as strong: "There are some cars I would not like to drive, but that's up to each driver to decide. As for the rules, I have no comment. I don't know enough about car designing to offer a

When he is not racing or testing, the World Champion relaxes with his own aircraft, with a game of tennis or by driving! So far, Rosberg's only Grand Prix victory has been in the Swiss Grand Prix at Dijon (below) but there must surely be many more to come. For 1983, Rosberg remains teamed with Frank Williams and designer Patrick Head (far left, centre), a partnership which has enjoyed quite remarkable success.

better solution to the current regulations. The only thing I would definitely like to see changed are the skirts back to the old sliding type. They were much more consistent than the present ones and made the car much more consistent and safer to drive."

Nor is Keke one of the crusaders demanding the circuits be changed. If anything, he takes the opposite stand, harping on endlessly about "ridiculous" and "absurd" chicanes, wistfully noting that the one corner at Hockenheim which offered a challenge — the blindingly fast Ostkurve — had been ruined by the addition of yet another switchback. Brands Hatch, he says, is one of the only circuits left on the GP calendar which remains a driver's track. What other World Champion in recent history would have jumped at the offer to compete in a small sedan race at the Nürburgring at the end of a long season, just because he believed it might be his last chance to lap the full 14-mile course? (ask Keke about his 7m 1s lap of the 'ring in an F2 car some years ago, and watch his eyes catch fire . . .).

Flying with Keke, I was often surprised by his quick grasp of a situation. Not surprisingly, he is just as sharp on the ground. Whether he's working out a tricky mental problem or thinking up a brusque remark to answer a stupid question. His command of the English language makes you forget that it's not his mother tongue, though sometimes his overly direct Scandinavian-style syntax can leave a listener in no doubt as to what he thinks of him or her. This has probably contributed to the stories appearing in many a newspaper or magazine which describe Keke as cold, arrogant, morose, unhappy or just about any other uncomplimentary remark you can think of. "I always treat a professional journalist professionally," he says with a shrug. "If I get asked a stupid question, I will give a

stupid reply, or if somebody is rude to me I will be the same way with him. I don't like bad press, but the people that give it to me are the ones who never talk to me or don't know me. You can draw your own conclusions from that . . ."

I can attest to the fact that Keke has a great sense of humour, is one of the most "human" GP drivers on the circuit, and enjoys nothing more than a night with friends having plenty of good food and drink.

He is also a hard business man. Business and pleasure are two things he will never mix. His years of living from hand to mouth on the wages of a computer operator trying to go FV racing (which contributed to a broken marriage in those early days), have left him with a strong sense of financial self-preservation. He has a healthy respect for money and enjoys the business opportunities that come out of his racing almost as much as the racing itself. Whether talking German, English, Swedish or his native Finnish, Keke can drive a hard bargain and he is always happy to sit on the other side of a table from somebody trying to sell him something and beat the poor man down a few pennies. Sometimes he loses things that he desperately wanted because he had made his bid and was not prepared to go up on his original offer and lose face on the deal.

Despite his aggressive bargaining tactics, he is an extremely fair man. Sponsors — and he now has many of them — get exactly what they pay for. Keke and long-time friend Ortwin Podlech, his business manager, see to that. After the Vegas race Keke returned to Long Beach for a few days of recuperation following Mansour Ojjeh's two day birthday/Championship party in San Francisco. Some of that time he spent personally modelling clothes from a Finnish fashion sportswear company with which he has just signed

an endorsement contract. This latest deal particularly pleases both Keke and Yvonne, who are both dedicated followers of style and fashion. Keke, in fact, was once part owner of a boutique in Finland and has impeccable taste in clothes.

"I really like the business aspect of racing even though it leaves you very little time to relax. Rest will come later, right now I have to work hard selling myself while there is something to sell . . ."

Preoccupied as he is with making money — and despite his lack of free time — Keke has little trouble spending it. He has a beautiful ranch-style home on the holiday island of Ibiza, a magnificent house in England (which he bought at the start of this season, just a few hundred yards away from Barbro Peterson's home), investment property in the States and, of course, the obligatory apartment in the tax haven of Monaco. He can also boast a collection of exotic, racy automobiles as well as his twin-engine Piper Seneca. The latter is on the block, for Keke has decided to get a bigger aeroplane "so I can relax in the back behind a full-time pilot."

With the Championship sewn up, the signs of relief on Keke's expressive features were obvious. "It's the greatest day of my life," he said in the Williams motorhome, as the noise outside began to swell. He puffed on the inevitable cigarette and downed some more champagne in between bites of Mansour's chocolate cake, squinting through the window at the anxiously waiting press. "Suppose I better get out there and tell them how I feel," he said with a sly wink.

People might be saying "Keke who?" today, but you can be sure it won't always be that way. After all, the same people once said "Jackie who?" but, like Stewart, Rosberg will not be slow in making the most of his success.

HOW THE TITLE WAS WON

FINAL CHAMPIONSHIP STANDINGS

1	Keke Rosberg	44	14	Nigel Mansell	7
2 =	John Watson	39	15 =	Carlos Reutemann	6
2 =	Didier Pironi	39	15 =	Gilles Villeneuve	6
4	Alain Prost	34	17 =	Andrea de Cesaris	5
5	Niki Lauda	30	17 =	Jacques Laffite	5
6	René Arnoux	28	19	Mario Andretti	4
7 =	Michele Alboreto	25	20 =	Jean-Pierre Jarier	3
7 =	Patrick Tambay	25	20 =	Marc Surer	3
9	Elio de Angelis	23	22 =	Manfred Winkelhock	2
10	Riccardo Patrese	21	22 =	Eliseo Salazar	2
11	Nelson Piquet	20	22 =	Bruno Giacomelli	2
12	Eddie Cheever	15	22 =	Mauro Baldi	2
13	Derek Daly	8	26	Chico Serra	1

The 1982 Grand Prix season was one of tragedy and controversy. Villeneuve died, rules were bent, the favourites faltered and in the end Keke Rosberg emerged with another well won Championship for Frank Williams. BRIAN LABAN looks back on a sad season and forward to a fresh start . . .

BEFORE the South African Grand Prix which opened the 1982 season in January, Keke Rosberg had scored just six points in his Grand Prix career. By September's finale, against the unlikely backdrop of that famous Las Vegas car park, Rosberg, with a single, spectacular Grand Prix win under his belt, was World Champion. It was the first time since Mike Hawthorn's Championship in 1958 that the Champion had won only one race — in Hawthorn's case one of ten, in Rosberg's one of 16, in another overcrowded calendar structured to please the TV networks and the faceless money men. Hawthorn's Ferrari was one of six Grand Prix teams in 1958; Rosberg's Williams was one of 17 and in 1982 no driver won more than two races. Interviewed by Bob Constanduros for *Automobile Sport,* John Watson mulled over the Championship which slipped from his grasp, with the astute observation '. . . the Championship was begging to be won by somebody'. How right he was.

In the overall context Rosberg will, without doubt, be remembered as a worthy Champion, a skilful and pure racer in every sense; but the tragic irony of 1982 was that, long before Rosberg donned the laurels, the purest and perhaps the most skilful racer of them all had died in a sickeningly needless practice accident and his heir apparent lay critically injured in a Heidelberg hospital, impotently watching as his title slipped away.

On an already grey day in May, Gilles Villeneuve, 30 years old, winner of six Grands Prix and by general consensus one of the best ever, died after crashing at Zolder. On his last lap on his last set of qualifying tyres, Villeneuve, out to prove a point, clipped Jochen Mass's cruising March. His Ferrari was torn apart as it landed, Villeneuve was thrown across the track and his injuries were fatal. He had not been a winner in the four already contested races of 1982 but on that last lap he was racing for pole position and for a principle. Two weeks before, his team mate, Didier Pironi had demoted Villeneuve to a seething second place in the undersubscribed San Marino Grand Prix. Thereafter, the two never again plotted to overcome the threat of Renault or Brabham or Williams; they never even spoke.

By August, Pironi had a commanding lead in the Championship, having added victory in Holland to his tally; and then he came periously close to becoming Ferrari's second loss of a sad season. In blinding rain at Hockenheim, lapping fast on new wets and already assured of pole position, Pironi's Ferrari slammed oblivious into the back wheel of Prost's slowly moving Renault and launched itself to destruction. Pironi was lucky to survive and kept his legs only by virtue of supremely skilful circuit rescue and subsequent surgery, and by flatly refusing to accept the horror of amputation. Pironi may yet race again, but the near certainty of Championship victory had gone.

With Pironi all too clearly out of the equation, the Championship was thus thrown wide open with five races to run; and such was the leaderless state of Grand Prix racing by the end of this sad season that each of those five races saw a different winner — four of them winning for the first time — and when the final flag fell, Pironi had still only missed his Championship by five tantalising points, to share runner-up spot with John Watson.

Watson, too, could look back ruefully on what might have been his but for a desperately frustrating run of six barren races in the second half of the season. Watson was one of the five two time winners who trailed the enviably consistent Rosberg (a scorer on the road in every round but three) to make up the Championship top six. Time and again through 1982, Watson, so often condemned as a non-trier and no-hoper, drove like a man inspired; his wins, overshadowed in Belgium and comic book brilliant in Detroit, were *racing* performances of the highest order, with good, old fashioned overtaking the name of the game. In fact Watson probably overtook more cars in this season than most Grand Prix drivers do in a lifetime — or at least, perhaps, until next season, when who knows what cat the 'new' cars will set among the pigeons.

Renault's frustrations seemed somehow less trying, just for their sad predictability. There was rarely much doubt that Prost and Arnoux would hog the limelight end of the grid, but there was also something approaching resignation for their ultimate fate. While Ferrari, for all their tragic losses, demonstrated unapproachable reliability in taking the Constructors Championship, Renault simply could not keep its fast but fragile turbo cars together for long enough to capitalise on their obvious speed. One or other Renault sat on pole for ten of the season's races and one or other led 13 out of the 16, but there were just three wins on the road and one by virtue of protests to show for such deceptively flattering pace.

The Brabhams too were undoubtedly quick with their BMW turbo engines, but one of the team's two wins came with the Cosworth-powered car, and who is to say that with another Cosworth-powered Champion in the record books the BMW route served the outgoing World Champion best? Brabham, never ones to shun attention, kept Grand Prix watchers on the edges of their seats with their vaunted, half-tank, soft-tyre pit stop stratagem through the second half of the season, finally demonstrating their well re-

Ferrari started 1982 in the best possible shape, with the new, Harvey Postlethwaite designed 126C2 and Villeneuve and Pironi (top left) on the driving strength. Either one of the Ferrari drivers might have been world Champion, the biggest danger, as demonstrated at Imola, Villeneuve's last race, being that the two would race each other. By mid season it did not matter, with Villeneuve lost and Pironi terribly injured, Ferrari eventually ran a driver line up completely different from that with which they set out, Tambay and Andretti (above left) providing at least some relief from the gloom. Reigning Champion, Nelson Piquet (trying hard with the Cosworth-powered car at Long Beach, above) had a frustrating season at Brabham, persevering manfully with fragile BMW turbo power while perhaps longing for Cosworth reliability (above far left); Derek Daly, looking on, spent his season with Williams in the shadow of Rosberg. Elio de Angelis has developed into a driver of great promise (left) and his deserved win in Austria was a real shot in the arm for the long-struggling Lotus team. Although Renault were joint top scorers with four wins in the 16 races, their season could only be regarded as a failure, with Arnoux (below left) and Prost regular front runners and equally regular retirements. The only other team to take four wins was McLaren, with two each for Watson and Lauda (right), Watson in particular being entitled to look puzzled as to just how the title managed to slip from his grasp in the second half of a season in which he showed real brilliance. Jacques Laffite's season with Ligier (right, below) was an unmitigated disaster and at the end of it all the ever enthusiastic Frenchman was probably happy to move back to his old boss Frank Williams' fold.

The Autodelta Alfas were one of the victims of 1982, although the Alfa name will still appear on the grids, with Euroracing pulling the strings and with Andrea de Cesaris (left) driving — much to the consternation of some others. At long last, the Tyrrell team was back in the limelight with Ken Tyrrell and Maurice Phillipe providing Michele Alboreto with the tools to do the job and Brian Lisle overseeing the operation (below, far left), just like the good old days. Balestre's initiatives during the season eventually paved the way for the new rules and 'flat bottom' cars such as the prototype Brabham (right) but not all his ideas were implemented, some of his thoughts on tyres being particularly difficult to come to terms with. Goodyear's grooved slicks were tested, briefly, at Zandvoort (below, left) where M. Balestre is seen speaking to Nigel Wolheim of Pirelli, who were less than 100% in favour of the new rules. Among the changes which will take force by 1984 is the outlawing of stops for fuel, rendering the pit stop strategy which Brabham finally tried in Austria (bottom) ultimately obsolete. Also now obsolete, as Ligier switches to Cosworth and Renault turbo power for 1983, is the glorious, if not entirely successful, Matra V12 engine (below).

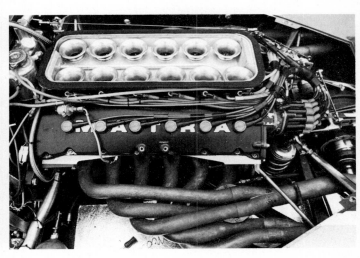

hearsed virtuosity at Österreichring shortly before both cars expired anyway. With fire-suited mechanics, pre-heated tyres and choreography worthy of Busby Berkely, the pit stop as theatre was magnificent; the pit stops as tactics was debatable and, of course, ultimately self defeating, because had it proved so advantageous as to be universal there would have been no further advantage.

There were other, more invidious, ways of gaining an edge to be found during 1982, and one of them cost Piquet and Rosberg first and second places in Brazil, handing Alain Prost his second 'win' in as many outings. Hamstrung by the inability to extract more power from normally aspirated engines, most of the front-running Cosworth teams had invoked the power/weight equation and built ultralightweight cars with actual weights below the permitted minimum. As the rules ostensibly allowed topping up of 'essential fluids' after the race and before final scrutineering, the lightweight cars now developed a previously unfelt need for water cooled brakes — and to feed them a water tank which could legitimately be topped up after the race. In apparent contradiction to the laws of Physics, the lightest cars seemingly had the biggest brake cooling problems, and consequently needed the biggest water tanks, a fairly accurate rule of thumb being that the amount of water needed was approximately the amount by which the car was light of 585kg.

In that the problem was at its worst at the beginning of a race, when the car with a full fuel load was at its heaviest, this water was obviously used up at a prodigious rate almost immediately and the cars then had to struggle round with no brake cooling other than God's fresh air and, of course, no water in their tanks.

Remarkably, the turbo teams, with heavier cars thanks to more complicated engine plumbing and heavier fuel demand, inferred from this that some cars could actually run below the weight limit during the race, and the protests flew thick and fast. Seen in this cynical vein, the water tank controversy was a clever and even mildly amusing exploitation of just another inevitable loophole, but it also bore some more worrying implications, in terms of what sacrifices might be made in the quest for lightness and how much that quest might cost, with carbon fibre monocoques and more and more titanium already moving building costs another quantum leap ahead. It was right that FISA should nip the trend in the bud, but sad that the rule making process can still admit of such glaring anomalies.

Not that the constructors are incapable of going around the rules as well as through them. With sliding skirts and hydropneumatic suspension systems both banned, near rigid suspension with telephone number spring rates became the order of the day. Thereby, no suspension movement, constant ride height and a surrogate role for 'rigid' skirts. The cars kept their massive downforce and almost mind boggling cornering performance but now they became, literally, a pain to drive and a dangerous liability when the inevitable accidents came.

Fears that the latest generation ground effect cars, exploiting rapidly escalating turbo power, were becoming dangerously fast were given weight as early as March, when Pironi escaped miraculously unscathed from a truly massive testing accident at Paul Ricard. Such have become the straight line speeds and extraordinary cornering capabilities of current cars that, even at this modern and oft dubbed 'safe' circuit, Pironi's Ferrari ended its high speed flight in what would on race day be a spectator area. Concern was dutifully registered but nothing was done and on race day Jochen

Mass's March played a chilling re-run of Pironi's accident, causing several minor spectator injuries but again with merciful (and again miraculous) deliverance from far worse.

The pressing need to slow the cars down was becoming indisputable and, remarkably, something actually happened within the rule making machinery. Throughout the year, FISA's widely reviled President, Jean-Marie Balestre, had submitted his own often fanciful, technically naïve, yet basically well intended proposals for sweeping changes. Aerodynamic restrictions, weight and tyre size reductions and a hugely complicated alternative to the despised and tragically exposed qualifying tyre system were among his targets, but there are too many vested interests within Grand Prix racing for change to be easy. The turbocharged runners are predictably cool on allowing the more nimble Cosworth cars to exploit lighter weight or better aerodynamics, and the Cosworth constructors are equally vociferous in branding the supercharging equivalency formula inequable. And so it goes on, with significant change effectively stifled by the so-called Concorde Agreement's well-intentioned stability clauses, under which fundamental change is only possible in cases of *force majeure,* notably over matters of safety, or by unanimous consent.

Unanimity is no common occurence in the desperately competitive and commercially charged Grand Prix arena, but shortly after the end of the 1982 season, the unthinkable actually happened; faced with a cry of *force majeure, all* the constructors agreed (some grudgingly) to accept far reaching technical changes which may lend Grand Prix racing a very different, and perhaps very exciting, aspect for next season.

For 1983, Formula One cars will run with a flat bottom between front and rear wheels, no skirts or other system to bridge the gap between bodywork and ground and with significantly different permissible wing dimensions. The minimum weight limit will be reduced to 540kg, now defined as being the weight with fuel on board, and checkable at random at the pits entrance during practice and after the race. Four-wheel drive is banned, as are cars with more than four wheels, and several technical regulations are revised to in-build even more effective crash protection structures. From 1984, fuel tank capacity will be reduced from 250 to 220 litres and fuel stops will be outlawed, rendering the Brabham philosophy instantly obsolete and effectively placing a power limit on the proliferating turbo engines which many regard as essential.

By November, hastily revised cars were testing and it was immediately apparent that, at a stroke, the rule changes had dramatically increased lap times and re-introduced a spectacular tendency to understeer, oversteer and corner any which way but on rails. Initial driver reaction was, mostly, ecstatic: back to being a real live driver instead of a high speed passenger; back to skill instead of balls. Phrases like 'throttle control' and 'sensitivity' came out as though they had never been away, and there was the euphoria of *knowing* that 1983 was to be the dawn of a new Golden Age of racing.

It may yet be so; the new rules certainly have the look of a great leveller, penalising the turbos' idiosyncratic response and unavoidable bulk, while breathing fresh life into the Cosworth's flexibility and compactness. And the cars will certainly be *different* to drive, if not more difficult. If the expected emphasis really does accrue to driver skill, then 1983 will be a year to remember, with so many reputations on such a narrow line. Time will tell.

THE GRANDS PRIX WINNERS

1950-1982

Jackie Stewart	27
Jim Clark	25
Juan Manuel Fangio	*24
Niki Lauda	19
Stirling Moss	*16
Jack Brabham	14
Emerson Fittipaldi	14
Graham Hill	14
Alberto Ascari	13
Mario Andretti	12
Alan Jones	12
Carlos Reutemann	12
James Hunt	10
Ronnie Peterson	10
Jody Scheckter	10
Denny Hulme	8
Jacky Ickx	8
Nelson Piquet	7
Tony Brooks	*6
Jacques Laffite	6
Jochen Rindt	6
John Surtees	6
Gilles Villeneuve	6
Giuseppe Farina	5
Alain Prost	5
Clay Regazzoni	5
René Arnoux	4
Dan Gurney	4
Bruce McLaren	4
John Watson	4
Peter Collins	3
Phil Hill	3
Mike Hawthorn	3
Didier Pironi	3
Patrick Depailler	2
Froilan Gonzalez	2
Jean-Pierre Jabouille	2
Peter Revson	2
Pedro Rodriguez	2
Jo Siffert	2
Maurice Trintignant	2
Wolfgang von Trips	2
Billy Vukovich	2
Michele Alboreto	1
Elio de Angelis	1
Giancarlo Baghetti	1
Lorenzo Bandini	1
Jean-Pierre Beltoise	1
Jo Bonnier	1
Vittorio Brambilla	1
Jimmy Bryan	1
Francois Cevert	1
Luigi Fagioli	*1
Pat Flaherty	1
Peter Gethin	1
Richie Ginther	1
Sam Hanks	1
Innes Ireland	1
Jochen Mass	1
Luigi Musso	*1
Gunnar Nilsson	1
Carlos Pace	1
John Parsons	1
Riccardo Patrese	1
Jim Rathman	1
Keke Rosberg	1
Troy Ruttman	1
Ludovico Scarfiotti	1
Bob Sweikert	1
Patrick Tambay	1
Piero Taruffi	1
Lee Wallard	1
Rodger Ward	1

*includes shared wins

THE GRANDS PRIX

*Grand Prix reports by **Phillip Bingham** and **Bob Constanduros***

PROST STRIKES FIRST

COMPLACENCY, already! That was the unnerving way in which rival teams might be tempted to describe the scene, as Alain Prost and René Arnoux stood proudly on the winner's rostrum at Kyalami in their Renault overalls. Renault's superiority had been so dazzling, so truly sublime, that it had obviously blinded even their own judgement.

Granted, the turbo powered French motor manufacturer *had* expected to be quick here, where the rarefied air at 6,000ft altitude generously gives the turbo cars as much as a 150bhp power advantage, and where the ageing Ford Cosworths wheeze like breathless asthmatics. They had confidently expected, too, a logical continuation of Alain Prost's near perfect end-of-season 1981 form, in which his last four outings had brought a second place and two satisfying victories. The highly acclaimed Frenchman had gone into winter hibernation more impatient than most for the arrival of the new season, confident that in 1982 the Renault turbos would be swift rather than susceptible, and his title chances realistic. He knew, too, that the anomolous atmosphere of this Johannesburg track could provide the ideal preface to the good story. Yes, Renault and Alain Prost had *expected* to win at Kyalami in January 1982, just as the company had won on their last visit here, in 1980.

But what they *hadn't* expected! A turbo powered superiority so distinct that Team Manager Jean Sage had scratched the first blemish on to the 1982 record, before René Arnoux, because of his faith in his boss's confidence, was forced into the second error. It was, said little tousle-haired René from the exalted heights of the victor's podium, a great privilege to be part of the Regie's first ever 1-2 Grand Prix success.

Except that it wasn't. Unbeknown to the smiling Frenchman, bubbling with patriotic diplomacy and grace, this was in actual fact 'only' a Renault 1-3!

Sure, it had been the sort of rare, commanding performance which is deserving of a 1-2. Arnoux, untroubled in qualifying in his RE30B, had claimed the first pole position of the year by nearly three-tenths of a second — as an early reminder that 'twas not only Prost who seriously intended to win the World Championship in a Renault. And Prost, from a third row start dictated by a first session engine failure and a premature, rain induced halt to the second session, was simply startling. Words can only whisper of the enormity of his achievement and of the pathetic vulnerability of his token rivals. This was the strongest recovery charge to victory seen in a post-war Grand Prix since Jim Clark's legendary Monza performance in 1967.

Making everyone else on the track look even sillier than they had done two days earlier when barricading themselves up in a room of the nearby Sunnyside Hotel, Prost passed Arnoux for the lead after a dozen laps — only to suffer his second rear puncture of the weekend mid-way round lap 41. He had to limp slowly around the remainder of the lap in order to preserve skirts and suspension, yes, and he had to sit stationary in the pits for over a quarter-of-a-minute while new Michelins were fitted all-round. He was

When the drivers finally decided to race at Kyalami, Alain Prost (above) was in a class of his own, making a storming recovery from a pit stop to change a punctured tyre to lead a Renault 1-3. On Thursday the drivers took the bus (below) to their hotel retreat and emerged for practice only on Friday (below right)

lapped by the entire field, and slipped a whole lap behind the new leader, team mate Arnoux.

But none of this was too much!

On fresh rubber and light fuel load, Alain Prost accelerated out of the pit lane towards one of the greatest bounce-back drives ever seen in Grand Prix racing. One by one, he did not so much pick-off the normally aspirated opposition as sweep past them. A simple task made all the easier by the disintegration of all the other turbo motors in the race. Within 33 laps Alain

had even made up the whole lap on Arnoux, representing a 2.6-second per lap improvement on his leading team mate's times, and a margin sufficient to reclaim the lead. On Michelins driven twice the distance of Alain's, and with a vicious circle vibration effect — the slower he was forced to drive, the more his tyres picked up rubber from the track and so worsened — Arnoux made no efforts to stave off his stablemate, although events later in the year suggest that he would have liked to.

Instead, Arnoux dutifully followed the

Hero of the Day around, quite content to collect second place. Better, he reasoned, to preserve the turbo and tyres. No matter that Michele Alboreto's well-driven Tyrrell 011 was managing to keep pace in his slipstream since being lapped, and no matter, either, that Carlos Reutemann's Williams FW07 was catching up. The Argentinian was in third place behind the two Renaults, yes, but as Arnoux's pit signals confirmed, even he was a lap behind. "REUT 1 LAP" said the message from TM Jean Sage. Logically, therefore, Arnoux let the Williams close the gap completely, and then politely moved over just five laps before the end and let Reutemann by . . .

. . . which was the epitome of innocent conceit. Alas, Reutemann had been on the *same* lap as the second placed Renault, just as the French team's timekeeper had cautiously believed. Sage, however, had disagreed. Reutemann simply couldn't be just a few lengths behind. The Renaults were that much quicker than everyone else. How could a Cosworth car *possibly* be catching?

But catch it did, to be waved gratefully by. So Reutemann, the much-maligned 1981 World Championship loser, the man who at the last minute accepted that his life would have little meaning without racing and so returned from a short winter's disillusioned retirement, filled the Renault sandwich. The runner-up from '81 became the runner-up in the first chapter of '82, and did so at a circuit suited to the new Turbo Era in a yester-year Cosworth car. An early indication that reliability and "the Devil you know" were still capable of chasing the championship, even in turbo torn '82.

Reliability, of course, the turbos all too frequently lack. Ignoring the runaway Renaults, Kyalami was no different. Again, the turbo-v-Cosworth war was a case of shattering speed versus obstinate obsolescence during qualifying — only to become fragility versus reliability in the race. A fresh and particularly poignant addition to the turbo ranks arrived at Kyalami, in the shape of four-cylinder BMWs, in the sleek new Brabham BT50s of world Champion Nelson Piquet and his new stable mate Riccardo Patrese. Yes, that's right: turbo power in the team owned by Bernie Ecclestone, the Formula One Constructors' Association figurehead through all the FOCA stalwarts' days of pious argument against turbo power on a variety of dubious "principles"!

The turbo coup, surely, was now complete. Turbo success, however, was not *quite* convincing. Not yet, at least. Piquet underlined the BMW's hefty potential by qualifying on the front row, and by flashing through the speed trap on the approach to Crowthorne corner at an awesome 200.1mph. In paltry comparison, the fastest that a non-turbo car could manage here during sample measurement was 173mph.

But in the race itself Nelson made a poorly start, spluttering away with a temporary boost deficiency, and then from an unspectacular seventh place threw it all into the catchfences under braking on lap four. Patrese, too, had difficulty getting away from the line cleanly, and his second row qualifying effort disintegrated with an oil leak, and predictable engine failure, after 16 laps.

Neither were the Ferraris much better. The recently unveiled 126C2 not only possessed the immense V6 turbo power with which opponents had become so frustrated last year, but now Briton Harvey Postlethwaite had designed a chassis which handled decently as well. This resulted in a second row start for Gilles Villeneuve, and a third row place for the other familiar face in the Italian camp, Didier Pironi. But Gilles — the only man seemingly capable of keeping the Renaults in sight — suffered engine failure after a mere half-dozen laps, while Pironi had to pit for fresh rubber after wearing his Goodyears out in a series of slides intended to compensate for sudden, inexplicable understeer. Like Prost, he re-joined a lap down, in eighth place and, also like Prost, his was an inspired charge, which took the Ferrari right back to second spot. But then the fuel injection began to stutter, and after two more pit stops the sole remaining turbocar other than the Renaults was also out.

Cosworths, then, dominated the minor points. The returning Niki Lauda showed all his old flair, precision, and off-track individuality in the McLaren MP4B, with its new carbonfibre bodywork and wings and revised underbody profile. Third in the race, he had also been quickest of all the "second division", normally aspirated cars during unofficial testing. In qualifying, a misjudged piece of braking saw him mount kerbs, clobber a catchfencing pole and bend a front upright — then cooly qualify seventh with this damage once he had noticed that it was about to rain! His team mate, John Watson, qualified two rows further up the grid, but finished sixth whereas the canny Lauda managed fourth. Between them at the finish was Williams newcomer Keke Rosberg, who had already shown that he was capable of racing more quickly than the identically equipped Reutemann, heading him easily in the opening stages, until his gear knob had come off in his hand and dropped into the footwell, causing all imaginable worries among the footwork!

Of the others, there was little of note that the results do not tell. They all raced hard and, after a long winter in which to sharpen the appetites, all raced with inspiration. But perhaps this was just as well: considering the other, off-track antics of the weekend (of which, more elsewhere), it is difficult to imagine the ill-treated crowd tolerating anything less.

SOUTH AFRICAN GRAND PRIX

Kyalami: 23 January 1982

77 laps of 2.55-mile circuit = 196.35 miles

RESULTS

1	Alain Prost	Renault RE30B-V6 turbo	1hr 32m 08.40s
2	Carlos Reutemann	Williams FW07C-Ford V8	1hr 32m 23.35s
3	René Arnoux	Renault RE30B-V6 turbo	1hr 32m 36.30s
4	Niki Lauda	McLaren MP4B-Ford V8	1hr 32m 40.51s
5	Keke Rosberg	Williams FW07C-Ford V8	1hr 32m 54.54s
6	John Watson	McLaren MP4B-Ford V8	1hr 32m 59.39s
7	Michele Alboreto	Tyrrell 011-Ford V8	76 laps
8	Elio de Angelis	JPS Lotus 87B-Ford V8	76 laps
9	Eliseo Salazar	ATS D5-Ford V8	75 laps
10	Manfred Winkelhock	ATS D5-Ford V8	75 laps
11	Bruno Giacomelli	Alfa Romeo 179D-V12	74 laps
12	Jochen Mass	March 821-Ford V8	74 laps
13	Andrea de Cesaris	Alfa Romeo 179D-V12	73 laps
14	Derek Daly	Theodore TY-Ford V8	73 laps
15	Raul Boesel	March 821-Ford V8	72 laps
16	Slim Borgudd	Tyrrell 011-Ford V8	72 laps
17	Chico Serra	Fittipaldi F8D-Ford V8	72 laps
18	Didier Pironi	Ferrari 126C2-V6 turbo	71 laps

Fastest lap: Prost, 1m 8.278s (134.45mph) — record
Winner's average speed: 127.86mph

RETIREMENTS

Jean-Pierre Jarier, Osella FA1C-Ford V8, 0 laps, accident; Nigel Mansell, JPS Lotus 87B-Ford V8, 1 lap, electrics; Nelson Piquet, Brabham BT50-BMW 4 turbo, 3 laps, accident; Gilles Villeneuve, Ferrari 126C2-V6 turbo, 6 laps, turbo; Eddie Cheever, Talbot-Ligier JS17B-Matra V12, 11 laps, fuel vaporisation; Riccardo Patrese, Brabham BT50-BMW 4 turbo, 18 laps, engine; Derek Warwick, Toleman TG181-Hart 4 turbo, 44 laps, accident; Jacques Laffite, Talbot Ligier JS17B-Matra V12, 54 laps, fuel vaporisation.

CHAMPIONSHIP POINTS

1	Alain Prost	9
2	Carlos Reutemann	6
3	René Arnoux	4
4	Niki Lauda	3
5	Keke Rosberg	2
6	John Watson	1

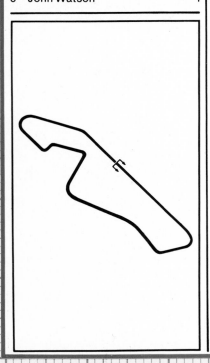

THE GRID

Arnoux 1m 06.351s	Piquet 1m 06.625s
Villeneuve 1m 07.106s	Patrese 1m 07.398s
Prost 1m 08.133s	Pironi 1m 08.360s
Rosberg 1m 08.892s	Reutemann 1m 09.306s
Watson 1m 09.306s	Alboreto 1m 10.037s
Laffite 1m 10.241s	Salazar 1m 10.624s
Lauda 1m 10.681s	Warwick 1m 10.685s
de Angelis 1m 10.685s	de Cesaris 1m 10.952s
Cheever 1m 11.005s	Mansell 1m 11.227s
Giacomelli 1m 11.285s	Winkelhock 1m 11.808s
Boesel 1m 12.077s	Mass 1m 12.100s
Borgudd 1m 12.366s	Daly 1m 13.418s
Serra 1m 13.467s	Jarier 1m 13.834s

Only one timed practice session was held, owing to a drivers' dispute.
Did not qualify: Mauro Baldi (Arrows A4-Ford V8) 1m 13.976s; Riccardo Paletti (Osella FA1C-Ford V8) 1m 15.504s; Brian Henton (Arrows A4-Ford V8) 1m 16.653s.

Alain Prost's Renault led the field from the start of the first race of the season (above) and went on to win but jubilation in the Renault pit (right) later turned to consternation. Keke Rosberg (below, during practice) was Williams' new hope

A SHAKY START

RENAULT'S thrown-way 1-2 in South Africa was not the only communications problem of the 1982 season opener. Not by a long way. Chaos and misunderstanding of a more universal order meant that the world's top racing drivers again made international headlines for reasons other than their highly paid adeptness behind the wheel. Quite the contrary, in fact: this time it was for their refusal even to sit behind the wheel, prompted by a unanimous fear that a plot was afoot to make them *less* highly paid.

The irony of it all was pungent. Before, at Jarama in Spain in 1980, there had been headlines and Grand Prix belittlement because of FISA versus FOCA. More recently, at this very same Johannesburg track just a year ago, it was a FISA versus FOCA power struggle again — and again only the FOCA teams had raced.

And now? Now *no-one* was intending to race. Now, the tables had turned so far that it was barely credible. Now, the FOCA representatives who had found their way onto FISA's Formula One Committee since the last "war" had wrought such influence that they were being accused of manipulating the drivers while simultaneously pretending to wash their hands of guilt by frowning upon FISA. Now, the controversial Super

Licence was here — but not, the drivers were going to make damn sure, to stay.

There were two particular thorns in the legally binding manuscript, which all drivers were obliged to sign agreement to before being issued with the Super Licence vital to participation in the 1982 World Championship.

Clause 1: "I am committed to the above mentioned team to drive exclusively for them in the FIA Formula 1 World Championship until . . ." (a specified date stipulated by the team). Thus there could be no team changing mid-stream; no opportunist moves by drivers from weak teams to stronger career possibilities in the event of driver retirements or injuries. Drivers were to be tied-down employees of the ruling constructors, they said, and not surprisingly they hardly welcomed the prospect.

And Clause 5: "I will do nothing which might harm the moral or material interests of the image of international motor sport or the FIA Formula One World Championship."

Hawk-eyed Niki Lauda noticed both the clauses and, as probably the highest paid racing driver ever, refused to sign the document and alerted his colleagues. A few other drivers said that they had been rather worried, yes, but that their team bosses had pressured them into signing.

FISA President Jean-Marie Balestre countered that the drivers, in the main, had signed the document, so why were they bickering about it afterwards? If they had signed, surely they agreed! Bernard Ecclestone argued heatedly with several "star" drivers, including his own

Brabham team member, World Champion Nelson Piquet — with the emphasis on "his own". That, it is clear, was the way he would like it. Nelson Piquet the Brabham employee. It is not the Piquets or Villeneuves or Laudas who attract the public interest, he purported, but whoever happens to be in the right car at the right time. As history will recall, he reasoned, drivers are expendable — but the sport and its support survives them.

And so the bitter acrimony raged. Appointed representative of the drivers' cause, Didier Pironi, *insisted* on their behalf that the clauses be changed. Otherwise there would be no drivers this weekend. Predictably, FISA refused.

So the world's top 30 racing drivers, a goodly portion of them millionaires, decided to strike. An almost unanimous action, with all the good intention, but also all the elements of farce, of a children's pantomime. To escape the influence of the constructors, all the drivers at Kyalami, with the sole exception of March's Jochen Mass, "escaped" from the circuit together in a coach — only physically to imprison themselves, one hour before official qualifying was due to start, in a room in the nearby Sunnyside Park Hotel, belonging to Grand Prix Drivers' Association Secretary Trevor Rowe.

Here, the drivers plotted their cause, and sent Pironi back to the battleground as an emissary. And here, like schoolboys in revolution, they locked themselves in, refusing to speak to incredulous pressmen or irate team managers or even to tearful wives and girlfriends. It was a strike that lasted the night, with

all on slung-down mattresses but with perked-up spirits. If nothing else, it was a uniquely talented gathering, as Elio de Angelis and Gilles Villeneuve played the piano, Lauda related anecdotes and Bruno Giacomelli sketched caricatures of various constructors on a blackboard.

From the hotel, Lauda kept in telephone contact with Pironi at the track, who negotiated on Thursday evening and negotiated again on Friday morning against the backdrop of a solitary racing car — that of Mass — lapping the circuit. Then, announced Pironi, agreement had been reached. At 10 am on Friday Lauda received the telephone call they had all been waiting for, and the 29 unshaven drivers caught the coach back to the circuit. Only 29? Yes: Toleman's Teo Fabi had added further colour to the pantomime by "just going to the washroom" and escaping in a car!

And with Business-as-Usual at Kyalami once more, Ecclestone criticised Piquet and deemed him unfit to drive on Friday morning — only for the Brazilian to go out and set a front row time in the afternoon! Ensign boss Morris Nunn, on the surface at least, withdrew his Grand Prix newcomer Roberto Guerrero because, he said, he was "in an inappropriate physical and mental condition to drive."

But drive, at last, the others did — only for the race to end with an unpleasant expectancy of recriminations, suspensions, fines, and more publicised squabbling. In the truest tradition of farce, it was unclear whether anyone had won, but certain that much had been lost.

ACTIONS being louder than words, Nelson Piquet made the final comment. Quite rightly so, one might say, considering that he was the Brazilian World Champion, at the Brazilian Grand Prix — but it was for all the wrong reasons.

He had won his home race, yes, and he had driven well to withstand a typical Gilles Villeneuve Ferrari challenge, which had ended with a not entirely untypical Villeneuve Ferrari excursion. Thereafter it had been straightforward; victory was a mere formality — compensation delivered to the crowd who, just twelve months earlier, had looked on in disbelieving anguish as their idol spun hopelessly across a wet track on dry tyres. This time, Piquet had got it right.

But — even at the circuit itself on race day, long before the whole event was riddled by cancerous Formula One politics — it was not quite as simple as that. In success there had been an ironic sense of failure, and in making it look oh so easy there had been misleading deception. True, the Ferrari and Renault turbo cars had been beaten — not, alas, by Brabham's own new turbo weapon, the four-cylinder BMW M1 unit, but instead by the venerable Ford Cosworth DFV which the team had spent so many pesetas trying to consign to history. And, as anyone could detect after witnessing the victory ceremony, perhaps winning — nay, even finishing — a modern day Formula One race was not quite so easy after all. Before popping the champagne cork, Champion Piquet reminded the world of the super-human, mind-over-matter performance that had been required to claim the title five months earlier in Las Vegas. In Rio, as in Vegas, there was an unusual preponderance of left hand bends, and again Piquet clambered out of his Brabham-Ford with aching neck and limbs. Also just as in Vegas, he eventually folded up helplessly and teetered down the steps of the winner's rostrum . . .

Despite the lessons of its clumsy, self-destructive start at Kyalami and its glaring absence from Argentina, the 1982 Grand Prix season showed no signs of improvement in Brazil. It was, rued Those That Know, still on the critical list. This circuit, with its long, motor-straining straight and fast, driver-straining turns, *should* be remembered as the place where Gilles Villeneuve showed his brilliance in a quick but inadequately handling Ferrari 126CK turbo, leading the pack bravely and against the odds just as he had at Jarama in 1981. The place where Nelson Piquet showed that Cosworth reliability could win him the title again, but that turbo perseverance was plainly throwing the chance away. Or the place where, with three more years of costly and frustrating development behind the first ever F1 turbo, Renault's latest version of the theme maintained Alain Prost at the head of the World Championship points table.

Instead, events would later dictate that this Brazilian Grand Prix be remembered more as the latest chapter in the fearful Turbo-Cosworth war. The place where the Cosworth ranks fought back, spitting insubordinately in the face of their much more powerful opponents with a shrewd but soon-to-be-outlawed "interpretation" of the weight limit rules' loopholes. No; this was not the race of the heroic Villeneuve or the omnipresent

Prost, or even of the exhausted Piquet. It was the nadir of contorted common sense, yet simultaneously the zenith of clever constructors' rule exploitation. The turning point in the short but stormy era of Cosworth car dieting.

The loophole, like all loopholes, was disarmingly simple once recognised. After a Grand Prix, cars are always permitted to top-up the systems with "essential fluids", before going on to the scales. That way, a car which started the race legitimately may not unjustly be considered beneath the weight limit because it has simply consumed excessive engine oil or coolant water during the course of a race. Coolant being that required by the engine, of course . . .

. . . but suddenly 1982-style F1 cars — or Cosworth cars at least — developed enormous braking problems. Their brakes were overheating, 'twas said, because of the ever-improved cornering and later braking. It was natural, 'twas also said, to require brake coolant to cure the problem. And the coolant bottles, of course, just *had* to be as enor-

mous as the "problem" they were introduced to solve. Fill them to the brim in the queue for the scales after the race, and shake your knowledgeable head ruefully at the amazing demands these cars make these days on brakes. But *before* the race, in that thin veil of secrecy called the team garage, merely inject the truly "essential" dribble.

Hence, instant disposable ballast. An equivalent to horsepower improvement, achieved in a fraction of the development time with unprecedented infallibility, and at a billionth of the cost. Little wonder that the turbo teams verged on tears.

It was that old chestnut again. To the *letter* of the regulations, Gordon Murray, Frank Williams *et al* were in the right, although to the *spirit* of the rules they were not. But why argue lightness other than on grounds of safety? Renault argued it, and indeed officially protested it, as did Ferrari. But then Renault also fielded a car here for Alain Prost which had its rear wing break away from the rest of the car not just once in untimed

At the end of a victorious home Grand Prix run, Piquet (above) was near total collapse while Carlos Reutemann (top right) just didn't want to hear about GP racing any more. The water bottles arrived in Brazil and not all were as small as this (above right) on Guerrero's non-qualifying Ensign. Villeneuve challenged Piquet only until he ended his race in the catch fences (below)

rassing absence of new Matra Murenas and Ranchos in their showrooms. No sales, no turbo.

And what of Brabham? The team's BMW turbo hope that disintegrated miserably at Kyalami two long months ago, just as it had so often and so expensively in the telemetry-observed winter test sessions. The cancellation of the Argentine Grand Prix, mainly because of "financial reasons", had given Brabham boss Bernie Ecclestone time to do some financial reasoning of his own. BMW had issued a Brabham-knocking statement after the SA race. The BT50-BMWs, they commented with quaint but controversial wording, suffered one basic problem: "The engines are too fast for the chassis."

Indeed?

So it was that Mr.Ecclestone, the Brabham team owner, sat down at a committee table as Mr.Ecclestone the chairman of a FOCA meeting, in Rio's Intercontinental Hotel. The F1 rules, he reminded, would be due for renewal when the Concorde Agreement expires at the end of 1984. Then, said the man who had reputedly invested over a million pounds in the BMW turbo project, turbos should be banned. They were too fast (a familiar phrase!) and too damned expensive. And besides, he said later, at the track, in early answer to any possible accusations of hypocrisy, if anyone else wanted to run his BMW engines, they could take the bloody things.

The on-track action of the weekend echoed those sentiments. Nelson Piquet waltzed to a win with Ford power. Villeneuve's challenge had been a strong one, the Ferrari powering away from the front row into an immediate, vulnerable but vociferously defended lead. He had not taken pole, losing three-tenths of a second to Prost's Renault RE30B, but Gilles was sure he *could* have taken it were it not for a moment's hold up on his All Out quick lap, by Keke Rosberg's Williams FW07. The race, he predicted, would be good — and it was, just like that classic Jarama '81 run. Until lap 30. Then, the chasing BT49D of Piquet made its bid. The Brazilian had charged through from a traffic-induced seventh on the grid, setting the race's fastest lap as early as lap four! Opposition was token — until he tackled leader Villeneuve. Then, the Ferrari driver left his braking fractionally too late and slid wide. Piquet lunged alongside, and Villeneuve found himself faced with the choice of tangling with his challenger, lifting off and losing all momentum as he swept by — or risking the dirt. Villeneuve being Villeneuve, the grass it was. He kept the loud pedal dug in and fought with the car. But it didn't quite work: one large, lazy spin and his race was over.

From this moment, Piquet had it made, running out to an 11-second victory and second place in the points chase.

Still heading that table was Prost. The Frenchman had qualified with the outright speed worthy of a win, but in the race the Renault was down-on-power, with a worsening tyre vibration, so he 'only' finished third. But remember: a string of third places *can* win the championship.

And second? Another man who had catapulted to the forefront of championship possibilities, Williams' '82 new-

comer Keke Rosberg. Taking over in the British team where the retiring farmer Alan Jones had left off, he had conducted himself in a hard-charging manner of which his predecessor would have been proud. It was clear, already, that if anyone could take a Cosworth-powered title this year, it was Rosberg.

His task was aided, of course, by the demise of others. Pironi had his pit stop; Prost his muffled engine; and René Arnoux his second unhappy race in succession in the other Renault. Again he proved his ability to mix it with team mate Prost, both cars passing and repassing each other and sowing the poisonous seeds of civil war. Like Prost, Arnoux suffered a weak engine — but, unlike the championship leader, he spun off in his efforts.

In spinning, the Renault was collected by Carlos Reutemann. The Argentinian, it became clearer, had returned to Grands Prix only to find himself teamed with another Jones-type hard-charger. He was 0.8 seconds slower than teammate Rosberg in qualifying, and equally lacklustre in the race. Before hitting Arnoux, he had tangled with the seventh placed McLaren MP4B of Niki Lauda, in an incident remarkably similar to his 1981 Zandvoort fracas with Jacques Laffite. That Dutch clash, it could be argued, cost Grand Prix racing's senior citizen the '81 championship, his last shot at the title: with an Argentina-Britain war looming in the Falklands, and with little satisfaction from his driving, Carlos Reutemann again retired. As in Las Vegas, it was an inglorious departure which did not impress Frank Williams.

Trailing Rosberg, then, Cosworth honour fell to John Watson, who qualified a mighty 1.8 seconds slower than team mate Lauda, but actually passed him in the race as the Austrian took to the dirt avoiding the errant Arnoux. Like Rosberg's or Prost's, Watson's was a quiet points accumulation, but one which would later add up to loud prominence.

Nigel Mansell brought the new Lotus 91 home fifth on its debut, happier on race rubber than he had been on qualifiers but plagued throughout by a porpoising problem so vicious that it led to several skirt breakages. Team mate de Angelis, like many others, retired with accident damage. But perhaps the strangest accident of all was the long, wayward spin of Riccardo Patrese's Brabham. From an early third place, he dropped back, tangled with Mansell, and then, on lap 34, indulged in an independent spin. He had blacked out with exhaustion.

Piquet, therefore, was not alone in his physical distress, in a car whose revised bodywork had unexpectedly reduced cool air flow into the cockpit. As an epilogue to the South African arguments, he had shown that, perhaps more than ever before, the Grand Prix driver does *earn* his wealth.

All that heat, all that effort — and then, tediously typical, all the post race protestations. Piquet's car, like the Williams of Rosberg, was a water-cooled lightweight. On those grounds, both their points were later to be taken away from them by a French court. Which meant that Monsieur Prost suddenly had nine more points instead of just four. Controversial decisions like that could also decide a championship . . .

practice, but twice. With red faces, Renault replaced the lightweight carbon-fibre wing mounting with a "conventional", metal mounting.

On the all-important grounds of safety, Ferrari also committed their own public violation. Pitting on lap 35 of the race with fuel starvation and worn Goodyears, Didier Pironi took on fresh rubber, and more fuel — with the engine still ignited, and with a fuel vent illegally open to atmospheric pressure, earning a subsequent protest from Ken Tyrell.

The all-pervading politics here forced the race itself into the shadows. An altogether new meaning to "politicking" developed in the Ligier team, with a rather unique turbo problem — Jacques Laffite was unhappy (just as he would still be, vocally, in the twilight of the season) and Guy Ligier likewise — because he couldn't even get his hands on a promised turbo motor in the first place. The V6 turbo that was to have marked Matra's return with Ligier was conspicuously absent — because Ligier's sponsor Peugeot-Talbot showed an emba-

BRAZILIAN GRAND PRIX
Rio de Janeiro Autodrome: 21 March 1982
63 laps of 3.13-mile circuit = 196.94 miles

RESULTS

1	Nelson Piquet	Brabham BT49D-Ford V8	1hr 43m 53.76s*
2	Keke Rosberg	Williams FW07C-Ford V8	1hr 44m 05.74s*
3	Alain Prost	Renault RE30B-V6 turbo	1hr 44m 33.13s
4	John Watson	McLaren MP4B-Ford V8	1hr 44m 36.12s
5	Nigel Mansell	JPS-Lotus 91-Ford V8	1hr 45m 09.99s
6	Michele Alboreto	Tyrrell 011-Ford V8	1hr 45m 23.89s
7	Manfred Winkelhock	ATS D5-Ford V8	62 laps
8	Didier Pironi	Ferrari 126C2-V6 turbo	62 laps
9	Slim Borgudd	Tyrrell 011-Ford V8	61 laps
10	Jochen Mass	March 821-Ford V8	61 laps
11	Jean-Pierre Jarier	Osella FA1C-Ford V8	60 laps
12	Mauro Baldi	Arrows A4-Ford V8	57 laps

Fastest lap: Piquet, 1m 36.582s (116.52mph) — record
Winner's average speed: 113.71mph

RETIREMENTS

Raul Boesel, March 821-Ford V8, 11 laps, accident; Derek Daly, Theodore TY-Ford V8, 12 laps, spun off; Andrea de Cesaris, Alfa Romeo 182-V12, 14 laps, loose undertray; Jacques Laffite, Talbot-Ligier JS17B-Matra V12, 15 laps, handling problems; Bruno Giacomelli, Alfa Romeo 181-V12, 16 laps, engine; Eddie Cheever, Talbot-Ligier JS17B-Matra V12, 19 laps, water leak; René Arnoux, Renault RE30B-V6 turbo, 21 laps, accident; Carlos Reutemann, Williams FW07C-Ford V8, 21 laps, accident; Niki Lauda, McLaren MP4B-Ford V8, 21 laps, suspension damage; Elio de Angelis, JPS-Lotus 91-Ford V8, 21 laps, accident; Gilles Villeneuve, Ferrari 126C2-V6 turbo, 29 laps, accident; Riccardo Patrese, Brabham BT49D-Ford V8, 34 laps, heat exhaustion; Chico Serra, Fittipaldi F8D-Ford V8, 36 laps, accident; Eliseo Salazar, ATS D5-Ford V8, 37 laps, engine.

*Piquet and Rosberg were subsequently excluded from the results following eligibility protests by Ferrari and Renault. Alain Prost was therefore deemed the winner.

CHAMPIONSHIP LEADERS

1	Alain Prost	18
2	John Watson	7
3	Carlos Reutemann	6
4 =	René Arnoux	4
4 =	Nigel Mansell	4
6 =	Michele Alboreto	3
6 =	Niki Lauda	3
8 =	Keke Rosberg	2
8 =	Manfred Winkelhock	2
10	Didier Pironi	1

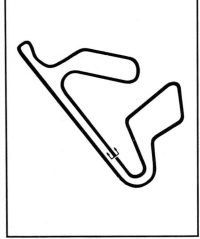

THE GRID

	Prost 1m 28.808s
Villeneuve 1m 29.173s	
	Rosberg 1m 29.358s
Arnoux 1m 30.121s	
	Lauda 1m 30.152s
Reutemann 1m 30.183s	
	Piquet 1m 30.281s
Pironi 1m 30.655s	
	Patrese 1m 30.967s
de Cesaris 1m 31.229s	
	de Angelis 1m 31.790s
Watson 1m 31.906s	
	Alboreto 1m 31.991s
Mansell 1m 32.228s	
	Winkelhock 1m 32.524s
Giacomelli 1m 32.769s	
	Boesel 1m 34.050s
Salazar 1m 34.262s	
	Baldi 1m 34.380s
Daly 1m 34.413s	
	Borgudd 1m 35.020s
Mass 1m 35.039s	
	Jarier 1m 35.081s
Laffite 1m 35.084s	
	Serra 1m 35.246s
Cheever 1m 35.288s	

Did not qualify: Teo Fabi (Toleman TG181-Hart 4 turbo) 1m 35.326s; Roberto Guerrero (Ensign N181-Ford V8) 1m 35.730s; Brian Henton (Arrows A4-Ford V8) 1m 35.748s; Derek Warwick (Toleman TG181-Hart 4 turbo) 1m 36.014s; Riccardo Paletti (Osella FA1C-Ford V8) did not pre-qualify.

Ready for action, but not for success; Gilles Villeneuve (left) again coped heroically with the powerful but still ill-handling Ferrari until, after having led, he spun out of the Brazilian GP while fighting off the challenge of Nelson Piquet. The Brabham driver went on to win on home ground, from Keke Rosberg's Williams (below) only for both to be deemed underweight following the water tank controversy. Both were subsequently excluded from the results and the nine points went to Alain Prost

41

IT was a surprise, for sure — in the words of the man himself. *No-one* had thought that it could happen so soon, least of all Niki Lauda. There had still been too many factors stacked against him.

Sure, he had single-mindedly endured a winter of physical torment and rigid army discipline, as only Lauda could. There had been the early morning running, the incessant exercises, the often terrifying, fast cross-country skiing. There had been the new motor racing financial games, with the lure of instant results but the possibility of embarrassing losses. There had been the carefully controlled diet; the right foods at the right time. There had also been the regulated sleeping pattern, so that even in escape from this long programme he was still fulfilling a requirement.

Willi Dungl had seen to all that, Willi the doctor who had helped Lauda bring himself back from the critical list after his fiery Nürburgring accident in 1976. Five-and-a-half years later, this time helping Lauda bring himself back from the disappointments of the private airline business to the more immediate satisfaction and profits of motor racing, Dungl could once more pronounce himself "delighted" with Andreas Nikolaus Lauda's fitness. It was a pity, he said, that a man being paid millions on his comeback by Marlboro should insist on smoking the damn things as well, but the motivation of the man was inspiring. The wiry Lauda, too, had never been more confident of his physical condition. He was fitter than he'd ever been, he reckoned. Fitter, probably, than anyone else in the Grand Prix world.

The contrast was incredible, rather like Lauda's self-confessed life story of "weedy, goofy-toothed school kid's rise" to one of the sharpest, most talented, and extraordinarily courageous men ever to feature in world class motor racing. Remember his attempt at a discreet comeback drive, in the McLaren MP4 at Donington Park last October? Photographers and newsmen had found their way in, to join the proud Marlboro personnel invited to the track to witness their latest *coup* in action. And that had made it all the worse. More witnesses to relate how Lauda had by no means been slow, but how he hadn't been exactly quick either. More tales of the wizened state of the man as he got out of the car, physically reluctant to drive any further. He was *exhausted!*

Lauda, then, may have been doubted by the unwary until the United States West Grand Prix around the streets of Long Beach in early April. Especially so because They believed he had only returned for the dollars, and because HE still believed that the cars nowadays were "rubbish; really terrible to drive." Even after a winter of testing and some quick times at the Paul Ricard circuit, Lauda complained persistently, often to people who didn't want to listen, about the gross and unnecessary discomfort of these new-style ground-effect machines with no suspension and even less respect for the well-being of the human anatomy.

Those things, perhaps more than anything else, lulled the optimists amongst Lauda's rivals into believing that the Austrian had not yet really come to grips with Formula One 1982 style. Those, the

moderate form of the MP4 on its Michelins, and Lauda's own honest confessions of his limitations. He had even made such admissions this very week, a couple of days before the Long Beach race. His return programme was simply "on schedule", he observed laconically. Which was to say that he was still climbing the progress curve at a reasonable pace, thank you very much, but that he had not yet reached the peak. That — and of course the first comeback win — would not come for a few races yet, he said . . .

In reality, it couldn't have come any sooner. Indeed, Niki Lauda did not so much score his first comeback Grand Prix win at Long Beach on Sunday afternoon, but on Saturday. With over half-an-hour of official qualifying still remaining, he knew he had it sewn-up.

Until that time, Lauda had been comfortably quickest. He had only used one of Saturday's two permitted, available sets of Q-tyres, for very good reason, and just like the Good Old Days he sat on the pit counter by his parked car, watching with interest as other front runners scrabbled desperately around the Californian streets in an attempt to oust him. Both the Renaults of Alain Prost and René Arnoux tried long and hard in

the dying minutes of qualifying, in spite of the inherent bottom-end throttle lag of their turbo motors, and in spite of the intense disgust of Renault's Sports President, Max Mongenot, who said that the circuit revisions — particularly the new chicane supposedly added to slow the cars down on Shoreline Drive — had been designed to favour the British constructors' Cosworth-powered cars. Both Renaults failed in their bid, but nevertheless reaped an excellent monopoly of the second row.

In a weekend of surprises, the only man to pip Lauda to pole — and only just, on the last timed lap, long after the pit personnel had turned away from the computer-timing video display, sure that Niki had it made — was young Andrea de Cesaris. The 22-year-old Alfa Romeo driver whose place at McLaren had been taken by Lauda had beaten the maestro at his own much-practiced art.

For de Cesaris, there were tears of latin joy after his superb qualifying performance, in which he stole the first pole of his career by a tenth-of-a-second. After the race it was all that he could do to hold back tears of a very different kind. He had led into the first corner without challenge, as Lauda had cautiously intimated he could if the Alfa left the line

more cleanly, and he had stayed in front for 15 laps. Over twenty-two glorious minutes in which to drag a reputation from the depths of impudent wreckless-ness to the suddenly exalted heights of a brilliant new star; time to revel in the rare sparkle of the V12-powered Alfa 182, making its finest showing of the year on a circuit that obliged the Michelins and emphasised the Alfa's magnanimous turn-in capabilities.

Ultimately, however, it was the Alfa Romeo's turn-*out* which cost de Cesaris dearly. It was lap 33 out of 75, with Lauda now in the lead and disappearing fast, but Andrea looking secure for second — until he thought he saw his engine smoking. That was his story afterwards; after he'd smitten the concrete retaining wall and savaged the suspension. He'd looked in his mirror, he said, at the engine. One moment's inattention cost the sort of result he'd been dreaming of all his life.

Lauda, by now, had long left the likes of Arnoux, Bruno Giacomelli, and Gilles Villeneuve, with whom he had circulated in a delicate nose-to-tail train in the opening stages. Arnoux had actually passed Lauda at the start, and held second place until lap seven. Then, the Frenchman fumbled a gear — at pre-

cisely the same instant that Lauda, close behind, was outbraked by Giacomelli. Lauda was laughing: the Alfa rammed the Renault, and both were out.

At this point it was clear to all why Lauda hadn't used his second set of qualifiers the day before. He simply hadn't needed them. The Michelin race rubber was not just a match for the supposedly sticky qualifiers, but even better. On race day, therefore, Lauda's lap times remained super-quick, and in his third outing as a second-time round Grand Prix driver, he'd cracked it.

Others, in contrast, cracked only their cars, hard against the concrete walls. World Champion Piquet's early season hiccoughs — helped none by his nine lightweight Brazilian points later being taken away from him — raced hard with Gilles Villeneuve's Ferrari, just as he had in his home Grand Prix. But he also ran wide and collected a wall, just as he had two days earlier. His Brabham-Ford team mate Riccardo Patrese also committed indiscretions in both qualifying and the race, although in the latter he battled from a lowly seventeenth place on the opening lap, soon to be deprived of a front fin, to take fourth spot. The points were his primarily because he had survived, as were those of Michele

Alboreto's fifth placed Tyrrell 011, and Elio de Angelis's sixth placed Lotus. Only second placed Keke Rosberg and third placed Villeneuve had what might really be described as a race, battling mightily until the Williams scrambled past the Ferrari, only for Gilles to retaliate immediately with an impossible outbraking attempt and half-spin, concluding the dice.

Those who didn't survive, nor look like scoring, were numerous in a race saturated with driver errors. They naturally included the perenially struggling tailenders, but they also included the likes of Ferrari's Didier Pironi — who crashed, on lap six — and John Watson, who had started on softer Michelins than Lauda, had to pit for a new set, and finished a forgotten seventh. It would have been incredible at the time to propose that Watson and Pironi would later lead the 1982 World Championship.

But then, was it not incredible, too, that Andrea de Cesaris had taken pole position for, and led, a Grand Prix? Or that Niki Lauda had bounced back to form in these "ridiculous" cars in just three races, and five months later would also be in the running for the World Championship when the final race came around?

Confounding most prophets, it took Niki Lauda only three Grands Prix to find his way back to the top step of the winner's rostrum (above left) — and that after a convincing display of the old psychology in practice. Then he was beaten to pole at the very last gasp by none other than the unpredictable Andrea de Cesaris, who actually led from the start (left) and for the 15 laps it took a cautious Lauda to find a way past. de Cesaris ultimately dumped the car unceremoniously into the wall and in that he was not alone; when Piquet collected the concrete the tow truck which removed his bent Brabham must have raised a few heartbeats (above right) and Giacomelli outbraked Lauda only to find the unfortunate Arnoux in his path and Super Rat on his winning way (right). Amidst all the carnage, Gilles Villeneuve survived with little more than the odd half spin to claim a third place which was eventually taken away after Ken Tyrrell protested the Ferrari's strange double wings (above)

UNITED STATES GRAND PRIX (WEST)
Long Beach: 4 April 1982
75.5 laps of 2.1-mile circuit = 160.8 miles

RESULTS

1	Niki Lauda	McLaren MP4B-Ford V8	1hr 58m 25.32s
2	Keke Rosberg	Williams FW07C-Ford V8	1hr 58m 39.98s*
3	Gilles Villeneuve	Ferrari 126C2-V6 turbo	1hr 59m 29.61s*
4	Riccardo Patrese	Brabham BT49C-Ford V8	1hr 59m 44.46s
5	Michele Alboreto	Tyrrell 011-Ford V8	1hr 59m 46.26s
6	Elio de Angelis	JPS Lotus 91-Ford V8	74 laps
7	John Watson	McLaren MP4B-Ford V8	74 laps
8	Nigel Mansell	JPS-Lotus 91-Ford V8	73 laps
9	Jochen Mass	March 821-Ford V8	73 laps
10	Raul Boesel	March 821-Ford V8	70 laps
11	Slim Borgudd	Tyrrell 011-Ford V8	68 laps

Fastest lap: Lauda, 1m 30.831s (84.42mph)
Winner's average speed: 81.47mph

RETIREMENTS

Manfred Winkelhock, ATS D5-Ford V8, 1 lap, accident; Eliseo Salazar, ATS D5-Ford V8, 3 laps, accident; Bruno Giacomelli, Alfa Romeo 182-V12, 5 laps, accident; René Arnoux, Renault RE30B-V6 turbo, 5 laps, accident; Didier Pironi, Ferrari 126C2-V6 turbo, 6 laps, accident; Alain Prost, Renault RE30B-V6 turbo, 10 laps, brake failure; Mario Andretti, Williams FW07C-Ford V8, 19 laps, suspension damage; Derek Daly, Theodore TY02-Ford V8, 22 laps, accident; Nelson Piquet, Brabham BT49D-Ford V8, 25 laps, accident; Jean Pierre Jarier, Osella FA1C-Ford V8, 26 laps, transmission; Jacques Laffite, Talbot-Ligier JS17-Matra V12, 26 laps, spun, unable to restart; Roberto Guerrero, Ensign N181-Ford V8, 27 laps, accident; Brian Henton, Arrows A4-Ford V8, 32 laps, accident; Andrea de Cesaris, Alfa Romeo 182-V12, 33 laps, accident; Eddie Cheever, Talbot-Ligier JS17-Matra V12, 59 laps, gearbox oil leak.

*Villeneuve was subsequently excluded from the results following an eligibility protest by Tyrrell.

CHAMPIONSHIP LEADERS

1	Alain Prost	18
2	Niki Lauda	12
3 =	Keke Rosberg	8
3 =	John Watson	8
5 =	Michele Alboreto	6
5 =	Carlos Reutemann	6
7 =	René Arnoux	4
7 =	Nigel Mansell	4
7 =	Riccardo Patrese	4
10 =	Elio de Angelis	2
10 =	Manfred Winkelhock	2

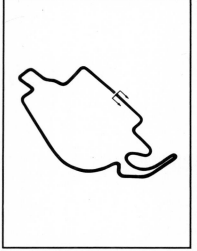

THE GRID

Lauda 1m 27.436s	de Cesaris 1m 27.316s
Prost 1m 27.979s	Arnoux 1m 27.763s
Piquet 1m 28.276s	Giacomelli 1m 28.087s
Rosberg 1m 28.576s	Villeneuve 1m 28.476s
Jarier 1m 28.708s	Pironi 1m 28.680s
Alboreto 1m 29.027s	Watson 1m 28.885s
Andretti 1m 29.468s	Cheever 1m 29.336s
de Angelis 1m 29.694s	Laffite 1m 29.587s
Patrese 1m 29.948s	Mansell 1m 29.758s
Henton 1m 30.474s	Guerrero 1m 30.168s
Daly 1m 30.919s	Mass 1m 30.476s
Borgudd 1m 31.033s	Boesel 1m 30.977s
Salazar 1m 31.825s	Winkelhock 1m 31.593s

Did not qualify: Teo Fabi (Toleman TG181-Hart 4 turbo) 1m 31.988s; Riccardo Paletti (Osella FA1C-Ford V8) 1m 32.146s; Chico Serra (Fittipaldi F8D-Ford V8) 1m 32.496s; Mauro Baldi (Arrows A4-Ford V8) 1m 33.701s. Derek Warwick (Toleman TG181-Hart 4 turbo) did not prequalify.

Ahead of schedule, the Rat was back. It took only three races for the returning Niki Lauda to win a Grand Prix, his McLaren MP4B (below right) excelling in Long Beach with its good Michelins and good grip. Also performing better than expected around the street circuit, Elio de Angelis took the Lotus 91 (above) to a championship point, although less fortunate was René Arnoux's Renault (below) which was attacked by Bruno Giacomelli's Alfa Romeo after only six laps

PIRONI STEALS THE SHOW

THEY put on a good show, the two Ferraris, but if the truth be known they had to. The 45,000 spectators at Imola on Saturday and the 100,000 on Sunday had come for nothing else. Indeed, they had come *knowing* that there would be nothing else, even had they wanted it, for there were only 13 cars in this Formula One race.

But a good show it was. René Arnoux led, while Gilles Villeneuve and Didier Pironi tucked themselves together nose-to-tail and chased. Then Villeneuve passed Arnoux, after applying 26 laps of harassment. Then Arnoux passed him back, and again the Ferrari pursued. The crowd loved it, cheering from beneath their Ferrari banners, and the TV stations loved it too. So what if the sulking FOCA teams weren't present? It only takes two cars to make a good race.

Then, as could almost be expected, Arnoux's Renault turbo spat the flames of failure and stopped. On lap 45, the lead once more belonged to Villeneuve and so, to the crowd's delight, did the race. Sure, Pironi took over where Arnoux had left off, and kept alive the show-business of cat-and-mouse. But Villeneuve did not let this concern him. Why should he? He knew Pironi was not only his team mate but also a good friend, and he knew, therefore, that he was only playing a game. Just something to keep the crowd happy and underline the fact that the likes of Brabham and Williams weren't missed. There was obviously no point in *really* racing. Not when they were running 1-2 like this, with 15 laps remaining in which to preserve engines and tyres. No point at all.

Not to Villeneuve, at least. If there was anything the confused and argumentative Grand Prix world could take for granted by now, it was that little Gilles Villeneuve was the biggest talent in their midst. In his own modest but self-assured manner, Gilles knew it too, sitting out front in the San Marino Grand Prix, in a position to discern that it would be far wiser to lap in the 1m 37s bracket and be sure of winning the race, rather than needlessly go nearly two full seconds per lap faster and risk running out of fuel, which was marginal in the extreme at this race. Of course he could go faster, if need be. Faster than anyone. But there was no need. Not to Villeneuve.

But it was because Pironi knew of the French-Canadian's immeasurable abilities as well, that the trouble started. The Frenchman, on this, his honeymoon week, with his new wife watching, wanted to prove otherwise. And he would exercise no conscience, it seemed, whether by fair means or foul.

Villeneuve had no doubt that it was foul, in every sense of the word. He was certainly not alone in his opinion, and of course he was in the best position in the world to judge. One only had to look at the two Ferraris' lap times, he pointed out. They told the real truth of the whole, unpleasant story.

While shadowing Arnoux, Gilles had been lapping in the 1m 35.5s bracket. He could have gone a little bit faster, even in race trim, as his considerably quicker qualifying performance of 30.25s shows. Then, as he might have expected, Arnoux's engine had blown. That left Villeneuve from Pironi, with the Ferrari pits hanging out a "Slow" signal. So, obli-

ging the team orders, Gilles dropped into the 1m 36.5s groove preserving car and, most importantly, conserving fuel. If only the bloody petrol lasted, the race would be his.

With Gilles going that much slower, Pironi had the chance to close up on his team mate — and, when Gilles made a mistake on lap 46, he slipped by. No problem, thought Villeneuve. His team mate was just playing to the crowd. He would surely maintain much the same sensible pace, and without doubt he would let Gilles re-take his rightful lead, and so ultimately the win, just a few laps before the end. Gilles had been in front when the Renault's engine had gone, and so by assuming the lead in a 1-2 situation he would naturally take the win. Team orders and common sense would prevail, just as they had when he had dutifully followed Jody Scheckter around at Kyalami in 1979, despite catching him hand-over-fist. He had been potentially quicker there, but had played the subservient shadow until

46

The signals from the pits (left), the stark contrast between Villeneuve's disillusionment (below left) and Pironi's jubilation (right) and the hard fact of the results of Villeneuve's last Grand Prix say it all, after Imola there would have been no quarter ... In simple numbers (below) this was a small Grand Prix named for a small country, but in quality it was immense, with René Arnoux leading, then splitting, then again leading the Ferraris (bottom) before succumbing to another engine failure and yet another retirement

had to take the initiative; to re-claim the lead and reinstate common sense.

That he did on lap 49 — only for Pironi to come charging by again four laps later! Once more the lap times dipped into the low 1m 35s region, and once more Villeneuve shook his head in disbelief. He re-took the lead, once and for all, he thought, on lap 59, the penultimate lap. Again he eased to 1m 37s, and later this policy would be proven to be totally correct when it was found that Ferrari no 27 finished the race with barely enough fuel for one more lap in its tanks.

But to the disbelief of the crowd, and of his team mate, Pironi did it again! On the last down-the-straight draft of the last lap he dived out of Gilles' slipstream to steal the lead, and the victory.

So Pironi sprayed the champagne from the highest step on the presentation podium, celebrating the second Grand Prix win of his career which, in a world of justice, should have been Gilles Villeneuve's seventh. The real, moral victor was left to stand back from the photographers and the crowd with pursed lips and angry thoughts. He had considered leaving Ferrari more than once these last couple of years, to go instead to win as often as his enormous talent deserved in a Brabham or a Williams. Every team in the world wanted him, so why not give it some thought? If Pironi was going to be at Ferrari again next year, he said, there was just no way that he could consider anything else.

There were little means, either, by which one could consider this San Marino race in any context other than the Pironi-Villeneuve split. Quite apart from the tragic consequences to which this rivalry would soon contribute, there was little else worth remembering in a race composed of only 13 cars, only half of which might be described as competitive. Although dangerously close to it, the Ferraris did not, of course, run dry of fuel, so that left Alboreto's Tyrrell third, 70 seconds behind. If Ken Tyrrell had genuinely broken away from the FOCA teams' boycott in order to please his Italian sponsors Ceramica (see separate story), then he had been wise.

Fourth, and a whole lap behind, Jean-Pierre Jarier scored the only championship points of the season in the large, Pirelli shod Osella FA1C, ahead of the ATS D5s of Salazar and Winkelhock.

Yes, both ATSs in the points! This was largely because Alain Prost's Renault lasted only six laps before its predictable engine failure, while the Alfa Romeos of Andrea de Cesaris and Bruno Giacomelli succumbed to electrical failure and an oil leak. Indeed, Salazar's fifth place was more ridiculous than it first seemed, for it was achieved despite a back row qualifying performance, six mighty seconds off the pace, caused by the absence of the Avon tyre truck, which forced him to use a dubious mixture of Avon cross-ply fronts and Pirelli radial rears. In the race itself, he even had time to stop to replace a broken gear lever. Adding an extra element of silliness to the ATS points finishes, Winkelhock's car was later disqualified for being 6kgs underweight. His transmission had been damaged, and the gearbox oil had genuinely leaked away — but new rules are new rules, even if, like the San Marino race itself, they make no sense.

Jody had pitted for new tyres. Or just as they had again at Monza in that same season, where Gilles realised only too well that a win was his last chance of keeping his championship hopes alive, but where he also obligingly followed the leading, but slower, Scheckter.

But at Imola three arduous and unrepresentatively unrewarding years later, the Ferrari system faltered. With the passing of each lap here, the tactics and the honour began to appear disconcertingly questionable. Once Pironi had

taken the lead, he did *not* slow down again, and neither did he give the marginal fuel consumption so much as a second thought. Gilles' conservative 1m 36.5s pace suddenly became Pironi's racing 1m 35.3s dash.

Enough was enough. How the hell could they go on like this, when there was the very real possibility of both stuttering dry of fuel and handing victory to the only staunch FOCA entry of the race, the infinitely slower, third-placed Tyrrell of Michele Alboreto? Gilles obviously

SAN MARINO GRAND PRIX
Imola (Italy): 25 April 1982
60 laps of 3.13-mile circuit = 187.95 miles

RESULTS

1	Didier Pironi	Ferrari 126C2-V6 turbo	1hr 36m 38.89s
2	Gilles Villeneuve	Ferrari 126C2-V6 turbo	1hr 36m 39.25s
3	Michele Alboreto	Tyrrell 011-Ford V8	1hr 37m 46.57s
4	Jean-Pierre Jarier	Osella FA1C-Ford V8	59 laps
5	Eliseo Salazar	ATS D5-Ford V8	57 laps

Manfred Winkelhock (ATS D5-Ford V8) finished in sixth place but was disqualified; Teo Fabi (Toleman TG181-Hart 4 turbo) was running in seventh place at the finish but was unclassified.
Fastest lap: Pironi, 1m 35.036s (118.63mph) — record
Winner's average speed: 116.66mph

RETIREMENTS
Derek Warwick, Toleman TG181-Hart 4 turbo, 0 laps, electrical problem on warm-up lap; Brian Henton, Tyrrell 011-Ford V8, 0 laps, transmission; Andrea de Cesaris, Alfa Romeo 182-V12, 4 laps, fuel pump; Alain Prost, Renault RE30B-V6 turbo, 6 laps, engine; Riccardo Paletti, Osella FA1C-Ford V8, 7 laps, suspension failure; Bruno Giacomelli, Alfa Romeo 182-V12, 24 laps, engine; René Arnoux, Renault RE30B-V6 turbo, 44 laps, engine.

The Brabham, Williams, McLaren, JPS-Lotus, Ensign, March, Fittipaldi, Talbot-Ligier, Arrows and Theodore teams withdrew their entries before first practice.

CHAMPIONSHIP LEADERS

1	Alain Prost	18
2	Niki Lauda	12
3=	Michele Alboreto	10
3=	Didier Pironi	10
5=	Keke Rosberg	8
5=	John Watson	8
7=	Carlos Reutemann	6
7=	Gilles Villeneuve	6
9=	René Arnoux	4
9=	Nigel Mansell	4
9=	Riccardo Patrese	4

THE GRID

Arnoux 1m 29.765s	Prost 1m 30.249s
Villeneuve 1m 30.717s	Pironi 1m 32.020s
Alboreto 1m 33.209s	Giacomelli 1m 33.230s
de Cesaris 1m 33.397s	Warwick 1m 33.503s
Jarier 1m 34.336s	Fabi 1m 34.647s
Henton 1m 35.262s	Winkelhock 1m 35.790s
Paletti 1m 36.228s	Salazar 1m 36.434s

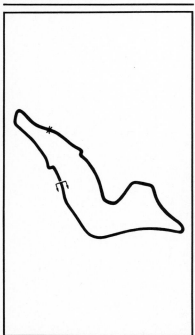

THE *RACERS* SAVE THE DAY

THERE were only 14 cars at San Marino because, in everyday language, the FOCA teams were sulking. Like little school-children unable to get their own way, they had stomped off in disgust.

The list was considerable. Brabham, Williams, McLaren, Lotus, Talbot, Arrows, Ensign, March, Fittipaldi, and Theodore — all these teams boycotted the race at Imola, taking their transporters half-way across Europe only to turn around and head back to base.

A FISA appeal court hearing in Paris had ignited the explosion, where representatives from Ferrari and Renault were present to listen to a defense made by the water-ballasted weight-saving cars used by the outlawed Brabham and Williams in the Brazilian GP. Unsurprisingly, the court "clarified" that cars should satisfy the 580kg minimum by visiting the scales after a race in exactly the same condition in which they had crossed the finish line. The topping up tactic was therefore over. This was unsurprising, said FOCA, because both Renault and Ferrari had threatened withdrawal if the decision hadn't gone their own way.

This "clarification" was not to take effect from the next race, San Marino, but was to be implemented retrospectively in Brazil — which meant that winner Piquet and runner-up Rosberg were both now disqualified, controversially handing the nine points for the win to the third-on-the-road Renault of Alain Prost.

Worse still, said the British teams, this decision was not merely a rule clarification. It was, they said, a new rule altogether. And unless blessed with unanimous team agreement, new rules were supposed to be forbidden by the FOCA/FISA Concord Agreement.

"The FIA appeal tribunal has sought to change the Formula 1 rules in a way which would render our cars ineligible for Grand Prix racing", commented an official FOCA statement. The supposed rule "clarification", they argued, effectively meant that cars would now have to start a Grand Prix compensating *beforehand* for weight loss during the race through natural consumption of essential fluids. That meant leaving the start line weighing 590kg instead of the previous 580kg. And that, they said, was a rule change. Facetiously pretending that they couldn't modify their cars in time, the FOCA teams asked for the San Marino race to be postponed until July. The request was declined, so in effect they went on strike, in spite of having condemned the drivers for striking in South Africa.

With vicious irony, the San Marino Grand Prix was entertaining without them. It mattered not in this instance that ten teams were absent, for two *drivers* had saved the day.

"IT'S war", Gilles Villeneuve had said, a few days after beating a hasty retreat from the Imola circuit in his Agusta helicopter. Then, he just *had* to make a quick getaway, to escape from the mobs before they started asking the idiotic or provocative questions. Then, he had exercised enormous self-discipline and kept his lips sealed. He had not gone away to sulk, as some might expect of a "loser", but had gone lest he be tempted to make any truthful, unpleasant remarks. Packing his bags and making a run for it, he had decided it best to do what he'd always done in this intense and emotional sport. Let his driving speak for itself — starting with the next race.

Which only made Belgium worse. This was the next race, yes, and Gilles Villeneuve certainly approached it with considerable resolve. But race he did not, the Gods didn't give him a chance. Zolder on Saturday 8 May 1982 was the last time Gilles Villeneuve drove a racing car — qualifying rather than actually racing — and the last opportunity the world had to appreciate the little man's monumental abilities, for he died doing what his countless fans will always love him for. Going All Out, pushing a 600bhp racing car to its outer limits, shooting for The Quick One.

It was the second qualifying session on Saturday afternoon. All weekend Villeneuve had displayed perhaps the only element that his widely-worshipped race driving had ever lacked: now the natural brilliance also had a side to it, a bitter no-holds-barred resolve. He hadn't spoken to Pironi since Imola, and he had now made it publicly clear that he intended "never to talk to Pironi again. Ever."

In the worst conceivable manner, he was so tragically, prophetically correct.

Villeneuve went out in a racing car for the last time on Saturday afternoon with just one intent. He was on his second (and therefore last permissible) set of qualifying tyres. Pironi had just been out, and Pironi had just improved Villeneuve's best time so far by 0.1s. Gilles had to beat it.

So Gilles went out knowing that he had just three laps before the super-sticky rubber would lose its effect; knowing that on the second and quickest of these laps he would again be forced to take the ludicrous qualifying risks that he had so often shaken his head about. No-one seemed to listen to his warnings, and no-one probably would, he'd said, until someone lost their life because of it. Only yesterday it had nearly happened to him: he was wound-up for a quick lap, squeezing-as-a-blur through traffic-gaps one wouldn't normally even admit existed, and then he had suddenly come across Jochen Mass' much much slower March. Rather than take an even greater risk than all the others already taken on that crucial lap, Gilles had stomped on the brakes, instantly wasting the Q-tyres in clouds of their own burning rubber.

But this time he couldn't afford to do that. This was the second and final qualifying session on Saturday afternoon's second and final set of Q-tyres. The final opportunity to take a place on the Zolder grid where, as he'd hoped so intensely since Imola, bitter words would no longer be needed because his driving *would* speak for itself.

And this time it was Jochen Mass,

again. It happened just over the rise after the first chicane, on the approach to a fast lefthander, and it happened in the worst possible way. Gilles thought the crawling March would adhere to its own line, as backmarkers are safest (or at least more predictable) to do, and let him find his own way by — but Jochen thought the Ferrari was so fast, so irrevocably committed to the perfect racing line, that he ought to move over. So the March flicked to the right at exactly the same moment that the Ferrari did likewise, and the result was horrendous. The Ferrari reared up high over the back of the March, literally took off, and somersaulted, the force tearing seat-harnesses clean out of the monocoque and chucking steering wheel, seat, and driver across the track through two layers of catchfencing. The empty Ferrari flung away many of its attachments in its crazy flight, before dive-bombing the track with the shattering magnitude of an air crash. The G-forces had been incalculable; the loss to the motor racing world was immeasurable.

In the St Raphael hospital in nearby Louvain at 9 o'clock that dark evening, the story of Gilles Villeneuve became legend.

Saturday, then, overshadowed the rest of the weekend, and indeed the rest

of the season for many. Yet although the Belgian Grand Prix suffered one of the worst qualifying sessions in years, it also witnessed one of the better race winning performances for quite some time.

Even John Watson was surprised at his success. His qualifying performances certainly hadn't hinted that the third Grand Prix win of his career was just around the corner, or that he was due to spring to a strong second place in the championship points standings. He had parked on the fifth row, 1.3 seconds slower than the Cosworth-class pace-setter Keke Rosberg in the new Williams FWO8, and almost as far behind his McLaren team mate Niki Lauda.

Again, it was almost as though Watson was forgotten in the shadow of Lauda: before Belgium the Austrian lay second in the championship, while the Irishman was merely amongst the evenly matched masses, in seventh spot, and before the race Lauda had got the soft Michelins to work, while Watson had not. Lauda therefore opted to race on the softer rubber on Sunday, which he considered worth maybe as much as half-a-second per lap. Watson could see the logic in this decision, but did not follow it. Not because he thought he knew better, nor even because he had a

The three drivers who stood on the rostrum at the joyless Belgian Grand Prix (left) would eventually go into the final race of the season each with a theoretical chance of taking the world title — Niki Lauda's chances also depending on the reinstatement of the points which he lost when he was disqualified from his third place here. Lauda's disqualification, when his McLaren was alleged to be marginally underweight, promoted Chico Serra (right) into the points, in sixth place. Predictably, in the absence of the Ferraris, a Renault, Arnoux's, led from the start (below) and equally predictably it soon broke its engine. Derek Daly's promising debut for Williams (below right) ultimately came to naught when he fell off just ten laps from home, finally caught out by chronic tyre problems.

specific win-or-bust gamble in mind. No, Watson simply *couldn't* use the softer option. He had worn the left hand fronts and rears out with persistent punctuality in qualifying, and this inexplicable quirk of his driving style would doubtless mean that he would destroy the rubber again in the early stages of the race.

So it was that Watson completed the opening lap way down in ninth place on harder Michelins, while Lauda sat confidently in third on stickier rubber.

And for this very reason Watson won the race.

Sure, Lauda's tyre choice did work to begin with. René Arnoux's leading Renault had expired with another turbo failure, on lap seven, and Alain Prost had tumbled helplessly down the order with handling so irksome and inconsistent that he had been forced to pit for new tyres while lying eighth on lap 17, and then finally ran out of road 42 laps later. This meant Rosberg's new FWO8 led its first race, confirming the considerable promise it had shown in both his and Jonathan Palmer's hands during testing — but Lauda, so far pleased with his tyre choice, was hard on his heels. And what Lauda didn't know was that Rosberg was finding his lead none too easy, either! The Finn was struggling with exceptionally heavy steering, the sort that

made manoeuvrability only a wish and understeer incurable. Lauda, he feared, would win this one.

But then two factors wrought entirely unexpected circumstances. In his arm-aching efforts, Rosberg finally clipped a kerb. That, he thought, was it. Race to Lauda. But no! He *had* torn a skirt, as he had suspected — but this had the effect of reducing the FWO8's frontal downforce enough to make it driveable again. At much the same time, Lauda's soft tyres began to lose their grip. He knew that because, shortly before mid-distance, he had Andrea de Cesaris' Alfa Romeo looming up in his mirrors. The Italian only had to follow Lauda for a couple of laps, before the McLaren driver found Nelson Piquet's Brabham-BMW spinning across his bows. Jumping on the middle pedal, Lauda was instantly relegated to third.

All this time, John Watson suffered no such problems. *His* McLaren was behaving perfectly, and one-by-one he picked off his opponents. Only Riccardo Patrese's Brabham BT50-BMW had been difficult to pass, but by the same token leader Rosberg was encountering difficulty getting past backmarkers as well. Lauda was easy — indeed, obliging — prey, and that promoted Watson to third. Until poor de Cesaris' gear linkage

broke.

So then it was Rosberg from Watson — and with the gap at 19 seconds and diminishing by as much as 1.5 seconds per lap, Watson needed just a dozen more laps in which to catch the Williams. There were actually 20 laps remaining, so Wattie had it made! Win number three and second place in the points standings.

Third place belonged to Eddie Cheever, who carved his way through from the seventh row of the grid most impressively in the ageing Ligier JS17-Matra V12, while in fourth place Elio de Angelis showed (not for the last time this season!) that a nearly-there pace can be quite quite adequate if allied to reliability. Brazilians Piquet and Chico Serra, in the still underfinanced and uncompetitive Fittipaldi F8C, completed the points finishers. Like his team-mate Patrese, whose spin in front of Lauda had spelt retirement, Piquet found the BT50's behaviour rather less than ideal. This was, however, the World Champion's first points finish of the year; in fact the only turbo points scored here. Both the Renaults had retired, of course, and Ferrari driver Pironi hadn't even started the race. Sadly, by 9 o'clock on Saturday evening, racing didn't seem to matter anymore.

BELGIAN GRAND PRIX
Zolder: 9 May 1982
70 laps of 2.65-mile circuit = 185.36 miles

RESULTS

1	John Watson	McLaren MP4B-Ford V8	1hr 35m 41.99s
2	Keke Rosberg	Williams FW08-Ford V8	1hr 35m 49.26s
3	Eddie Cheever	Talbot-Ligier JS17B-Matra V12	69 laps
4	Elio de Angelis	JPS Lotus 91-Ford V8	68 laps
5	Nelson Piquet	Brabham BT50-BMW 4 turbo	67 laps
6	Chico Serra	Fittipaldi F8D-Ford V8	67 laps
7	Marc Surer	Arrows A4-Ford V8	66 laps
8	Raul Boesel	March 821-Ford V8	66 laps
9	Jacques Laffite	Talbot-Ligier JS17B-Matra V12	66 laps

Niki Lauda (McLaren MP4B-Ford V8) finished in third place but was disqualified.

Fastest lap: Watson, 1m 20.214s (118.85mph) — record
Winner's average speed: 116.20mph

RETIREMENTS
Eliseo Salazar, ATS D5-Ford V8, 0 laps, accident with Giacomelli; Bruno Giacomelli, Alfa Romeo 182-V12, 0 laps, accident with Salazar; Manfred Winkelhock, ATS D5-Ford V8, 0 laps, engine; René Arnoux, Renault RE30B-V6 turbo, 7 laps, turbo; Nigel Mansell, JPS-Lotus 91-Ford V8, 9 laps, clutch; Teo Fabi, Toleman TG181-Hart 4 turbo, 13 laps, brakes; Michele Alboreto, Tyrrell 011-Ford V8, 29 laps, engine; Derek Warwick, Toleman TG181-Hart 4 turbo, 29 laps, drive shaft; Brian Henton, Tyrrell 011-Ford V8, 33 laps, engine; Andrea de Cesaris, Alfa Romeo 182-V12, 34 laps, transmission; Jean-Pierre Jarier, Osella FA1C-Ford V8, 37 laps, engine; Mauro Baldi, Arrows A4-Ford V8, 51 laps, engine; Riccardo Patrese, Brabham BT50-BMW 4 turbo, 52 laps, accident; Alain Prost, Renault RE30B-V6 turbo, 59 laps, accident; Jochen Mass, March 821-Ford V8, 60 laps, engine; Derek Daly, Williams FW08-Ford V8, 60 laps, accident.

CHAMPIONSHIP LEADERS

1	Alain Prost	18
2	John Watson	17
3	Keke Rosberg	14
4	Niki Lauda	12
5=	Michele Alboreto	10
5=	Didier Pironi	10
7=	Carlos Reutemann	6
7=	Gilles Villeneuve	6
9	Elio de Angelis	5
10=	René Arnoux	4
10=	Eddie Cheever	4
10=	Nigel Mansell	4
10=	Riccardo Patrese	4

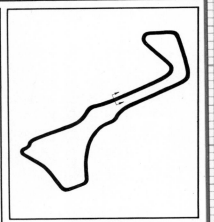

THE GRID

Prost 1m 15.701s	
	Arnoux 1m 15.730s
Rosberg 1m 15.847s	
	Lauda 1m 16.049s
Alboreto 1m 16.308s	
	de Cesaris 1m 16.575s
Mansell 1m 16.944s	
	Piquet 1m 17.124s
Patrese 1m 17.126s	
	Watson 1m 17.144s
de Angelis 1m 17.762s	
	Winkelhock 1m 17.879s
Daly 1m 18.194s	
	Cheever 1m 18.301s
Giacomelli 1m 18.371s	
	Jarier 1m 18.403s
Laffite 1m 18.565s	
	Salazar 1m 18.967s
Warwick 1m 18.985s	
	Henton 1m 19.150s
Fabi 1m 19.300s	
	Surer 1m 19.584s
Serra 1m 19.598s	
	Boesel 1m 19.621s
Mass 1m 19.777s	
	Baldi 1m 19.815s

Did not qualify: Roberto Guerrero (Ensign N181-Ford V8) 1m 20.116s; Jan Lammers (Theodore TY-Ford V8) 1m 20.584s; Riccardo Paletti (Osella FA1C-Ford V8) and Emilio de Villota (March 821-Ford V8) did not prequalify. The Ferrari entries were withdrawn following Gilles Villeneuve's fatal accident in practice. Didier Pironi (Ferrari 126C2- V6 turbo) had recorded 1m 16.501s and Villeneuve (Ferrari 126C2-V6 turbo) had recorded 1m 16.616s.

Eddie Cheever drove brilliantly with the aged JS17 (right) to make it through from a seventh row grid position to an impressive third at the flag. This should have been the faithful JS17's final fling as the JS19 was to be unveiled at Monaco but there was life in the old thing yet. For the last time, on Saturday afternoon, Gilles Villeneuve (below) went for broke. When Villeneuve died the sport lost one of its all time greats and the loss was all the sadder for the sheer senselessness of it all.

RICCARDO'S LOTTERY

HE stood on the rostrum with the Monegasque royal family, looking dazed. Had he really won? What had happened to the others? Prost? Yes, he'd seen the Renault lying wrecked at the side of the track just after the chicane. At that moment, he'd taken the lead. But on a surface made lethal by light rain, anything could have happened. And it had. He'd had a spin and surely been overtaken by two other cars. What had happened to them? Andrea was here, and so was Elio but . . .

Any race in which the lead changes three times in the last three laps is bound to be confusing, especially at Monaco where adversaries may be parked up the odd side street or in the tunnel. And for Riccardo Patrese, as he collected his prizes from Prince Rainier, there might have been a slight uneasiness. After all, he had been pushed, and his engine had started. Might there be a protest?

In fact those final four laps of the 76-lap Monaco Grand Prix threw up quite a few questions. René Arnoux had made a superb start and had led the first 14 laps on a dry track until a torn skirt resulted in a spin at the swimming pool, and there it had stalled. Unable to restart, the little Frenchman's Renault (with new fuel injection system) had been winched off the track and out of the race. But Alain Prost had received the leadership with open arms. Even when it began to rain, on lap 60, he had taken care not to make any mistakes. He hadn't enjoyed the slippery conditions, but had at least maintained a seven second lead over Patrese's Brabham. And then quite suddenly, coming out of the chicane on the harbour front, the Renault slewed across the track, slamming into the guardrail on either side of the road, shedding wheels and debris.

Politically, questions might have been asked in the Renault house. After all, both men had apparently spun out of the race when in the lead. But the conditions excused Alain, and anyway, shortly before, Derek Daly had crunched the rear end of his Williams into the Armco at the same spot, and his gearbox later ran out of oil, most of which had probably escaped because of the impact.

Patrese was now in the lead, and with only a couple of laps to go. Yet on the very next lap, braking for the old Station Hairpin, the back end of the Brabham broke away and the car went into a spin. Although he didn't feel himself being pushed, the marshals had instantly judged him to be in a dangerous position and begun to move his car. Riccardo simply dropped the clutch and the Cosworth burst into life.

By this stage, however, both Didier Pironi and Andrea de Cesaris had overtaken the Brabham. For some time Pironi had been signalling to the clerk of the course to stop the race, no doubt partly because his Ferrari was spluttering badly. He could but hope that he would complete the full distance. Andrea, on the other hand, had driven an excellent race for Alfa Romeo, as had team mate Giacomelli, albeit briefly, for the first few laps. Normally known as a crasher, Andrea had kept his cool in the slippery conditions on the world's tightest track, where those Armco barriers — to which Andrea had been constantly attracted the previous year — seem perilously close.

But going up the hill for what would be his last lap, and heading for second place, his Alfa suddenly spluttered and died. De Cesaris parked in Casino Square, bitterly disappointed. Pironi, meanwhile, was trying to get the last drops of five star into the Ferrari's V6, but in the tunnel the pump ran dry and the red car came to a halt. In the murk, Patrese's Brabham swept back into the lead, and an efficient official duly greeted him as the winner when he crossed the start/finish line.

Those last few laps made the Monaco Grand Prix an odd race. There was Elio de Angelis on the rostrum — he was actually fifth — while of the first six classified finishers, only three actually took the chequered flag. Marc Surer, who was classified ninth and last would have been placed fifth if the results had been based on those who actually took the chequered flag. And if Patrese hadn't taken advantage of his push, and had remained stationary, Nigel Mansell would have won the Monaco GP as the next driver still running. As it was, the JPS driver was only classified fourth. It brought into doubt that old maxim: to finish first, first you have to finish. Pir-

Alain Prost (left) inherited the lead for Renault when Arnoux spun and could not restart, but with the race all but run Prost fell foul of the slippery conditions. Patrese (below left) was probably the most surprised winner of the year after the chaotic closing laps. Ligier's new JS19 skirt system (below) did not meet with the approval of the scrutineers and the team had a thoroughly miserable weekend. Pironi (right) and Derek Daly (bottom) both led the closing stages of this strange race but Pironi ran out of fuel and Daly ran out of gearbox oil thanks to damaging the box (below right) in a late half-spin.

oni, de Cesaris, Daly and Prost were classified second, third, sixth and seventh, but not one of them actually finished . . .

That was the more controversial side of the Monaco GP, and how the winner stepped warily onto the rostrum. By the damp paddock after the race, a disappointed Piquet was holed up on his boat, not willing to discuss a disappointing race which ended with a broken turbo and gearbox problems after he had dropped to 18th place on the first lap. The McLaren team had had a poor race as well. Watson was still second in the

championship, and the team still led the Constructors series, but neither driver finished. Watson got up to eighth before stopping with electrical trouble, while Lauda got no higher, if a little further, before his engine threatened to blow through lack of oil.

The JPS Lotus team, on the other hand, had a varied weekend, but notched points-scoring performances from both cars. Mansell, eleventh on the grid, had climbed to seventh by half distance, only to drop back to tenth after a stop for a new tyre. Team mate de Angelis was last on the first lap, but in spite of a

bump with Pironi's Ferrari (in which the red car's nosecone went flying) he was heading for fourth place, only to be pipped by his team mate on the very last lap.

Both Tyrrell and ATS had their moments. Alboreto had tussles with both Rosberg and Daly only to damage the suspension with six laps to go. Henton, however, came home eighth. At ATS, Winkelhock put on a superb performance, leading Lauda for 15 laps, but retiring with a broken differential after 30. Salazar had earlier been surprised when the fire extinguisher went off on its own. His car was parked on the track on the uphill section for around 50 laps.

And what of Williams? Remarkably, Keke Rosberg was making his Monaco début. In the past he could usually be found at the Tip-Top with Fred Opert by Saturday night, never having qualified for Monaco. But there's always a first time, and Keke proved it by putting his Williams into sixth on the grid. He overtook Alboreto and was disputing fourth place with de Cesaris for several laps when he jumped a kerb after a clash with the Alfa and the Williams' suspension was damaged. Daly, eighth on the grid, was heading for fourth place when he thumped the barrier with the back end of the Williams, but was still classified sixth, even though he was in the pits by that stage.

Monaco has more than its fair share of hard-luck stories, and this year was no exception. Even though the field was one Ferrari short, five cars still failed to get through pre-qualifying, and another six didn't make it onto the grid. Amongst these were both Theodore and Ensign, both teams being left tyre-less after Avon's withdrawal from GP racing. March, who had apparently bought the Avon stock and abandoned Pirelli, were in no better state, neither of the works cars qualifying. Guerrero managed to practice on old tyres in his Ensign, while the Theodore sat on its jacks and bare wheels until Goodyear came to the rescue for the rest of the season. Michelin later bailed out Ensign, but neither car qualified at Monaco.

Only marginally happier were the men at Ligier. Their new JS19 was due to make its début at Monaco after recent testing, but when it was presented for scrutineering, Messrs Cadringher and Barrabino, representing FISA and the ACM respectively, ruled that the long skirts, running all the way to the back of the car, and the rear wing extensions were not legal. Skirts behind the rear wheels would have to be taken off. Unfortunately, this also robbed the car of around 30 per cent of its downforce, and far from having an exciting and competitive new car, Laffite and Cheever had an awful new car in a totally different configuration to that in which it was designed. They qualified 16th and 18th and were both glad to be out of it before half distance.

The Magic of Monaco comes in various guises. Some, like Riccardo Patrese, can scarcely believe their luck. Others, like the Renault team, had every reason to wonder what had gone wrong. Apart from Pironi's second place, the race really had very little effect on the championship. However, it was Patrese's first Formula One win, and the Brabham-Cosworth BT49's last. Two races later, the new régime would take over.

MONACO GRAND PRIX
Monte Carlo: 23 May 1982
76 laps of 2.06-mile circuit = 156.41 miles

RESULTS

1	Riccardo Patrese	Brabham BT49C-Ford V8	1hr 54m 11.26s
2	Didier Pironi	Ferrari 126C2-V6 turbo	75 laps*
3	Andrea de Cesaris	Alfa Romeo 182-V12	75 laps*
4	Nigel Mansell	JPS-Lotus 91-Ford V8	75 laps
5	Elio de Angelis	JPS Lotus 91-Ford V8	75 laps
6	Derek Daly	Williams FW08-Ford V8	74 laps*
7	Alain Prost	Renault RE30B-V6 turbo	73 laps*
8	Brian Henton	Tyrrell 011-Ford V8	72 laps
9	Marc Surer	Arrows A4-Ford V8	70 laps
10	Michele Alboreto	Tyrrell 011-Ford V8	69 laps*

*not running at finish

Fastest lap: Patrese, 1m 26.354s (85.79mph)
Winner's average speed: 82.21mph

RETIREMENTS

Bruno Giacomelli, Alfa Romeo 182-V12, 4 laps, broken stub axle; René Arnoux, Renault RE30B-V6 turbo, 14 laps, spun off, unable to restart; Eliseo Salazar, ATS D5-Ford V8, 21 laps, fire; Eddie Cheever, Talbot-Ligier JS19-Matra V12, 27 laps, engine; Jacques Laffite, Talbot-Ligier JS19-Matra V12, 29 laps, handling problems; Manfred Winkelhock, ATS D5-Ford V8, 31 laps, differential; John Watson, McLaren MP4B-Ford V8, 35 laps, ignition; Nelson Piquet, Brabham BT50-BMW 4 turbo, 49 laps, engine and gearbox; Niki Lauda, McLaren MP4B-Ford V8, 56 laps, engine; Keke Rosberg, Williams FW08-Ford V8, 64 laps, accident; Alboreto, 69 laps, suspension; Prost, 73 laps, accident; Daly, 74 laps, accident damage to gearbox; Pironi, 75 laps, out of fuel; de Cesaris, 75 laps, out of fuel.

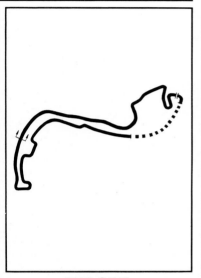

CHAMPIONSHIP LEADERS

1	Alain Prost	18
2	John Watson	17
3	Didier Pironi	16
4	Keke Rosberg	14
5	Riccardo Patrese	13
6	Niki Lauda	12
7	Michele Alboreto	10
8 =	Elio de Angelis	7
8 =	Nigel Mansell	7
10 =	Carlos Reutemann	6
10 =	Gilles Villeneuve	6

THE GRID

	Arnoux 1m 23.281s
Patrese 1m 23.791s	
	Giacomelli 1m 23.939s
Prost 1m 24.439s	
	Pironi 1m 24.585s
Rosberg 1m 24.649s	
	de Cesaris 1m 24.928s
Daly 1m 25.390s	
	Alboreto 1m 25.449s
Watson 1m 25.538s	
	Mansell 1m 25.642s
Lauda 1m 25.838s	
	Piquet 1m 26.075s
Winkelhock 1m 26.260s	
	de Angelis 1m 26.456s
Cheever 1m 26.463s	
	Henton 1m 26.690s
Laffite 1m 27.007s	
	Surer 1m 27.019s
Salazar 1m 27.022s	

Did not qualify: Mauro Baldi (Arrows A4-Ford V8) 1m 27.209s; Jan Lammers (Theodore TY-Ford V8) 1m 27.523s; Jochen Mass (March 821-Ford V8) 1m 27.885s; Derek Warwick (Toleman TG181-Hart 4 turbo) 1m 28.075s; Jean-Pierre Jarier (Osella FA1C-Ford V8) 1m 28.264s; Roberto Guerrero (Ensign N181-Ford V8) 1m 28.653s. Raul Boesel (March 821-Ford V8), Teo Fabi (Toleman TG181-Hart 4 turbo), Riccardo Paletti (Osella FA1C-Ford V8), Chico Serra (Fittipaldi F8D-Ford V8) and Emilio de Villota (March 821-Ford V8) did not prequalify.

There is absolutely nothing to rival the dramatic setting of Monte Carlo (left), even if nowadays Grand Prix racing has all but outgrown the famous streets. In the middle of a fine season, Alboreto (above) was a somewhat disappointing tenth in Monaco but his disappointment was nothing compared to that of Alain Prost (below) who crashed out of a commanding lead with just three laps left to run.

REMEMBER the football games at the Spanish GP in 1980, the San Marino in 1981, and the South African of 1982? Well, they went into extra time at Detroit in June of '82. The newest, slowest, bumpiest and silliest Grand Prix circuit wasn't quite ready to welcome the field, which had made a mad dash from Monaco to Michigan for one of the biggest culture shocks of the decade. When the teams (less Toleman) got there, they found a very much substandard circuit, lacking in run-off areas, speed, security, character and interest. The organisers lacked experience and efficiency, despite having abundant enthusiasm and charm. Quite simply, it wasn't ready. Out came the footballs and frisbees for the start of what was a pretty weird weekend.

It wasn't really until the race had been stopped a few laps after the start, and then restarted again, that some real racing got under way. And then John Watson dodged and darted around the concrete blocks of what used to be called Motor City to overtake no less than ten different drivers, win the first Detroit GP and put himself into a six point lead in the World Championship. He had started from a lowly 17th on the grid after the single practice session, yet everything had come right on this 2.59-mile circuit where rhythm and flow would mean so much. Not for the first time in 1982, nor the last, Wattie proved to be an overtaking and *racing* maestro.

The latest of street circuits for some reason was spared the usual (and supposedly mandatory) pre-Grand Prix race, so the teething troubles were reserved for race weekend. And the only racing that took place up until late Friday evening was earlier in the week on boats on the lake. Even then, the lake was rough and the weather was threatening. On Saturday afternoon, it rained.

By Friday evening, the pleasant but lackadaisical race organisers had their circuit together. This in itself was remarkable. Circuit inspector and adviser Robert Langford had actually discussed the feasibility of the circuit nine months previously with the writer, on the eve of the 1981 Italian GP; even then, he mentioned the 135 manhole covers which dotted the proposed circuit; add to that problem the crossing of a railway line, corners so tight that cars threatened to stall, a recently laid $800,000 surface and the almost total absence of any lifting gear to remove crashed cars and you had an utterly remarkable circuit.

Under some duress, practice took place over 24 hours late. Originally a test session had been laid on for Thursday so that drivers could familiarise themselves with the circuit. That went by the wayside as there simply was no circuit, so too did the first two sessions of official practice. Late on Friday, the cars went out for an unofficial practice session, which would be followed on Saturday by two official sessions. By this stage, the puzzled but long-suffering spectators were just beginning to wonder why this form of racing was supposed to be the best in the world.

Even those official sessions were odd. It was dry for the first, and wet for the second. The field, already three short without one Ferrari and both Tolemans, was further reduced by one on the Friday, when Jan Lammers crashed the Theodore and broke his thumb. On Sat-

urday morning, Nelson Piquet's BMW engine soon broke and he had electrical trouble in the spare car. It wouldn't pick up coming out of corners and the World Champion ended up with the slowest time: 28th fastest. When it rained in the afternoon, it sealed the World Champion's fate. He didn't even practice. Nelson wasn't going to race in Detroit.

There were some other remarkable changes in this lottery of practice. Take Roberto Guerrero. At Monaco, he hadn't qualified. He'd only had old tyres. But with brand new Michelins, he was on the sixth row of the grid. Daly, Laffite, Patrese, Arnoux, Alboreto and Watson were all further back. Manfred Winkelhock was similarly astonishing. Only Prost, de Cesaris, Rosberg and Pironi were quicker. And just to confirm it, Manfred was fastest in the warm-up. Once again, the Alfa Romeos were well up, with de Cesaris second fastest to the inevitable Renault. Giacomelli was sixth quickest.

Both Osellas made the race, but Jarier's suspension broke in practice and then he crashed on the warm-up lap and had to start in the spare car. Poor Paletti, for his second race, also failed to make the start after crashing during the warm-up.

The scramble through the streets of Detroit had certain predictable results. For instance, a Renault led, there were quite a few shunts, and the race was stopped. Prost took off from pole position followed by de Cesaris and Rosberg, but Keke's continual rival was soon out with broken transmission on his Alfa. Baldi and March driver Raul Boesel tangled on the first lap and Winkelhock crashed on the second. Jarier's race lasted until lap three when the spare Osella's electrics failed. Rosberg was just beginning to draw in Prost's tyre-troubled Renault when out came the red flag. De Angelis and Guerrero had tangled at the first corner, and although de Angelis had continued, the Ensign was broadside across the track, and Patrese had gone off avoiding the stationary car. Then a Brabham brake duct had caught fire, and although it was ultimately put out by fire extinguisher, this only added to the panic. Out went the word to stop the race, and out went the red flag. It was all rather embarrassing, and was then followed up with a ridiculously long delay before the show got under way again. And Grand Prix drivers don't like making two starts in a day. But teams don't mind. They busily set about renewing anything that looked wrong on the 18 surviving cars.

Finally the race got under way again,

and this time for real. In fact it turned out to be a lively race, with lots of overtaking. This time Prost's Renault was in better form than in the first 'heat', and the Frenchman led the first 16 laps. Team mate Arnoux was way back in eighth place, having clipped a wall in the dry session of practice and never having set a competitive lap time. But his Renault was soon in trouble with a misfire, and it appeared to be contagious. Prost's car suffered the same malady, and on the 24th lap, Rosberg swept into the lead. Five laps later, Prost decided to have his fuel system sorted out, and pitted. Although both cars finished, the

Renault challenge was over.

But the man who really livened up this race was Watson. Thirteenth at the restart, he swiftly picked off Mass and de Angelis in one lap, and then Arnoux and Mansell in the same fashion a little later. He was now in ninth place, and overtaking Daly a little later promoted Wattie to eighth. Laffite put up a spirited defence of seventh, but he too was overtaken, and Prost's pit stop promoted the McLaren driver to sixth.

Ahead of him were Rosberg, Pironi, Cheever, Lauda and Giacomelli. The first to go was the Alfa driver. He was overtaken easily enough, but then a lap later he tried to get his position back. He drove for one of those perpetually decreasing gaps, his front wheel rode over the McLaren's rear wheel, and while the Italian combination bounced out of the race, the British duo powered ever onwards. In a flash, Watson was past Lauda, Cheever and Pironi, and into second place. No one appeared to be able to stop him. And Rosberg wasn't in any position to defend the lead, suffering the lack of third gear. On lap 42, the McLaren took the lead, and that was the last anyone saw of him until the chequered flag came out after two hours and 62 of the 75 proposed laps.

The lead, then, wasn't in doubt. And it might so easily have been a McLaren one-two. Just as Giacomelli had been spurred on, so too was Lauda on being overtaken by Watson. He soon passed Cheever, and Pironi was the next to go. Only Rosberg stood between the Austrian and second place. But on lap 40, he dived into another shrinking gap between Rosberg and the wall. Like Giacomelli previously, he bounced off the Williams into the concrete and out of the race.

Two cars that were well-placed to take up good positions were the two Ligier JS17s that had made the trip in preference to the impotent JS19s. Cheever had been involved with Giacomelli and Pironi for most of the race and held fourth place on lap 41 when Lauda went out. Laffite was just one place behind. Cheever had already had a demonstration on how not to overtake at Detroit, and had found that his Ligier had been superior under braking to the Ferrari. But team mate Laffite hadn't been so lucky, and had knocked his nose wing askew when he tried to slither by Pironi's car.

Cheever, however, was able to go ahead to greater things, and soon picked off Rosberg's Williams, now also suffering from falling fuel pressure. Indeed Laffite also got by, but then the Matra engine began to lose power, and he dropped down the order again, so into third place came Pironi's Ferrari, scoring more points. Rosberg survived to finish fourth ahead of team mate Daly who spent much of the race shadowing Laffite who finally finished behind him in sixth.

For everyone it had been a matter of survival, and the first to be unrewarded for staying away from the walls was Jochen Mass's March, while Marc Surer finished eighth. There was a total of 12 finishers, including both Renaults. The first Detroit Grand Prix was not a wild success, and perhaps Rosberg summed it up best later in the year when he was asked if Las Vegas was as bad as it had been the previous year and he replied "No, we've been to Detroit since then!".

From a driver's eye point of view, the hastily contrived Detroit circuit was nothing if not spectacular (left) with tight corners and unyielding concrete walls virtually everywhere. It was a troubled weekend right from the start; with practice curtailed there was plenty of time for football games and for non-qualifying World Champion, Nelson Piquet to practice (above left) for later encounters with Eliseo Salazar. As John Watson's storming drive to victory saved the weekend from total ignominy, the locals probably let him get away with the speeding fines (above right). When the race was red-flagged after a handful of laps (below) the already frustrated drivers probably wondered why they had come at all, but in the end it had at least shown how not to do it next year . . .

DETROIT GRAND PRIX

Detroit: 6 June 1982

62 laps of 2.59-mile circuit = 160.57 miles

RESULTS

1	John Watson	McLaren MP4B-Ford V8	1hr 58m 41.04s
2	Eddie Cheever	Talbot-Ligier JS17-Matra V12	1hr 58m 56.77s
3	Didier Pironi	Ferrari 126C2-V6 turbo	1hr 59m 09.12s
4	Keke Rosberg	Williams FW08-Ford V8	1hr 59m 53.02s
5	Derek Daly	Williams FW08-Ford V8	2hr 00m 04.80s
6	Jacques Laffite	Talbot-Ligier JS17-Matra V12	61 laps
7	Jochen Mass	March 821-Ford V8	61 laps
8	Marc Surer	Arrows A4-Ford V8	61 laps
9	Brian Henton	Tyrrell 011-Ford V8	60 laps
10	René Arnoux	Renault RE30B-V6 turbo	59 laps
11	Chico Serra	Fittipaldi F8-Ford V8	59 laps
12	Alain Prost	Renault RE30B-V6 turbo	54 laps

Fastest lap: Prost, 1m 50.438s (84.42mph)
Winner's average speed: 81.17mph

The race was stopped by red flag after six laps and restarted with grid positions as race positions. The results were determined on aggregate time for both parts, the race distance being determined by the number of laps completed within two hours.

RETIREMENTS

Riccardo Paletti, Osella FA1C-Ford V8, did not start; Raul Boesel, March 821-Ford V8, 0 laps, accident with Baldi; Mauro Baldi, Arrows A4-Ford V8, 0 laps, accident with Boesel; Manfred Winkelhock, ATS D5-Ford V8, 1 lap, accident; Jean-Pierre Jarier, Osella FA1C-Ford V8, 2 laps, electrical problem; Andrea de Cesaris, Alfa Romeo 182-V12, 2 laps, broken driveshaft; Riccardo Patrese, Brabham BT50-BMW 4 turbo, 6 laps, accident; Roberto Guerrero, Ensign N181-Ford V8, 6 laps, accident; Eliseo Salazar, ATS D5-Ford V8, 13 laps, accident; Elio de Angelis, JPS-Lotus 91-Ford V8, 17 laps, gearbox; Bruno Giacomelli, Alfa Romeo 182-V12, 30 laps, collision with Watson; Michele Alboreto, Tyrrell 011-Ford V8, 40 laps, accident; Niki Lauda, McLaren MP4B-Ford V8, 40 laps, collision with Rosberg; Nigel Mansell, JPS-Lotus 91-Ford V8, 44 laps, engine.

CHAMPIONSHIP LEADERS

1	John Watson	26
2	Didier Pironi	20
3	Alain Prost	18
4	Keke Rosberg	17
5	Riccardo Patrese	13
6	Niki Lauda	12
7 =	Michele Alboreto	10
7 =	Eddie Cheever	10
9 =	Elio de Angelis	7
9 =	Nigel Mansell	7

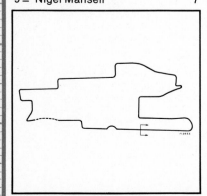

THE GRID

Prost 1m 48.537s	de Cesaris 1m 48.872s
Rosberg 1m 49.264s	Pironi 1m 49.903s
Winkelhock 1m 50.066s	Giacomelli 1m 50.252s
Mansell 1m 50.294s	de Angelis 1m 50.443s
Cheever 1m 50.520s	Lauda 1m 51.026s
Guerrero 1m 51.039s	Daly 1m 51.227s
Laffite 1m 51.270s	Patrese 1m 51.508s
Arnoux 1m 51.514s	Alboreto 1m 51.618s
Watson 1m 51.868s	Mass 1m 52.271s
Surer 1m 52.316s	Henton 1m 52.867s
Boesel 1m 52.870s	Jarier 1m 52.988s
Paletti 1m 54.084s	Baldi 1m 54.332s
Salazar 1m 55.633s	Serra 1m 55.848s

Did not qualify: Emilio de Villota (March 821-Ford V8) 1m 56.589s; Nelson Piquet (Brabham BT50-BMW 4 turbo) 1m 57.779s; Jan Lammers (Theodore TY-Ford V8) no time.

The Toleman entries of Teo Fabi and Derek Warwick were withdrawn due to transport problems.

*After the pitiful shambles of the early part of this first Detroit Grand Prix weekend, John Watson's stunning and spectacular performance in the restarted race must have seemed like manna from heaven to the beleagured Motor City promoters. Watson was simply in a class of his own; with the right tyre choice, the McLaren for once giving of its best, and his head down, Wattie stormed through the field from nowhere to take a real **racing** victory and a six point championship lead.*

THE red light came on — and stayed on. The pole-winning Ferrari driven by Didier Pironi began to creep forwards, but the driver braked ... once, twice, a third time. Only this time, the engine stalled. And at the same instant, the green light finally came on. Pironi's orange-gloved hand shot into the air as the rest of the field swerved around the Ferrari. Those lined up behind the car swerved later and later, until suddenly Boesel's March clipped the Ferrari and slid towards the pit rail where it tangled with other cars. From the penultimate row of the grid, Riccardo Paletti, having his first standing start in a GP, shot straight into the back of the stationary Ferrari at over 100mph. The driver died that evening.

The previous day, the bespectacled Italian had admitted that he wasn't too sure if he was good enough to be a Formula One driver. He didn't in fact meet FISA's Super Licence requirements, and on the other two occasions that he'd qualified to start a GP, his Osella had let him down each time before he got onto the grid. It was desperately sad that this charming young man should lose his life before his career had even begun.

There were other unfortunate ironies. Here, on this Circuit Ile de Notre Dame, the 40,000 spectators had one man in their minds: their recent hero, Gilles Villeneuve. In his memory, the circuit had been renamed the Circuit Gilles Villeneuve. Yet on this day of remembrance, another driver had lost his life in another unnecessary and pointless accident. And finally, the other driver innocently involved was Didier Pironi. The Frenchman had had a hard time from the Canadian public after the Imola race, and the subsequent death of their hero. He was blamed and, just to remind him, there were portraits of the Canadian driver everywhere. But Didier had proved the diplomat, as he had at Kyalami, and explained his situation to his former team mate's fans. No sooner had he overcome that hurdle than he had the grave misfortune to be involved in another driver's fatal accident.

After the accident, there was the inevitable delay, but even so, there were few drivers who knew that Paletti had died of his injuries. So the competition got under way in earnest. Remarkably, just one race after non-qualifying, Nelson Piquet won the 70 lap race, from team mate Riccardo Patrese. Two races earlier at Monaco, Cosworth had proved stronger than BMW turbo. On this occasion, BMW turbo proved faster than Cosworth, but either way it was a Brabham race and their first 1-2 since the Italian Grand Prix of 1978.

After setting fourth quickest time in practice, the signs were already hopeful that after the previous weekend's disaster, this would be a Brabham day. Montreal is a circuit full of significance for Piquet, however. It was there that he assumed the mantle of team leadership when Lauda walked out of the team in 1979, and it was there that he lost the championship after banging wheels with Alan Jones on the first lap in 1980.

And now he was fourth on the grid at the re-start. In front of him were three turbos: Pironi's spare car, which wouldn't be as well set up as his now wrecked car, and the two Renaults, whose reputation for reliability and error-free driving was already beginning to suffer. The chances of a good race

looked promising — providing the BMW engine held together.

As suspected, poor Pironi was out of it from the start. He'd dropped to ninth by the 22nd lap when he pitted for new tyres and engine adjustments, and ultimately finished an ignominious ninth. Alain Prost put up little resistance to Piquet's charge, and by lap three, the Brazilian was in second position. Ahead, there was only Arnoux, and on lap nine the Brabham nosed ahead of the Renault. Arnoux tried to stay with Piquet but, 19 laps later, the Renault challenge was over. Arnoux spun and stalled the car, while a lap later, Prost, whose engine had been losing power, finally decided to call it a day.

Shortly before, he had been overtaken by the fast closing Patrese. The Italian driver had dropped to tenth on the opening lap, but had overtaken Rosberg, Watson, Pironi, de Cesaris and Cheever to pick up second place when the Renaults retired before half distance. Although Piquet eased up at the end, there was never any question of Patrese catching the BMW-engined car. The World Champion had reaped reward for his perseverance, and the men from Munich could

celebrate their first Formula One win. Nine points kept Piquet in the championship race, but Patrese's six were more advantageous.

Both drivers might have looked stronger in the championship but for two cars running out of petrol with just two and four laps to go. Eddie Cheever, again in the JS17 which had now been made legal, having failed scrutineering in Detroit, had started only 12th on the grid. Yet within eight laps he was up to fourth. He was overtaken by both Patrese and de Cesaris (both of whom he'd already overtaken within the first two laps), but with the Renault retirements the American appeared to be heading for a safe fourth place, only for the engine to splutter and die. After Eddie had parked the car right opposite his pit, and made suitably disgruntled noises about wasted trips, he was able to watch Andrea de Cesaris suffer the same fate — for the second time in three races. As at Monaco, the Alfa cruised silently to a halt; this time Andrea might have picked up third place.

Consequently, instead of finishing a lonely fifth, John Watson suddenly found himself on the rostrum in third

Both Cheever and de Cesaris were unfortunate not to finish in the points in Canada — both running out of petrol in the closing laps. At the restart (below left) Pironi went into a short-lived lead with the spare Ferrari, only to drop back to an eventual ninth place while turbo honour was upheld by Nelson Piquet giving the BMW engine its first win (right). A week earlier, Piquet had been a non-qualifier and had the BMW failed here its future could have been very short. Nigel Mansell's skirmish with Giacomelli's Alfa (below) was the start of a very difficult period for the Englishman.

place. And the four points came in very useful, thank-you, for now John was ten points clear of his nearest rival, the unfortunate Pironi.

Cheever and de Cesaris weren't the only ones to suffer from a petrol shortage. The man who should have taken fourth place was Derek Daly. Nether Williams driver was particularly happy at Montreal, and although Rosberg had started seventh, Daly was back in 13th place. But while the Finn dropped down the order with a porpoising problem, and then retired when the gearbox fell apart, Daly was quietly climbing up through the field. And just as he was about to take advantage of the misfortunes of others, he suffered the same shortage, and spluttered to a halt.

Suddenly promoted from seventh place to fourth in the space of three laps was Elio de Angelis. He had started in tenth place, but dropped to 15th on the first lap. He overtook an unhappy Lauda, soon to retire with clutch trouble, a similarly troubled Rosberg and Pironi — and then fourth place fell into his lap. He'd been overtaken by team mate Mansell on that first lap, but Nigel slid into the back of Giacomelli's misfiring Alfa,

which was already heading for the pits. The shunt might not have been too serious but for Nigel's hand getting caught in the steering wheel and wrenching his arm, which took a considerable time to heal.

Also out of luck early on was Brian Henton who was thumped by Eliseo Salazar, driving the only ATS to get into the race, after a rash of accidents. Henton remained in the car as it was lifted off the circuit, and later drove back to the pits, but his persistence wasn't rewarded. Alboreto was also strangely off-form, never running higher than eleventh and retiring with a blown engine.

Behind the first four came two anomalies of motor racing. The first, in sixth place, is quite simple. De Cesaris had picked up third place at Monaco, even though he hadn't taken the chequered flag. This time he was classified sixth, even though, again, he hadn't taken the flag.

The second anomaly was Marc Surer. Badly injured for the second time in two years at Kyalami earlier in the year, Surer had returned to the fray in Belgium, yet three races later he was in the points with a typically gutsy drive. He

may only have been 16th on the grid, but he stuck at it as he usually does and fifth place was his reward.

After the accident, the race restarted with only 23 runners. Both Osellas were absent from the grid, but so too was the Theodore. After Lammers had broken his thumb at Detroit, Geoff Lees had been called in to take his place. He had qualified 25th and better than Henton, Winkelhock, de Villota and Serra (there were no Tolemans, again incidently) but like Boesel and Salazar, Geoff was involved in the startline accident, although unlike his fellow drivers, he was ultimately unable to start the race.

So the Canadian GP became a celebration for Brabham, and a pretty miserable weekend for everyone else. The weather reflected most people's attitude, and there had been other problems with the Canadian event, such as the local underground going on strike and severely upsetting people's plans to visit the race. In terms of the championship, Watson and McLaren were looking good. The begging questions were: how much longer were Renault going to have problems, and could Brabham maintain the pressure?

CANADIAN GRAND PRIX
Circuit Gilles Villeneuve, Montreal: 13 June 1982
70 laps of 2.74-mile circuit = 191.80 miles

RESULTS

1	Nelson Piquet	Brabham BT50-BMW 4 turbo	1hr 46m 39.58s
2	Riccardo Patrese	Brabham BT49D-Ford V8	1hr 46m 53.38s
3	John Watson	McLaren MP4B-Ford V8	1hr 47m 41.41s
4	Elio de Angelis	JPS Lotus 91-Ford V8	69 laps
5	Marc Surer	Arrows A4-Ford V8	69 laps
6	Andrea de Cesaris	Alfa Romeo 182-V12	68 laps*
7	Derek Daly	Williams FW08-Ford V8	68 laps*
8	Mauro Baldi	Arrows A4-Ford V8	68 laps
9	Didier Pironi	Ferrari 126C2-V6 turbo	67 laps
10	Eddie Cheever	Talbot-Ligier JS17-Matra V12	66 laps*
11	Jochen Mass	March 821-Ford V8	66 laps
12	Brian Henton	Tyrrell 011-Ford V8	59 laps

*not running at finish

Fastest lap: Pironi, 1m 28.323s (111.68mph) — record
Winner's average speed: 107.932mph

RETIREMENTS

Nigel Mansell, JPS-Lotus 91-Ford V8, 1 lap, accident; Bruno Giacomelli, Alfa Romeo 182-V12, 1 lap, accident; Roberto Guerrero, Ensign N181-Ford V8, 2 laps, clutch; Jacques Laffite, Talbot-Ligier JS17-Matra V12, 8 laps, handling problems; Niki Lauda, McLaren MP4B-Ford V8, 17 laps, clutch; Eliseo Salazar, ATS D5-Ford V8, 20 laps, engine; René Arnoux, Renault RE30B-V6 turbo, 28 laps, spun off; Alain Prost, Renault RE30B-V6 turbo, 30 laps, engine; Michele Alboreto, Tyrrell 011-Ford V8, 41 laps, engine; Raul Boesel, March 821-Ford V8, 47 laps, engine; Keke Rosberg, Williams FW08-Ford V8, 52 laps, gearbox.

CHAMPIONSHIP LEADERS

1	John Watson	30
2	Didier Pironi	20
3	Riccardo Patrese	19
4	Alain Prost	18
5	Keke Rosberg	17
6	Niki Lauda	12
7	Nelson Piquet	11
8 =	Michele Alboreto	10
8 =	Elio de Angelis	10
8 =	Eddie Cheever	10

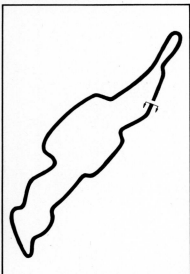

THE GRID

	Pironi 1m 27.509s
Arnoux 1m 27.895s	
	Prost 1m 28.563s
Piquet 1m 28.663s	
	Giacomelli 1m 28.740s
Watson 1m 28.822s	
	Rosberg 1m 28.874s
Patrese 1m 28.999s	
	de Cesaris 1m 29.183s
de Angelis 1m 29.228s	
	Lauda 1m 29.544s
Cheever 1m 29.590s	
	Daly 1m 29.833s
Mansell 1m 30.048s	
	Alboreto 1m 30.146s
Surer 1m 30.518s	
	Baldi 1m 30.599s
Jarier 1m 30.717s	
	Laffite 1m 30.946s
Guerrero 1m 31.235s	
	Boesel 1m 31.759s
Mass 1m 31.861s	
	Paletti 1m 31.901s
Salazar 1m 32.203s	
	Lees 1m 32.205s
Henton 1m 32.325s	

Did not qualify: Manfred Winkelhock (ATS D5-Ford V8) 1m 32.359s; Emilio de Villota (March 821-Ford V8) 1m 34.045s; Chico Serra (Fittipaldi F8D-Ford V8) 1m 37.678s.

The race was stopped after a fatal start line accident to Riccardo Paletti (Osella FA1C-Ford V8) and restarted. The entry of Jean-Pierre Jarier (Osella FA1C-Ford V8) was withdrawn from the re-start and Geoff Lees (Theodore TY-Ford V8) was unable to restart due to damage sustained in the accident.

Wet practice (above) was very wet indeed. The Arrows team (right) had a very promising weekend for once; Surer and Baldi qualified together in 16th and 17th slots, Surer went on to score a couple of hard earned points for fifth place and Baldi came home 8th.

DIDIER Pironi's face and body were bright pink, but that wasn't unusual. Didier sweats a lot when racing, but it never matters, and there's rarely a difference between race-winning pink and midfield pink. In the Haribo motorhome at the bottom of the Zandvoort paddock, he was more relaxed than ever. There had only been one slight worry and that had been whether René Arnoux was alright after his horrific accident. Once he'd checked up on that, Didier had gone to relax and cool off. His story of the race was uncomplicated: "all the work we do to win is done before the race. I knew that our tyres were better than Michelin's, and I knew the Renaults would have a tyre problem. I didn't have to push them very hard."

Rarely are Grand Prix victories that easy, but Didier was certainly uncomplicated about winning this rescheduled Dutch Grand Prix. He had almost been glad to get back to Europe after the Canadian tragedy, and the difficulties with the Canadian people concerning his former team mate. Now he had a new team mate in Patrick Tambay, and the Ferrari team were back to working away at the World Championship. Although the Renaults had started from their habitual front row, Didier had been fourth quickest and Tambay, despite a misfire, had been right behind him on the grid. Turbo cars filled five of the first six places. Only Niki Lauda upset the clean sweep.

Didier's victory even looked easy. He'd overtaken Piquet as the Brazilian had made a poor start to finish the first lap behind the two Renaults. Coming out of the chicane on the second lap, he had calmly pulled past Arnoux's car, and had quickly realised that Prost was in tyre trouble. Leaving Arnoux behind, he soon hauled in the other Renault driver and, at the start of the fifth lap, calmly outbraked the leading Renault into the first corner. Within one lap, he had drawn out a second, within another 12 he had a six and a half second lead. Only a slightly blistered tyre, which never worsened, caused any bother at all. At the end of it all, Didier cruised to a halt and admitted that he had been thinking of Gilles Villeneuve. Later, he would tot up the points, and realise that he'd hauled himself to within one point of non-scoring championship leader John Watson.

After the tight Monaco, Detroit and Montreal circuits, Zandvoort marked the start of the European summer of faster tracks. This, surely, would be where the championship would be won by the turbocharged engines. There were more turbocharged cars in the field than ever before, apart from at Kyalami at the start of the season. There were two Ferraris and, after Piquet's win in Canada, Patrese too had a turbo BMW in the back of his Brabham. Although Teo Fabi failed to qualify because of a preparation fault, even Toleman were beginning to look competitive. Derek Warwick was 13th on the grid, largely thanks to new, narrow Pirelli tyres. It was ironic that the turbos should be so competitive now. Exactly 15 years and one month previously, at this very circuit, the Cosworth engine had made its pole-winning and race-winning début. If things went according to a logical plan, it would be here that the engine would begin its decline. But how often, in motor racing, do things go according to plan?

Ferrari's plans went perfectly that day, even if replacement driver Patrick Tambay did suffer a recurrence of his practice misfire during the race and finish a lowly eighth. Fifteen years previously, the team had just lost Lorenzo Bandini at Monaco, but Chris Amon, Mike Parkes and Ludovico Scarfiotti finished fourth, fifth and sixth behind Clark's new Lotus-Cosworth and two Brabham-Repcos.

This time, it seemed that the tables were turned. Ferrari was on top of the job. Pironi did make short work of the two Renaults, and it was an unhappy Saturday for the French team. After Pironi had overtaken them and drawn away, the Renault men were left in relative peace for nearly ten laps. But Piquet recovered from his poor start, overtook both tyre-troubled Watson and Tambay on the second lap, and knuckled down to catching the Renaults. It took him 12 laps to catch Arnoux and he then demonstrated to all and sundry that BMW's turbo power is every bit as good as Renault's, by coolly overtaking Arnoux on the pit straight.

If that didn't shock Arnoux, then what came next certainly did. The Frenchman began to suffer slight vibration which he attributed to his tyres. But, as he braked for the corner at the end of the main straight on lap 22, his front left steering arm suddenly broke, and the wheel quickly broke off and bounced away. Brakeless and with no steering, poor Arnoux was helpless as his Renault shot off the track and ploughed into the sand, reared onto two wheels, buried its nose in the tyres protecting the barrier at the end of the straight, and reared up on that in a snowstorm of black bouncing tyres. Amazingly, little René was lifted out of the car with nothing worse than a brui-

sed ankle, but his look was particularly wide-eyed afterwards, as though he'd nearly met his maker.

Prost undoubtedly eased up a little at the sight of a similar car to his leaning at a crazy angle against the armco, and steadily Piquet closed in on the second-placed Renault. On lap 31 of the 72 lap race, he swooped past, and two laps later, Prost guided his smokey Renault into the pits and retirement.

So there were two turbos in the lead, but two more potential leaders were out. Patrese had never looked particularly happy either and had pitted to have his gear selection tightened, although he would eventually finish 15th and last. Warwick had climbed up to ninth and had set fastest lap, probably helped by the fact that his rear wing had flown off. He had stopped to have a new one fitted, only to retire shortly after with an oil leak.

An unwitting protector of the turbos' lead was Patrick Tambay. He had soon

settled down in fifth place but with an impressive queue behind him, reminiscent of the Ferrari queues of the previous year. This time, Lauda, Giacomelli, Rosberg, Patrese, Watson and later Warwick were involved. Of these, only Rosberg and Lauda would move up; the rest would drop back. Patrese and Warwick have already been dealt with. Poor Watson found himself on a dud set of tyres and ultimately pitted for some new ones on lap 37, by which time it was too late to improve his position. Giacomelli's exhausts broke which lost him power.

Rosberg, however, got by Giacomelli on the eighth lap and then tigered past Lauda a lap later. Three laps after that, he overtook Tambay and set off in a rather lone pursuit of Piquet. Keke, in fact, suffered a blistered front left within 15 laps, but at half distance he began to put some pressure on. Steadily the gap between second placed Brabham and third placed Williams diminished. With 20 laps of the 72 lap race still to go, the gap was around seven seconds, for Piquet had just lost three seconds behind Salazar's ATS. With ten laps to go, Keke pulled out all the stops, but Piquet was confident of holding off the charging Williams. Despite being held up by Alboreto's damaged Tyrrell, Piquet crossed the line 0.7s ahead of Rosberg. Keke moved up to third in the championship, however.

Lauda took a lot longer to overtake Tambay's Ferrari. Just before half distance, the Ferrari's misfire (caused by poor fuel pick-up) reappeared and, as the car spluttered out of corners, Lauda pulled past into fourth place on lap 40. Two laps later, Daly did the same, only to suffer a blistered front left tyre like Rosberg. But with twenty laps to go, the Williams began to misfire, and into the picture came Alboreto. With just two laps remaining, Alboreto challenged Daly for fifth place at the first corner. The two cars tangled and spun but Daly got going and kept his fifth place. Alboreto, however, got caught on the grass and bent a rear wheel. He staggered round for the last two laps, but lost his sixth place to Baldi. Michele was furious with Daly afterwards, and tried to take a swing at him. Baldi was delighted with his sixth place and Pirelli's new tyres, but team mate Surer had had to pit for a new set of the same tyres.

Not so delighted were the three tobacco-sponsored teams. Ligier's new JS19 was still handling badly and Cheever failed to qualify. Laffite had to use a JS17 after his JS19's clutch broke in the warm-up, but the older car handled so badly that he gave that up in disgust after four laps. Nigel Mansell wasn't fit to drive his Lotus following his Montreal accident, but replacement driver Roberto Moreno had never driven a 91 and didn't have the confidence to qualify, while de Angelis quit due to poor handling. And both Rothman's Marchs suffered damaged valves. Jan Lammers, back in the Theodore again, suffered the same problem.

But the over-riding feeling after Zandvoort was that the turbo era had begun. Watson would have trouble defending his championship lead, and that it was doubtful that a Cosworth would get a look-in until Dijon or Las Vegas! That theory was due to be proved wrong just a couple of weeks later as the faithful Cosworth notched its 149th win.

With the race re-scheduled to a July Saturday there were almost as many people in the pits as in the grandstands when the flag fell (top left). It may be a long time before Didier Pironi again stands on the rostrum (above left) but he is determined to do so. Apparently neither Arnoux nor the photographers read the notice (above near left). Roberto Moreno (left) had a frustrating weekend, failing to qualify the Lotus, while his countryman, Nelson Piquet, just held on for second (above) and Ferrari debutant Tambay drove around engine problems to an encouraging eighth place.

With growing concern being expressed in many quarters over the ever increasing cornering speeds of the latest generation F1 cars, there were those who questioned the wisdom of building an extra grandstand on the outside of Zandvoort's notorious Tarzan corner — approached at maximum speed on the long straight. In recent years both John Watson and Derek Daly have had huge accidents exactly here having run out of brakes into the corner. This year it was René Arnoux's turn to test the barriers after a suspension breakage on his Renault (far right). Mercifully, the 'spherical impact attenuators' (or old tyres) again did their job and Arnoux was virtually unharmed but yet again it was a disturbing case of what might have been. There were no such dramas for Didier Pironi (below) who cruised to a comfortable win for Ferrari, bringing him within a point of John Watson in the title chase.

DUTCH GRAND PRIX
Zandvoort: 3 July 1982
72 laps of 2.62-mile circuit = 190.23 miles

RESULTS

1	Didier Pironi	Ferrari 126C2-V6 turbo	1hr 38m 03.25s
2	Nelson Piquet	Brabham BT50-BMW 4 turbo	1hr 38m 24.90s
3	Keke Rosberg	Williams FW08-Ford V8	1hr 38m 25.62s
4	Niki Lauda	McLaren MP4B-Ford V8	1hr 39m 26.97s
5	Derek Daly	Williams FW08-Ford V8	71 laps
6	Mauro Baldi	Arrows A4-Ford V8	71 laps
7	Michele Alboreto	Tyrrell 011-Ford V8	71 laps
8	Patrick Tambay	Ferrari 126C2-V6 turbo	71 laps
9	John Watson	McLaren MP4B-Ford V8	71 laps
10	Marc Surer	Arrows A4-Ford V8	71 laps
11	Bruno Giacomelli	Alfa Romeo 182-V12	70 laps
12	Manfred Winkelhock	ATS D5-Ford V8	70 laps
13	Eliseo Salazar	ATS D5-Ford V8	70 laps
14	Jean-Pierre Jarier	Osella FA1C-Ford V8	69 laps
15	Riccardo Patrese	Brabham BT50-BMW 4 turbo	69 laps

Fastest lap: Warwick, 1m 19.780s (119.22mph)
Winner's average speed: 116.40mph

RETIREMENTS

Jacques Laffite, Talbot-Ligier JS17-Matra V12, 4 laps, handling problems; Derek Warwick, Toleman TG181-Hart 4 turbo, 15 laps, split oil union; Chico Serra, Fittipaldi F8D-Ford V8, 18 laps, fuel pump; Raul Boesel, March 821-Ford V8, 21 laps, engine; Brian Henton, Tyrrell 011-Ford V8, 21 laps, throttle linkage; René Arnoux, Renault RE30B-V6 turbo, 21 laps, accident; Alain Prost, Renault RE30B-V6 turbo, 33 laps, engine; Andrea de Cesaris, Alfa Romeo 182-V12, 40 laps, handling problems; Jan Lammers, Theodore TY-Ford V8, 41 laps, engine; Jochen Mass, March 821-Ford V8, 60 laps, engine.

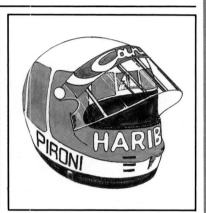

CHAMPIONSHIP LEADERS

1	John Watson	30
2	Didier Pironi	29
3	Keke Rosberg	21
4	Riccardo Patrese	19
5	Alain Prost	18
6	Nelson Piquet	17
7	Niki Lauda	15
8 =	Michele Alboreto	10
8 =	Elio de Angelis	10
8 =	Eddie Cheever	10

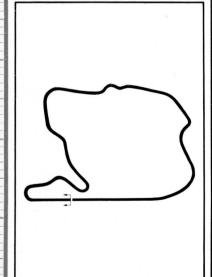

THE GRID

Prost 1m 14.660s	Arnoux 1m 14.233s
	Piquet 1m 14.723s
Pironi 1m 15.825s	Lauda 1m 15.823s
Tambay 1m 16.154s	Rosberg 1m 16.260s
Giacomelli 1m 16.513s	de Cesaris 1m 16.576s
Patrese 1m 16.630s	Watson 1m 16.700s
Daly 1m 16.832s	Warwick 1m 17.094s
Alboreto 1m 17.237s	de Angelis 1m 17.620s
Baldi 1m 18.020s	Surer 1m 18.296s
Winkelhock 1m 18.352s	Serra 1m 18.438s
Henton 1m 18.476s	Laffite 1m 18.478s
Boesel 1m 18.658s	Jarier 1m 18.953s
Mass 1m 19.083s	Salazar 1m 19.120s
Lammers 1m 19.274s	

Did not qualify: Roberto Guerrero (Ensign N181-Ford V8) 1m 19.316s; Teo Fabi (Toleman TG181-Hart 4 turbo) 1m 19.414s; Eddie Cheever (Talbot-Ligier JS19-Matra V12) 1m 19.646s; Roberto Moreno (JPS-Lotus 91-Ford V8) 1m 21.149s. Emilio de Villota (March 821-Ford V8) did not pre-qualify.

THE big blue and red car came up beside the red Ferrari, a direct confrontation between British and Italian turbocars. The two rocketed over the start/finish line and into Paddock bend. But in the braking area, the contest was decided. The Ferrari was the first to slow, the blue and red car shot ahead. A great cheer went up from the throng of people overlooking the corner, reflected all the way round the track as the Toleman pulled away. Derek Warwick was in second place, and all the Englishmen at Brands Hatch were right behind him.

Underneath that blue and white helmet, Derek gave himself a little chuckle, the kind that even the coolest and proudest can't resist when they really feel pleased with themselves. It may have been nicknamed the Belgrano, or even the Flying Pig, but this Toleman was going well. From 16th on the grid, Derek had picked up five places on the first lap to complete it in eleventh place. Immediately ahead had been Tambay's Ferrari, but that was swiftly dealt with. Alain Prost's Renault quickly went the same way, and after a couple of laps watching the two Alfas, Warwick demoted them, too.

On lap seven Derek Warwick was already in a points-scoring position. His new Pirelli tyres were performing well, the Hart engine felt strong, it was more than a match for Elio de Angelis's Lotus when Derek came up to challenge on the 13th lap. The other Derek, Daly, put up stiffer opposition but, in the end, his fate was the same as all the others. Then there was only the Ferrari and Niki Lauda's distant McLaren ahead.

Once the Ferrari was disposed of, there was plenty of time for the Toleman driver to settle down and bide his time. Lauda was some way ahead, but only a third of the race had been run. The Toleman powered on, carrying with it the hopes of many of the 90,000 spectators present, let alone those watching on TV. In Sweden, where a Formula Two race was being run, the news that Derek Warwick was in second place behind Niki Lauda was greeted with astonishment. The news had come via Austria; could it be wrong? No, the Toleman forged onwards.

But on lap 41, going up the hill to Druids, the Hampshire driver felt a slight vibration. He changed down, cranked the wheel over to the right, guided the car round the hairpin, and stamped on the accelerator. A sickening clunk came from the rear end. Derek's heart sank and, with it, the hopes of all those spectators. A driveshaft had broken, and there was nothing to be done. Toleman had been there, they'd tasted points for the first time in the team's history. But fate had decided otherwise. Later, looking at his left rear tyre, Derek wondered if he would have made it to the end anyway . . .

But he wasn't the only one that was disappointed that day. The crowd had been behind him, but also behind that other more British than British team, Williams. After a gutsy demonstration of high speed car control in practice, and several engaging PR exercises by microphone, and by personal appearances in the pits, Keke Rosberg had the crowd behind him. The man himself was more determined than ever. After his third place at Zandvoort two weeks previously, Keke had actually had the inter-

While Derek Warwick was giving the bulky Toleman its moment of glory and raising patriotic hopes all around the circuit, his former team mate Brian Henton (above) was having perhaps his best outing of the year to take fastest lap with his somewhat battered Tyrrell. Henton eventually finished eighth, after a pit stop but the team, who had made elaborate plans, including pressurised refuelling equipment (below left) for their own stop, never made it that far. Nigel Mansell (below right) fought valiantly in spite of his injured wrist, but eventually had to give in to the pain. Having taken pole in truly stunning fashion, Rosberg's problems on the grid (right) must have been bitterly disappointing. Tambay's race was far less dramatic (right below) until he inherited third place one lap from home.

vening weekend to himself. He had relaxed for the first time for weeks, but he'd given up drinking even his occasional modest glass of wine. He'd felt desperately out of place at a high-spirited Williams party on the Saturday, but Brands Hatch was a race he really wanted to win. He felt it might be his last opportunity before Las Vegas. His father was coming over from Finland to watch.

On the Friday, Keke had put in a superb lap which had remained good enough on Saturday. Keke had watched nervously as the Brabhams got close, but he had won 100 bottles of champagne for his pole position. However, Frank Williams had taken his 60 per cent . . . Then things had begun to go wrong. Even on the hardest Goodyears in unexpectedly sunny English weather, the car

had understeered badly during Sunday morning's warm-up. The settings were changed, but the car handled just as badly.

But even before then, Keke's hopes were dashed. A vapour lock in the fuel system left him stationary as the others went out on their final warming-up lap. All that work had been wasted. Keke would have to start from the back. Even so, he was 15th on the first lap, then shot through the field in fantastic style, later overtaking Tambay, Prost and Giacomelli and reaching sixth place on the 12th lap. At that stage, he was 23 seconds behind leader Lauda, but still hadn't given up hope. When the tyres blistered, he realised that it was all over and, in the end, fuel vapourisation sidelined the car. The crowd had been be-

could thus start with less than full tanks, and softer tyres which could also be changed. Brabham had ostensibly adopted the idea. Expensive refuelling gear, fireproof overalls for 12 mechanics and a heater to warm the new tyres had all been purchased, while the team had got the act together in 12 seconds during tests at Donington.

So Nelson was intent on building himself a big lead. With nine laps gone, he was ten seconds clear. But on the tenth lap, the Brabham cruised round Paddock bend with a dead engine: the fuel metering unit belt had come off, as it had at Monaco, and the car's race was run. Only later did it transpire that the re-fuelling trick was a hoax — at Brands anyway. The Brabham, for what it was worth, was on full tanks . . .

And into the lead swept Niki Lauda. He had followed Nelson past his stationary team mate at the start, had been content to let the Brabham pull away, and was now inheriting a comfortable lead. After that, Niki was able to relax. It was a real 'no problem' race. He had a comfortable ten seconds here and there to play with, and that's just what he did. No one expected it to be that easy, it rarely is, and certainly not in the face of the turbos, but sometimes things just go perfectly . . .

Despite the shock of being overtaken by Warwick's Toleman, Pironi kept second place, although he was nursing his Goodyear rubber which had found hot weather at Brands Hatch slightly surprising. Derek Daly suffered from the same problem. Despite having to dodge the startline carnage, Derek picked off de Cesaris, Alboreto and later de Angelis to hold third place by the tenth lap. Warwick pushed him down to fourth, but then his tyres went off sufficiently to necessitate a pit stop. Despite dropping to eleventh, Derek came back to finish fifth.

He finished by closely challenging de Angelis in fourth, and by being closely challenged by Prost just behind him. And those three were only a couple of seconds behind Tambay's third placed Ferrari. Handling and an engine problem meant that the Ferrari driver started only 13th on the grid, but quiet unhurried progress promoted him to third place when he overtook de Angelis's misfiring Lotus on the very last lap. The Italian had run out of fuel.

Perhaps the most disappointing performance was that of Prost. Brands obviously didn't suit the Renault men, for Arnoux started sixth and Prost was eighth. The survivor of the two found the handling appalling at first, probably due to a damaged skirt, but it improved, and only Daly's weaving at the end kept the Renault man in sixth place.

While Lauda went on his winning way, poor Watson was walking home. He hadn't started particularly high up, and then had to take to the grass to avoid the startline shunt. He was down in 16th place when a fast starting Chico Serra, having his last race in the Fittipaldi F8, tangled with Jean-Pierre Jarier on lap two. The Fittipaldi overturned, luckily without injury to the driver, and Rosberg just scraped past. But Watson spun to avoid the damaged cars, stalled the engine and failed to get going again. With Pironi scoring six points, Watson lost the championship lead, and team mate Lauda was now only six points behind.

hind him in his struggle and just as when Warwick pulled out, there was a sense of deflation as the Williams retired.

He had, however, won Cosworth's only pole position of the season, and one of only two non-turbo poles.

If Keke was the main Cosworth hope against the turbos, then now the turbos should have come into their own. But things hadn't gone well for them from the start. It wasn't a good day to be on the front row of the grid. There was Riccardo Patrese with probably the greatest chance he'd had all year. Front row of the grid and the poleman had gone missing. Effectively, he was on pole. He selects first gear, but not carefully enough. Drops the clutch, there's a slight crunch and then nothing. The Brabham didn't move. It could have been Montreal all

over again, but fortunately Arnoux, two behind Patrese came up and thumped the BMW department of the Brabham. Both of them slid off towards the grass, but Arnoux's front wheel bounced into the path of Fabi's Toleman. For the first and only time in the season, Teo had qualified quicker than Warwick . . . and now this. Three turbos out, Daly and particularly Watson delayed by having to take to the grass in avoidance.

So Piquet, who should have had Rosberg in front of him on the grid, has the ideal line for a superb start. Furthermore, his team appeared to have a trick up their collective sleeves. Keith Duckworth had had the idea first, when he said that the ideal turbo engine would require so much fuel that a car would have to make a pit stop during the race, and

BRITISH GRAND PRIX
Brands Hatch: 18 July 1982
76 laps of 2.61-mile circuit = 198.634 miles

RESULTS

1	Niki Lauda	McLaren MP4B-Ford V8	1hr 35m 33.81s
2	Didier Pironi	Ferrari 126C2-V6 turbo	1hr 35m 59.54s
3	Patrick Tambay	Ferrari 126C2-V6 turbo	1hr 36m 12.25s
4	Elio de Angelis	JPS Lotus 91-Ford V8	1hr 36m 15.05s
5	Derek Daly	Williams FW08-Ford V8	1hr 36m 15.24s
6	Alain Prost	Renault RE30B-V6 turbo	1hr 36m 15.45s
7	Bruno Giacomelli	Alfa Romeo 182-V12	75 laps
8	Brian Henton	Tyrrell 011-Ford V8	75 laps
9	Mauro Baldi	Arrows A4-Ford V8	74 laps
10	Jochen Mass	March 821-Ford V8	73 laps

Fastest lap: Henton, 1m 13.028s (128.84mph)
Winner's average speed: 124.70mph

RETIREMENTS

Riccardo Patrese, Brabham BT50-BMW 4 turbo, 0 laps, startline accident; René Arnoux, Renault RE30B-V6 turbo, 0 laps, startline accident; Teo Fabi, Toleman TG181-Hart 4 turbo, 0 laps, startline accident; Chico Serra, Fittipaldi F8D-Ford V8, 2 laps, accident with Jarier; Jean-Pierre Jarier, Osella FA1C-Ford V8, 2 laps, accident with Serra; John Watson, McLaren MP4B-Ford V8, 2 laps, spun off, avoiding Serra and Jarier; Roberto Guerrero, Ensign N181-Ford V8, 3 laps, engine; Nelson Piquet, Brabham BT50-BMW 4 turbo, 9 laps, injection pump belt; Nigel Mansell, JPS-Lotus 91-Ford V8, 30 laps, pain from wrist injury; Derek Warwick, Toleman TG181-Hart 4 turbo, 41 laps, CV joint; Jacques Laffite, Talbot-Ligier JS19, 42 laps, gearbox; Michele Alboreto, Tyrrell 011-Ford V8, 44 laps, handling problems (running at finish but unclassified); Keke Rosberg, Williams FW08-Ford V8, 51 laps, fuel pressure; Marc Surer, Arrows A4-Ford V8, 59 laps, engine; Eddie Cheever, Talbot-Ligier JS17-Matra V12, 61 laps, engine; Andrea de Cesaris, Alfa Romeo 182-V12, 66 laps, electrical problem.

CHAMPIONSHIP LEADERS

1	Didier Pironi	35
2	John Watson	30
3	Niki Lauda	24
4	Keke Rosberg	21
5 =	Riccardo Patrese	19
5 =	Alain Prost	19
7	Nelson Piquet	17
8	Elio de Angelis	13
9 =	Michele Alboreto	10
9 =	Eddie Cheever	10

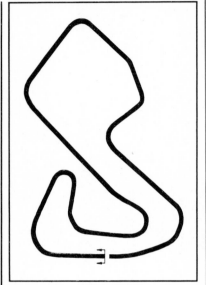

THE GRID

	Rosberg 1m 09.540s
Patrese 1m 09.627s	
	Piquet 1m 10.060s
Pironi 1m 10.066s	
	Lauda 1m 10.638s
Arnoux 1m 10.641s	
	de Angelis 1m 10.650s
Prost 1m 10.728s	
	Alboreto 1m 10.892s
Daly 1m 10.980s	
	de Cesaris 1m 11.347s
Watson 1m 11.418s	
	Tambay 1m 11.430s
Giacomelli 1m 11.502s	
	Fabi 1m 11.728s
Warwick 1m 11.761s	
	Henton 1m 12.080s
Jarier 1m 12.436s	
	Guerrero 1m 12.668s
Laffite 1m 12.695s	
	Serra 1m 13.096s
Surer 1m 13.181s	
	Mansell 1m 13.212s
Cheever 1m 13.301s	
	Mass 1m 13.622s
Baldi 1m 13.721s	

Did not qualify: Manfred Winkelhock (ATS D5-Ford V8) 1m 13.741s; Jan Lammers (Theodore TY-Ford V8) 1m 13.815s; Eliseo Salazar (ATS D5-Ford V8) 1m 13.866s; Raul Boesel (March 821-Ford V8) 1m 13.968s.

Derek Warwick was in inspired form with the heavy and largely unloved Toleman TG181 'General Belgrano' (right) clawing his way up to second place, cheered to the echo by the fiercely patriotic crowd, before a broken driveshaft brought his run to an end. For Lauda (below), always a favourite in Britain, the fairytale return rolled on with another fine win.

RENÉ Arnoux was adamant. He stood there with his eyes wide, rather as he had after his big shunt at the Dutch GP. But this time he was pleading that he'd done the right thing. *This* wide eyed expression was wide-eyed innocence. René, so often the meek and mild, was showing that he could think things out for himself, thank you, and wasn't going to be pushed around. He wasn't in motor racing to let someone else win, and certainly not some namby pamby favourite who can't win races for himself.

René, you see, had just disobeyed team orders that had decreed that he should slow down and let Alain Prost win no matter what position they were in. It had been agreed before the start of the race, for Alain had 19 points against René's four, and the former was therefore in with a better chance of winning the World Championship. As both Renaults were again on the front row of the grid, there had to be some sort of discussion regarding team tactics. Under those conditions, it was decided that provided neither driver was in direct confrontation with another driver outside the team, Arnoux should let Prost past.

Once both the Brabhams had dropped out before their planned pit stops at half distance, the Renault men found themselves comfortably in the lead. Both had their problems however. Arnoux, the faster in practice, began to suffer serious vibration at half distance, and was seriously worried that he might have to make a pit stop. In the end, it was discovered that he'd chipped a rear wheel rim. Prost, meanwhile, had dropped back with sub-standard roadholding caused by a cut right hand skirt.

But with ten laps of this 54-lap race run, Arnoux had a 23 second lead. And it was then that team manager Jean Sage hung out a sign saying "1 Alain, 2 René". Arnoux would actually have to slow by 2.3s a lap. Perhaps he could just park it? No such thought entered his head. The board came out a lap later with the same message. Nothing happened. The Renault men were getting a little desperate on lap five, and out went the board again. No reaction. It was getting a little late when the two boards were hung out with just two laps to go, and it was almost futile to hang the board at the start of the last lap. The guy just wasn't interested. Arnoux wanted to win, and win he did.

His mechanics were delighted, the bosses weren't so thrilled. When a major company such as Renault spends a fortune in trying to win the World Championship, it expects its directors to do the job properly, to have control over staff, whether floor cleaners or drivers, and to impress upon those people exactly the nature of the major objective: to win the World Championship for Renault. The factory and Company name comes first. Still, it wasn't an enviable position for the Larousses of this world. A competitive instinct would surely agree that Arnoux deserved to win. But the company man would say Prost. No, not an enviable position for a man of Larousse's experience to be in.

Later that afternoon, while Renault wondered if they should celebrate or not, but made the best of it anyway with good grace (who wouldn't, having scored a one-two at home?), Alain Prost explained that the atmosphere between himself and Arnoux was inflammatory.

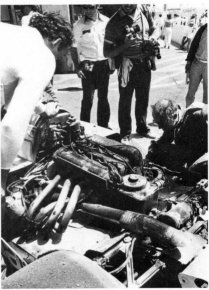

Renault would have to choose between Arnoux and Prost for next year. As the crowds began to leave the sun-baked circuit, black smoke began to fill the sky to the south of the circuit as one of the South of France's infamous bush fires took hold on the surrounding countryside, fanned by a strong Mistrale. It reflected the atmosphere within the Renault camp: there was no smoke without fire. Within a month, René Arnoux was rumoured to be joining Ferrari, and before the end of the season it had been announced. Renault had made its choice: Prost had always been the favourite. He would stay the favourite, and remain with the team. Arnoux was the outcast.

It was, in fact, a remarkably fiery weekend. Take the Brabham pit. Thanks to the pit stop idea, it was one of the best equipped to take care of fires, and it had to be. The hot weather and a surfeit of oil leaks meant that there was at least one engine fire per practice session. Fortunately, the team had gas-loaded fire extinguishers, and a quick squirt put out the fire and didn't leave any residue. With the normal ·powder-filled extinguishers, the mechanics would have spent around 24 hours a day changing engines.

When the Brabhams were going, they went well. Although Renault dominated practice, the other two major turbo teams monopolised the next two rows. Patrese shared row two with Pironi, and Piquet shared row three with Tambay, although in each case the Ferrari was the quicker. Once again, the Brabham men were planning on stopping at around the 25 lap mark, and hoping to pull out all the stops during the first half of the race. The plan went well. Patrese was in the lead by lap three, and Piquet had followed him through to hold second place by lap five. The Renault men weren't being duped into following the flying Brabham-BMWs.

But on lap eight, the first chink in the Brabham armour appeared. The BMW engine in the back of Patrese's Brabham threw a piston, causing the engine to burst into flames. Not wanting a long walk home, and knowing that his team was well-equipped for fire fighting, Riccardo cruised back to his pit and retirement. Piquet, meanwhile, had taken over the lead and pounded around, building up a 22 second lead by the 24th lap. It was almost time for the pit stop. The mechanics in their blue overalls were waiting, but then Piquet cruised to a halt with a broken valve spring, almost certainly the result of twice over-revving that day. The Brabham challenge was

René Arnoux was unconcerned about his indiscretion (left and below) and the team was delighted by victory (right), but the Renault management was less than totally impressed by the lack of discipline. Brabham had an expensive weekend at the punishing French circuit (below far left) and, once again, the sophisticated pit-stop arrangements (below left) went unproved. Keke Rosberg was best of the Cosworth runners, in fifth place, but he was given a run for his money by the ever impressive Alboreto (below right).

over.

That left the two Renaults in the lead to the end and their logical pretenders were the two flame-red Ferraris. Pironi had started third and Tambay fifth. It was important for them both to finish, particularly Pironi for this would mean building up his lead in the World Championship. The main problem for them was tyres, and neither driver had much hope of staying with the Renaults, but at least they cruised home third and fourth. Didier, indeed, remained in the lead of the World Championship and opened up his lead to nine points over John Watson.

The Cosworth men, you see, were in quite a lot of bother. They knew that they would be far outclassed by the turbos at this circuit, and their only possible respite was in getting round the corners a lot quicker than the turbo men who relied on their straight line speed. Both Goodyear and Michelin test a lot at Ricard, but the combination of a hot track, more supporting races than at any other Grand Prix in the world (and therefore more rubber on the track) and the ambitions of engineers and drivers alike, meant that tyre choice was a lottery.

Daly shot up to be the first non-turbo during the opening laps, but was in the pits within 13 laps for more tyres after a puncture. Team mate Rosberg took it slightly easier in the opening stages, waiting for Watson to retire with a broken battery cable and later for Lauda to pit for tyres. In between time, he overtook Giacomelli — who also pitted later for tyres. Keke found himself first non-turbo after 17 laps, and there he remained to the chequered flag. But even he was in trouble with his tyres and, at the end, Michele Alboreto came through to challenge him, failing by just 1.4s.

In spite of the heat, there were 16 finishers. Embarrassingly enough, two of the last three were Ligiers. The two cars had at least three tyre changes between them, and the drivers appeared still to be sorting out the cars, but at least they finished. After putting on a brave show to return for his home Grand Prix, Nigel Mansell had again decided against driving for the JPS Lotus team because of his Montreal arm injury. Rather than give one of their test drivers another crack at qualifying, the team had called in Geoff Lees as a replacement. Although suffering from suspected glandular fever, Geoff put the car on the 24th spot on the grid and was going well until he suffered a puncture, but in the end he finished 12th. Chico Serra, driving the new Fittipaldi F9 for the first time, failed to qualify.

Motor sport is rarely blessed with good luck, it sometimes seems, but there was no doubt that it had a lucky escape at Ricard. On their tenth laps, Jochen Mass and Mauro Baldi came together at Signes, the very fast right hander at the end of Ricard's long Mistrale straight. The corner is taken virtually flat in a Formula One car, and Didier Pironi had already had one enormous accident there earlier in the season. This time, Baldi's Arrows spun into the catch fencing, but Mass's Rothmans March flew through the air, into the debris fencing and on into the crowd. There, it burst into flames briefly, landing upside down on Mass and some spectators. A dozen spectators suffered burns and other minor injuries, while Mass suffered back trouble for the second time in three years (the same thing happened to him in Austria in 1980) and did no more F1 for March in 1982. It was just remarkable and so lucky that no one was killed. Ricard is the safest circuit in Europe. To have anyone killed — particularly spectators — at the French circuit would have placed the sport in serious jeopardy.

Instead, life went on as normal. The trucks packed up, and headed for home, leaving Didier Pironi in the lead of the championship . . .

FRENCH GRAND PRIX

Paul Ricard: 25 July 1982

54 laps of 3.61-mile circuit = 194.94 miles

RESULTS

1	René Arnoux	Renault RE30B-V6 turbo	1hr 33m 33.22s
2	Alain Prost	Renault RE30B-V6 turbo	1hr 33m 50.52s
3	Didier Pironi	Ferrari 126C2-V6 turbo	1hr 34m 15.34s
4	Patrick Tambay	Ferrari 126C2-V6 turbo	1hr 34m 49.46s
5	Keke Rosberg	Williams FW08-Ford V8	1hr 35m 04.21s
6	Michele Alboreto	Tyrrell 011-Ford V8	1hr 35m 05.56s
7	Derek Daly	Williams FW08-Ford V8	53 laps
8	Niki Lauda	McLaren MP4B-Ford V8	53 laps
9	Bruno Giacomelli	Alfa Romeo 182-V12	53 laps
10	Brian Henton	Tyrrell 011-Ford V8	53 laps
11	Manfred Winkelhock	ATS D5-Ford V8	52 laps
12	Geoff Lees	JPS-Lotus 91-Ford V8	52 laps
13	Marc Surer	Arrows A4-Ford V8	52 laps
14	Jacques Laffite	Talbot-Ligier JS19-Matra V12	51 laps
15	Derek Warwick	Toleman TG181-Hart 4 turbo	50 laps
16	Eddie Cheever	Talbot-Ligier JS19-Matra V12	49 laps

Fastest lap: Patrese, 1m 40.075s (129.87mph) — record
Winner's average speed: 124.99mph

RETIREMENTS

Jean-Pierre Jarier, Osella FA1C-Ford V8, 0 laps, driveshaft; Teo Fabi, Toleman TG181-Hart 4 turbo, 0 laps, electrical problem; Eliseo Salazar, ATS D5-Ford V8, 2 laps, accident; Riccardo Patrese, Brabham BT50-BMW 4 turbo, 8 laps, engine; Mauro Baldi, Arrows A4-Ford V8, 10 laps, accident; Jochen Mass, March 821-Ford V8, 10 laps, accident; John Watson, McLaren MP4B-Ford V8, 12 laps, electrical problem; Elio de Angelis, JPS-Lotus 91-Ford V8, 17 laps, fuel pressure; Nelson Piquet, Brabham BT50-BMW 4 turbo, 23 laps, engine; Andrea de Cesaris, Alfa Romeo 182-V12, 25 laps, accident.

CHAMPIONSHIP LEADERS

1	Didier Pironi	39
2	John Watson	30
3	Alain Prost	25
4	Niki Lauda	24
5	Keke Rosberg	23
6	Riccardo Patrese	19
7	Nelson Piquet	17
8 =	Elio de Angelis	13
8 =	René Arnoux	13
10	Michele Alboreto	11

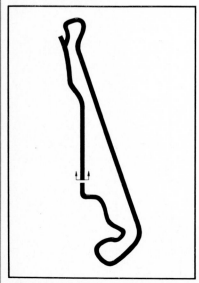

THE GRID

Arnoux 1m 34.406s	Prost 1m 34.688s
Pironi 1m 35.790s	Patrese 1m 35.811s
Tambay 1m 35.905s	Piquet 1m 36.359s
de Cesaris 1m 37.573s	Giacomelli 1m 37.705s
Lauda 1m 37.778s	Rosberg 1m 37.780s
Daly 1m 38.767s	Watson 1m 38.944s
de Angelis 1m 39.118s	Warwick 1m 39.306s
Alboreto 1m 39.330s	Laffite 1m 39.605s
Jarier 1m 39.909s	Winkelhock 1m 39.917s
Cheever 1m 40.817s	Surer 1m 40.335s
Fabi 1m 40.421s	Salazar 1m 40.673s
Henton 1m 40.852s	Lees 1m 40.974s
Baldi 1m 40.997s	Mass 1m 41.579s

Did not qualify: Jan Lammers (Theodore TY-Ford V8) 1m 41.714s; Roberto Guerrero (Ensign N181-Ford V8)) 1m 42.270s; Chico Serra (Fittipaldi F8D-Ford V8 and Fittipaldi F9-Ford V8) 1m 42.414s; Raul Boesel (March 821-Ford V8) 1m 43.099s.

For once, the Renaults held together for the duration and they couldn't have chosen a better place to do it, sweeping to a convincing 1-2 victory in front of an enthusiastic home crowd. Arnoux (right) led the Renaults home but when the cheering died down there would be some explaining to be done ... Ricard's long straights put an enormous strain on engines and the Brabham team's BMW turbos (below) suffered a frighteningly expensive run of breakages in both practice and the race.

IT was a lousy day. On some lousy days, when the rain falls incessantly, drivers sit around in the pits and wait for the weather to improve. Others are more conscientious: they go out in all that spray and damp and slither about just in case it's the same on race day. Some aren't even allowed to go out in the rain, such are the parts/engine supply problems of their particular teams.

But when there are new rain tyres to test, the drivers have to drive. And Didier Pironi was out on the track that Saturday morning, testing new rain tyres. The championship leader was leaving nothing to chance. If it was going to be wet on Sunday, then he would have tested his tyres and be ready to fit them and set up the car to make the most of them. He had done a number of laps and was heading for the pits. By his own admission, he was doing around 175mph which doesn't sound like cruising to you or I. In front of him was Derek Daly and, just at the end of the long straight, running from what was now the third chicane to the entrance to the stadium, the Williams driver jinked to the right.

There was just a moment to reflect that Derek might be moving over for Didier, before the words RENAULT Elf on Prost's rear wing shot through the spray towards the Ferrari driver. Then came the sickening thump and the Ferrari was launched off the Renault's rear tyre and high into the air. There was another sickening thump, and then silence as the wrecked Ferrari slid to a halt. The rescuers were there in seconds. Nelson Piquet and Eddie Cheever both stopped. Piquet, sickened by what he saw, took off Didier's helmet, but then could stand it no longer and drove slowly back to the pits.

Didier was conscious almost throughout the rescue operation, which took over 30 careful minutes. Then he was helicoptered away to Heidelberg University Hospital. There were rumours around the pits that he would lose a leg, then, later, that he would never race again, that he would surely retire. But his recovery was little short of miraculous. Enzo Ferrari promised him a drive for the 1983 season when he was ready, but first of all, both arms had to mend, and both legs, particularly the badly damaged right ankle. At one time, Didier had over 100 metal screws holding him together.

On that soggy Saturday morning, the 1982 World Championship lost a major contender. Many observers would argue that Pironi should have won the World Championship. Others would simply point out that he didn't. Some of his own colleagues and countrymen would remark that it is unlucky to have a huge accident, just as it is unlucky to have a startline shunt, or blow an engine. All three cost a driver points, but doing considerable speed in the wet tends to stretch that luck. Whatever, Didier Pironi was out of the World Championship. In the end, he finished second equal with John Watson. But for that accident, he would almost certainly have won the title. But as most racing drivers will point out, that accident was avoidable.

Race day was grey; one of those still, murky days which have no life in them. The six turbos, from Ferrari, Renault and Brabham, were due to start from the first six places on the grid. Pironi's Ferrari wasn't withdrawn — there's money for pole position — although Lauda's

McLaren had been, so Surer had joined the back end of the grid. After that one dry day of practice on Friday, the times were incredible. The turbo men were just running away. The times for the first six men on the grid varied from 1m 47.9s to 1m 49.7s. Then came a gap of nearly three seconds to the first normally aspirated car: Michele Alboreto's Tyrrell. It was obvious that there were two races here.

The first one was soon led by Nelson Piquet in his lightweight Brabham. Team mate Patrese had a full fuel load, but Nelson was acting as hare. By lap 15, he had a 20 second lead and it was increasing all the time. The projected pit stop was expected around half distance of

this 45 lap race, but Nelson never got that far.

He was easily faster than anyone else on the track, particularly Eliseo Salazar's struggling ATS. Nelson's fastest lap was no less than six seconds faster than Eliseo's. On lap 19, the Brazilian gave the Chilean hand over fist as they went from chicane number one to the silly new creation shortly before the Ost Kurve. As Eliseo got to this ridiculously narrow affair, he looked in his mirror and saw Nelson charging up behind him. Eliseo pulled over to give him room to brake, but the Brazilian dived for the ever-narrowing gap. The two cars tangled and spun to a halt. In full view of the world, via TV and satel-

At long last, 'Mr Nice Guy' got to stand on the top step of the rostrum (above) and, although his thoughts were of Villeneuve, Pironi and his own family, he could savour a well earned victory — albeit in a grey race run on a Grade A grey day. Pironi's accident was of truly horrifying proportion and it is a great tribute to the circuit medical team and the hospital doctors that the outcome was not even more catastrophic. When Nelson Piquet arrived on the scene (top right) he was literally sickened by the severity of the situation and returned to the pits feeling totally helpless. For once, Arnoux's Renault (above right) held together from flag to flag and, in spite of a worsening vibration problem, René managed to coax the car home behind Tambay to put French drivers first and second. Quite predictably, Hockenheim had been a turbo race and the best of the rest was Rosberg (right) who inherited third place when the often unlucky John Watson succumbed to suspension failure with nine laps to run.

lite, the sport's World Champion grabbed the hapless Chilean, thrust both fists into his full face helmet, and then aimed a futile kick at the ATS driver: "the dago always kicks," remarked an English team member with colonial geniality after the umpteenth replay on TV. It was almost laughable, if it wasn't for the fact that we're meant to respect our World Champions, and admire their perspicacity, accuracy and good judgement. And poor Mr Schmid had been put in a very embarrassing position: for one German car to knock out another at home when the BMW-engined version had been leading ... it couldn't have been worse, especially when Mr Schmid was so hoping for BMW engines to power Winkelhock's

ATS in 1983. Poor Eliseo later got the sack after he'd qualified at Monza and Winkelhock hadn't.

There was little joy to be derived from the gloom of Hockenheim and, although Piquet's antics provided light relief in a flippant sort of way, only Tambay's victory at the end of the day could actually make one smile. It had, after all, been a grim weekend, particularly for Ferrari. But Tambay had overtaken Prost's misfiring Renault on the fourth lap, and disposed of Arnoux's version on the tenth. When the Brabham had spun out of the race, Tambay was left with a comfortable lead to the end. Mr Nice-Guy had won his first Grand Prix. Even at that moment, his thoughts had been filled

with memories of Gilles Villeneuve, the maimed Didier Pironi, and his family, friends and supporters who had so long believed in him and given him the morale to carry on when things got tough. It seemed rather sad that Patrick couldn't enjoy his first win and think of it as his own, but that was the way he wanted it.

It was also sad that he had won in such a boring race. Arnoux could do little about the Ferrari because once more he was suffering from a vibration which had him thinking about new tyres. Team mate Prost headed for the pits when lying fourth to have his misfire seen to, but he emerged from the car a few laps later when the trouble was traced to the fuel injection pump. Patrese, on full tanks as insurance against his team mate's half tanks, didn't even last as long as Piquet. On lap 14, having just inherited fourth place when Prost pitted for the first time, Patrese's BMW engine gave up the ghost and the first Brabham was out.

As Patrese cruised to retirement, he was overtaken by John Watson's Marlboro McLaren. With Pironi obviously sidelined for the rest of the season, Watson had the best chance of overhauling him and taking the championship lead. He'd overtaken Cheever, Alboreto, Rosberg and the ailing de Cesaris with his gearbox troubles, as well as Prost and Patrese. With Piquet retired, Wattie found himself in a very handy third place. But, with just nine laps left, his McLaren's front suspension suddenly buckled at the 'silly' chicane, and slid off the track and into retirement, for the fourth time in as many races.

Into third place, but a lap behind, came Rosberg with all manner of problems, yet seemingly unchallenged. He'd been overtaken by Laffite shortly after half distance but, like Ligier team mate Cheever, the French driver was in dire trouble with skirts very soon after, and neither Ligier finished. Once again, Michele Alboreto followed Rosberg home after qualifying an excellent sixth but falling back in the early stages. Bruno Giacomelli scored his first points of the season, leading home Surer. The Swiss driver had been allowed into the race when Lauda withdrew and, starting from the back, had overtaken 12 others to finish a fine sixth.

If Pironi's Ferrari had been withdrawn earlier, Irishman Tommy Byrne would have made his Grand Prix début on his first attempt. Some thought that he had been purposely left out as his experience had been limited to Formula Three and only three sessions in the Theodore, but his time would come. Nigel Mansell was back on the grid again, qualifying 18th but still in pain from his injured arm. He eventually finished ninth, two places ahead of Chico Serra who brought up the tail end in the Fittipaldi F9's first race.

But now the championship had taken on a new look. The expected turbo domination hadn't fully materialised. Pironi was out of action, Watson had had a run of retirements, and creeping into the picture was Rosberg. He was still three points behind Watson, and Prost was only two more behind him. The next few races, particularly on turbo ground at Österreichring, would surely favour the Renaults and even give championship hopes to Patrese and Arnoux back in sixth place.

GERMAN GRAND PRIX
Hockenheim: 8 August 1982
45 laps of 4.22-mile circuit = 189.85 miles

RESULTS

1	Patrick Tambay	Ferrari 126C2-V6 turbo	1hr 27m 25.18s
2	René Arnoux	Renault RE30B-V6 turbo	1hr 27m 41.56s
3	Keke Rosberg	Williams FW08-Ford V8	44 laps
4	Michele Alboreto	Tyrrell 011-Ford V8	44 laps
5	Bruno Giacomelli	Alfa Romeo 182-V12	44 laps
6	Marc Surer	Arrows A4-Ford V8	44 laps
7	Brian Henton	Tyrrell 011-Ford V8	44 laps
8	Roberto Guerrero	Ensign N181-Ford V8	44 laps
9	Nigel Mansell	JPS-Lotus 91-Ford V8	43 laps
10	Derek Warwick	Toleman TG181-Hart 4 turbo	43 laps
11	Chico Serra	Fittipaldi F9-Ford V8	43 laps

Fastest lap: Piquet, 1m 54.035s (133.33mph)
Winner's average speed: 130.43mph

RETIREMENTS
Manfred Winkelhock, ATS D5-Ford V8, 3 laps, clutch; Jean-Pierre Jarier, Osella FA1C-Ford V8, 3 laps, spun off; Mauro Baldi, Arrows A4-Ford V8, 6 laps, engine; Eddie Cheever, Talbot-Ligier JS19-Matra V12, 8 laps, broken skirt; Andrea de Cesaris, Alfa Romeo 182-V12, 9 laps, accident damage; Riccardo Patrese, Brabham BT50-BMW 4 turbo, 13 laps, engine; Alain Prost, Renault RE30B-V6 turbo, 14 laps, fuel injection; Eliseo Salazar, ATS D5-Ford V8, 17 laps, accident with Piquet; Nelson Piquet, Brabham BT50-BMW 4 turbo, 17 laps, accident with Salazar; Elio de Angelis, JPS-Lotus 91-Ford V8, 21 laps, handling problems; Raul Boesel, March 821-Ford V8, 22 laps, accident; Derek Daly, Williams FW08-Ford V8, 25 laps, broken valve spring; Jacques Laffite, Talbot-Ligier JS19-Matra V12, 36 laps, broken skirt; John Watson, McLaren MP4B-Ford V8, 36 laps, suspension breakage, accident.

CHAMPIONSHIP LEADERS

1	Didier Pironi	39
2	John Watson	30
3	Keke Rosberg	27
4	Alain Prost	25
5	Niki Lauda	24
6 =	René Arnoux	19
6 =	Riccardo Patrese	19
8	Nelson Piquet	17
9	Patrick Tambay	16
10	Michele Alboreto	14

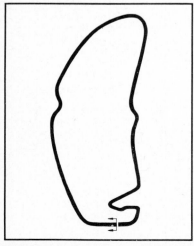

THE GRID

Pironi* 1m 47.947s	Prost 1m 48.890s
Arnoux 1m 49.256s	Piquet 1m 49.415s
Tambay 1m 49.570s	Patrese 1m 49.760s
Alboreto 1m 52.625s	de Cesaris 1m 52.786s
Rosberg 1m 52.892s	Watson 1m 53.073s
Giacomelli 1m 53.887s	Cheever 1m 54.211s
de Angelis 1m 54.476s	Warwick 1m 54.594s
Laffite 1m 54.982s	Winkelhock 1m 55.223s
Henton 1m 55.474s	Mansell 1m 55.866s
Daly 1m 55.876s	Jarier 1m 56.250s
Guerrero 1m 56.489s	Salazar 1m 56.537s
Baldi 1m 56.680s	Boesel 1m 57.245s
Serra 1m 57.337s	Surer 1m 57.402s

*Didier Pironi was unable to start and his space on the grid was left unoccupied.

Did not qualify: Tommy Byrne (Theodore TY-Ford V8) 1m 59.007s; Rupert Keegan (March 821-Ford V8) 1m 59.951s; Teo Fabi (Toleman TG181-Hart 4 turbo) no time.

Niki Lauda (McLaren MP4B-Ford V8) recorded 1m 52.683s but withdrew from the race due to a wrist injury.

Having been forced to pick themselves up from the crushing blow of Villeneuve's fatal accident, the Ferrari team were again plunged into the depths of despair by Didier Pironi's dreadful accident at Hockenheim. Once again Patrick Tambay did everything that could have been expected of him, and more, and his well judged win in Germany (below), coupled with encouraging news of Pironi's condition, did wonders for the team's morale.

COLIN Chapman was literally bowled over. It had been a fantastic weekend. The announcement that Lotus would be using Renault engines in 1983 had taken the press by surprise, and had sent journalists scurrying from team to team to find out what engines *they* would be using in 1983. Then Elio had started his black JPS Lotus 91 from seventh spot on the grid, and had held station right behind the five turbos in front as one by one they had dropped out. He had kept his cool when Rosberg had reeled him in, and had won the closest Grand Prix for a decade. The Chapman cap had been unearthed by Hazel and had been sent flying for the first time since the Dutch Grand Prix almost four years earlier, in its traditional greeting for a Lotus winner. Now, as Elio turned into the *parc ferme,* an excited Chapman was running alongside. As the Lotus slowed, Chapman bent down. And suddenly the 91 leapt forwards, throwing the Lotus boss into the air. Yes, Colin was literally bowled over.

In the motorhome later, Elio was concerned for his team patron's health, but fortunately Chapman was unhurt. Anyway, the excitement, the champagne dispensed by motorhome hosts Mike and Ann Murphy and the throng outside were enough to cure anything. Peter Warr was vainly trying to get through to Elio's father in Sardinia and, outside, a friend of Elio's was busily signing facsimile autographs for fans who really didn't seem to care if it was the real thing or not. In the middle of it all, Williams sponsor co-ordinator Charlie Crichton-Stuart came into congratulate the rival team: "We don't mind losing a close race like that" he said. "Well done".

The race had reached a thrilling climax. The latest Williams tweak had been to start with relatively low pressure in the tyres, so that for most of the second half of the event, the car would be at its best after the tyres had heated up and the pressure was just right. At the same time, the all-important ride height would also be correct. So Keke had plummeted from sixth on the grid to ninth in the early stages. Within nine laps, he was back up to sixth, and began to shadow Elio's rise through the field, albeit some seconds behind the Lotus driver.

In the second half of the race, The William's rising tyre pressure allowed Keke to press on. On lap 33 of the 53-lap race, he moved up to third and began to chip away at the gap between himself and de Angelis, now in second place. When leader Prost pulled off the track on the 49th lap, Keke was still around ten seconds behind the flying de Angelis, but the Williams was just as fleet, and as each lap was reeled off, the gap came down and down. The two cars were just yards apart as they went into that final lap. Those in the pits could only listen to the oohs and aahs from the spectators in the grandstand opposite. They couldn't see the battle being fought on the hillside behind them as the black JPS Lotus and the green and white Williams wound down the hill for the last time. But as Keke essayed and slid his Williams beside the Lotus, the Italian driver retaliated, and the crowd reacted accordingly. As the two cars swung around the final bend, the Williams darted out from behind the Lotus. Whatever

By this margin (above), Elio de Angelis scored his first Grand Prix win and Keke Rosberg didn't, leaving de Angelis to celebrate (below right) and Rosberg to wait for just one more race. Fourth place was slim reward for Tambay's magnificent recovery after a puncture and pit stop (below left) probably caused by picking up debris from the Alfa-initiated startline chaos (bottom). Unlike Tambay's, Brabham's pit stops were expected and carefully rehearsed (above right), though to no avail.

tactics he had used around the circuit on that last lap — and Keke never blamed him for them — Elio kept his car arrow straight on the run to the line. The Williams inched alongside but as they flashed across the start/finish line, Elio's hand punched the air. He had won, the crowd cheered, Jackie Stewart congratulated Frank Williams and in the excitement, the Longines men forgot to check the final winning margin!

There was something pleasantly old fashioned about this dash to the line. For a start, it was Cosworth's 150th Grand Prix victory. Lotus had won the first race with the V8 back in 1967 and here they were winning the 150th. In that final run, there hadn't been anything complicated like turning up turbo boost and that sort of thing. It was good, raw, normally aspirated V8 versus normally aspirated V8.

In fact the whole weekend was slightly paradoxical, for after all the fuss of the turbos throughout practice and the early part of the race, it was, after all, the normally aspirated engines that provided the excitement. It was hard to imagine that a brace of turbos could ever provide similar excitement.

But Österreichring, after all, was supposed to favour turbos. The height of the surrounding Styrian mountains provided rarified air — a disadvantage to non-turbos — which got increasingly stuffy throughout each hot day until a nightly thunderstorm cleared it again. The exceptionally fast nature of the circuit also favoured the turbo men. Add to that all the chat about turbos stirred up by the Lotus/Renault agreement and you had a thoroughly turbo orientated weekend. The announcement that Toleman's new turbocar would run later in the week, after the race, increased the turbo talk.

And the cars and drivers further emphasised the situation. A week earlier, Patrick Tambay had won his first Grand Prix. Now Ferrari's, Renault's and Brabham's drivers had all won a Grand Prix. In practice, none of them disappointed. After some modifications to the wastegate of their BMW turbo, which appeared to eliminate the all-too-common engine fires, the Brabhams were on top form with fastest and second fastest times, Piquet in front of Patrese. Prost was next quickest in front of Hocken-

heim victor Patrick Tambay in the lone Ferrari, while Arnoux was the main one to suffer from problems with Renault's fuel injection. The second Renault was fifth quickest. The Toleman team, looking forward to later in the week, were also competitive with 15th and 17th fastest times.

The hills around the circuit were packed on race day with multi-national spectators expecting a three-cornered battle between Italian, German and French turbos. But it was to be a battle of attrition. Once again, tapes were laid on the pit road in order to guide the Brabhams to their resting places — would they get as far as making their pit stops this time? The Brabhams on their half tanks just ran away with the opening laps. Within two laps they were followed by the Renault pair for poor Tambay had a puncture on his Ferrari and had to stagger round half a lap on three tyres and shredded rubber. The pit stop for a new tyre dropped him to 21st and last, so it was remarkable that he ultimately finished fourth out of the seven finishers.

The Brabham men swopped places, with Patrese taking over the lead and soon to drop Piquet who suffered a blistered tyre. But before he could stop to change it, Arnoux pitted from fourth place and retired shortly after with more injection trouble. One turbo delayed, one out. Two laps later, rather earlier than planned, Piquet ducked into the pits. The tyres were changed, fuel sloshed in and he was on his way in 18 seconds, although it actually cost him 31s on the road. And that was good enough to drop him to fourth place, behind Patrese, Prost and de Angelis.

When Piquet rejoined, one could see that his engine had lost its edge. Rosberg was just behind the Brabham turbo, and going just as quickly. Fractionally before half distance, Patrese brought the second Brabham into the pits. His stop was three seconds quicker — and he remained in the lead, three seconds ahead of Prost. Now it was a run to the flag. Not so. Four laps later, Patrese was guiding his Brabham into the second part of the wrongly-named Texaco 'chicane' when the car suddenly snapped sideways, slid across the grass and up a bank. Fortunately, it went no further, although it did give a lady in a deck-chair,

who claimed to have all the right passes, a nasty surprise. The spectators behind the bank (and behind a fairly flimsy fence) found themselves staring at the back end of the leading Brabham, and no doubt they saw that it was covered with oil. For although it looked at first as though the Italian had made a mistake, it had been his engine blowing that had locked the rear wheels and sent him off the track. Just three laps later, Piquet's electrics caused his engine to cut. Three down, two left.

Apart from Tambay, who was just about to hand over the honour of last place to Serra, there was only one turbo left in the race: Alain Prost's. He had an enormous lead over the rest of the field, and there were only five laps left when suddenly the yellow and black French car slowed with flames licking from the exhausts. It couldn't be true, thought Alain Prost, as the car cruised to a halt with broken fuel injection. From the race's point of view, it really didn't matter, for it promoted the de Angelis/Rosberg battle to that for the lead. The turbo rout was complete.

As if to emphasise that rout, Jacques Laffite brought his JS19 into third place for its first ever finish, although its handling had been dreadful. Niki Lauda lost fourth place to Tambay at about the same time that Prost retired, while Mauro Baldi picked up sixth place and his second ever championship point. Team mate Marc Surer had risked losing his head by persevering with an atrocious misfire in a hurriedly prepared spare Arrows, but ultimately he gave up — so it must have been very bad. Serra was the seventh finisher.

As well as the turbo mob, there were a lot of other unhappy faces that day. De Cesaris and Giacomelli were as red as the Marlboro livery of their Alfa Romeos after colliding on the grid when trying to avoid (but hitting) Daly's stalled Williams. Keegan was also involved, while the retirements rose to five when Alboreto crashed on the second lap. Guerrero spun and stalled on the seventh lap and, nine laps later, Winkelhock did the same.

Never had there been so many English and Irish-men in one race, but none of them had happy stories to tell. Apart from Daly and Keegan, Warwick was soon out with broken suspension on lap eight, when sixth, and Grand Prix debutant Tommy Byrne followed him across the grass after being caught out by a detached side pod on the 29th lap. John Watson was never really in the hunt and retired with a broken engine. Both Mansell and Henton got into the top six only to pull out with engine trouble. The Tyrrell driver had done particularly well, but the Lotus man dashed for home as quickly as possible. While Elio was almost deadheating with Rosberg, Nigel almost deadheated with the arrival of his first child, born to wife Rosanne in England.

In championship terms, the picture was beginning to change. With poor Pironi in hospital, Rosberg was now only six points behind, having overtaken the consistently unlucky Watson. Lauda, meanwhile, had overtaken Prost, and de Angelis had moved into sixth place ahead of turbo trio Patrese, Arnoux and Tambay; Ferrari's 'stand-in' had scored in each of the last four races.

By all rights, the Austrian Grand Prix should
have seen a turbo-power tour de force, with
its long, fast sweeps and situated as it is
high in the Styrian Hills. Again, however, the
turbo charge failed, leaving Keke Rosberg
(above) and Elio de Angelis to fight out the
most spectacular finish of the year. For
either driver it would have been a maiden win
but it was de Angelis who hung on to return
Lotus to the winner's circle by the narrowest
of margins, notching up the remarkable Cosworth engine's 150th Grand Prix win in the
process.

AUSTRIAN GRAND PRIX
Österreichring: 15 August 1982
53 laps of 3.69-mile circuit = 195.69 miles

RESULTS

1	Elio de Angelis	JPS Lotus 91-Ford V8	1hr 25m 02.21s
2	Keke Rosberg	Williams FW08-Ford V8	1hr 25m 02.23s
3	Jacques Laffite	Talbot-Ligier JS19-Matra V12	52 laps
4	Patrick Tambay	Ferrari 126C2-V6 turbo	52 laps
5	Niki Lauda	McLaren MP4B-Ford V8	52 laps
6	Mauro Baldi	Arrows A4-Ford V8	52 laps
7	Chico Serra	Fittipaldi F9-Ford V8	51 laps
8	Alain Prost	Renault RE30B-V6 turbo*	48 laps

*Prost was classified 8th although not running at finish.
Fastest lap: Piquet, 1m 33.699s (141.87mph)
Winner's average speed: 138.07mph

RETIREMENTS

Andrea de Cesaris, Alfa Romeo
182-V12, 0 laps, accident with Giacomelli; Bruno Giacomelli, Alfa Romeo
182-V12, 0 laps, accident with de Cesaris; Derek Daly, Williams FW08-Ford
V8, 0 laps, also involved in startline
accident; Rupert Keegan, March
821-Ford V8, 1 lap, steering damage
after startline accident; Michele
Alboreto, Tyrrell 011-Ford V8, 1 lap,
accident; Roberto Guerrero, Ensign
N181-Ford V8, 6 laps, driveshaft; Teo
Fabi, Toleman TG181-Hart 4 turbo, 7
laps, transmission; Derek Warwick,
Toleman TG181-Hart 4 turbo, 7 laps,
rear suspension breakage; Manfred
Winkelhock, ATS D5-Ford V8, 15 laps,
spun off; René Arnoux, Renault
RE30B-V6 turbo, 16 laps, turbocharger; Nigel Mansell, JPS-Lotus 91-Ford
V8, 17 laps, engine; Eddie Cheever,
Talbot-Ligier JS 19-Matra V12, 22
laps, engine; Riccardo Patrese, Brabham BT50-BMW 4 turbo, 27 laps, acci-
dent; Marc Surer, Arrows A4-Ford V8,
28 laps, electrical problem; Tommy
Byrne, Theodore TY-Ford V8, 28 laps,
spun off; Nelson Piquet, Brabham
BT50-BMW 4 turbo, 31 laps, engine;
Brian Henton, Tyrrell 011-Ford V8, 32
laps, engine; John Watson, McLaren
MP4B-Ford V8, 44 laps, engine; Alain
Prost, Renault RE30B-V6 turbo, 48
laps, fuel injection.

CHAMPIONSHIP LEADERS

1	Didier Pironi	39
2	Keke Rosberg	33
3	John Watson	30
4	Niki Lauda	26
5	Alain Prost	25
6	Elio de Angelis	22
7 =	René Arnoux	19
7 =	Riccardo Patrese	19
7 =	Patrick Tambay	19
10	Nelson Piquet	17

THE GRID

Piquet 1m 27.612s	Patrese 1m 27.971s
Prost 1m 28.864s	Tambay 1m 29.522s
Arnoux 1m 30.261s	Rosberg 1m 30.300s
de Angelis 1m 31.626s	Alboreto 1m 31.814s
Daly 1m 32.062s	Lauda 1m 32.131s
de Cesaris 1m 32.308s	Mansell 1m 32.881s
Giacomelli 1m 32.950s	Laffite 1m 32.957s
Warwick 1m 33.208s	Guerrero 1m 33.555s
Fabi 1m 33.971s	Watson 1m 34.164s
Henton 1m 34.184s	Serra 1m 34.187s
Surer 1m 34.422s	Cheever 1m 34.620s
Baldi 1m 34.715s	Keegan 1m 34.770s
Winkelhock 1m 34.984s	Byrne 1m 34.985s

Did not qualify: Raul Boesel (March 821-Ford V8)
1m 35.149s; Jean-Pierre Jarier (Osella FA1C-Ford
V8) 1m 35.206s; Eliseo Salazar (ATS D5-Ford V8)
1m 35.271s.

CROWNING GLORY

THE party was still going on at eleven o'clock that night. There, in the middle of Dijon, on a largish traffic island, were about 30 Finns, steadily becoming more and more intoxicated. But what the hell! It isn't every day that a Finn wins a Grand Prix! And that day, a Finn had won the Swiss Grand Prix, and another Finn had won the Finnish Grand Prix. If that sounds cockeyed, that's because Hannu Mikkola had just won the 1000 Lakes rally, often known as the Finnish GP. But that wasn't necessarily the cause for celebration in Dijon. After all, one of those rallying Finns wins the 1000 Lakes every year. But a Finn winning a pukka GP was something else. Leo Kinnunen had never really made it as a GP driver, and nor had Mikko Kozarowitzky. Come to that, Keke's career had looked a bit sticky until Frank Williams had given him a drive. But now he led the World Championship by three points, and was eleven ahead of Alain Prost. Could he become the first Finnish World Champion?

While the Finns were celebrating, the French were worrying. What on earth was wrong with Renault? The two cars had started from the front row of the grid, despite a nasty shunt by Arnoux in practice. Once Nelson Piquet had pulled out of second place to make his routine pit stop, the two yellow and white cars had appeared to control the race. With just a few laps remaining, one of the Regie's PR men was busily unloading crates of champagne from a refrigerated van in the paddock. It was looking that good. All but one of the last four Formula One races to be held in France had been won by Renault; why not this one? Rosberg's Williams was threatening, but surely he couldn't overtake both Renaults?

In fact there was every reason to be wary. With just 15 laps remaining of this 80-lap race, Arnoux was closing on his team mate, and Rosberg was closing on both. And there was little that Prost could do about either of them. One of his Renault's skirts was badly worn, making the car's handling very difficult. Behind him Arnoux was closing inexorably. After the Le Castellet race a month earlier, there was little doubt that if Arnoux could win, he would — and to hell with Prost's championship chances.

But with ten laps remaining, that worry at least was dispelled. The second Renault began to misfire badly, and Arnoux lost three places in three laps. Finally he headed for the pits where more fuel was sloshed into the tank. René accelerated out of the pits and then suddenly the engine died. He cruised round the first corner, and parked the car on the outside of the track. For the second time in two races, the fuel injection pump had packed up. It would become three times within a couple of weeks, but already there was frustration within the team: "It's amazing. How much longer can this go on? Why can't they do something about it? It's totally the team's fault. It's not bad luck. It's just plain bad," screamed a member of the Renault team, far too closely involved to want to be named.

Rosberg, who had been about to pounce on René's Renault before it went sick, was elevated to second place, and now his sights were reset on leader Prost. Keke began to catch him at an impressive rate. There was a very strong

likelihood that a Renault would not win this race after all. The man with the chequered flag was so worried that his Francophile conscience began to affect him badly, and he made moves to end the race. Fortunately, the Williams team was one of the closest to the start/finish line, and Williams team manager Peter Collins restrained him.

With two laps to go, the Williams was right behind the Renault. And at that juncture, René Arnoux decided that there was nothing more he could do to his stricken Renault. He ran across the track, right in front of his team mate. Prost eased his foot from the accelerator, as the overalled figure ran across in front of him. His attention had been distracted for a moment, and at the next downhill lefthander, he ran slightly wide. The Williams was through in a flash. After another lap and a half, Keke should have received his first Grand Prix chequ-

ered flag. But by now the flagman had the jitters and was unwilling to do his bit. Swiss clocks, if not Swiss officials, gave the results after 80 laps. Keke won, Alain was second.

It was a thrilling end to a fine battle, but one which encompassed so much more than just those last few laps. The Brabhams were in there for a while, the leaders had to run through a great queue of cars which was bottled up behind Patrese for much of the race, and John Watson drove a superb race for no reward.

For the Brabham team, the Swiss GP provided possible proof that the pit stop idea wasn't the ideal solution. Piquet started from sixth on the grid on half tanks while Patrese started from third with full tanks. The higher man on the grid might have been better off with half tanks, in retrospect. On lap four, their paths crossed as Piquet relieved his team mate of third place and went on to

86

Keke Rosberg's first Grand Prix win was the result of a typically committed charge (above left) as the Renaults faltered yet again. Keegan and Alboreto were both caught out by spins, Alboreto (left) getting going again to finish seventh, but March's stand-in couldn't restart. 'Like a brood of chicks following the mother hen' (below left) — the frustrated queue behind Patrese's Brabham. 'Why doesn't Keke like me?': de Cesaris (above left) was another guilty of getting in the way, but not even Andrea would deny Rosberg (above right) his day today. Derek Warwick and Marc Surer (below) looked good in the early stages, but not for long.

demote Arnoux to that position on lap 11. Nelson remained second until the obligatory stop for tyres and fuel on lap 40, exactly half distance. The actual stop took less than 15 seconds, but it cost the driver twice that much. He hadn't really pulled out enough during the first half of the race, and he rejoined in only fifth place. And then he promptly suffered tyre vibration and was unable to improve on his position. After Arnoux's retirement, he finished fourth.

He rejoined just in front of team mate Patrese. From his third place, he had dropped to seventh in the first 17 laps. First Piquet, then Rosberg, followed by McLaren men Lauda and Watson, had overtaken, but after that, his position stabilised.

Those who had overtaken him had been part of a mammoth queue which had built up behind the unwieldy Brabham. They were the escapees in fact, be-cause Daly, Laffite, de Cesaris and Alboreto were still left behind. Later, they were joined by Cheever, de Angelis and Mansell, all of whom had an excellent view of the Brabham's rear end, but could do no more than battle with one another like a brood of chicks following the mother hen.

It is one of the strange things about modern motor racing that drivers can get into such a situation. Of those that had overtaken the Brabham, some did a full lap and came up to overtake it again. Amongst them was Rosberg, although not without his problems. Gaining hand over fist on Arnoux, Keke came up behind de Cesaris's queue-bound red and white Alfa and there he remained for lap after lap as Arnoux began to pull away again. In all, Keke lost ten seconds there, and he had some harsh words for Andrea afterwards. It wasn't the first time that the two had come together, but

long after the season had ended Andrea was still bleating 'Why doesn't Keke like me?' Ultimately, Keke got by the seventh placed Alfa, only for Andrea to slide wide and down to tenth.

Lauda got by the Brabham nice and early on, and at one time looked as though he might be a potential challenger to Rosberg, but then he dropped back to finish a safe third. Just before the 20 lap mark, his team mate John Watson had looked much stronger. Wattie had started 11th, dropped to 13th, and then picked off Marc Surer and Michele Alboreto on lap 4, and then Giacomelli, Laffite, de Cesaris and Daly in successive laps. On lap 17, he overtook Patrese and moved up to sixth, but the manoeuvre cost him dearly. A skirt flopped out and John had to pit, losing three laps. But he was on form that day, and even though he would be lucky to pick up a point, he raced hard, and overtook many of those that he'd overtaken before the stop for a second time. He finished only 13th, poor reward for the drive, and, in failing to score for the sixth time in as many races, was joined on 30 points in the championship by Lauda.

Only one of the men behind Patrese would actually get a point, and the lucky one was de Angelis, winner of the previous round at Österreichring. Neither JPS Lotus had been on form in practice, particularly Mansell, who had started last on the grid. Elio, at least, had been 15th, and moved into the top ten just before half distance. He gained a place when Alboreto lost three with a spin while trying to overtake Patrese, and then overtook a tyre-troubled Daly. When de Cesaris dropped back, Elio picked up seventh, fought off a challenge from Alboreto and then inherited sixth when Arnoux retired.

Others weren't so fortunate. Alboreto was seventh, not far behind, and Mansell had come through superbly for eighth, despite a misfire. Daly was immensely frustrated in ninth, having scarcely raced at all, while de Cesaris finished tenth. Giacomelli had pitted for tyres and finished twelfth, behind Henton, while Surer had started well in his home Grand Prix in the latest Arrows (a Williams FW08 lookalike) but had had to pit for new tyres and a new skirt and finished 15th. No one else had really starred, although both Keegan and Warwick had had good fortune in the early stages, but both had dropped out before 30 laps had elapsed.

And if Ferrari hadn't had a miserable season already, a new problem had arisen. Patrick Tambay had suffered a pinched nerve after the Österreichring event and had suffered from an insensitive right arm throughout the Dijon weekend. He had only done a minimal number of laps, but on Sunday morning he had decided not to race so, for the second time in a year, there had been no Ferrari on the grid.

The joy, then, was restricted to the Williams camp and the Finns. Keke had become the third first time winner in as many races. The night of the race, while the Finns were celebrating in Dijon, Keke was in Geneva, and the Williams test truck passed through there the next day on its way to Monza. Keke, his fans and his team wanted to win that World Championship, and preparations to do well at Monza began in earnest almost as soon as the Dijon race was won.

SWISS GRAND PRIX
Dijon-Prenois (France) 29 August 1982
80 laps of 2.36-mile circuit = 188.88 miles

RESULTS

1	Keke Rosberg	Williams FW08-Ford V8	1hr 32m 41.09s
2	Alain Prost	Renault RE30B-V6 turbo	1hr 32m 45.53s
3	Niki Lauda	McLaren MP4B-Ford V8	1hr 33m 41.43s
4	Nelson Piquet	Brabham BT50-BMW 4 turbo	79 laps
5	Riccardo Patrese	Brabham BT50-BMW 4 turbo	79 laps
6	Elio de Angelis	JPS Lotus 91-Ford V8	79 laps
7	Michele Alboreto	Tyrrell 011-Ford V8	79 laps
8	Nigel Mansell	JPS-Lotus 91-Ford V8	79 laps
9	Derek Daly	Williams FW08-Ford V8	79 laps
10	Andrea de Cesaris	Alfa Romeo 182-V12	78 laps
11	Brian Henton	Tyrrell 011-Ford V8	78 laps
12	Bruno Giacomelli	Alfa Romeo 182-V12	78 laps
13	John Watson	McLaren MP4B-Ford V8	77 laps
14	Eliseo Salazar	ATS D5-Ford V8	77 laps
15	Marc Surer	Arrows A4-Ford V8	76 laps
16	René Arnoux	Renault RE30B-V6 turbo	75 laps*

Eddie Cheever (Talbot-Ligier JS19-Matra V12) was running at the finish but was unclassified; *René Arnoux was not running at the finish.

Fastest lap: Prost, 1m 07.477s (125.97mph) — record
Winner's average speed: 122.28mph

RETIREMENTS
Roberto Guerrero, Ensign N181-Ford V8, 4 laps, engine; Derek Warwick, Toleman TG181-Hart 4 turbo, 24 laps, engine; Rupert Keegan, March 821-Ford V8, 25 laps, spun off; Raul Boesel, March 821-Ford V8, 31 laps, gearbox oil leak; Teo Fabi, Toleman TG181-Hart 4 turbo, 31 laps, engine; Jacques Laffite, Talbot-Ligier JS19-Matra V12, 33 laps, skirts; Jean-Pierre Jarier, Osella FA1C-Ford V8, 44 laps, engine; Manfred Winkelhock, ATS D5-Ford V8, 55 laps, broken engine mounting.

CHAMPIONSHIP LEADERS

1	Keke Rosberg	42
2	Didier Pironi	39
3	Alain Prost	31
4 =	Niki Lauda	30
4 =	John Watson	30
6	Elio de Angelis	23
7	Riccardo Patrese	21
8	Nelson Piquet	20
9 =	René Arnoux	19
9 =	Patrick Tambay	19

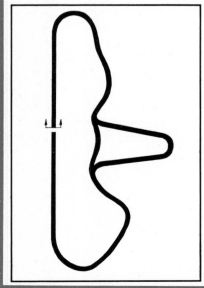

THE GRID

	Prost 1m 01.380s
Arnoux 1m 01.740s	Patrese 1m 02.710s
Lauda 1m 02.984s	de Cesaris 1m 03.023s
Piquet 1m 03.183s	Daly 1m 03.291s
Rosberg 1m 03.776s	Giacomelli 1m 03.776s
Tambay* 1m 03.896s	Watson 1m 03.995s
Alboreto 1m 04.069s	Laffite 1m 04.087s
Surer 1m 04.928s	de Angelis 1m 04.967s
Cheever 1m 05.001s	Jarier 1m 05.179s
Henton 1m 05.391s	Guerrero 1m 05.395s
Winkelhock 1m 05.451s	Warwick 1m 05.877s
Keegan 1m 06.011s	Fabi 1m 06.017s
Boesel 1m 06.136s	Salazar 1m 06.168s
Mansell 1m 06.211s	

*Patrick Tambay (Ferrari 126C2-V6 turbo) did not start due to injury.

Did not qualify: Chico Serra (Fittipaldi F8D- and F9-Ford) 1m 06.339s; Tommy Byrne (Theodore TY-Ford V8) 1m 06.990s; Mauro Baldi (Arrows A4-Ford V8) 1m 07.836s.

Winners and losers: Keke Rosberg (above left and below) at last scored his first Grand Prix win, while René Arnoux (below left) was again thwarted by engine problems having held second place in the early laps.

THE zip of the Renault motorhome canopy shot skywards. Through the resulting hole came a hand clutching a camera. The hand wandered vaguely, the camera clicked, and then disappeared, almost as quickly as it had appeared. Hopefully, somewhere on that film, one fanatic Italian fan had a picture of Ferrari's new driver, the one who had just won the 1982 Italian Grand Prix, and who would drive for his beloved Scuderia the following year. The little fellow who had stood on the top step of the rostrum that very afternoon, between Patrick Tambay and Mario Andretti: René Arnoux.

That afternoon, Ferrari drivers past, present and future had delighted probably the biggest, noisiest, smelliest and most enthusiastic yet dishonest crowd ever to invade a Grand Prix circuit. They had totally ignored the potential World Championship battle taking place, being far more interested in the red Ferrari's fortunes than those of the Ulsterman, the Finn and the Frenchman who were fighting for the honour of World Champion in the final throes of the 1982 World Championship.

Perhaps, on reflection, they were right. The World Championship battle that afternoon wasn't of the greatest excitement. But then neither was the battle at the front. The main interest was that there were two Ferraris (for the first time since the French Grand Prix) and both of them were in the top three. Admittedly the two Ferraris were being led by René Arnoux's Renault — but then that very week, he'd signed to drive for Ferrari. Any Italian fan's day was complete, with Ferrari drivers past, present and future filling the top three places.

The excitement had begun a few days previously when Mario Andretti had stepped off a trans-Atlantic flight at Malpensa. Press, TV cameras and thousands of fans had been there to welcome him 'home'. The doors of the Boeing opened, and out stepped Mario, arms wide in an embrace. He would have been a perfect under-study to the Pope. And the crowd loved it. Before the Italian GP weekend began, Mario had a few days of acclimatisation with the team for whom he had last driven an F1 car ten years previously.

Then came official practice. The fans turned up in their thousands, climbing over fences, wheedling their way into the hallowed (but overcrowded) paddock and waving to their friends on the pit balcony as they succeeded in the ultimate deception by sneaking into the pits. There, along with far too many others, they could live out every minute of the Ferrari team's weekend.

And what a weekend it was! Patrick Tambay, virtually recovered from his Austrian maladies, was nearly half a second faster than anyone else on the Friday. But the next day, it was Mario's turn. Sure, Tambay was the first to improve, but then the 42-year-old veteran pulled out all the stops to put himself on pole position. His time was greeted with cheers from the crowd that must have echoed across the Monza park. Only Nelson Piquet's Brabham-BMW prevented an all-Ferrari front row. The excitement was intense, but it was wholly Ferrari orientated. The brief appearance of Alfa Romeo's two-year-old turbo engine in the back of one of the 1982 cars went almost unnoticed — perhaps justifiably so.

The fever of practice was caught by thousands of locals who poured in from Milan and the industrial towns roundabout for the race, armed with scaffolding to build their own grandstands. One wonders how many half-finished buildings in Milan fell down that day because their supports were otherwise occupied at Monza. It would be hard even to estimate the size of the crowd, and certainly, if only for tax reasons, the official figures are predictably vague.

The race itself was pretty well sorted out by the seventh lap. Andretti had a sticking throttle right from the start, so Piquet led into the first tight chicane in his spare car after an electrical problem troubled his race machine. But within seconds, he also realised that he had clutch problems and was only fifth at the end of the first lap. Tambay took over the lead for part of that first lap, and then Arnoux came screaming up from sixth on the grid to overtake the Ferrari on the start/finish straight. And, from there on, the little Frenchman was untroubled by other cars. He had his own problems to contend with which might have made life difficult if the others hadn't had theirs. From the tenth lap onwards, René was in handling trouble, and a fuel leak allowed petrol to burn his bottom from the 20th lap.

Piquet was plummetting down the

'Son of Belgrano', the new, carbon fibre monocoque Toleman TG183 made its first race appearance (above), showing great promise during practice but then being eliminated in a first lap accident. Jean-Pierre Jarier too had a miserable weekend to cap a miserable season, culminating in a wheel falling off his fragile Osella (below). The Ferraris have no such problems, even when driven Andretti-style (right). Andretti's performance, pole position and third place with a less than perfect car, put an awful lot of other people's efforts into none too flattering perspective . . .

order and soon to retire, but Patrese at least held second place early on for four laps before he began to suffer the same fate. By lap eight, both Brabham-BMWs were out. So Tambay reappeared in second place on lap six, and was never to lose that position. However, he was unable to do anything about Arnoux's ill-handling Renault as he was suffering exactly the same problem: bad handling caused by a worn left hand skirt.

Arnoux first, Tambay second: it was decided pretty early on. Third took a little longer to settle. After the changing fortunes of the first six laps, Alain Prost moved into third place ahead of Mario Andretti. As Arnoux had shot into the lead from sixth on the grid, so Prost had dropped to tenth on that first lap having been badly held up behind Andretti. But his recovery was rapid. After all, he was still very much a World Championship contender. He'd recovered five places by the fourth lap, and another two by the seventh. He had overtaken one Ferrari, much to the crowd's disappointment, and he soon showed that he had every intention of doing the same thing to the other. He was closing inexorably on the red car when suddenly the Renault's en-

gine died. Then it picked up, only to die again. In this way, Prost regained the pits on the 27th lap. The mechanics swiftly attempted to put things right, and sent Prost on his way again. The Renault accelerated cleanly out of the pits — and almost immediately died. This time there was no restarting. His fuel injection had gone on the blink yet again, and this time it had cost him any chance of the World Championship.

Prost's retirement reinstated Andretti to the top three. The American was still suffering from a sticking throttle, but it began to improve towards the end. But by that stage, there was nothing further to be done. Third place, however, was a fine reward, and certainly restored his credibility which perhaps suffered at Long Beach earlier in the year.

The rest were largely in another race. And in amongst this other race were two men racing for the World Championship, and very attentive to the fortunes of Prost. Generally speaking, the leader of the 'rest' was racing in a position in the top six. Although the crowd's adulation was strictly reserved for Ferrari, the local team, Alfa Romeo, did well during the opening stages. The two drivers

qualified eighth and ninth, although they might have done better but for the diversion of their flag-waving turbo presentation. By lap 10, de Cesaris was in sixth and Giacomelli seventh, but Andrea had to duck into the pits to have his ignition sorted out. That elevated Bruno briefly to fifth place, until John Watson came along. He'd disposed of team mate Lauda on the first lap and was clearly in a mood for racing. He needed those World Championship points badly. When he came up to take Rosberg for sixth, Keke put up little resistance. He was biding his time, and he badly wanted to finish this race. Wattie went on to overtake Giacomelli quite easily, but then realised that there was little more to be done, and he settled for a safe fifth place. At least he would finish, after a string of six retirements. The race became that much more valuable when he inherited fourth on Prost's retirement. Not only had one championship contender dropped out, but he had picked up more points.

Only a lap previously, Rosberg had begun his quest for points. Giacomelli was only just ahead of him, but the Alfa's engine was too powerful in a straight line. But passing the pits for the 24th time, Rosberg's Williams just had the edge on the Alfa. This time he'd made it. As Rosberg powered through, Giacomelli waved a finger. Rosberg waved his fist: the same to you too! Into the first chicane, the Williams felt unstable, further round, it felt worse. Rosberg slowed, it must be a puncture. But it wasn't. The rear wing had fallen off. That's why Bruno had been pointing. After days of trouble-free testing, this had to happen. Once the wing had been replaced, Rosberg set off with customary brio, but it was now too late. He finished out of the points. He wasn't World Champion yet, as he explained to press men after the race, crushed by the mob against the Williams motorhome door. But he was confident; there was a slight smile after each reply, and you have to be confident to step out of your retreat into an Italian mob!

The other placings were won thanks to regular driving. Lauda was never happy and retired with brake problems, Laffite's gearbox packed up early on, although Cheever rescued a point for Ligier on the very weekend that he signed for Renault, while Alboreto picked up two points in a steady drive. Mansell just missed a point after starting a lowly 23rd on the grid, while de Angelis made little impression.

And there were disappointments. Daly, Guerrero, Henton and Warwick were all eliminated on the first lap in a pair of connected incidents. Particularly unfortunate was the involvement of Warwick, who was driving the new Toleman TG183, of which so much had been expected and which certainly *looked* promising on its first competitive appearance, qualifying 16th.

And there were disappointments off the track too. Prost left the circuit already thinking about next year, and how a year previously, everyone had reckoned him the favourite for 1982. The favourite had failed. Watson had his sights set on a good race in Vegas — with a fine performance and a win, he would win the championship, although it was a tough task. And Rosberg was almost there ... but not quite.

Italy's answer to the Red Arrows, the Frecci Tricolori *eclipsed most of the weekend action with their absolutely stunning displays (top) while René Arnoux (above) irreverently beat his new team's current drivers into second and third places. The return of Andretti (right, with Forghieri) to Ferrari and to Monza brought the* tifosi *flooding in — with or without tickets . . .*

ITALIAN GRAND PRIX
Monza: 12 September 1982
52 laps of 3.60-mile circuit = 187.40 miles

RESULTS

1	René Arnoux	Renault RE30B-V6 turbo	1hr 22m 25.73s
2	Patrick Tambay	Ferrari 126C2-V6 turbo	1hr 22m 39.80s
3	Mario Andretti	Ferrari 126C2-V6 turbo	1hr 23m 14.19s
4	John Watson	McLaren MP4B-Ford V8	1hr 23m 53.58s
5	Michele Alboreto	Tyrrell 011-Ford V8	51 laps
6	Eddie Cheever	Talbot-Ligier JS19-Matra V12	51 laps
7	Nigel Mansell	JPS-Lotus 91-Ford V8	51 laps
8	Keke Rosberg	Williams FW08-Ford V8	50 laps
9	Eliseo Salazar	ATS D5-Ford V8	50 laps
10	Andrea de Cesaris	Alfa Romeo 182-V12	50 laps
11	Chico Serra	Fittipaldi F8D-Ford V8	49 laps
12	Mauro Baldi	Arrows A5-Ford V8	49 laps

Roberto Guerrero (Ensign N181-Ford V8) was running in thirteenth place at the finish but was unclassified.

Fastest lap: Arnoux, 1m 33.619s (138.58mph) — record
Winner's average speed: 136.39mph

RETIREMENTS
Brian Henton, Tyrrell 011-Ford V8, 0 laps, accident with Daly and Warwick; Derek Warwick, Toleman TG183-Hart 4 turbo, 0 laps, accident with Daly and Henton; Derek Daly, Williams FW08, 1 lap, accident damage; Teo Fabi, Toleman TG181-Hart 4 turbo, 2 laps, engine; Jacques Laffite, Talbot-Ligier JS19-Matra V12, 5 laps, gearbox; Riccardo Patrese, Brabham BT50-BMW 4 turbo, 6 laps, clutch; Nelson Piquet, Brabham BT50-BMW 4 turbo, 7 laps, clutch; Jean-Pierre Jarier, Osella FA1C-Ford V8, 10 laps, brakes — accident; Niki Lauda, McLaren MP4B V8, 21 laps, handling and brakes; Alain Prost, Renault RE30B-V6 turbo, 27 laps, fuel injection; Marc Surer, Arrows A4, 28 laps, engine; Bruno Giacomelli, Alfa Romeo 182-V12, 32 laps, handling; Elio de Angelis, JPS-Lotus 91-Ford V8, 33 laps, sticking throttle.

CHAMPIONSHIP LEADERS

1	Keke Rosberg	42
2	Didier Pironi	39
3	John Watson	33
4	Alain Prost	31
5	Niki Lauda	30
6	René Arnoux	28
7	Patrick Tambay	25
8	Elio de Angelis	23
9	Riccardo Patrese	21
10	Nelson Piquet	20

THE GRID

Andretti 1m 28.473s	Piquet 1m 28.508s
Tambay 1m 28.830s	Patrese 1m 29.898s
Prost 1m 30.026s	Arnoux 1m 30.037s
Rosberg 1m 31.834s	Giacomelli 1m 32.352s
de Cesaris 1m 32.546s	Lauda 1m 32.782s
Alboreto 1m 33.134s	Watson 1m 33.185s
Daly 1m 33.333s	Cheever 1m 33.377s
Jarier 1m 33.531s	Warwick 1m 33.628s
de Angelis 1m 33.629s	Laffite* 1m 34.029s
Guerrero 1m 34.058s	Surer 1m 34.343s
Henton 1m 34.379s	Fabi 1m 34.780s
Mansell 1m 34.964s	Baldi 1m 34.977s
Salazar 1m 34.991s	Serra 1m 35.230s

*Jacques Laffite recorded a time of 1m 34.029s in the final practice but the time was disallowed as his car was found to be underweight.

Did not qualify: Rupert Keegan (March 821-Ford V8) 1m 35.323s; Manfred Winkelhock (ATS D5-Ford V8) 1m 35.701s; Raul Boesel (March 821-Ford V8) 1m 35.747s; Tommy Byrne (Theodore TY-Ford V8) 1m 36.032s.

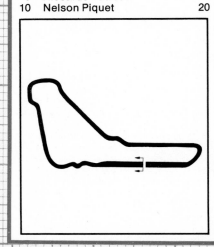

THERE were some good bets in Las Vegas, and there were some bad ones. Keke Rosberg was a bad one. The guy's far too smart to want to go and win this race. It's in his nature to give his all, at least it was at the start of the season but, since then, he'd calmed down, learned to be careful, and not take chances. Sure as anything, he wasn't going to go rip-roaring around this mess of concrete blocks chancing his arm. Look at it from his point of view: was he going to throw it all away for the sake of some Caesars Palace laurel leaves? No way. That was Wattie's job, not his. In this town, where chance is offered at every doorway, Keke wasn't taking any.

He was right, of course. John Watson had to win this one outright and Keke finish out of the points for him to lose the championship. Then FISA threw in a wild card to keep everyone guessing when they delayed the findings of their inquiry into Niki Lauda's disqualification from the Belgian race until after the Las Vegas event. Belgium? Yes, Belgium, back at the beginning of May when Niki lost four points for being two kilos under weight. If his appeal was upheld, then Lauda would gain four points, which would give him a remote chance of winning the title. As it was, they didn't uphold the appeal, but by that stage it was all over. Before the race, there was still some doubt.

In fact, psychologically, Watson was much more worried about Lauda at Las Vegas than he was about Rosberg. With Keke, everything was cut and dried. If Wattie couldn't win, he wasn't champion. If Keke dropped out, he had a chance, but there was always the possibility that Niki would be in there too, also determined to maximise his chance just in case the appeal should go in his favour.

As it turned out, Lauda was never particularly on form throughout the weekend. Watson qualified, ninth, four places ahead of his Marlboro McLaren team mate. He drove another storming race, overtaking no less than seven other drivers, except that two factors stood in the way of his World Championship. The first was that having qualified superbly in third place, Michele Alboreto was perfectly placed to take over from the Renaults when they failed. And he was just too far ahead of John to be caught. The second factor was that far from being fazed by the competition and the occasion, as Carlos Reutemann had been a year previously, Keke just hung in there quite coolly. He never overtook anyone who was on the same lap as himself, but was twice overtaken by other cars, once by Watson. The first to overtake him was Mario Andretti, again filling the second Ferrari seat. For the first 26 laps, they were running close together, and had just taken over fifth and sixth places when the Ferrari's rear suspension broke, sending Mario spinning off, and giving Keke what looked like a nasty moment. But the Williams driver denied it and, from there on in, he remained constantly in fifth place until the chequered flag came out. He was World Champion, yet it seemed strange to those who had followed his career for long that his most uninspired motor race — and Keke is known for inspiring drives — netted him the greatest accolade a driver could earn.

Eddie Cheever rounded off his variable fortunes with Ligier with a splendid third place in Vegas before packing his bags and heading for Renault. As Alboreto took the flag for Tyrrell's first win in too many years, Ken Tyrrell had plenty to smile about (above right). John Watson (right) drove brilliantly once again, but it was not enough, the championship had slipped from his grasp in mid season, to be snatched up by Keke Rosberg and the ever meticulous Williams team (far right).

There were others who were just as happy. Michele, of course, was delighted. He had driven the sort of race that had won the race for Jones the previous year and, just to underline it, he also scored fastest lap. It was the ninth win of the season by a normally aspirated engine, against seven by the turbo men.

In second place, John Watson would normally have been happy with his performance, again overtaking so many people. But Wattie was a little bemused on the rostrum. He knew how close he'd come to the World Championship, and it had slipped from his grasp. After the race, he jetted off to a Pacific island for some peace, but there he thought more and more about that lean spate of six races in the second half of the season. When he got back to England, the very thought of those lost opportunities aroused him.

If it was any consolation to him, Renault had more reason to be upset than anyone. This Las Vegas Grand Prix reflected most of their races this season. For the fourth time in 1982, Alain Prost started from pole position. For the 12th time in the season, it was an all-turbo front row, and half of those, as here in Las Vegas, had been all-Renault front rows.

Arnoux steamed past his team mate on the second lap when Alain missed a gear, but the yellow and black cars remained in the lead, until positions swapped again on lap 15 when René slowed with electrical trouble. René ended his four-year Renault career in the pits five laps later, leaving Prost to defend the Regie's honour on his own. But there were clearly problems by two thirds distance when Alboreto began to close on the Renault. Alain's Michelins were picking up rubber and sending the wheels out of balance. Under braking, the driver was being shaken like a Bloody Mary. He was easy prey for Alboreto. The Italian swept by on the 52nd lap, around two thirds distance. Prost struggled manfully with his problem, but there was nothing he could do about the determined Watson and future team mate Cheever as they came up on him. Rosberg might have been the next to try, but for once he wasn't interested, and Alain

was allowed to score for fourth place.

While the World Championship tussle obviously grabbed the headlines, there were some other factors about this Las Vegas Grand Prix which might have stood out had it been a mid-season round. In a way, the grid was quite topsy turvy. Alboreto third, Cheever fourth, Warwick tenth, Laffite eleventh: they might well have swopped places with Piquet 12th, Lauda 13th, Daly 14th, Giacomelli 16th and de Cesaris 18th. Three races previously, Elio de Angelis had been on the top step of the rostrum. With only 20th time in practice (and 21st by his team mate), it looked unlikely here. There seemed to be an end-of-term feeling about Las Vegas.

One part of the end-of-term feeling is a lack of money: end of budget. Some of the smaller teams were feeling decidedly poor as the season ran to a close. Having blown two engines at Dijon, Guerrero and his manager had had to bail out the Ensign team for Monza, but they managed to get to Las Vegas. Guerrero put in his best performance of the year with 15th on the grid, but then blew

another engine in the morning warm-up and was unable to start the race. For the sixth time in the season, a Grand Prix got under way with less than the authorised number of starters. That always seems such a waste when there are eager potential non-qualifiers fighting it out at the unfashionable end of the pits during qualifying, and who will be destined for the 'early bath' syndrome.

Guerrero had defeated the two Alfas in practice, and no doubt some of the spirit had gone out of their fight thanks to rumours that the whole operation was going to be closed. It wasn't, but there was a major shake-up six weeks later which left Giacomelli out in the cold. Baldi was chosen in preference, even though his off-track excursions at Las Vegas were only rivalled by Salazar's.

There was more Italian trouble at Osella where designer Herve Guilpin made sure that none of the blame for recent failures and Jarier's lucky escape in practice was attributed to him. The French driver had set a time good enough for 20th on the grid when the front suspension broke and sent the

Osella headlong into a concrete wall. It wasn't the first, second or even third breakage of the year, and Jarier was taking no further part in practice or in Osella's history. Few could blame him.

And then there was poor Patrick Tambay. He withdrew once again having set a time good enough for eighth on the grid, just a fraction slower than Andretti's, but his pinched nerve was again causing him trouble. Tambay was the ninth driver of the season to be unable to take part in a Grand Prix because of injury, fatal in two cases.

And so the season wound down in a muggy parking lot in the Nevada desert. The championship was won and lost — it just seemed so sad that there were so few people in Las Vegas who appreciated it! Spectator attendance was estimated at less than 30,000, the smallest crowd of the season, and there were rumours that even the Las Vegas hoteliers didn't want to play any longer. But the powers that be had already foreseen that eventuality: some unknown and untried part of New York City would be the scene of the 1983 championship finale.

CAESARS PALACE

Caesars Palace, Las Vegas: 25 September 1982

75 laps of 2.268-mile circuit = 170.1 miles

RESULTS

1	Michele Alboreto	Tyrrell 011-Ford V8	1hr 41m 56.88s
2	John Watson	McLaren MP4B-Ford V8	1hr 42m 24.18s
3	Eddie Cheever	Ligier JS19-Matra V12	1hr 42m 53.33s
4	Alain Prost	Renault RE30B-V6 turbo	1hr 43m 05.53s
5	Keke Rosberg	Williams FW08-Ford V8	1hr 43m 08.26s
6	Derek Daly	Williams FW08-Ford V8	74 laps
7	Marc Surer	Arrows A5-Ford V8	74 laps
8	Brian Henton	Tyrrell 011-Ford V8	74 laps
9	Andrea de Cesaris	Alfa Romeo 182-V12	73 laps
10	Bruno Giacomelli	Alfa Romeo 182-V12	73 laps
11	Mauro Baldi	Arrows A4-Ford V8	73 laps
12	Rupert Keegan	March 821-Ford V8	73 laps
13	Raul Boesel	March 821-Ford V8	69 laps
14	Manfred Winkelhock	ATS D5-Ford V8	62 laps

Fastest lap: Alboreto, lap 59, 1m 19.639s (102.522mph)
Winner's average speed: 100.1mph

RETIREMENTS

Jacques Laffite, Ligier JS19-Matra V12, 5 laps, electrics; Nigel Mansell, Lotus 91-Ford V8, 8 laps, accident; Riccardo Patrese, Brabham BT50-BMW turbo, 17 laps, clutch; René Arnoux, Renault RE30B-V6 turbo, 20 laps, engine; Nelson Piquet, Brabham BT50-BMW turbo, 26 laps, broken spark plug; Mario Andretti, Ferrari 126C2-V6 turbo, 26 laps, broken suspension and accident; Elio de Angelis, Lotus 91-Ford V8, 28 laps, engine; Derek Warwick, Toleman TG183-Hart turbo, 32 laps, broken spark plug; Tommy Byrne, Theodore TY02-Ford V8, 53 laps, spun; Niki Lauda, McLaren MP4B-Ford V8, engine.

FINAL CHAMPIONSHIP STANDINGS

1	Keke Rosberg	44
2 =	John Watson	39
2 =	Didier Pironi	39
4	Alain Prost	34
5	Niki Lauda	30
6	René Arnoux	28
7 =	Michele Alboreto	25
7 =	Patrick Tambay	25
9	Elio de Angelis	23
10	Riccardo Patrese	21

THE GRID

Prost 1m 16.356s	
	Arnoux 1m 16.786s
Alboreto 1m 17.646s	
	Cheever 1m 17.683s
Patrese 1m 17.772s	
	Rosberg 1m 17.886s
Andretti 1m 17.921s	
	*Tambay 1m 17.958s
Watson 1m 17.986s	
	Warwick 1m 18.012s
Laffite 1m 18.056s	
	Piquet 1m 18.275s
Lauda 1m 18.333s	
	Daly 1m 18.418s
*Guerrero 1m 18.496s	
	Giacomelli 1m 18.622s
Surer 1m 18.734s	
	de Cesaris 1m 18.761s
Henton 1m 18.765s	
	*Jarier 1m 19.220s
de Angelis 1m 19.302s	
	Mansell 1m 19.439s
Winkelhock 1m 19.767s	
	Baldi 1m 20.271s
Boesel 1m 20.766s	
	Keegan 1m 21.180s
● Byrne 1m 21.555s	

*Did not start
● Allowed to start in place of Tambay

Did not qualify: Teo Fabi (Toleman TG181-Hart 4 turbo) 1m 21.569s; Eliseo Salazar (ATS D5-Ford V8) 1m 21.583s; Chico Serra (Fittipaldi F8D-Ford V8) 1m 22.387s.

Suppose they held a motor race and no-one came... Even the lure of the World Championship being decided right out there in the car park was not enough to lure more than a handful of curious spectators away from the more immediate business of gambling in the casinos of Las Vegas. In this bizarre setting (far right), Keke Rosberg (right) drove with uncharacteristic self restraint to clinch the championship in his first season with a competitive car, while Michele Alboreto (below) confirmed that he is a man of the future with a brilliantly paced victory. With more traditional settings becoming ever more emasculated and television revenue rendering dedicated, on the spot enthusiasts merely coincidental, is this the future face of Grand Prix racing?

THE TEAMS

A look back at the winners and the losers of 1982, including BOB CONSTANDUROS's team by team analysis of all the Grand Prix runners.

Piquet 27·61
2 Patrese 27·97
Prost 28·86
29·52
4
Arnoux 30·26
6 Rosberg 30·30
deAngelis 31·62
8 Alboreto 31·81
Daly 32·06
10 Lauda 32·13
deCesaris 32·3
12 Mansell ·32·88
Bruno-G 32·95
Laffite 32·95
Warwick 33·24
16 GUERRO 33·59
Fabi 33·97
18 Watson 34·16
34·18
20 SERRA 34·18
Marc 34·42
22 Cheever 34·62
Mauro 34·71
24 K.EGAN 34·77
Winklehk 34·9
26 BYRNE 34·98
Boesel 35·14
28 Jarier 35·20
Salazar 35·2

THE SADDEST YEAR

At the beginning of 1982, the Ferrari team, with two of the best drivers in the world and, at last, a chassis to match its power looked set for championship victory. By mid-season, as BRIAN LABAN reports, it had all gone tragically wrong, but the team still did not give up.

NOW in his 85th year, Enzo Ferrari is no stranger to tragedy. He still grieves for his son Dino who died in 1956 and, motor racing being the cruel sport that it is, for the drivers who have inevitably died in Ferrari racing cars. They were great drivers: Ascari, practising at Monza in 1955, Peter Collins and Luigi Musso in 1958, Von Trips in 1961, Bandini in 1967. They were all bitter blows to Ferrari, but 1982 was perhaps the bitterest year of all in racing terms as the team suffered the immeasurable tragedy of the loss of Gilles Villeneuve and the horror of Didier Pironi's accident at Hockenheim. To Enzo Ferrari, Villeneuve in particular was almost a son; at his annual meeting with the Press in September, Ferrari remarked 'I was fond of Villeneuve; in my eyes he was one of my family . . .'. That Ferrari could continue after Villeneuve's death is no sign of callous indifference, but an underlining of the total and almost religious sacrifice which Ferrari makes to his sport; and in spite of all the terrible tragedy of 1982, the Scuderia again emerged as World Champion Constructor — this for the seventh time.

At the beginning of the season Ferrari had cause for optimism. Gilles Villeneuve and Didier Pironi were by any standards a formidable driver line up: Villeneuve simply a brilliant, natural talent completely incapable of giving less than his all, and Pironi a much matured Grand Prix winner. Their results in 1981, including two

wins for Villeneuve, were achieved in spite of the Ferrari rather than because of it. The 1496cc V6 turbo could demonstrably boast prodigious power, almost certainly more than any competitor, but the woeful inadequacies of the 126C chassis were such that the advantage was only usable in a straight line. The engine was light and compact but the chassis was badly overweight and sadly lacking of grip. The two Ferrari drivers had a frustrating season fighting to overcome the handling deficiencies and many rivals had an equally frustrating time bottled up behind the red cars in corners and left for dead on the straights.

For 1982 it should all have come good. Over the winter, Dr Harvey Postlethwaite progressed from trying to make a silk purse of the 126C sow's ear and came up with a completely new car, the 126C2. Using the most modern of materials and technology and looking conspicuously more compact than its unloved predecessor, the

When Enzo Ferrari welcomed both Didier Pironi and Gilles Villeneuve to Maranello (above) the future looked assured, but by the end of the year, with Villeneuve dead and Pironi badly injured, Ferrari was relying on two completely different drivers.

126C2 was truly a new generation of Ferrari — and not a moment too soon. The new monocoque was built up from folded Nomex honeycomb bonded around carbon fibre composite bulkheads. Principally, the tub was considerably narrower than before, allowing more room for ground effect producing side pods. The engine remained virtually unchanged, used as a stressed unit bolted directly to the rear of the monocoque and driving through the familiar transverse gearbox.

126C2s were used right from the beginning of the season, the first pair appearing at Kyalami, avidly watched by virtually every other team, all knowing that if Postlethwaite had come up with a chassis to match the KKK turbocharged engines the season might well be very one sided. Certainly the car was a vast improvement on its predecessor, but contrary to early fears it was not immediately right. The cars had obvious potential but ultimately suffered mechanical and electrical problems, Villeneuve retiring and Pironi struggling on to a lowly 18th place.

Before the Brazilian Grand Prix, Pironi was fortunate to escape unharmed from a *very* big testing accident at Paul Ricard in which the first of three cars was destroyed. The accident was eventually put down to driver error.

It was apparently no error that Ferrari misinterpreted the rule book at Long Beach and had Villeneuve disqualified from third place after his laughably Heath Robinson, yet technically legitimate, double rear wing had been protested. Seemingly, Ferrari had sacrificed championship points to make a political point about the difference between the letter and the spirit of the regulations, a barbed gesture to those Cosworth teams now using water cooled brakes . . .

Thanks to the same controversy, Ferrari were somewhat short of opposition at Imola but what should have been a welcome one-two turned sour when Pironi led team leader Villeneuve home to a 'two-one' finish. Villeneuve was furious, Pironi unrepentant and whether or not the two would ever have made it up became tragically academic two weeks later when Villeneuve was killed at Zolder. Emotionally triggered criticism of the strength of the Ferrari chassis, which broke up in the accident, was grossly unfair and deeply saddening to a man of Ferrari's integrity. The simple truth is that in an impact of such proportion the inevitable happened. Ferrari, deeply affected by the loss of Villeneuve, requested that FISA withdraw the racing number 27 in memory of his driver but when a second car appeared at the Dutch Grand Prix it bore witness to the fact that FISA had refused the request. Fittingly, perhaps, the new Ferrari driver would be Patrick Tambay, one of Villeneuve's closest friends, stepping in after a great deal of soul searching, having turned his back on Formula 1 in disgust after the South African shambles. With the team back to full strength, in numbers at least, Pironi further raised the spirits with a comfortable win in Holland.

Thereafter, both drivers were consistently in the top four but there was also further tragedy and disaster. At the Canadian Grand Prix, Pironi's car stalled at the start on the front row of the grid and the unfortunate Riccardo Paletti, rushing, unsighted from the back row, tore headlong into the back of the Ferrari, Paletti dying the same evening from terrible injuries. Having survived another major testing accident at Ricard it then fell to Pironi to run into the back of another car: in blinding spray during practice at Hockenheim he hit Alain Prost's near stationary Renault and was again fortunate to survive, suffering particularly horrific leg injuries. Tambay's first ever Grand Prix victory the following day, as news of Pironi became more optimistic, lifted the team from the depths of despair.

Before Hockenheim, Pironi was drawing into a comfortable championship lead; the Ferrari engines, with a closely guarded emulsified water injection system, showing reliability as well as power, a trick which the other turbo teams were seemingly still a long way from mastering. There was little reason to believe that Pironi would not be World Champion, but that was not to be.

As this nightmare season drew to a close there were further problems. Having driven a masterful race in Austria, to recover from a pit stop and last place to finish fourth, Tambay missed the Swiss Grand Prix, victim of excruciating back pain caused by the pounding of the virtually suspensionless modern Grand Prix car.

As Pironi's championship lead was inexorably whittled away, there was just one more high spot for Ferrari to set against the lows. To satisfy Monza's fanatical *tifosi*, Ferrari made the inspired move of bringing Mario Andretti, Italian-born and hero worshipped, back to the wheel of a car from Maranello. As Andretti took pole position the Grand Prix became fairy tale. In the race Andretti could only finish third, plagued by a sticking throttle, behind Tambay and the man who Ferrari had just announced would be his driver for 1983: René Arnoux.

In the end, Pironi lost the title to Keke Rosberg by a single point, the Constructor's Cup being scant consolation. Alongside the new cars for Tambay and Arnoux for 1983, there will be a third Ferrari for Didier Pironi. Pironi has vowed that he will return and Ferrari will wait. In modern Grand Prix racing he is unique.

He was in all ways a purist — a throwback to the days when the driver was supreme. Like the romantic heroes of racing past, Gilles drove with his heart, to win. Motor racing was his magnificent obsession, an obsession that left no room for half-measures. He never failed to push himself to the limit. For a driver who lived with as relentless a passion for the sport as did Gilles, there was only one way to race — flat out.

Perhaps because of his exuberance each time he donned a helmet and stepped into a racing car, or perhaps because he fought to master his unique talent, he touched a resonant chord in everyone. After just four years of Formula One competition, the little French-Canadian's fans were legion; the name Villeneuve was synonymous with speed.

After his death, the public outpouring of grief probably surprised even the most avid racing enthusiast; rarely has a motorsport figure so captured the imagination of people the world over as did Villeneuve.

Of course, reaching the upper echelons of racing had its rewards; Gilles became one of the sport's highest paid drivers. There was the home in Monte Carlo and the ski chalet in the mountains. There were the mandatory toys, such as the 1400 horsepower speedboat and his prize Agusta helicopter. But through it all Gilles never really changed from the early days in Formula Atlantic. He shunned hotel life on the road, preferring to park his motorhome at the track and to enjoy home-cooked meals with his wife Joann. He never really considered himself rich. Asked what he would do if the FISA-FOCA struggle ended in the cancellation of the 1981 season, Gilles replied, "I'll put my jeans on and work in a garage. I can do that".

It was only when Gilles' driving talent was put on the line that he ever became conscious of his value. In 1980, when Williams indicated an interest in the Ferrari driver, Gilles and his agent, Gaston Parent, sat down to serious negotiations. But when Frank Williams learned what they wanted, he was floored. "I can't afford you", said Williams. "You're right," snapped Gilles, "you can't afford me".

While most of his colleagues at Ferrari may have feared to speak the truth to the aged boss, Gilles was painfully direct. For him there was no room for cover-ups or excuses, and he was deeply respected for that.

Nor was he reluctant to make a stand on an issue, if he felt strongly about it. It was Villeneuve who led a protest against the dangerously overcrowded pits at Zolder, in 1981, and he was equally active, one year later, when the dispute over drivers' rights, threatened the running of the South African Grand Prix. In the midst of that controversy, Gilles, firm in his beliefs, said: "We gave in to the Federation last year, but we refuse to compromise this time. If we get down on our knees to them now, they'll dictate to us forever".

He was just as candid about the present rules which forced him and his colleagues to drive ground-effect cars that left little room for driving flair. "The current cars are so difficult to drive," he would complain. "They bounce around so much and the grip is unbelievable." Gilles' ideal Formula One car . . . "would be like the ones we have now, but with no turbo, or ground-effects, and a 5-litre, normally-aspirated engine, instead of a 3-litre, that would develop something like 750bhp; and big wheels and tyres like thay had back in 1975 or '76. That would be the real Formula One!".

If Gilles approach to racing was straightforward and uncomplicated, that was not surprising to anyone who knew his background. Born the son of a sewing machine contractor in the small rural town of Berthierville, Quebec, Gilles' early racing was modest. At 13 years old he was cutting his teeth in snowmobiling; by the time he left school he had decided to race on the professional snowmobile circuit. It was solid training and Gilles believed it helped him achieve his precise car control, especially in the wet. It was also punctuated by some of his worst spills. Gilles' father, Seville, still remembers a race when Gilles fell off the snowmobile, and another machine "passed right over his head. His helmet was crushed into bits but he wasn't injured".

By 1973, Gilles was signed to a professional contract with a factory snowmobile team and wound up that season capturing the World Championship. He then convinced the factory team to finance a season in Formula Ford, and with their help went on to capture "rookie of the year" honours.

But while racing was important to Gilles by this time, it still wasn't his full-time occupation. When he decided in the off-season to become a professional driver, in the Formula Atlantic series, he mortgaged his home and, with a small amount of money he had made in snowmobiling, bought his first ride. But it was to be a disappointing year. Deeply in debt and needing results to attract the sponsors, Gilles broke his leg mid-way through the season. He was able to make it back for the final race of the year, although his chances for that season were effectively wiped out and so was his money.

It was typical of Villeneuve that he was undeterred. "In fact," he offered, "if this accident has done anything, it's to make me go faster". Gilles raised the stakes on his racing career by selling his house to finance his 1975 Atlantic season. Gilles, Joann and their two children moved into the cramped quarters of a motorhome that they parked in his hometown of Berthierville when they weren't on the road to another track. It was by no means an easy decision for a man who carried the responsibilities of home and family, but it was even more daring for a man who had nothing to go by. No one in Canada, least of all an Atlantic driver from a small town in rural Quebec, had made it into Formula One.

But Gilles was determined and confident. Gaston Parent recalls that, "he never doubted in his mind that he was going to Formula One. He believed in his own success unquestionably".

Gilles' investment started to pay dividends that first full year in Atlantic. He won his first race — in the rain at Gimli, Manitoba — and finished fifth in the standings. The next year was picture perfect as he signed with Ecurie Canada to drive a March 76B for what had to be the most professional team on the circuit.

Gilles won the Atlantic championship that year, along the way winning an incredible nine-out-of-ten Canadian races. Then, at the Formula Atlantic race in Trois-Rivieres, Quebec, not far from his

GILLES VILLENEUVE

The death of Gilles Villeneuve in an accident during practice at the Belgian Grand Prix robbed motor sport of one of its greatest talents. NOEL NEELANDS pays tribute.

hometown, he got his first chance to test his mettle against a handful of Formula One drivers.

Gilles proved equal to the task, outpacing the likes of James Hunt, Alan Jones, Patrick Tambay and Vittorio Brambilla right from the beginning. In the process he so impressed James Hunt that the future World Champion returned to England with strong praise for the French-Canadian. Clearly, Gilles was on the brink.

Not long after, Gilles got a 'phone call from Teddy Mayer of McLaren, to discuss a contract for 1977. His Formula One debut came in the British Grand Prix at Silverstone in what was to be the first of four races with McLaren. After a couple of spectacularly quick practice sessions, punctuated by some lurid spins, the word was out — Villeneuve was a prize catch but a potentially costly driver.

McLaren decided to pass on Gilles, but Ferrari was unperturbed by the reckless image. Former Ferrari driver Chris Amon had returned from the Can-Am circuit extolling the virtues of the driver from

Quebec. Villeneuve had taken over Amon's Can-Am seat in the Dallara sponsored by Walter Wolf, leaving Amon to run the team. It didn't take long before Amon, duly impressed with Gilles' quickness and car control, was on the 'phone to Modena urging the Commendatore to sign him.

It was a dizzying next few months for Gilles. He received a 'phone call from Ferrari, and, after only three hours of negotiations, the agreement was signed. The next day he was on the track testing his new mount and barely 24 hours later was back on a flight to Canada, complete with Lauda's modified seat. The seat would go into the number 2 Ferrari waiting for Gilles at Mosport for the Canadian Grand Prix.

This was all heady stuff for a driver who had just wrapped up his second consecutive Formula Atlantic title. It was, perhaps, unmerciful as well, considering Gilles' complete lack of preparation in the Ferrari. In any case, the next two races did nothing to ease the image of recklessness that still dogged Gilles and threatened to make his Formula One career short-lived. Following some exuberant but ragged driving in Canada, Gilles capped the season with a horrific accident at Fuji, Japan, that catapulted his car into a spectator area. Rumours spread quickly that Ferrari had found Gilles' spills too costly and his contract for 1978 would not be renewed. But it was apparent by this time that the Commendatore had a special understanding for the real Gilles and his strong will to win. He quickly put the reports to rest, saying that the man who doesn't try will never have accidents and will never aspire to the World Championship.

So, with a new lease on life, Gilles once again threw himself into testing the new Ferrari and settling into relative job security with a contract inked for 1978. 1978 was a learning experience for Villeneuve, and he made giant strides in poise and maturity. By midseason his Formula One driving style began to take on an air of precision as well as quickness, and by the final race of the year, in front of a hometown crowd, *le petit grand homme* was hitting his stride. It was a faultless afternoon for Gilles as he took the lead from the Lotus of Jarier and sailed home the winner of the Canadian Grand Prix. He was the first Canadian ever to win a Grand Prix and the feeling of partisan warmth and jubilation that swept through the grandstands as Gilles made his final tours was heart-rending. For Gilles it was a fairy-tale come true — his first win in Montreal's first Grand Prix. Never again would Gilles regard the Canadian Grand Prix as anything but 'his race'.

Even though his Ferrari team mate, Jody Scheckter, captured the World Championship in 1979, he referred to it graciously as 'Gilles' Year'. And well it might have been a championship year for Villeneuve if bad luck hadn't plagued him on so many occasions. But Gilles pressed on regardless. In Zandvoort, his last title hopes slipped through his fingers when a rear tyre deflated and sent him into the catch-fencing. It was typical Villeneuve stuff: Gilles slamming the Ferrari into reverse, flat tyre and all, pounding up a cloud of dirt and smoke as he managed to get himself pointed in the general direction of the pits, then willing the crippled car the final stretch, tyre and bodywork shredded and his day ultimately over.

The following year was a long struggle for Villeneuve, his abilities in so many races far surpassing those of his Ferrari chassis. But here again was the fabric of determination that shaped his image. This was the year of countless pit stops for fresh tyres, and spirited but hopeless drives that offered little in the way of points.

1981 dawned with the introduction of the Ferrari turbocar, and once more he was saddled with a machine that didn't match his potential. Gilles jokingly referred to the oafish-handling Ferrari as his "big red Cadillac", a car strong on power but lacking in agility.

But here was Villeneuve at his best. It was not an easy task, taming the wild and unpredictable 126CK. It twitched and bounced and gave Gilles fits. Eventually he made it respond to his touch, deftly tossing the scarlet Ferrari around the circuits of Monaco and Jarama and scoring back-to-back wins. It will be recorded that Jarama was the sixth and final Grand Prix victory of his career. Happily, it will be remembered as a classic.

For the 1982 season Gilles had worked feverishly on the newly-designed Ferrari chassis. Despite a "stolen" victory at Imola by number two man Didier Pironi and the subsequently strained team relations, he was confidently looking forward to the rest of the season. Gilles, it appeared, had been blessed — finally — with the chassis he needed to take him to the World Championship.

By Belgium, Gilles was ready to crest the wave. Sadly, the chance never came. On that chalk-grey afternoon in the pine woods of Zolder, Gilles died the only way he could — racing on the limit.

Gilles, yours was a rare and magic talent that will not soon be forgotten. Like the epitaph of the legendary Nuvolari, to whom you were so often compared, 'You will travel faster still upon the highways of heaven'.

FIGHTING BACK

When Didier Pironi crashed at Hockenheim in August he came horribly close to losing his life, but less than eight weeks later, in his hospital room, he spoke to JABBY CROMBAC, Editor and Grand Prix correspondent of *Sport-Auto,* of his remarkable recovery and future plans.

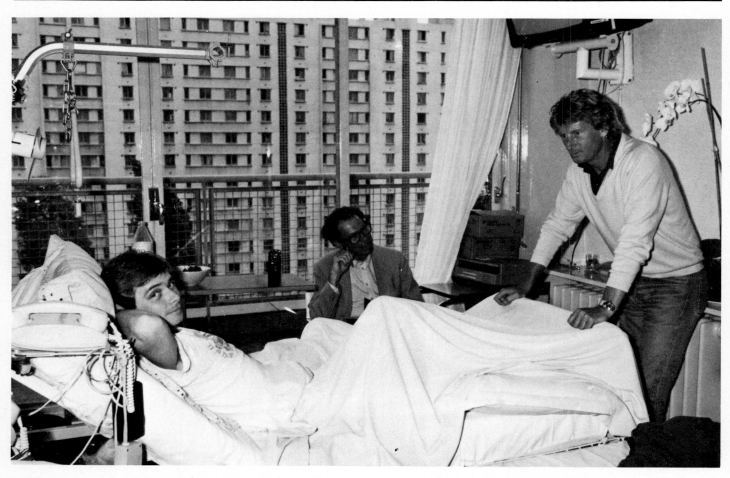

SIDELINED By an enormous accident at Hockenheim during the first practice day for the German Grand Prix in August, Didier Pironi has only taken part in eleven out of sixteen Grands Prix this season, but he nevertheless tied for second place in the final points standings with John Watson, just five points behind the new champion, Keke Rosberg. The latter scored no less than 21 points during the races in which the injured Pironi was unable to participate.

Fifty two days after his accident, the Frenchman talked to us from his hospital room in Paris. Slightly paler and thinner, Didier still displayed the tremendous physical stamina which had astonished the surgeons who have taken care of him and proved a tremendous asset in his fight. The man who was considered lost to motor racing by most press reports following his accident is achieving such a comeback that one can talk of a miracle. A miracle which has been made possible by Pironi's stamina and iron will, but also by the way he has been treated both at the Heidelberg hospital immediately after his crash, by Professor Michkowsky, and in Paris by Professor Letournel. The latter was already well spoken of after taking care of Patrick Depailler following his serious hang-gliding accident.

Although it is unusual after such a traumatic experience, Didier retains excellent memory of the accident, and told us how it happened:

"It was raining hard and I was testing new rain tyres. I was about to stop in my pit, and I was following Daly to avoid getting in his way as he seemed to be on a flying lap. Just before the braking area for the right turn at the entrance to the Stadium, he was on the correct line, to the left. He turned towards the right and I only had time

to think that he wanted to let me through then, suddenly I saw the back wing and the rear wheel of Alain Prost's Renault. I was doing about 175mph and he was going so slowly it looked as if he was stopped. It was obviously too late to do anything about it, and I felt only a slight bump when I hit his rear wheel and took off, climbing in the air like an aircraft. I could see the tips of the trees! I was completely aware of what was going on, and I thought 'this time, this is it!' The Ferrari then dived towards the earth on the right of the track, and I shut my eyes pending the crash.

"When I opened them again I had blacked out. It was like being in the night. I could hardly distinguish the faces of the people who came to my rescue, and it took about fifteen minutes before I could see properly again. I remember seeing Nelson Piquet first, but he did not talk to me. Then I recognised Professor Watkins, the FISA's doctor. I heard a surgeon say: 'We have to chop his right leg off to get him out of this!' This shook me up and I said 'No way!' I think this gave them the incentive to try a little longer to extricate me without cutting my legs off.

"After half an hour I was put on a stretcher, which was lifted into the helicopter, a Bell Jet Ranger. This was the first time I felt some pain, when they bumped my right leg against the helicopter.

"I then arrived at the hospital, where I was brought into the operating room. I underwent several operations at Heidelberg, but the first one lasted seven to eight hours and Professor Michkowsky did a fantastic job to reinstate blood circulation, especially in the right foot. At the time, he thought my ankles would remain blocked, but fortunately this was not the opinion of Professor Letournel, who was constantly in touch with him before, during and after the operation. He came to see me at Heidelberg, before I was brought back to Paris, and he was full of praise for the work of his German colleagues.

"The most difficult time for me was the next week: because of the open fractures, there was a great risk of infection and this would have meant the loss of my right leg. For this reason, I was kept in an aseptic room.

"After 13 days in Germany, I was flown back to Paris, and two days later the surgeon operated on both my arms. The left one had just been put in plaster because it was necessary to open it to straighten it up, and they did not want to take this risk earlier on. On the morning of the operation, they found that the cubitus of my right arm was also broken. This operation went well, except that they did not put me fully to sleep. After a few minutes I woke up to hear the doctor order 'Take this muscle to the side — pull a little

Recovering in a Paris hospital (left), having been transferred from Heidelberg, Pironi is joined by Crombac and by Jean-Pierre Jabouille, whose own racing career came to a premature end after an accident in Canada in 1980 which badly shattered his legs. Mauro Forghieri returns to the Hockenheim pits carrying Pironi's helmet (above) immediately after the accident, his team cast once again into despair.

tighter!' Fortunately I felt no pain, but I tried desperately to signal that I was awake, and finally I managed to move a bone he was touching, so he said 'He is awake. Put him asleep!' They gave me another shot and I passed out. But when it was over I was able to narrate the operation to the surgeon, who was quite astonished!

"I have about 20 screws in both arms, and 53 in the left leg alone. In the right one, they will graft some bone next Thursday, and only then will they put the screws in. Altogether I shall then have over 100 screws in my four limbs.

"I never felt very great physical pain, and it is mostly at night that I have a bad time, and need some drugs to go to sleep. After this week's bone grafting, I hope to be able to sit up in an armchair and soon start 're-education'. If everything goes well, I should be able to walk on crutches by Christmas time.

"Since my accident, Commendatore Ferrari has called me on the phone twice a week. He has told me: 'The day you feel fit to try a racing car again, come to Fiorano and we shall put a car at your disposal. The day you feel fit to *race* again, we shall provide you with a car and team, like this year.''

"I am determined to take up this generous offer and race again next season. Obviously I shall start by testing, and if I am not fit enough I shall give it up.

"This is my first accident, and I think when I am able to resume a normal life I shall have different ideas about life and the importance one should give to each matter. I will know the real value of life.

"As regards motor sport, I shall obviously continue my campaign through the Professional Racing Drivers' Association to improve the drivers' safety, although the circumstances of my accident are not within the factors to which we are giving priority in our quest for safety. But this season was tragic enough to need no more incentive to take care of these things, even if our new World Champion doesn't look at it the same way."

SEFAC FERRARI

WHAT an incredible year for Ferrari: finishing the year with two different drivers to those with whom they started, winning the Constructors Cup and being placed second in the Drivers' series with a driver who had missed five races. Ferraris could have started 32 times; in fact they started 22 times. The team started with the new carbon fibre 126C2 but, if there was a telling factor, it was the reliability of the V6 engine which used an intriguing but undisclosed emulsifying technique to cool the fuel with water. Of those 22 starts, Ferraris finished in the points on 14 occasions. At the same time, the team had to deal with at least six wrecked cars. Yet throughout this, Mauro Forghieri's men were hard at work with development: as well as the water cooled injection, there was the twin wing which caused Gilles Villeneuve's disqualification at Long Beach, new suspension at Detroit, the longitudinal gearbox in Holland, revised wastegate in Austria and a stronger monocoque for the Swiss GP at Dijon. No team could have had an unhappier year, yet with such extraordinary success at the end of it.

DIDIER PIRONI
IT was a year of success and sorrow, of controversy and diplomacy for the Parisian. He was at the forefront in the drivers strike at Kyalami, won a controversial San Marino GP in front of his team mate who was to die two weeks later. He had to deal with the Canadian fans later in the season, and suffered the extreme misfortune to be involved in Riccardo Paletti's fatal accident. Then he won in Holland, finished second at Brands Hatch, and third a week later in France. Leading the World Championship, he was hospitalised in an appalling crash two weeks later. By the end of the season, only one driver had overtaken him to claim the title. No conclusion can be drawn from a year of such mixed emotions.

PATRICK TAMBAY
KYALAMI'S politics caused this most cosmopolitan of Frenchmen to quit F1 before the season had barely begun. The death of his friend, Gilles Villeneuve, provided an opening at Ferrari which, after much soul-searching, Patrick filled. In all but one of the six Grands Prix he drove, he scored points. But injury caused him to pull out of two events, otherwise his score might have been greater. Even so, he achieved more than was expected of him: he scored nearly twice as many points as in his previous four years of GP racing.

BUSINESS AS USUAL

Two years after the big split, Niki Lauda and Grand Prix racing decided that they still needed each other after all and in a blaze of publicity the twice World Champion came back to 'driving around in circles'. MIKE DOODSON looks behind Lauda's highly successful 'second coming'.

SUCCESSFUL come-backs are indeed rare in motor racing. Although the occasional sports car driver achieves it, in Grand Prix racing it seems that the indefinable qualities which add up to "will to win" get lost after a champion's retirement (sometimes even before he announces his departure). In Montreal in 1979, on the day that he walked away from the sport, Niki Lauda announced that he had lost that urge.

Lauda's famous statement about why he had lost interest in "driving around in circles" could have haunted him when he returned to the sport in 1982. Not even McLaren International's joint Managing Director Ron Dennis, who had stayed in monthly touch with Niki throughout his retirement, and who eventually persuaded him back into a car, was absolutely convinced that the Austrian would be the same driver whose talents had won world championships in '75 and '77, and whose "will to win" had brought him back from death's door after the fiery accident at the Nürburgring in 1976. In the McLaren/Lauda contract, Dennis inserted a "get out" clause which could be invoked after three races . . . But Lauda, as usual, broke all the rules. He scored points for fourth place in his first GP with Dennis' McLaren team and won his third, at Long Beach. It was through the streets of the Californian city that we had the best indication that the old magic was still there, for while every other driver in the field slashed and struggled with his car and its steering, Lauda delicately *flowed* between the concrete walls, caressing them at every turn but never once looking as though he would even kiss them, let alone embrace them.

For Lauda, the return started with a flight to London in his private Falcon jet in October 1981. Unusually, he brought his wife Marlene, who had just presented him with Mathias, their second son, but he did not tell her until they had arrived at Heathrow what he intended doing. He just said, "Off you go to Harrods, darling. I'm going to

test a Formula 1 car at Donington Park." The scenes at Donington were amazing. News of the test had leaked out and by midday the gates were besieged with pressmen and a TV crew. If Dennis had worried about being able to put his hands on the rumoured three million dollars which Lauda was asking, it was obvious now that persuading his sponsors would be much easier.

As Tyler Alexander, the American engineer and McLaren director who looks after Niki's car at the circuits, said, "he's one of those guys who likes a challenge — even more so when the cynics said he was doing it for the money."

Lauda may not have needed the money. He won't admit it, although there is no doubt that Lauda Air, the airline which he had founded with the money which his racing career had amassed between 1973 and 1979, was in the the same sort of trouble as any other business of its type. There were penalty clauses invoked when he cancelled the DC10 wide-body jet which he had ordered from the makers in Long Beach and his hopes of taking on the national Austrian Airlines had been frustrated by government opposition. Austrian Airlines was itself already losing money and didn't want to concede its route monopoly.

What is sure is that the airline business had to go on the back burner: Lauda Air's two Fokker F27 turboprop aircraft have been leased to an Egyptian company, and the two smaller jets are being used now for executive travel. The airline has not gone bust: its 30 employees, to whom Lauda is utterly loyal, are still working from their headquarters in Vienna.

Lauda had not, of course, driven for McLaren before his "second coming." Comparisons with his "before" style are therefore difficult to make, although John Watson believes that Niki still drives in the old, neater pre-ground effects manner which requires comparatively early braking and early acceleration away from the corner.

Watson himself had to "unlearn" that style two years ago. There have been several occasions this year when Lauda has been slower in a race than Watson (it's invariably the other way around in qualifying), so maybe Wattie's right. "But I wouldn't be too dogmatic about it," says Alexander, "because it's all tied up with the choice of tyres, for example — and it seems that Wattie's definitely harder on tyres than Niki is".

The current wing cars — rigid suspension, non-sliding skirts, etc — were unknown to Lauda before the Donington test. "He approached it all very professionally", recalls Alexander: "he drove the thing, sussed it out and obviously said to himself 'God it's awful . . . but I'll have to learn to cope with it.' Then he went off to prepare for it physically".

In two years behind a desk at his airline HQ, Niki had started to develop a roll of fat around the waist line. The muscular arms were a trifle flabby. He had acquired a taste for evil smelling cheroots and a daily glass of whisky. To get back into physical shape he called up his old trainer Willi Dungl, a fifty-ish, gnome-like man who's worked with all types of sportsmen.

"Dungl soon had him working out," reports one of Lauda's friends, the Austrian journalist and TV commentator Heinz Prüller. "I spent a day training with him, and it was hell. Up at seven, half an hour's jogging before breakfast, and then an hour and a half of cross-country skiing. Before lunch we would do some downhill skiing, there was more cross-country in the afternoon and then he'd have us in the pool for swimming and underwater massage. The final torture was half an hour in the gym doing stretching exercises".

An essential part of this punishment is 'Dungl's diet', apparently based on muesli and fruit juices, with fish rather than meat as a protein source, invariably washed down with herbal tea. Dungl comes to virtually every GP to supervise the exercise and to prepare the unappetising gruels; in return for the same treatment John Watson pays half the little trainer's expenses. In Brazil, where there were no motorhomes in which to hide, the two drivers solemnly sat in their garage between practice sessions ingesting these healthful substances. If you look at the results (Watson a winner in Belgium and Detroit, Lauda with wins at Long Beach and Brands Hatch), it is difficult to argue with Dungl's recipes for success.

Lauda's off-track priorities have changed somewhat since the old days. Like Piquet with Ecclestone, he has sold all his publicity rights to his team in exchange for a lump sum. The ever-present Parmalat cap (worn at all times except when the Nomex balaclava is rolled over the Nürburgring scars) brings in part of the reputed three million dollar salary, as also no doubt does the pit lane procedure, seen at most races, in which the champion extracts a gasper, flamboyantly lights it up and inhales deeply, with evident relish. In theory the brand should be Marlboro, but at Zandvoort Niki attempted unsuccessfully to disguise a package of Winstons. At least he tried . . .

He lives with Marlene and the boys in their comfortable house at Hof, near Salzburg, where few journalists or other outsiders are ever invited. There is also a summer home belonging to his in-laws in Ibiza, 100 metres from Keke Rosberg's hideaway, where he likes to escape as often as possible. Frequently he climbs out of his racing car after a GP, takes a quick shower, then makes for his own Falcon jet at the local airfield in order to leave immediately for Ibiza. "By rights he should be knackered," says James Hunt, who's flown with him after a race, "but instead it seems to refresh him to get behind the controls of a plane. Come to think of it, he was always like that . . .".

Looking back on his season, there were two glaring errors in Niki's driving. The first was at Detroit, where frustration got the better of him and he attacked Rosberg in an ill-advised move that ended with the McLaren parked in the wall. Since the race had been re-started, it wasn't even necessary for Niki to have passed Keke to finish ahead on combined placings; he blamed himself entirely. He then hurt himself at Hockenheim when he slid wide during qualifying and wrenched his wrist as the car went through the catch fences and walloped the wall. "That was a real boob," says Alexander, "because he went off when he was 1.5 seconds fastest in the 'Cosworth' class. He was just pissed off because he had been blocked by someone — and of course he couldn't start the race.

Let's see now, if we assume that he would have won, say, at least six points at one of those races, and maybe a couple from the other, then Keke wouldn't have finished so well up, and probably Niki would have arrived at Vegas with perhaps a two point advantage in the world championship . . .

The hard facts of the sport, of course, are that there are no 'ifs' and 'buts'. He failed to win a third title in his comeback year; that is undeniable. Next year is McLaren's first with the Porsche-built TAG turbo, and the evidence says that turbos cannot be reliable in their first year. Porsche may be able to prove otherwise, and evidently Lauda thinks so, too. He'll be in there pitching: of that you can be sure.

McLAREN INTERNATIONAL

ALTHOUGH the MP4 looked outwardly similar throughout 1981 and 1982, John Barnard substantially changed his carbon fibre car under the skin. The aerodynamics were in a constant state of development, and the car was tuned to fine limits. The result was that the team had one of its best seasons for some years. The drivers won two races apiece, a feat emulated only by Renault's men. Furthermore, McLaren finished second to Ferrari in the Constructors Championship and the drivers finished second equal and fifth in the World Championship. Without doubt, the team was the best Cosworth-runner, and would appear to have two of the more regular and experienced drivers, both of whom proved capable of race-winning performances. The team's biggest disappointment was losing Lauda's third place in Belgium when his car was less than two kilos under weight. If their protest had been successful, it would have meant that both drivers would have gone into the last race with the possibility of winning the World Championship.

JOHN WATSON
THE Ulsterman had his best-ever season in Formula One. His drives in Detroit, Dijon and Las Vegas proved that he is a very competitive racing driver. He wasn't over-shadowed by Niki Lauda, but took each race as it came. Regrettably, he had six consecutive non-scoring races, partially his own fault, and partially that of the team. But for a damaged skirt at Dijon, he would almost certainly have been nine points better off.

NIKI LAUDA
THE world's best-known racing driver set himself a task, and succeeded in fulfilling it. He returned, and won his third race. He won again at Brands Hatch and picked up another 12 points elsewhere. He proved to be a diplomat at Kyalami, but also a very good racing driver. He has, perhaps, more commitment than he did in 1979 when he quit.

INTERVIEW

A RACER'S YEAR

Time after time through 1982 John Watson proved that, given the right equipment, he will beat the best of them. In mid-season it really looked as though this would be his year but then, as he explained to BOB CONSTANDUROS, the championship slipped from his grasp.

FOR John Watson, it was the best Grand Prix season ever. He won two races, finished second in the championship, and dazzled spectators with some superb drives. The man himself is modest, he admits to being introvert, and talks about 'satisfaction' rather than real enjoyment. There's good reason for that, but it's important for John to enjoy his races.

"No, I don't think it was an enjoyable year. In terms of results it was, but then they are only a part of it. It was my best season ever but, taking it from an overall point of view, I think it was the worst motor racing season that I've ever been involved in. I should have had more feeling of enjoyment, instead of just being satisfied. I gained satisfaction from Belgium this year, and to some extent Brazil. And a race that I put a lot of effort into for no reward was Dijon. I started in the middle of the grid, got up to sixth place and then a skirt flopped out, so I had to make a pit stop. When you lose three laps like that, there's not much point in trying hard, but I drove really hard. Prost, Rosberg, Niki and I were the only ones racing as far as I could see, and I overtook the group behind Patrese twice. I thought my overtaking manoeuvres in that race were very good and well-judged."

Overtaking is an important part of motor racing, not only for spectator enjoyment but also for the driver. "There are some people that can race, and there are some people that are fast in racing cars. I think my ability as a racing driver is broader than others and because I can race, I can overtake people. I think I did more overtaking this season than probably most of the rest of the field put together. At each race, because I didn't start at the front of the field, I passed lots of cars. Even in Las Vegas, where it's hard to overtake, I got by eight or nine cars."

John never disputed that a Cosworth-engined car would win the championship this year. "I predicted that before the start of the season, Renault *ought* to win the championship. On paper, everything was in favour of Prost winning. But I also felt on that, while that was the situation, a Cosworth car would win the championship in the end, and I felt that there were only two teams running Cosworths that had that ability and capacity: McLaren and Williams."

And Watson desperately wanted to win that championship. Last year, Watson said he was worried that team mate Lauda might overshadow him. But that didn't happen.

"I believe that both of us received 100 per cent effort from the team, but he gets himself involved in every aspect: whether testing or development. He's very successful in doing that. I knew this, but

I knew that I shouldn't try and fight it. Even so, at certain stages of the year, the cars would be set up in the way that Niki had treated them at the circuit, but it wasn't the way that I wanted mine set up because we drive our cars differently. So I would lose a lot of time during practice getting my car right. That's why I would quite often race better than I had qualified."

The championship went well for John until after Canada. Then came a string of non-points scoring finishes. "I felt a lot of disappointment after Las Vegas. There had been a spell of six races after Canada and up to Monza where I didn't score, and the more I think about that, the more it annoys me. To finish equal second in the championship and not score in six races — it's no different to Pironi, he missed five races. It's infuriating because, as it turned out, the championship was begging to be won by somebody. The problems in those six races were both my fault and the team's, a combination of circumstances. All those things come down to a consistency: consistency from me and consistency from the team. Niki had problems earlier in the season which I didn't have. I had a very good first half season, I had a very bad second half. In the last two races, I scored what I thought was a good fourth place in Monza, and a good second, if disappointing, at Las Vegas. I overtook a lot of people, I did something that a lot of other people didn't do at Las Vegas: I raced. Not very many others did, but I raced bloody hard. It was still a disappointment."

But John was already looking ahead. His plans weren't settled for the coming year, but he knew what he wanted. "I would like to drive for McLarens next year. I think they have a very well-balanced driver situation, and I think that the team has the potential to do more than they did this year. I look at the team as being two years old, and I think that what it has achieved in two years is outstanding. I'm sure that next year we'll be more competitive than we have been this year."

But John still had some interesting ideas on the 1983 championship. "There are going to be a lot of turbocharged cars in 1983, and that raises the level of competitiveness, and then you'll get all the turbocharged cars pushing one another. All they had to do this year to win the championship was to finish, and they couldn't even do that. But next year, they're going to have to race, so it's possible for a well-prepared, competitive Cosworth-engined team, purely through consistency, to win the championship. It may not even win a race. It could be that next year, the World Champion may not even win a race . . . ."

BEATEN FAVOURITE

With four wins in the bag, Renault could count themselves the season's joint top scorers, but the race wins could not disguise a dreadful catalogue of missed opportunities and internal strife. DIDIER BRAILLON, Deputy Editor of the authoritative *Grand Prix International*, looks at the Regie's problems.

WITH two victories by Alain Prost, at Kyalami and (after Piquet's and Rosberg's disqualification) Rio, and two others by René Arnoux, at Paul Ricard and Monza, Renault Sport can pride itself, together with McLaren International, on winning the largest number of Grands Prix in 1982.

Yet, at the heart of the French team, there is a good deal of disillusionment. Widely regarded as the favourite at the beginning of the season, Renault let slip both the world titles which it was chasing — the drivers and manufacturers titles — in spite of the obvious competitiveness of its cars.

Technical problems, as well as some human problems, changed

what should have been a successful year into a season full of frustration and disappointments. A sample survey of the specialised press during the closed season, showed Renault to be the clear favourite in the race for the 1982 World Championship. In fact, the start of the season was highly promising for the yellow and black single-seaters of the Regie Renault. Alain Prost won the opening race at Kyalami, and then was declared winner of the second event, the Brazilian GP at Rio, after both Nelson Piquet's Brabham and Keke Rosberg's Williams, were disqualified because they were deemed to be underweight. With 18 points already in the bag, Prost must have seen himself as a potential World Champion. He was soon to be very disappointed as a long and frustrating period of failures hit the French team. The Renault RE30Bs were still among the most competitive cars in terms of sheer speed, as confirmed by the numerous pole positions achieved by Prost and Arnoux, but success just refused to come their way. For seven Grands Prix, from Long Beach to Zandvoort, Alain did not score a single point and the bad luck which started for René at Rio stayed with him until Brands Hatch, or in other words for nine, miserable races. In a season punctuated by recurring mechanical breakdowns, often at times when the drivers looked ready to harvest the fruit of their labours, and with a surprising number of accidents, the engineers never lost faith but soldiered on behind director Gerard Larousse. The team never *appeared* to lack confidence and even when things seemed blackest they worked relentlessly. Perhaps in some ways, the failures brought them closer together.

Yet the cynics were already suggesting that Alain Prost, disappointed by the total lack of reliability of the Renault equipment, was thinking of changing teams in 1983 and that René Arnoux, who in both Monaco and Montreal spun off without any obvious reason, was no longer at the peak of his art.

It was the French Grand Prix, at Paul Ricard, that proved that, for the moment at least, the doubters were wrong. Arnoux won the race

in front of Prost, after the two French single-seaters had out-manoeuvred the Ferraris. It should have been an occasion for rejoicing but there was a strained atmosphere at the finish. To increase Prost's championship chances, he of the two drivers being in much the better position for the World Championship, Jean Sage, the team manager, had on five occasions ordered the leader to give way to his team mate. Arnoux, leading by 25 seconds, completely ignored this instruction, to the evident satisfaction of many journalists who did not like the attempt to interfere to such an extent. Prost, whose calm and polite mask suddenly broke, afterwards allowed himself some angry comments and thereafter stopped

Prost worked well with Larousse and the engineers (left) throughout the year, but not, in the end, with Arnoux (above). The V6 turbo (below) has tremendous power but dreadful reliability.

speaking to Arnoux, except in cases of absolute necessity, a decision which he stood by until the end of the season. This internal division, together with reprimands for René Arnoux, whose car was from then on treated very much as number two by Larousse and the chief mechanic Daniel Champion, made the end of the season extremely strained. The split proved to be quite amusing at times, such as when Arnoux, knowing that he would be driving for Scuderia Ferrari in 1983, showed his new employers that he could be faster than his "team mate".

Other problems, technical ones, made a lot of people more restless. These largely revolved around the electronic injection, with which the KKK twin-turbo V6 1500cc engine was fitted from Monaco onwards. There, the unit gave no trouble. In fact, contrary to all expectations, it was after the Renault Sport engineers thought the testing was over that the electronic injection started to give problems, notably at Hockenheim, Zeltweg, where Prost lost certain victory, Dijon and at Monza. The cause of the breakdowns was failure of the injection pump, most probably because of overheating. Curiously the chief engine man Bernard Dubot and his colleague Jean-Pierre Menrath had terrible difficulties in determining the cause of the problem.

René Arnoux nevertheless managed to win a magnificent race at Monza, once again beating the Ferraris. For Arnoux, as for Prost, the improved fortunes came miles too late for him to win the championship or to prevent one of the normally aspirated cars from winning it.

Renault pioneered turbocharging in Formula 1 and have persevered with it at every type of circuit since 1977. For the last three seasons Renault has admitted that the Championship was its aim and goal, but so far they have reaped very little reward. The principal cause of this lack of success must be the unreliability of the V6 engine, based on a block built ten years ago for the two-litre European F2 Championship and later equipped with a turbocharger for Le Mans. To carry the mantle of pioneer is not easy and Renault have, on several occasions, suffered the drawbacks not only within its own ranks but also in dealing with its suppliers, such as the manufacturers of the KKK turbo or the valve spring specialists, Schmitthelm. The unknown pitfalls and the ultimate restrictions of turbocharging can only be learned by trial and error. Ferrari, whose V6, with the well publicised water injection, has managed to reach a degree of reliability equal to the legendary Cosworth, and

Had Renault found reliability, the familiar sight of the back of the car (above) might have been more worrying to other drivers.

"second generation" turbo engines such as the BMW and Hart with production derived blocks, perhaps face an easier future.

Next season, in addition to its own entries which will be handled by Alain Prost and Eddie Cheever, Renault Sport is to supply the V6 turbo to the Lotus Team and, following a request from the French Government, to Ligier. Having a larger number of engines on the track should certainly help in determining more quickly than has so far been possible the remaining problems still handicapping the French 1500cc V6. The results obtained by the Lotus and Ligier teams with equal engine power should also enable Renault to form a more accurate opinion of the real worth of its chassis, drawn under the direction of Michel Tetu, something which has obviously been difficult so far.

After the missed opportunities of 1982, 1983 will be another very important year for the Renault team, when hard results will be more important than ever.

EQUIPE RENAULT~ELF

A Renault led all but three of this year's 16 races at one time or other, yet the record shows that they only won three on the road. A fourth was awarded later, although this was one of the three never led by either driver. So what went wrong? Clearly, the new RE30Bs which appeared at the beginning of the year were fast enough. They were stiffer and lighter than the original RE30, with different front suspension and revised aerodynamics. Although there was continuous development as one might have expected, the major developments were the Monaco-type engine with its electronic fuel injection and new turbo butterflies, and later the hydraulic ride height leveller. But the biggest question is, what happened to the pre-season favourites? No less than eleven times the drivers had some sort of incident, either their own fault (such as Arnoux at Monaco) or not (Prost at Monaco and Arnoux at Zandvoort). That cut their possible points scoring races to 21 and, between them, the two drivers scored points on another ten occasions. Of the remaining eleven races, Renaults retired on nine occasions: twice with broken turbos, three times with engine problems and four times with the dreaded fuel injection problem which so decimated the season's final races. To some extent, Renault can certainly blame the drivers, but they also had their own problems. Just when it looked as though they'd mastered the game, they found that they hadn't. And it will become more difficult as more turbos appear.

ALAIN PROST

THE pre-season favourite won more races making his reputation than when trying to defend it. In 1982, he won just one race on the road (South Africa), but was later awarded Brazil. He led seven of the races during the year, and team orders said he should have won the French GP. In the end, he came second in that race as he did later in the Swiss. The team's fuel injection problem cost him dearly at the end of the season; he had to settle for fourth in the championship. Four accidents, not all his fault, made him a wiser driver by the end of the year.

RENÉ ARNOUX

NOW an ex-Renault driver, the little man from Grenoble had his share of glory and controversy. He won both the French and Italian GPs in dominating style, but made mistakes early in the season, contributing to an embarassing tally of no less than seven terminal race accidents — again, not all his own fault. He proved that he is no longer the meek and malleable number two by disobeying team orders at Ricard, by dominating that race and the Italian, and by his occasional stupid mistake. But he remains a very quick driver.

TAG WILLIAMS TEAM

THE Williams situation wasn't unlike that of Ferrari, although fortunately without the disasters the Italians suffered. Frank effectively lost both his drivers from 1981 and, because of the dithering involved, perhaps found himself with less than an ideal team, at least as far as he was concerned. In terms of cars, the team ran FW07s up to the Belgian GP and, while the FW07s used were light, the FW08 had been built as a lighter and stronger car than its predecessor. It had also been built as a six-wheeler, but had only appeared briefly in that configuration. Remarkably, there was no carbon fibre in the chassis, and only two small titanium parts. The team concentrated on aerodynamics and latterly fuel pump cooling. In Germany, the front suspension was stiffened and fitted with wider track. The team's main attribute is the care taken in preparation: there's the flat patch, long and late nights, constant work on the spare car, a separate test team and the constant attention to ride height for maximum ground effect. And if Ferrari had their disastrous bad luck, it could be said that Williams had theirs too: Rosberg losing his second place in Brazil, Carlos Reutemann retiring, the team not going to San Marino, Rosberg's pole-winning car failing to start at Brands Hatch, and the wing falling off in Italy. In the end, however, the Williams team won its third title in four years.

KEKE ROSBERG
FRANK Williams didn't rate Keke that highly at the start of the season. He had the attack of an Alan Jones, but not the guile. He tried to win races from the front: at Zolder he made a mistake and lost the lead, in Detroit he slipped to fourth. Then the attitude changed: conserve the tyres, attack at the end. It just failed in Austria, but it was successful at Dijon. He won only one race, was disqualified from second in Brazil, but he worked hard for his World Championship. Despite his attacking style, he spun only four times during the season's races and testing, and only damaged one side wing. He stayed on the road, and won the championship.

DEREK DALY
IT was a year in which he and his supporters expected so much, yet there were only eight points at the end of it. After starting with Theodore, Daly did the last 12 races with Williams. He fitted in with the team well, raced hard, but qualified disappointingly. With Rosberg doing most of the testing, Derek was at a disadvantage but, overall, it was a disappointing year.

109

JONES

At the end of 1981, having helped Frank Williams to the top, Alan Jones retired; Carlos Reutemann hung up his helmet a few months later. IAN PHILLIPS, Racing News Editor of *Autosport*, London, looks back.

REUTEMANN

WHEN Alan Jones left the winner's rostrum at Las Vegas in 1981, having just scored his 12th Grand Prix victory, he also claimed he was leaving Grand Prix racing. There followed rumour and counter-rumour during the winter that he would change his mind, but he didn't. He remained in his native Australia, winning the national GT Championship, but never so much as came back to Europe. Ferrari tried to entice him back for the final two Grands Prix of the year following Didier Pironi's accident, but still he said "no".

But there is still a strong feeling that Alan Jones will be back, and probably with very little prompting. The Williams team, for whom he won the World Championship in 1980, would welcome him with open arms. True, his replacement, Keke Rosberg, won the title for the English team this year and did everything expected of him, but Jones was part of the furniture — he'd grown up with Williams Grand Prix Engineering and scored 11 of his 12 wins with them. Replacing Jones meant more than just finding a driver who could do the job.

Racing was in Alan Jones's blood from birth, his father Stan being Australia's number one in the mid-fifties. But truthfully, few others than Alan himself and his then invalided father could have been convinced of a successful career for Jones Jr after seeing his early races in Formula 3 in Britain in 1970 and 1971. There was a lot of Aussie bluff and bravado, but precious little sign of any outstanding ability and life was tough too.

The family car business in Melbourne had collapsed and Stan Jones had had a stroke. Alan, newly married to his lovely wife, Beverly, had to turn street trader of VW caravanettes and, later, boarding house owner/caterer in London to penniless fellow Autralians, in order to make ends meet. But he kept racing, and the first signs of success came in 1973 when he led the John Player F3 Championship to the final round, although a poor engine destroyed his chances of the title: he needed to finish first, but could only manage sixth.

Jones then wanted out of F3, but the fuel crises of the time made life tough again, and 1974 began with a one off drive in a three year old Atlantic March at Silverstone. As luck would have it, Jones won that race, and a month later he netted a drive in a new car run by former racer Harry Stiller. Although he only finished fourth in the Championship, he did enough to earn himself a Grovewood Award, having led the last 10 races of the year.

Jones had an impressive one-off F5000 drive at the end of the year and was planning more for 1975, but speaking at that year's London Racing Car Show he said: "If somebody offered me an F1 drive tomorrow, I'd probably take it, whatever the car. It seems to me that if somebody wants an F1 driver he'll look in his own back yard first. It's important to get into F1 and just do what you can

PERHAPS the way Carlos Reutemann retired mirrored his whole career. First of all he announced he was going to quit after Las Vegas in 1981, then he changed his mind and came back to lead the Williams team in the first two Grands Prix this year, before again retiring, this time for good.

His Grand Prix career spanned 146 races and 12 wins but, while everybody acknowledged that, on his day, the handsome Argentine was probably the best in the world, his career was marred by indecision, bad decision and moodiness. Too often he switched teams at the wrong time, was indecisive about the settings on his car, and subsequently drove in a sulk. Sadly, it is probably those bad points which will be longest remembered about Reutemann, not his outstanding ability to produce scintillating practice laps which decimated the opposition, or his super-smooth racing rhythm which enabled him to leave the pack as if they were in another class, or mount come-back charges which nobody could answer to. Carlos Reutemann was a very special driver and one whose ability deserved a Championship crown, but who, perhaps, in the end has only himself to blame for the fact that in years to come he will only be recalled as a man who won 12 Grands Prix and threw away the championship in his final year.

A deep and thoughtful man, Reutemann was never political or controversial, and it is ironic that in his first race in Europe he hit the headlines through controversy. Having been a triple Argentine touring car champion, he came to Europe in 1970 to drive an Argentine-backed F2 Brabham and at Hockenheim had the misfortune to take off the King of F2, Jochen Rindt, at the end of the first lap. From then on, though, it was upwards all the way. Reutemann finished runner-up to Ronnie Peterson in the 1971 championship and, but for a series of poor tyre choices would almost certainly have won it.

In 1972 he was due to drive for the now Ecclestone-owned Brabham Grand Prix team and lead Ron Dennis's semi-works Brabham F2 team. His Grand Prix career started in sensational fashion when he took pole position in his first event in front of his home crowd, but it wasn't until South Africa in 1974 that he scored his first win.

That first season was ruined by a heavy practice accident at the with the equipment you've got."

And that is exactly what he did. Harry Stiller did a deal to buy a Hesketh, and gave Jones his Grand Prix début at Monaco, where he qualified 18th in a big field. Stiller's money ran out after just four races, but Jones had done enough to be taken on by Graham Hill's Embassy team as a stand-in driver for the injured Rolf Stommelen, and he did four more races for them in between British F5000 races in a RAM Racing V6 March-Ford, in which he took two wins and five fastest laps from seven starts. Alan Jones had arrived, but there was another winter of worry before he landed a full time Grand Prix drive for the Durex Surtees team.

Jones and Surtees made a sensational debut together when the gritty Australian led James Hunt *et al* for the first 20 laps of the non-championship Race of Champions at Brands Hatch. That, though, was to be the high spot of a year which was fraught with frustration and which produced just three points finishes. At the end of it Alan decided to quit Formula 1 and race in America, where he was already winning F5000 races.

However, before he had returned from his winter holiday in Australia, AJ found himself back in Formula 1, replacing his former F3 sparring partner Tom Pryce in the Shadow team after the Welshman tragically lost his life at Kyalami. Despite having missed the opening races, it was Jones' best year to date, and he crowned it with his first Grand Prix win — and Shadow's — at the wet Austrian Grand Prix. His future seemed assured, but the Shadow team was rife with politics which were just not to Alan's liking, and before the season ended he announced his boldest move ever — he was to join Frank Williams.

Williams, at this stage, was still just the king of the survivors. Having escaped the clutches of Walter Wolf, who bought his original team, Frank had started Williams Grand Prix Engineering with Patrick Head and had run Patrick Neve in a March during 1977.

traditional Easter Monday Thruxton F2 meeting. His Rondel Brabham lost a wheel and the ensuing accident put Reutemann in hospital with a broken ankle. Ecclestone then banned him from competing in F2 and, other than the odd sports car drive, he never drove anything but Grand Prix cars again.

Reutemann drove for Brabham for five seasons, scoring four of his Grand Prix victories for them. But in his final year Ecclestone decided to run Alfa Romeo engines and the troublesome season upset Reutemann, so that he left to drive for Ferrari in the final race of the year. For two years he drove for Ferrari, winning five races, four of them in 1978, when he finished third in the championship behind the all conquering ground-effect Lotuses. At the end of the year Reutemann left Ferrari for Lotus. It was a bad move. Jody Scheckter took the championship with three wins with Ferrari, while Reutemann's best results were two seconds in the Lotus and only sixth place in the Championship. He switched teams again.

Reutemann joined the Williams team at the start of 1980 to run alongside Alan Jones. However, it was Jones who had inspired the team to championship winning form and it was inevitable that the Australian should take the honours. Reutemann was a superb num-

Jones's career as a driver followed many similar routes to Williams' own fortunes as an entrant, but between them they had a burning ambition to succeed and with the announcement of Head's simple, straight-forward FW06 car a partnership was forged which was to take the World Championship in 1980 and two successive Constructors' titles.

1978 was the year of ground-effect and domination by Lotus, but leading the battle for third place more often than not was Jones in the Williams. Between them they only managed 11 points that year, although these included a sensational second place at Long Beach. At the same time, Jones won the CamAm Championship with nine pole positions, nine fastest laps, and five wins from the nine races in Carl Hass's Lola.

Head's first ground effect car came in time for the European season in 1979, and that long awaited success was just around the corner. Sadly, it wasn't Jones who scored the first win for Williams, his team mate Clay Regazzoni did this at Silverstone after Jones retired with a huge lead. But wins in Germany, Austria, Holland and Canada followed, which gave Jones third place in the final Championship table, making him the hot title favourite for 1980.

Nobody was disappointed. Five wins and two seconds were the highlights of what was a superb all round season. Jones was a racer's champion. He always drove hard and clean. He could never be classed as a natural in the Jim Clark/Jackie Stewart mould, but in recent years there cannot have been a more determined and ruthless performer.

Too often World Champions rest on their laurels and collect the substantial rewards of the title in the succeeding year; the edge goes off their racing and interest wanes. The fact that Alan Jones won only the first and last Grands Prix of 1981 perhaps suggests a familiar pattern. No way. With the confidence of a champion he drove better than ever and, for all those who support the cause of non-political, thoroughbred motor racing, Alan Jones was perfection. He was sorely missed by everyone in 1982. He went home to rest and enjoy the trappings of success that ten years of sweat had rightfully earned. Those that appreciated his skill and admired him for his decision to quit for the reason he did, still hope that he will come back — the Australian humour recharged, the beer gut perhaps a little enlarged, but essentially still a racing driver in the true sense of the word. Again, going back to what he said before his 85 race Grand Prix career started in 1975: "I never thought that I wanted to race cars as an ambition — I just thought it would be natural that I should, just part of growing up." One thing Jones never was: a quitter. And even though he's now grown up, racing cars and winning at the highest level is still what Alan Jones is about.

ber two and, with a win at Monaco and an enviable finishing record, he claimed third in the championship.

Williams retained the same team for 1981 with Jones, by contract, number one again. However, it was Reutemann who took an early lead in the championship and became involved in the controversy of the Brazilian GP, where he refused to let Jones past him while they ran in 2-1 formation. From then on there was no love lost between the two drivers. As so often happens, a reigning World Champion immediately has an off-year to follow his success, but really Jones' was without luck. Reutemann, with wins in Brazil and Belgium and consistent finishing, took a commanding lead in the championship from April onwards. But then followed one of his typical moody sessions and he let the lead slip. Going into the final race at Las Vegas he still had a one point lead. He put in one of his typically brilliant practice laps to take pole position — but right from the drop of the flag he seemed to have resigned himself to not taking that crown and he slipped down the field rapidly and threw away the title. There were no real excuses, he just didn't make use of his reserves of talent on that day — the day that counted.

Reutemann wasn't a man of many words and he slipped quietly away, back to his farm in Argentina and announced his retirement. He had felt at Williams that Alan Jones was always going to get the superior treatment, but when it became clear that Jones was not going to come out of retirement, Carlos did. He came back to lead the Williams team and drove with verve in the season opener at South Africa to take second place. At the next race in Brazil he was overshadowed by his new team mate, Keke Rosberg. It was apparent that he didn't have his heart in the job and didn't particularly like the new breed of suspensionless cars. As a master of the art of driving, his superior ability was never again going to be a major factor until the cars became more conventional. Again he quit, this time for good.

Ironically, Rosberg went on to win the championship but, good as he is, he will never have the class of Reutemann. He was a rarity among Grand Prix drivers and even approaching 40 years of age he was still, when motivated, the cleanest, smoothest, quickest driver around.

TEAM LOTUS

THE season marked Colin Chapman's return to the winner's circle after an absence of almost exactly four years. The team began the year with last season's 87s, before its derivative, the 91, appeared in Brazil. The carbon fibre chassis proved strong, particularly when both Mansell and de Angelis crashed at Monza. It had variable wheelbase which allowed for three different configurations, particularly for fast and slow circuits. There was also a slightly less stiff monocoque available and, by the British GP, one of the cars was fitted with new, pull-rod-type suspension. The team suffered a blow when Mansell was injured in Canada, and test driver Roberto Moreno failed to qualify in Holland. Geoff Lees stepped in for Mansell in France and drove a good race, despite a pit stop for new tyres after being forced off the track. The team's win in Austria, plus the announcement that Renault would be supplying engines next year for one car, provided a tremendous boost, and the John Player Special team scored a total of 30 points during the season.

ELIO DE ANGELIS

THE high point, of course, was Elio's win in Austria. It proved that Elio is a greatly matured driver, for he thought out his race, and reaped the benefits. Prior to that, his points had been won with three fourth places and two fifths. He had a few accidents, but Colin Chapman holds him in high regard, and he'll be driving for Lotus again next year.

NIGEL MANSELL

THE Midlander had a difficult year, virtually abbreviated by his arm injury in Canada which took longer to heal than he would admit. Prior that that incident, he scored points on two occasions: a third in Brazil and fourth in Monaco. But Nigel had more incidents than his fair share this year. With his tremendous determination, he will be a wiser man in 1983.

TEAM TYRRELL

AFTER years in the doldrums, Ken Tyrrell returned to the winner's circle in 1982. The 011 first appeared in mid-1981, but it was constantly developed throughout the season to be a winner in the final race of the year at Las Vegas. Pull-rod suspension appeared on the cars at Kyalami at the beginning of the season and the car was soon under the weight limit and, later in the European season, the team tried a fast circuit set-up by varying the front track. Although a wider track was used at Brands Hatch, Henton set fastest lap at the Kent circuit. Aerodynamic modifications such as a revised engine cover were also made for the faster European circuits. Although complaints were rarely made, the team was financially stretched, having virtually no sponsorship for most of the season. However, Candy transferred their sponsorship from Toleman to Tyrrell for Imola, and Denim Musk sponsored the cars for the final two races. But this lack of finance and Slim Borgudd's unsettled bills hindered development, particularly on the number two car, and Henton hadn't the same equipment as number one driver Alboreto. Even in this unsponsored state, the team beat both Talbot-Ligier and Alfa Romeo in the Constructors Championship.

MICHELE ALBORETO

IN his first season of Formula One, Michele was undoubtedly one of the finds of the year. He frequently qualified well, and his just reward at the end of the year was a win in Las Vegas. His best result, prior to that, was a third at Imola, followed by three fourth places in Brazil, Long Beach and Hockenheim. Apart from his points-scoring finishes, he twice finished seventh. From 18 starts, he finished ten times, which is a good record.

BRIAN HENTON

HAVING started with Arrows, Brian replaced Slim Borgudd at Tyrrell when Marc Surer returned to the Arrows team. The ex-Toleman driver never had the same equipment as Alboreto, but he was a fairly regular finisher with only two accidents on the debit side. His best race was in Austria where he was lying fifth before retirement. Although he failed to score points and was regularly further back on the grid than Alboreto for the reasons already mentioned, it wasn't a totally fruitless season, if only in terms of experience gained.

DRIVING AMBITION

In only his second season of Grand Prix racing, Michele Alboreto showed without doubt that he has the potential to be a future World Champion — and, Ken Tyrrell believes, a great World Champion. PINO ALLIEVI of Gazetta della Sport, Italy, spoke to the fast rising star.

FOR Ken Tyrrell's rising star, the climax of a season of steady and continuous improvement came at the very last race, when Michele Alboreto won a memorable first Grand Prix victory at Las Vegas, and in motor racing the last race is the one that people remember most easily. Alboreto won in the artificial setting of the world's gambling capital, a place that seems to spring from nowhere into the bare desert, and there is an irony in that because Alboreto himself is quite the opposite of anything one might consider as a gambler. The 26-year-old, Milan based driver has very clear cut ideas about his future and his approach to building his motor racing career is both mature and totally professional.

Ever since his schooldays, Alboreto's one and only dream has been to become a successful racing driver and he has dedicated every day of his life to making that dream come true — while seemingly remaining oblivious of the setbacks he has endured. For Michele, obstacles are not a cause for sulking or self pity, but simply a part of the experience which one must go through to reach the top. After the win in Las Vegas, Alboreto can count himself a driver in the very top class.

'I'm still the same person I was before', he had said on stepping from his car after that first win, and he's still the same person now, a couple of months later and despite the inevitable round of prize givings, autograph signing and applause. For Michele, Las Vegas is already history, just a stepping stone to the new era that is opening up for him.

Alboreto is the son of a hard working, well-to-do Lombard family who traditionally base all their values on hard work and who consider each success simply a stimulus to push one on to even greater heights.

'My father, Vittorio, is in the sports goods business and my mother, Flora, works in a kindergarten in Rozzano; she looks after the children she so dearly loves', says Alboreto, 'so I grew up in a family that wasn't wealthy but that wasn't beset with financial worries either'. If one wants to discover the real background of a Formula 1 driver it is often very revealing to start with the family. Often, that seems the only way to understand a driver who lives and works in a world full of people who are where they are more because of their bank account than their ability, where arrogance replaces modesty and where lies sometimes hide the truth.

'I can say that what I really had to offer was my love for the sport and that hasn't changed since I first started. I was quite good at school and I was always a conscientious student in class, but I was so keen on motor racing that more often than not I would go to Monza instead of going to classes at the technical institute. The first Grand Prix that I saw was with my father in 1968. I remember Hulme winning with the McLaren and Ickx's Ferrari coming third.'

His parents' reactions to these occasional diversions were predictable: 'well, they weren't very happy to start with. They only began to accept when they realised that my interest for the sport was not just a childish infatuation but that I was taking things very seriously. So I never had any problems with my parents, in fact sometimes both my mother and my father were of considerable help to me from the psychological point of view. I honestly couldn't ask for anything more from them'.

But his father did do something more for Michele: he bought him a motor bike, which Michele sold almost immediately so that he could buy himself a Formula Monza racing car. Quite a lot of money was involved in the deal, so Alboreto split the cost with a friend, but unfortunately the friend did not pass his driving test and the partnership collapsed! Whereupon, Simone Vullo comes onto the scene.

Businessman Vullo is considered by many to be Michele's most trusted admirer and adviser. Vullo gave Alboreto his own racing car, saying 'if you're faster than me in it you may as well keep it'. That was in 1978, when Alboreto was employed as a clerk in a children's wear company, but from there on his career was going from stride to stride, through Formula 3 and Formula 2 into Formula 1, where he made his début with Tyrrell at Imola in 1981. His backing came from Candy who, as Tyrrell's sponsor, insisted on having an

Italian driver in Italy.

Alboreto readily admits he owes a lot to Tyrrell — 'everything I know, but especially he taught me never to give in, to fight hard all the time. Tyrrell is a very stubborn person, but quite honestly I don't know whether that is an advantage or a disadvantage!'

In 1981, Ken Tyrrell predicted that Alboreto would win a Grand Prix in 1982 and after Las Vegas, having been proved right, he also predicted that Michele could be World Champion in 1983. In fact, Tyrrell has described Alboreto as a worthy successor to Moss, Clark and Stewart, but Michele is typically modest on that point, saying 'frankly I think Ken exaggerates a bit, but deep down I would really like to think that I was wrong!'

And talking of mistakes, Michele is refreshingly honest when it comes to admitting his own. When he went off in Austria, he freely admitted that it was his own fault: 'there's no point in denying it, in Zeltweg I went off because I was stupid. I admitted it and I don't want to tell lies because if in any future race I go off because something in the car broke I want my team manager and my mechanics to believe me and not think that I am trying to hide behind an excuse'.

He is quite sure who he sees as the most complete driver in Formula 1 at the moment: 'in my opinion, Niki Lauda; he has a lot of charisma and his total professionalism tends to lead you on'. Of Lauda's battle for safer cars, Alboreto says 'in this business, complete safety doesn't exist. The important thing was to reduce the dangers as much as possible, and now I think that we are on the right road'. He is enthusiastic, too, about the new, flat bottom cars: 'there'll be a bit more wheel banging in the corners, but it's nothing to worry about. I wasn't a very clean driver in F3 and these things were quite normal, then I learned how to drive more neatly, so if necessary I'll use all the experience I had with the smaller formula cars'.

In terms of experience Alboreto doesn't single out any one driver who has taught him a specific lesson — 'nobody in particular, I want to try and learn from everybody. When for about ten laps I was right next to Lauda, I tried to understand his driving style, but even if I'm next to less capable drivers I always try to understand why they do certain things. I watch everybody very carefully!'.

He is adamant that his new found fame doesn't cause problems, 'no, it doesn't bother me. I think I'm a fairly quiet person and I would race with exactly the same enthusiasm on an empty race track'. He is also aware that, especially with Ferrari's interest, this quiet lifestyle probably can't continue: 'I'm obviously very proud of Ferrari's interest in me but I've still got plenty of time to enjoy my peace and quiet. Even if I was to drive a Maranello car tomorrow, nothing in my character would change so far as my lifestyle is concerned, but I would be different inside. It's like starting all over again, I would be motivated even more to go even higher, because I'd be a part of the world's most famous racing team'.

In spite of Ferrari's rare wooing of an Italian driver (Arturo Merzario was the last Italian to race a Ferrari F1 car, in 1973, and Ludovico Scarfiotti was the last Italian Ferrari winner, in Italy in 1966) Alboreto will stay with Tyrrell at least for 1983.

Alboreto then promises to continue being himself, and so far he has succeeded. After every event he goes back to his proud parents. It is a very personal thing because he knows that his mother worries. 'I always look at the races on television', she says, 'I watch on my own because I don't want to bother other people with my anxiety'.

Very often, Michele's fiancée is with him at Grands Prix: 'We've known each other for eight years now and we get on very well together' says Nadia. Michele's hobbies are tennis and music (both classical and modern), he reads fiction and detective stories and most of the films he sees he sees on aeroplanes! But this seemingly ordinary young man is somebody quite different when he is in the cockpit of a racing car. He is very determined and his colleagues know that he is both difficult to overtake and very committed when overtaking others. In Formula 1 there is no place for slow decisions.

JUST IMAGINE...

1982 was a strange year for outgoing World Champion Nelson Piquet and for the Brabham team itself. As MIKE DOODSON, Sports Editor of *Motor* magazine reveals, the changeover from Cosworth to BMW power was by no means straightforward and the rewards are still to come.

IT was Brabham designer Gordon Murray who said halfway through the 1981 season, on looking over the turbocharged Ferrari V6 engine, "just imagine how that thing would go if they put it in a decent chassis". The unstated flip side of Murray's observation was surely: "wouldn't it be great if we could get an equally reliable turbo into our Brabham chassis".

Well, the Ferrari engine found its way into a decent chassis in 1982, and Murray put a powerful BMW turbo into the BT50 development of his excellent BT49 chassis. Ferrari's irresistible combination of speed and reliability should have brought them a driver's title as well as the constructors' championship this year, and the reasons why they didn't achieve the "double" are too painful to be repeated here. But given the appalling unreliability of Renault (and its drivers), Brabham should have been there to take over when Ferrari's momentum faltered after Zolder and Hockenheim. The reasons why they didn't do so will doubtless be the cause of some heart-searching in Munich over the winter.

Immediately after Nelson Piquet had wrapped up the 1981 world championship at Las Vegas, the Brabham team returned to England in a mood of justifiable confidence. The BMW-engined BT50 (detailed largely by Murray's talented assistant David North) had already been running for several months. The BMW engineers were on the point of making an important breakthrough with Bosch in the development of some super-complicated electronickery which would greatly reduce those two bugbears of turbo technology, throttle lag and excessive fuel consumption. And the team had signed up Ricardo Patrese, a potential race winner in his own right, as Piquet's number two.

It seemed that the Bosch engineers had done everything right, because a three day test at Donington Park at the end of October had Piquet enthralled. "The BMW is 20mph faster on the straight

than the Cosworth", he said, "and we don't have one single reliability problem. We will beat Ferrari and Renault, that is for sure".

Well, it didn't work out quite like that. The "productionised" version of the Bosch electronic ignition and fuel injection systems was far from perfect, as another crop of holed engine blocks was to prove in a disastrous test at Ricard. At the annual BMW Christmas party in Munich, Nelson spent the evening in earnest discussions with BMW Sales Director Schoenbeck, who had just announced the joint intentions of Brabham and BMW to start the 1982 season in South Africa with two turbocars. Back at Chessington, however, caution dictated that Bernie Ecclestone should hang on to his collection of 20 or more Ford V8s . . .

Paradoxically, in South Africa it was the Brabham side of the partnership which seemed to have slipped up. The two BT50s were so astonishingly quick in a straight line that Nelson flippantly suggested providing the marshals with rifles ("if I have an accident at this speed, I would prefer to be shot than to hit the bloody barrier"), but they were less good in other departments. The handling was definitely "off", and the braking capacity insufficient. It was fading brakes that sent Piquet harmlessly into the catch fences; fortunately his "armed marshals" idea had been ignored. Patrese was out with engine trouble almost before the start.

Murray's decision to bring out the Ford engines for the next two races, at Rio and Long Beach, did not sit at all well with the board in Munich: as was to happen again throughout the year, the German press took an anti-BMW line, rubbing salt into wounds which were reopened every time the news escaped of more engine failures. The revised 'C' versions of the BT49, when they appeared in Brazil, were so extensively remodelled that it was clear that Murray did not propose to compromise his chances of winning the championship by making do with last year's machinery. When Piquet won convincingly in Rio, the BMW board gritted its corporate teeth and started sending unfriendly telexes to Chessington . . .

Relations between the two sides reached their nadir before the start of the European season. BMW Motorsport's boss, the pragmatic Dieter Stappert, was instructed to demand a full test of the revised turbocars at Zolder. When they arrived (with Murray and North conspicuous by their absence) it was evident that only the minimum of the necessary work on improving the brakes and revising the aerodynamic sidepod profiles had been done. "That test was critical", recalls Stappert: "if we'd had reliability problems of any kind, I'm sure the board would have withdrawn from racing. Then FOCA boycotted the San Marino GP at Imola — and the board issued an ultimatum".

That ultimatum was the sternest message yet to arrive on the desk of Brabham owner Bernie Ecclestone. It insisted that the BMW cars be raced at Zolder, evidently over-ruling a decision that Murray had taken not to race them until the later part of the summer, when the rapid circuits like Hockenheim and Österreichring came round on the calendar. Murray quietly acquiesced, the German press got out its biggest BMW-beating stick — and in only the BMW turbo's fifth race Nelson Piquet scored a fabulous, convincing victory in the Canadian GP at Montreal. His engine ran faultlessly, backed up in second place (it must be pointed out) by Patrese with a Ford-engined BT49. In the pits afterwards, Stappert looked as though a heavy load had been taken off his shoulders: "the only problem is that it's three in the morning in Munich and all the directors will be in bed", he said with a wry grin.

The achievement of Montreal healed up some of the breaches in the partnership. Piquet himself had always been keen to accelerate development of the turbocar ("let's get the bugs out of it so that it's a winner in '83"), while the brass in Munich had some of the heat taken off their backsides by this unexpectedly early success. But the fairy story did not have a particularly happy ending, because Montreal was the BMW's first and last victory so far. And the German press, astonished by the success of the company it had vilified, now reversed its stance and made it plain that BMW was expected to win *every* GP henceforwards.

It was quite remarkable nonetheless that Brabham had been able to win at all. Miracles don't often happen in racing, but Murray's achievement in combining separate programmes for the development of BMW- and Ford-engined cars must put many other teams into the shade. "If you count Bernard, we have only 41 people working here", said team manager Herbie Blash: "Frank Williams has at least twice that number".

There were some embarrassments in store, alas, for BMW. The BT49s were put away in July, and two BMW cars became the norm on the grids. They did not, however, feature too often at the finish: Piquet finished second to Pironi at Zandvoort, and at Dijon he and Patrese picked up modest fourth and fifth placings. The Brazilian's unalloyed enthusiasm for the engine, or more particularly for those who are developing it, had deteriorated to such an extent by Las Vegas that he had become openly critical. "We had exactly the same problem during practice that we had in South Africa. The engineers say that they'll have it all sorted out by next year. But do they mean the beginning of the year or the end of it?"

Attention has been focussed on the BMW frailties by Murray's brilliant pit stop tactics. In theory, by starting the cars on half-full tanks, and soft rubber, they can build up sufficient lead to make a stop for 25 pressure-fed gallons of fuel and four freshly warmed-up Goodyears. The ploy was due to be inaugurated at Brands Hatch, but pit stop fans didn't get to see one of the Brabham crew's express stops until two races later, in Austria: at Brands and Hockenheim both cars were out with engine troubles before they could stop.

Stappert nevertheless insists that there is nothing intrinsically unreliable about turbo engines. "There is no reason why they should not eventually be as reliable as, for example, the Cosworth-Ford. The only difference is that a minor fault in a turbo engine very rapidly develops into a serious problem".

Paradoxically, the Brabham team left Las Vegas this year with much the same mission as in 1981: to chase reliability in the engine, and to sort out a new car (Murray is working on a BT51). Behind them, the two parties have much more experience than they did a year earlier. The Brabham-BMW, an efficient, compact four cylinder engine mounted in an elegant, economically engineered chassis, coupled with the most sophisticated electronics ever harnessed to a racing machine, is still potentially the fastest and most reliable F1 car.

Even Piquet, who has the most to lose, recognises that. "Switch to another team?" he replied angrily to a questioner, "I have spent more than two years working on this project. I'm not going to let some wanker come in now and get the fruit from all my efforts. I want to win the championship again — and this is the car to do it with".

MOTOR RACING DEVELOPMENTS

IT was a year of transition for the Brabham team; a year dedicated to the switch from Cosworth power to BMW's turbo engines. But this wasn't a clean break. After using BMWs at Kyalami which was advantageous to turbo power, the team reverted to Cosworths for the next two races, then back to two BMWs for the Belgian GP, and then one BMW and one Cosworth for the next three events. Piquet's win in Canada precipitated the change to two turbocars for the rest of the year. The cars themselves underwent little development, but Paul Rosche's men from Munich were kept busy with new KKK turbos at Detroit, new injection in Britain, an emphasis on cooling including a mini-fridge and the use of dry ice from the German GP onwards and wastegate modifications in Austria. Brabham, meanwhile, continued their tests with carbon fibre brakes, and set themselves the task of refuelling and changing all four tyres mid-race. For three races, the mechanics stood and waited for a car to appear, only for the BT50s to fail (or in the case of the German GP, crash) before the allotted pit stop. But it wasn't a perfect solution, as the Swiss GP demonstrated, when Piquet stopped and finished fourth, and Patrese didn't and finished fifth. In 23 starts, turbo power scored 22 points; in seven starts, Cosworth power scored 19 points, or 28 if you include the disputed Piquet win in Brazil.

NELSON PIQUET
THE 1981 World Champion willingly devoted himself to a year of acclimatising to BMW turbo power. But before that became a full-time job, he won nine points in Brazil, and made a rare mistake in South Africa. From then on, he settled down to driving a turbo, and found that life was varied: non-qualification one weekend in Detroit, a win the next in Canada. He only gave up hope of winning the championship again when he provided the sport with unwanted publicity by thumping Eliseo Salazar at Hockenheim, which somewhat tarnished his image.

RICCARDO PATRESE
PATRESE settled down to do the job allotted him with a sensible, hard-working attitude. It was as though he had never changed, and was still driving for Arrows, but now his ability came to the fore. He only scored points four times but, like Piquet, they included those for a win and a second place, both in Cosworth-powered cars. Often quicker than his teammate, Riccardo scored one more point in the World Championship.

EQUIPE TALBOT-GITANES

BY the end of 1982, Guy Ligier had lost his Talbot partner, both drivers, and the use of the Matra turbo engine. His team had scored a total of 20 points, the best being Eddie Cheever's totally unexpected second place at Detroit. The team started the year with the heavy JS17 at a time when everyone else was turning out very light cars. In an effort to improve the older models, the team varied the track, but the new JS19 was ready for Monaco, and it immediately aroused the scrutineers' attention. Its slab-sided rear end extended to the ground, and the technical men promptly ordered a reduction in skirt length of 20 centimetres. This, in turn, meant a reduction in ground effect of 30 per cent of that available. The team then went back to square one in an effort to recoup this loss, and it wasn't until after the French GP that the problem was resolved. By this time, the team had lost six GPs. The drivers had JS17s for the North American double-header, and it was with this outdated tool that Cheever scored his six points. Ligier himself, Laffite and Talbot all lost patience at various stages, and poor Cheever was totally at a loss with his JS19 in Holland, and couldn't qualify the old JS17. Matra weren't too impressed and the team will use Cosworths and, eventually, Renault turbos, next year.

JACQUES LAFFITE
HAPPY Jacques wasn't so happy by the end of the season. He is one of the few elder statesmen of F1 racing, and it was because of his experience and determination that he had already signed for Frank Williams for 1983 by October 1982. Laffite had been fiercely loyal to both Ligier and latterly his brother-in-law, team engineer Jean-Pierre Jabouille. He had simply lost patience — but he didn't show it on the track. He has proved himself to be a fighter in the past, despite his approaching 40. Two points-scoring races, the best being third in Austria (where he won last year) don't do him justice.

EDDIE CHEEVER
EDDIE has driven for a different team in each of his four years of Grand Prix racing — and that doesn't include Theodore, for whom he never qualified. He's a very mature 25 year old and, although he became very disillusioned with the Ligier team, he never gave up. The result was a second, two thirds and a sixth: more points than he'd scored in the previous four years put together. He's not a crasher, doesn't break cars, and doesn't let his disappointment get to him. He should be a useful asset to Renault next year.

AUTODELTA ALFA ROMEO

AT the end of the 1981 season, it looked as if Gerard Ducarouge had steered his Italian team out of the doldrums. The final races of the year — as in previous years — had been better than those earlier in the season. But by the end of 1982, Alfa Romeo had so little to show for their season that there were rumours that the team would be disbanded. The team started off with 179Ds in South Africa, but their neat carbon fibre 'McLaren Alfa Romeo' made its debut in Brazil, and proved to be very light. By Belgium, a B-version of the new 182 had appeared with revised suspension and aerodynamics and a narrower body, but this was never raced. Accidents in Long Beach, Canada and Austria, plus a storm in the team's home base of Milan, held up development. Only aerodynamic modifications and emphasis on cooling improvements were noticeable in the second half of the season. The public debut of the team's two-year old turbo engine at Monza must have given little confidence to the team. There were promising moments, such as de Cesaris's pole position at Long Beach, but a measly seven points was all the team could muster by the season's close.

ANDREA DE CESARIS
IT was a better year for the fast but accident-prone driver of 1981. He took a fine pole position in the 182's second race at Long Beach, and was leading at Monaco when he ran out of petrol. He ran out of petrol again at Montreal after crashing in practice. And he will be a wiser man after tangling with team mate Giacomelli in Austria. But his total of accidents doesn't rival that of the previous year, and Andrea seemed more relaxed yet just as competitive in 1982. He still upset a number of drivers on the track — notably when Rosberg was trying to lap him at Dijon — which rather underlines that Andrea is still only 23.

BRUNO GIACOMELLI
A disastrous season for the senior Alfa driver: just two points won during the season from a fifth place in Germany. It was hard to remain hopeful throughout the season, and Bruno was becoming frustrated by the end of it. There were moments when he practised well, but fewer when he raced so promisingly. He is becoming an experienced driver but with no machinery with which to profit from that experience.

TEAM RAGNO ARROWS

IT wasn't an easy season for Arrows: the team started the season with the new A4, a lighter and longer version of the A3. Then Surer put himself in hospital during pre-race testing at Kyalami, Tambay walked out of the team before the strike-troubled race, and neither replacement driver Henton nor Baldi qualified. Surer had recovered from his injuries by Belgium, but it wasn't until Pirelli supplied the team with new breed tyres that the drivers began to score points, albeit for only three six places and a fifth. Development on the A4 centred on the suspension, but Dave Wass was already working on the A5 by mid-season which meant that the A4 remained undeveloped. The team's second new car in a year appeared at the Swiss GP and was immediately dubbed "Arrows's Williams", so similar was it to the FW08. This was a development car for the 1983 season, and certainly proved promising. But out of 30 possible starts, the cars only started 22 times, and with an inexperienced Baldi, and a recovering Surer, there was little that the team could hope to accomplish.

MARC SURER
THE brave Swiss driver admitted at the season's end that he still hadn't recovered from his second major accident in three years. He is a very under-rated driver whose courage is never in doubt but, as in 1980, his injuries prevented him from doing his best. Even so, he scored a brave fifth in Canada and showed tremendous tenacity and determination to finish his races. Only engine trouble prevented an excellent finishing record.

MAURO BALDI

THE 1981 European F3 champion had a somewhat disappointing first F1 season, including five non-qualifications, but few are the F3 drivers who can step into F1 and shine instantly, so it must be regarded as a year of acclimatisation for the Italian. He usually stayed out of trouble, but was responsible for precipitating Jochen Mass's dive into the crowd at Circuit Paul Ricard. However, he picked up two sixth places, at Zandvoort and Österreichring, which was no mean feat.

ATS WHEELS

A tough year for ATS in which their drivers brought them just four points, gained from two races early in the season. There might have been another, but for Winkelhock's disqualification at Imola for being under-weight. The team tried hard with the 1981 car, and there was a continuous stream of developments, including aerodynamics, suspension modifications, and new bodywork at Monaco. Later, both wide and narrow track were tested, plus a new engine cover. All this was accomplished despite rather too many accidents. The North American double-header at Detroit and Montreal saw the team struggling to ready two raceworthy cars, which affected those two races and the following Dutch event. A similar situation had arisen after Long Beach. But it was during the fast half of the season that the points were scored; the second half was totally devoid of top six scores, and it was only from Canada onwards that the drivers began to fail to get onto the grid. Both non-qualified three times, and this was almost certainly caused by the problems of chassis availability. However, during this latter half of the season, the team were desperately searching for more downforce and complaining of too little grip.

MANFRED WINKELHOCK
THE German's second crack at Formula One was certainly better than his first, with Arrows two years previously. He showed more promise than the two points gained in Brazil would indicate. At Monaco, he was running ahead of Lauda, but after the accidents in North America, his performances tailed off somewhat. However, he was the favoured driver in this Anglo-German team, and has probably earned himself a second year with ATS as a passport to BMW turbo power.

ELISEO SALAZAR

BEFORE the end of the season, the Chilean driver had been thrown out of the team. It hadn't been an easy season as number two, although he had picked up two points in the poorly supported San Marino GP. The publicity earned from tangling with Piquet at Hockenheim was a mortal blow, and Eliseo failed to qualify in two out of the following four races. Most of the testing was carried out by Winkelhock, and Eliseo had little moral support from the team. He would probably have done better if he'd remained with Ensign.

OSELLA AUTOMOBILI

AN extraordinary, end-of-season outburst by Herve Guilpin, the team's designer, probably summed up the team's season: a disaster. Although Guilpin tried hard with consistent development, there was an element sadly lacking: reliability. This wasn't simply allied to poor preparation, but the actual material of the parts, or the amount of time that they remained on the car. Quite simply, there were too many breakages on Osellas this year. In turn, this meant that a large number of cars were damaged in the resulting accidents which put further demands on the team. At least seven chassis were damaged during the year. Although Jarier's two end-of-season breakages remain the more memorable, his suspension broke in Detroit and at Imola, and the steering broke in Germany. Jarier failed to qualify on three occasions, and Riccardo Paletti was killed in the first race he actually started, although he had qualified at both Imola and Detroit. Osellas actually started only 12 out of a possible 23 races. By the end of the season, Osella had no drivers, no designer (unless there was a drastic change of policy) and no cars.

JEAN-PIERRE JARIER

IT was a very discouraging year for the ever hopeful Jarier. Although he failed to qualify on three occasions, he never appeared to give up until the last couple of races when the number of breakages on his car got through to even him. On occasions, such as at the Monza race, he practised very respectably, and he scored three points for his fourth place in the poorly supported San Marino GP. But the 36-year-old Frenchman is still looking for his break, and will probably be moving to his eighth GP team in 1983.

RICCARDO PALETTI

POOR Riccardo Paletti never had a chance to show whether or not anything might have come of his Grand Prix career. Rushed (not entirely unwillingly) into the Osella team by his erstwhile F2 sponsors, Paletti could gain experience only in the hard nosed reality of competition. With growing confidence and ability he had qualified in Detroit only to relinquish his car to Jarier for the race and when he suffered his fatal accident in Canada he was making his first ever Grand Prix standing start, having started the boycotted San Marino Grand Prix from the pit lane.

FITTIPALDI AUTOMOTIVE

THE team ran a single car in 1982, a stiffened version of the F8 for Chico Serra. Although it proved to be heavy, the team worked hard on it for the first couple of races, before devoting their time to the new F9 which was a stronger, lighter, and cleaner version designed by Richard Divila. This first appeared at the British GP, complete with pull-rod suspension, but its first race was to be in Germany. Although there was some sponsorship on the car, the team still wasn't flushed with money, but help was forthcoming from Pirelli whose tyres were more promising in 1982 than in the previous season. However, as in the previous years, the team had trouble qualifying, and including San Marino, the car failed to start seven of the year's 16 Grands Prix. The team's one saving grace was the single point that Serra won in Belgium, which at least helped the team's limited finances with their FOCA membership.

CHICO SERRA

AFTER one season learning the hard facts about F1, Chico's second season with the Fittipaldi team was scarcely any better. He did, however, score that single point in Belgium, but the happiest he looked all season was when ex-Fittipaldi team mate Keke Rosberg stepped onto the top step of the rostrum at Dijon. Poor Chico was a regular struggler around the 26th mark on the grid, which is always worrying. He had a number of incidents, notably at Dijon, and a nasty one at Brands Hatch when he tangled with Jarier. It would be nice to see him in a better car.

POWER TO THE PEOPLE

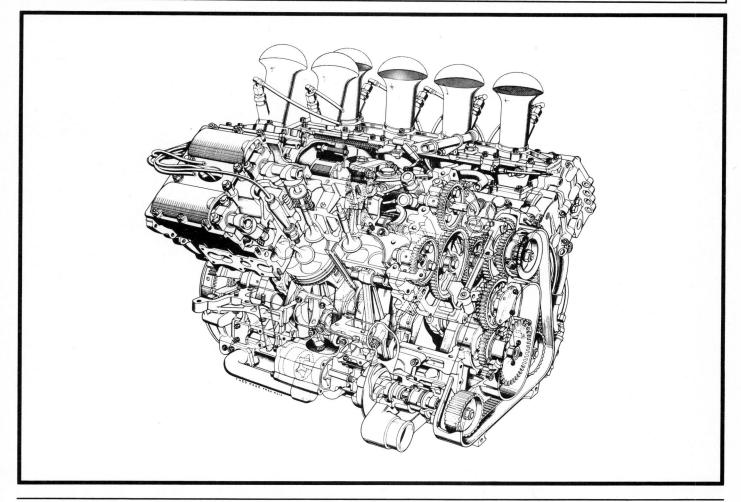

The Ford Cosworth DFV did not exactly bring Grand Prix racing for everyman but it did offer genuinely competitive power off the shelf, giving Grand Prix racing a very different character. BRIAN LABAN looks at the fifteen-year reign of the most successful engine in racing history.

THE start of the 3-litre Grand Prix formula, on 1 January 1966, was heralded as 'The Return of Power', but in reality many teams were struggling in the early days to find *any* suitable power unit. The likes of Honda, Ferrari and BRM could boast their own engines, McLaren struggled with an Indy derived Ford V8, Cooper went with Maserati and Brabham made the marvelously opportunist move of running the reliable, adequately potent and relatively inexpensive Oldsmobile based Repco V8. After the withdrawal of Coventry Climax, other 'kit-car' teams, notably Lotus, had an engine problem and initially relied on stopgap adaptations from the old 1½-litre formula or the anachronistic 2½-litre Tasman formula. And so it might have gone on but for the Ford Motor Company's supreme sensitivity to the marketing main chance and the skills of Cosworth Engineering.

Lotus was the catalyst which Ford needed to set the ball rolling. The Lotus and Ford connection was already well established through the two's collaboration on various roadgoing cars and Colin Chapman was probably preaching to the converted when he mooted a Grand Prix engine to Ford's Head of Public Affairs, Walter Hayes. Nevertheless, when Ford commissioned former Lotus engineer Keith Duckworth to develop such an engine on their behalf, the proviso was that the engine was, initially, for Lotus alone.

It is motor racing folklore that Ford's up-front investment in its Grand Prix project was £100,000 and equally legend that Ford has enjoyed quite extraordinary returns on that far sighted investment.

Duckworth's Cosworth Engineering Company (formed in 1958, with Mike Costin the other partner) was a natural choice for Ford, thanks to a reputation built on Formula Junior, Formula 2 and Formula 3 power units, all based on Ford production engines and, in some cases, already enjoying limited Ford backing. Lancastrian Duckworth eventually accepted the brief for the Formula 1 engine on condition that he first build a Ford-derived, four-cylinder, four-valve, 1.6-litre Formula 2 engine on which to evolve basic format.

The four-cylinder Formula 2 engine was designated FVA, for Four-Valve A-series, and the Formula 1 engine, with impeccable logic, the DFV, or Double Four Valve. While the highly successful Formula 2 engine was based on a Cortina production block, the Formula 1 engine would be built from scratch, block and all. Duckworth resisted the all too logical trend towards multiplicity of cylinders in favour of compactness and relative simplicity; from the outset the DFV was designed to be used as a fully stressed chassis element, carrying suspension pickups and mounting flushly onto the rear of an abbreviated monocoque, thereby relieving the chassis designer of much of the difficulty implicit in accommodating a wide V8. The width arose from the more or less unavoidable 90-degree configuration, with gear driven twin overhead camshafts per bank operating two pairs of inclined valves per cylinder around a central, single plug. A single plane crank allowed relatively simple exhaust layout and all the ancillaries, such as pumps and electrical equipment, were neatly packaged around the outside of the block or nestling within the V. Bore and stroke dimensions of 85.6 x

64.8mm gave a capacity of 2993cc and the earliest DFVs produced around 405bhp at 9000rpm.

The first engine was delivered to Lotus on 25 April 1967, meaning that the proposed Monaco Grand Prix début in May was out of the question. In fact, the DFV's first public appearance was at the Dutch Grand Prix at Zandvoort, in June, married to the exceptionally neat Lotus 49. Remarkably, that was also the first time that Jim Clark had ever driven the Ford-engined 49, what little development had been possible being undertaken by Graham Hill — and occasionally even by Chapman himself.

In a last gasp effort, Hill put the Lotus onto pole at Zandvoort and when he succumbed to camshaft problems while leading, Jim Clark took up the running, won the engine's début race and wrote the first chapter of the Cosworth legend.

On 15 August 1982, Elio de Angelis, appropriately enough in a Lotus 91, just held off Keke Rosberg to win the Austrian Grand Prix and notch up the DFV's 150th Grand Prix win — a record unapproached by any other engine in racing history.

In those fifteen remarkable years the DFV has changed the face of Grand Prix racing. In 1968 the engine became available outside the Lotus camp — in those days at a commercial price of £7500 — and with Lotus, McLaren and Matra it took eleven of the year's races and its first World Championship, with Hill and Lotus. Since then the DFV has powered eleven more World Champions; its more lightly stressed (and nowadays larger capacity DFL) long distance derivative has twice won Le Mans; and the turbocharged, 2.6-litre, 850bhp DFX is now as indispensible to the Indianapolis brigade as the Offenhauser was when roadsters ruled the roost, powering six winners since its introduction in 1975.

In the DFV and its derivatives, teams who would otherwise have been without a suitable power unit have found a ready made and — more important — genuinely competitive package. The DFV and the commercialisation of Grand Prix racing arrived on the scene pretty well at the same time and the two have thrived together, the proliferation of 'kit-car' teams which the engine made possible being the staple of racing as it has become in the last decade and a half. Without the DFV it is likely that the very face of Grand Prix racing in particular would now be vastly different, for richer or poorer depending on one's vested interests.

Through all that time, from 1967 to 1982, the V8 has evolved gradually rather than in great bounds — eloquent testimony to the quality of Duckworth's first thoughts. Today, a front running Cosworth probably gives in excess of 500bhp from a unit some 40lb lighter than the original and, if anything, more reliable.

When Jackie Stewart ran up the engine's half century in Canada in 1972, 450bhp was the commonly quoted output and the DFV was already being written off by seasoned observers, anticipating, rather too soon it transpired, the rise of the V12. When Jody Scheckter notched up the DFV's 'ton', for Walter Wolf at Monaco in 1977, power was up to perhaps 465bhp and the twelves were still the main threat. In response, Cosworth produced a series of 'development engines', lightweight, all magnesium units with a little more power, a lot less weight and sealed to keep prying eyes from the inner secrets. The engines were fast but fragile and by 1978 development was back to evolution rather than revolution.

Some credibility might have attached to the twelve cylinder superiority theory in light of Niki Lauda's two championships for Ferrari in 1975 and 1977 and Scheckter's repeat performance in 1979, but when it came right down to it, the DFV just kept on winning, with 27 more victories in the 1980s, including eight in 1982 — or more than all the turbos, now the main threat, put together.

That said, it would be facile to suggest that the engine can go on winning forever, but what the future holds for Cosworth in Formula 1 terms is a secret kept very close to the chest. Cosworth is highly successful in commercial terms as well as in competition, the Northampton based company employing some 220 skilled individuals and the Manufacturing Division alone occupying some 40,000 sq ft of workshops. Additionally the company has its own foundry and forge with the metallurgists, physicists and design engineers to go with them. Cosworth foundry processes are now universally used and the organisation's use of often self-designed computer operated machine tools is second to none. This machinery and expertise undertakes diverse projects for dozens of outside customers, but racing — and particularly Formula 1 — are in the blood at Cosworth. Aside from the often rumoured desmodromic valve gear for the DFV there are few fundamental changes possible, but the evolution will certainly continue. Keith Duckworth is still adamant that, within the letter of the current regulations, turbocharging is illegal as the turbine constitutes an auxiliary engine of an illegal type and, given his way, he would be working to a fuel consumption formula with more freedom for pioneering work with a social conscience. Whether or not Duckworth brings the rule makers around to his way of thinking — and he strives tirelessly to do so — Cosworth is certain to take up the challenge, but the DFV will be a very hard act to follow.

When the Ford Cosworth DFV was originally commissioned, the intention was to build a batch of just seven engines, but within a year the DFV's success had guaranteed a long queue at Cosworth's door. In 1969, with Matra, Brabham, McLaren and Lotus as the leading users, the engine scored a clean sweep, winning all 11 Grands Prix from pole position, with fastest lap in each and netting the World Championship for Jackie Stewart. In 1973 the engine missed out by a single pole position (taken by BRM) on repeating that performance over a 15-round season. By 1977, although the DFV continued to allow previously undreamed of quality in depth, the threat of the twelves had prompted Duckworth to devise a magnesium block version of the engine (above), offering a weight saving of 45lb on the standard 356lb unit, and Max Mosley described the DFV as 'probably the biggest single factor in the popularity of modern grand prix racing'. Even Enzo Ferrari could find praise for the engine, observing: 'undoubtedly the Cosworth DFV engine has — thanks to Ford — brilliantly solved the problems of those competitors who wish to race Formula 1 cars and could not undertake such a heavy planning, construction and industrial commitment with their own means'. At Indianapolis as in Grands Prix, the Cosworth (in DFX guise) has continued that same quality in depth, taking over the role of the once dominant Offy as essential equipment and adding to Cosworth's tally with 1982 Indy winner Gordon Johncock (below). The tally also, of course, included another Drivers Championship with the Williams team (right), but now Keith Duckworth sees a fuel flow formula as the most relevant way ahead.

MARCH GRAND PRIX

THE March team began the season with re-engineered 811s, Pirelli tyres and limited sponsorship. But Rothmans stepped in before Brazil, and it might have seemed that all the team's problems were solved, particularly as there was an option for three years. Rather than build a new car immediately, Adrian Reynard continued to work on the old model, with little success. This was very much due to staying faithful to Avon, when that tyre company ceased its official F1 operation. Other customers went elsewhere with varied results, and the Pirellis came good. March continued to founder around the non-qualifying mark. The inclusion of de Villota in the team did nothing to help, the Spaniard failing to start a race and finally quitting. Rothmans, expecting better results, became disillusioned and ceased their involvement. Reynard left the team, but the cars received pull-rod suspension and Michelin tyres for the last two races. Even that didn't help. A number of accidents, including the one that side-lined Jochen Mass in France, held up the team's efforts. Not a single point was won.

JOCHEN MASS

THE German driver made his comeback to F1 after an absence of a year. He finally drove his 100th GP in Detroit, but his disappointing performance must be allied with the team's. He had the misfortune to be involved in Villeneuve's fatal accident, and later to be flipped into the crowd in France. He remains a competitor, though whether nowadays as a top-line F1 driver is in question.

RAUL BOESEL

IT was a difficult F1 debut year for the Brazilian, and he failed to qualify five times. A bad testing accident at Snetterton prior to the British GP dented his confidence badly, and he had high hopes of doing well on the Michelins and with the new suspension at Monza. But again, he failed to qualify. His season was one of learning F1 the hard way.

RUPERT KEEGAN

CALLED in to replace Jochen Mass for the last five races, Rupert surprised some of his critics who reckoned him a lost cause. He qualified for three out of the five races and, in some cases, his efforts were really last minute fliers. He proved an able replacement driver.

ENSIGN RACING

THE team started the season with a new car drawn by Nigel Bennett, and a new driver in Columbian Roberto Guerrero. The combination matured well during the season, and the team worked hard on development — for as long as the money lasted. But poor Mo Nunn again ran short of funds, and the team ended the season as they had begun: by withdrawing the car from a race, but this time due to lack of engines. In between times, Guerrero had failed to qualify on five occasions and, at Monaco, the team had hit rock bottom due to a lack of tyres. Fortunately, one race after Avon's withdrawal, Michelin came to the rescue until the end of the season. The main problem in the second half season was porpoising, and Nigel Bennett tried to cure it with 10 different aerodynamic settings at Brands Hatch. Sadly, there were no points for the team, but they did prove to be competitive on occasions.

ROBERTO GUERRERO

AFTER a year in Formula Two, Guerrero took another bold step upwards to Formula One. There's a homeliness about the Ensign team which must be reassuring to any driver, and Mo Nunn is rarely rude about his men. So Guerrero was in the perfect mental situation to improve, and this he did. The financial bothers at the end of the season no doubt made him mechanically sympathetic, but he had a promising first year and, generally speaking, stayed out of trouble.

THEODORE RACING

THE little Theodore team had another difficult year, taking no less than four different drivers to 15 races, but actually starting only six. The team started the year with the previous year's model, before Tony Southgate's new car with a narrow bottom and stiffer chassis appeared in Brazil. Derek Daly started all three races in which he drove for the team, but when he went off to Williams, the team ran Jan Lammers who only started one race, and was subsequently replaced by Tommy Byrne. Southgate continued to develop the car, varying the front track and producing new side pods. New pull rod suspension appeared at Monza but with little success. The lot of the little teams is a hard one and, like Ensign, Theodore found themselves without tyres at Monaco when Avon withdrew. Although Goodyear came up with tyres for the rest of the season, it did little to improve the team's chances. Like March, Ensign and Toleman, Theodore failed to win a championship point.

THE DRIVERS

DEREK Daly, Jan Lammers, Geoff Lees and Tommy Byrne all drove for the team in 1982. Daly, despite starting the season with the completely unmodified 1981 car, and then taking over the new car, at least started all his three races. He provided the team with their only finish of the year, 14th at Kyalami. Jan Lammers qualified for the Detroit race, but broke his finger in a practice accident, so did not start. His place at Montreal was taken by Geoff Lees, who also qualified, only to be involved in the startline shunt and he was unable to restart. Lammers started his home Grand Prix but, after not qualifying at Brands Hatch and Ricard, was replaced by F3 driver Byrne for the rest of the season. Byrne qualified for Austria, but spun off, and was allowed to start in Las Vegas, where he also crashed. Variety proved not to be the spice of life for Theodore.

TOLEMAN MOTORSPORT

THE Toleman Group set out for its second season in Formula One with last year's driver Derek Warwick, and Italian Teo Fabi. Although the cars remained the same TG181 as used last year, some development work was done on them, particularly during the early part of the season before the team began work on the new TG183. New suspension appeared in Brazil, Warwick had revised bodywork in San Marino and the C version of the car appeared in Holland, principally allied to new suspension. Despite these few changes, the car was remarkably competitive on a number of occasions, setting fastest lap in Holland, and running an incredible second in Britain. Much of this can be allied to Pirelli's new tyres which worked so well on other cars as well as the Tolemans. A good deal may also be attributed to Warwick, who frequently qualified very well. These were the high spots of the season; there were also the low spots. The team lost its major sponsorship after three races, and the name of a Toleman subsidiary appeared on the car: Cougar Marine. There were high hopes for the TG183, a very much neater Toleman which made its debut at Monza, but although these weren't immediately fulfilled, there is no reason to believe that the team won't be competitive next year.

DEREK WARWICK

HIS second season of Formula One was a lot more lively than his first: the team didn't go to North America so, of a possible 14 races, qualifying for all but two was a good effort. Although some say Warwick was on half tanks at Brands Hatch, the team denies this, so it was a particularly fine race. The Hampshire man continues to work well with the team, and his spirits remain buoyant. Hopefully, persistence will be rewarded. Renault made advances to the Englishman at the end of the year, and Ferrari also showed genuine interest.

TEO FABI

POOR Teo holds the record number of non-qualifications for the year with seven. In all, Teo started the same number of races but even then he suffered bad luck, such as being involved in the start-line shunt at Brands Hatch. It was an instructive, if joyless, task being Toleman number two in 1982, but there is hope for the future.

**ROAD RACING
INTERNATIONAL**

LE MANS

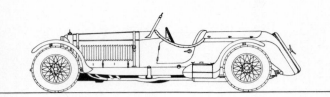

ALFA ROMEO 8C, 2.3-litre s/c
1835.55 miles at 76.48mph

1937

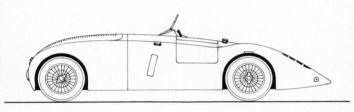

BUGATTI 57G 'TANK', 3.3-litre s/c
2043.03 miles at 85.12mph

1923

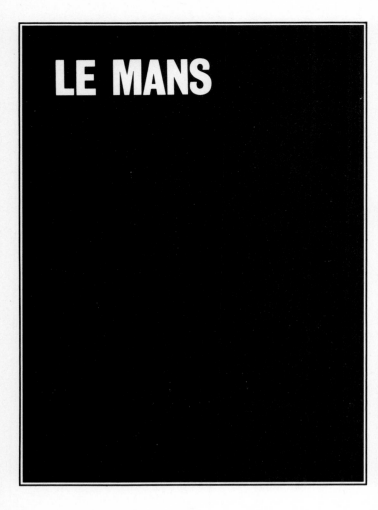

CHENARD & WALCKER, 3-litre
1372.94 miles at 57.20mph

1950

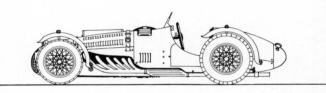

TALBOT-LAGO, 4.5-litre
2153.12 miles at 89.71mph

1928

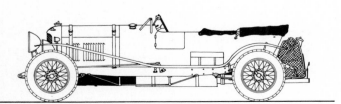

BENTLEY, 4½-litre
1658.60 miles at 69.11mph

1955

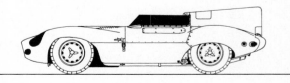

JAGUAR D-TYPE, 3.4-litre
2569.60 miles at 107.07mph

EVOLUTION OF THE WINNERS

1966

FORD GT40 MK11, 7-litre
3009.35 miles at 125.39mph

In the sixty years and fifty races since Lagache and Leonard won the first Grand Prix d'Endurance the Le Mans car has evolved from modified road car to sophisticated two-seater racer. These drawings, by BOB HINE of Grand Prix Models, show how the breed has developed — through some of the most significant winners in the race's illustrious history.

1970

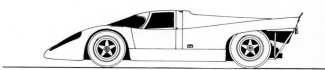

PORSCHE 917K3, 4.5-litre
2863.15 miles at 119.30mph

1959

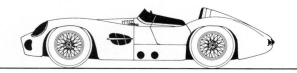

ASTON MARTIN DBR1, 3-litre
2701.65 miles at 112.57mph

1976

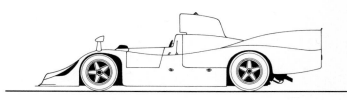

PORSCHE 936, 2.1-litre t/c
2963.89 miles at 123.49mph

1963

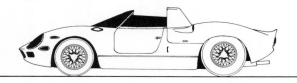

FERRARI 250P, 3-litre
2834.51 miles at 118.10mph

1982

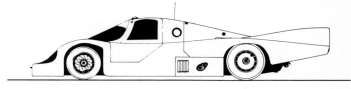

PORSCHE 956, 2.6-litre t/c
3044.15 miles at 126.84mph

STUTTGART STEAMROLLER

Porsche still have a little way to go to match Ferrari's record of nine wins at Le Mans, but with win number seven impressively in the bag at the fiftieth running of the classic, they are within striking distance. IAN BAMSEY watched the Stuttgart machine roll on . . .

4.00AM. A cold, in places misty, French dawn is breaking. The darkness of a long, tiring Le Mans night is fading fast, to reveal a predictable pattern to the 50th running of the world's most famous motor race. Works Porsches, designed and prepared to the fabled Stuttgart Standard of Excellence, are steamrollering the classic event. A bleary-eyed, still boyish looking Jacky Ickx tells a French reporter that he cannot believe that his car will go for another 12 hours without a problem, but only Ickx could believe that — and in his heart he probably doesn't, anyway.

The threat of a works Porsche breakdown is probably no greater than the threat to the team posed by the sole surviving opposition Group C car — another Porsche, the Joest built, 936 based Belga 936J, crewed by Bob Wollek and the Belgian Martin brothers. But this car, in third place behind the two leading works Porsches, is trying to do a David versus Goliath act with none of the tricks that David had. Works Porsche Team Manager Peter Falk smiles and chooses his words thoughtfully: "no problems . . ."

Throughout the hours of darkness the No1 factory car of Ickx and Derek Bell has performed almost faultlessly. The greatest worry has been a misfire between 6000 and 7000rpm — cured by simply richening the mixture. Stuttgart's first Group C car — its first monocoque racing car, and its first ground effect racing car — may be some 60 kilos overweight and, some have said, over engineered, but it is doing everything asked of it. The opposition from the fastest field Le Mans has ever seen has fallen apart in its wheeltracks.

The 956 did just what was asked of it right from the start of practice. Turning its wheels for the first time ever in anger, within no time Ickx's car was under the lap record. Pole position was secured early on in the proceedings, without the aid of qualifying tyres, at an average of 146.27mph. The previous year's 936 sports/racer had been a fraction slower than that, despite a 16mph higher top speed and the use of Q tyres. True, the Ickx 956 had a 'qualifying' engine fitted — but it was the same Indy derived 2.65-litre unit that powered the 936, with smaller twin KKK turbos to aid fuel consumption.

The 911 fathered Porsche flat 6 ran at 1.2 bar — good for 615bhp — in qualifying trim. The 'enduro' engines for the race ran at 1.1 bar and gave 590bhp. No other car at the event had that sort of power and no other car could match the 956 combination of speed on the long, long Mulsanne straight and downforce-aided grip through the turns. The car that came closest had an '81 predecessor, 550bhp and aerodynamics developed in conjunction with the Williams Grand Prix team. It didn't leave its drivers with the same grin, though. Bell called the 956 "a lovely, forgiving car to drive" and neither he nor Ickx had to push it to its limit.

Jochen Mass put the sister car he was sharing with Vern Schuppan alongside, on the front row, before a tyre blow-out caused bodywork damage. The works team's only severe headache of practice was the problem afflicting the third works car of Al Holbert/Hurley Haywood. This had a gremlin in its braking system

129

and languished back on the seventh row, 10 seconds off the pace. However, the engine in the Ickx/Bell car did lose pressure in one cylinder during the second session. Better then than in the race . . .

The Porsche performance was all the more impressive when one considered the fact that all three cars were brand new for the meeting. A prototype car, raced earlier in the season at Silverstone, remained untouched under a tarpaulin. This car had completed a 24 hour computer simulated rolling road Le Mans test without a hitch. Following that, three identical replicas were constructed for the race.

Race the 956s certainly did, but only during the opening stages of the event. The opposition forced the pace from the start but the No1 and No2 Porsches flew the flag upfront until the first pitstops at 47 minutes, all three works cars coming in on the same lap. Ickx stopped again 51 minutes later to hand over to Bell, and the Englishman was strapped in with firm instructions to "cool it". Economy of petrol was a paramount consideration during this year's fuel restricted 24 hours.

Considerations of economy were still to the fore when Ickx swept into the pits at 9.30am the following morning — three laps ahead of schedule. The perceptive Belgian had suddenly felt something strange about the handling as he negotiated the Ford chicane directly before the pits entry road. Rather than worry if this really was a problem, he came straight in. Sure enough, it was — a puncture which thankfully hadn't been given a chance to damage the car. But the question now was, could the 956 be refuelled here and now, or should it stop again after its scheduled number of laps?

With only 25 fuel stops allowed during this new CIA regulations running of the race and fuel tank capacity limited to a maximum of 100 litres, a very wary eye had to be kept on fuel consumption. But by 9.30am, with no serious opposition outside of its own team, conservative driving had kept the lead Porsche's consumption well within the limit. The car *could* afford to take on fuel three laps early.

Prior to the start, Porsche had carefully calculated the fuel consumption necessary to go the distance on the maximum permissible 2600 litres as being a rate of 107 litres/hr. With a metered fuel flow of 50 litres per minute from the pits dispenser and 2500 litres to take on board during the race, the car would be stationary in the pits for almost a full hour. Divide 2600 litres of fuel available by actual running time of 23 hours and you get a figure of 113 litres/minute — or 107 if you want a safety margin.

Having calculated the necessary consumption rate, Porsche provided digital cockpit readouts to allow drivers to keep an eye on the rate they were achieving. Ickx' and Bell's careful driving had kept their figures well below 107 and left both complaining that this "race" was more like an economy run! The average speed of their car varied by less than 1km/hr throughout the last five hours of darkness!

The pace of the No1 car certainly *was* cooled after the second pitstop. Neither of its highly experienced drivers had been unduly concerned when the Holbert/Haywood car, driven more agressively, went past during the night; Ickx and Bell became firmly established in the lead when both sister cars hit minor problems.

The American-crewed car lost the lead at 12.30am when Haywood reached over to check the door latch — and the door flew off into the night. That cost 20 minutes in the pits. Later the car stopped for repairs to a faulty wheel bearing and yet again for a front suspension rebuild, the bearing problem having caused suspected damage. The unlucky 956 had dropped as low as ninth overall, 21 laps behind, by 8.00am on Sunday morning. By this stage Jurgen Barth, Porsche factory test driver and Le Mans veteran (he has taken part in every race since '71, winning with Ickx and Haywood in '77) had been drafted in to reinforce the driving strength.

By breakfast time, the No2 956 had lost two laps to the leader thanks to a couple of unscheduled overnight stops, the first to cure a faulty rev limiter, the second to fit a new filter in the fuel line. But now, at 8.00am, all three cars were running like trains. Peter Falk could again report, "no problems", in stark contrast to every other Team Manager still in the pitlane. The repercussions of that could not be fully appreciated until Sunday lunchtime, by which time, although the hard trying third 956 had only made up two laps of its massive 21 lap deficit to the leader, it had nevertheless moved into third overall.

With half an hour to run, at 3.30pm on Sunday, the three Stuttgart steamrollers were able proudly to line up 1-2-3, in numerical order *and* order on the road, to **cruise** home to a triumphant finish. But the cars never quite made that triumphant finish — as they approached the start/finish area for the last time the crowd swarmed onto the track, completely blocking it.

This year there weren't sufficient gendarmes to restrain the masses — another economy measure! Thus it was that Ickx and Bell, notching up sixth and third wins respectively, were credited with 359 laps, rather than 360, at an average of 204.128kph — faster than their 1981 winning average despite all the economy measures. They also won the ACO's prize for the Thermal Index of

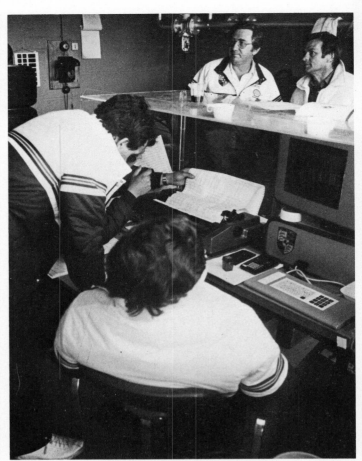

Porsche's Mission Control (above) masterminded a clean sweep, the first non-Porsche home being the Prancing Horse Farm Ferrari (right).

THE MIRAGE DISAPPEARS

MARIO ANDRETTI had two clear goals in mind as he sat on the grid, awaiting the start of the 50th Anniversary Le Mans 24 Hour race: to match Graham Hill's feat of winning the World Championship, the Indianapolis 500 and Le Mans 24 Hours and to match the feat of the Rosiers in 1950, by making his win a family one. Sharing the car with the 1978 World Champion and 1969 Indy 500 winner was son Mike, just up from karting and coping well with the 200mph Harley Cluxton entered Mirage M12 — lapping almost as fast as dad. Sitting on the fifth row, where the car had qualified despite a clutch problem, and with the knowledge that he had a strong back up team headed by former Aston Martin, Ford and Gulf Porsche Team Manager John Horsman, Andretti could feel justifiably hopeful of his prospects. But just minutes before the off, his dreams were shattered by officials insisting that the car be pushed to the paddock, excluded due to a technical infringement.

It was the first Andretti knew of the infringement, to which the team had been alerted at 2.40pm — less than one and a half hours before the start. The oil coolers were positioned behind the gearbox, a clear breach of the technical regulations. It hadn't been pointed out at pre race scrutineering, but the emphasis there is on safety not technical conformity, the Stewards explained — the onus is on the entrant to ensure that his car is legal. Full technical conformity is checked post race. But the team having failed to respond to the 2.40pm warning, the car never got as far as starting it.

The Mirage was checked (above right), given the seal of approval (right) and then denied the chance to race (below right).

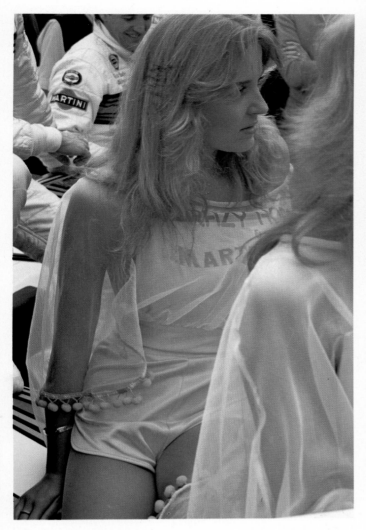

There were attractions (above) other than the vaunted Porsche v Ford battle which fizzled out as the Fords (the Ludwig/Surer C100 is above right) fell by the wayside.

Efficiency.

The Porsche 956 had certainly proved itself to be an effective, efficient weapon. The last 1-2-3 scored by a manufacturer in a World Championship race was by Ferrari at Daytona in 1965. What's more, Porsche cars were also fourth and fifth overall at Le Mans 1982. The meeting wasn't only a good weekend's work for Porsche's most highly prized European salesmen, it also saw a job very well done by the company's leading American salesman, IMSA GT frontrunner John Fitzpatrick. He brought a brand new 'Moby Dick' style Porsche 935 home in fourth overall.

San Diego resident, ex-patriot Brit, Fitzpatrick teamed up with former BMW flag waver David Hobbs (another ex-patriot, of course) and took delivery of a Reinhold Joest built tubular frame 935 (in the style of the factory 'whale' of 1979) for the meeting. Fitz's backer, J.David, had requested a Porsche be used for the event and with no Group C cars available the English former IMSA Champion reckoned that a Moby Dick was the next best thing, quick on the straight and reliable. "Those DFL cars will never last, so we should be able to do well . . ."

Sure enough, the Joest built car ran sweetly throughout Saturday afternoon/evening and on into the early hours of Sunday morning. "Like a clock" Hobbs mused as he watched it trundle past. The only delays of note had been when Fitz missed a pit call and ended up pushing the car home from the Ford chicane, and when Hobbs had been kept in the pit lane for five and a half minutes during the clearing up process after someone else's shunt. He should have joined the train behind the pace car, but the pace car never came past . . .

By half distance the Fitz machine had got into the top six, thanks to the fragility of the faster Group C cars, and hopes ran high in the Tim Schenken run pit. Alas, at 6.15am Fitz brought the car in sounding rough, and a blown head gasket looked to spell the end of a highly encouraging performance. But with commendable initiative, the mechanics managed to isolate number three cylinder and keep the car running on five cylinders.

Fitzpatrick/Hobbs kept going strongly enough to pick up fourth overall, first in class; a magnificent achievement which provided some consolation for Joest, whose Group C machine lost a potential third place (splitting the works cars) when it retired close to the finish.

Both Joest and arch rival Kremer entered a one-off Porsche based Group C cars for the event. Kremer went for a strikingly shaped 936 derivative with a 2826cc 935 twin-turbo motor mated to a five-speed gearbox, Joest for a more conservative looking 936 derivative with a 936 2517cc twin-turbo mated to a four-speed gearbox. The major difference between the two cars was in the amount of development they had been given — Joest's had raced at Monza, Silverstone and Nürburgring, Kremer's was new for the event.

The Joest 936J, in the hands of former Le Mans winner Bob Wollek and the Belgian long distance specialists, the Martin brothers, Jean-Michele and Philippe, qualified on the second row, just a fraction slower than the 'well-within-potential' pacesetting factory Porsches while the Kremer C-K5, in the hands of Americans Danny Ongais, Ted Field and Bill Whittington, was some six seconds slower. A bigger difference came in the relative race performances — the Kremer car retired during the second hour with driveshaft failure, while the Joest machine went on and on and on . . .

The performance of the 936J was most commendable. It kept the works cars on their toes throughout the hours of darkness, when all the other C-car opposition crumbled. The engine began to misfire as dawn came, but with two hours to go the Belga-backed machine still held a three lap advantage over the third Rothmans car and had sufficient speed to keep it at bay. Then the engine went bang.

So it was, that of 29 Group C cars which started the race, only three finished in a competitive state and only six finished at all. In stark contrast to the fragility of the new generation, 18 cars of the old Group 5/IMSA GT 'Silhouette' generation started the race and nine finished. Highest placed of them was, of course, the Fitzpatrick 935, and this was followed home by second in the IMSA GT class Kremer 935K3 of Danny Snobeck/Francois Servanin/René Metge, also running on less than six cylinders. Fifth overall, its performance provided some cheer for the Kremer brothers.

The highest non-Porsche at the finish was another IMSA GT entry, the Ferrari 512BB of the Prancing Horse Farm Racing stable, crewed by journalist Pierre Dieudonne/Carson Baird/Jean-Paul Liebert, which came home sixth overall. In eighth overall, the British 935K3 of John Cooper/Paul Smith/Claude Bourgoignie won the Group 5 class, having dropped back from a potential top six finish with turbo maladies on Sunday morning. Another strong IMSA GT showing had been posted by another 512BB, the NART entry for Alain Cudini/John Morton/John Paul Snr. This car vied overnight with the Fitzpatrick car for the IMSA GT lead and looked set to take

the class until it expired a few hours from home.

Porsche and Ferrari, the most successful marques in the history of Le Mans, carved up the top nine places among themselves, with just one exception, in the form of the seventh placed Aston Martin engined Nimrod entered by Viscount Downe and sponsored by Pace Petroleum. This was a semi-works entry — a works Nimrod also started the race, likewise powered by a 5.3-litre V8, good for around 550bhp.

The major drawback of the Bulldog British Nimrod-Astons, flat bottom, Lola T70 descended cars, penned by Eric Broadley, was one of weight — both cars tipped the scales at something in excess of 1000 kilos. On the Mulsanne the works car (Tiff Needell/Geoff Lees/Bob Evans) topped 205mph but the Downe machine (Ray Mallock/Mike Salmon/Simon Phillips) was some 10mph slower. However, early in the race, Needell had cause to regret his extra helping of top speed. The car started fishtailing away from the slight, flat out Mulsanne kink and the oscillations, caused by a deflating tyre, got worse and worse until the inevitable happened and the Nimrod struck the barrier a hefty blow. Thankfully, Needell escaped unharmed, no doubt due to the car's inherent strength.

That same strength saw the other weighty example pound its way up the lap chart from a lowly 23rd position on the grid. With six hours run, it was in the top six and as midnight came and went the Nimrod continued its steady progress, battleship sturdy. By dawn it was in fourth place. Third looked on the cards when the Joest 936's engine went flat but shortly after the 20-hour mark the Aston V8 itself went off song.

The electrics were changed, but to no avail — the engine got worse and the car started losing places. Eventually, with just two hours to run, the engine died altogether but thankfully Mallock was able to coax it back into life, to get back to the pit where a change of fuel pressure relief valve allowed the car to struggle on. Victor Gauntlett — Chairman of the sponsoring Pace Petroleum company and a Director of Aston Martin and Nimrod Racing Automobiles — swore that he would carry it home if it couldn't make the finish under its own steam, but that wasn't necessary — the car limped into seventh place.

At least one of the two Aston engined C cars had finished among the Porsches and Ferraris — the highest places of the numerous Ford engined C car entries was tenth overall. The race was billed as 'Porsche versus Ford', but by half distance it was no contest. There were 18 Ford entries, the majority running the latest version of the Cosworth DFV engine, the DFL in 3.3 or 3.9-litre forms. However, there were serious doubts about the effectiveness of the DFL due to a suspected vibration problem, which was to manifest itself to a frightening degree . . .

Keith Green, Manager of the Rondeau team which won Le Mans in 1980, suggested that at least one of his three works entries should run a conventional 3.0 DFV but all the drivers insisted on going for glory. The 3.9 DFL offered an extra 60bhp, essential to match the potential pace of the turbocharged Porsches. Thus the

Francois Migault/Gordon Spice/Xavier Lapeyre Rondeau, the Jean Rondeau/Jean Ragnotti Rondeau, the Jean-Pierre Jaussaud/Henri Pescarolo Rondeau and the two Zakspeed run works Ford C100s for Klaus Ludwig/Marc Surer and Manfred Winkelhock/Klaus Neidzweidz all ran DFLs, as did two Lola T610s for Guy Edwards/Rupert Keegan (works car) and Brian Redman/Jim Adams/Ralph Cooke (Cooke Racing). These cars spearheaded the Ford challenge.

Of the three marques, only the Rondeaus were flat bottomed, but only the Lola, its aerodynamics developed in the Williams wind tunnel at Didcot, England, could match the speed of the Porsches on the Mulsanne. Rondeau had an appalling practice but the Fords and the Lolas showed a good turn of speed and in the early stages the Edwards/Keegan car had a good run, dicing with the Porsches. Alas, things started going wrong in the second hour when the Lola's doors started belling and it dropped right out of contention, eventually to retire with head gasket failure.

The second Lola retired during the third hour, out of petrol on the circuit due to a simple miscalculation. An hour and a half later the Ford C100 of former Le Mans winner Ludwig stopped with terminal electrical problems. This had been the quickest Ford engined car in

---

Rondeau didn't even come close to repeating their race-winning performance of 1980, the top finishers being the Christian Bussi car in 15th place and the Primagaz car (following, below) in 10th. Three other cars retired within four laps of the 150-lap mark.

TREADING NEW GROUND

Racing cars don't run on treaded tyres unless it's raining. Everyone knows that. The smooth, wide racing slick has become such a familiar part of the contemporary scene that everyday treaded tyres look somehow out of place. But out of place or not, such tyres appeared on two Porsche 924s, entered (with Porsche backing) by BF Goodrich. BF Goodrich was at Le Mans to prove that its everyday Comp T/A High Tech radials could run trouble free through the rigours of the classic endurance marathon, and prove just that the American tyre giant did. The cars were a pair of Carrera turbos, prepared by Brumos Racing and by Herman + Miller in the USA, and supported by Stuttgart. They were, of course, the only cars in the race running on street tyres and not surprisingly needed to use slicks in practice to lap fast enough to qualify for the event. But once in the race, outright speed was of less importance and the Goodrich high performance road radials kept Jim Busby/Doc Bundy/Marcel Mignot circulating fast enough and long enough to win the poorly supported IMSA GT class in 16th position overall. Sadly, teammates Paul Miller/Patrick Bedard/Manfred Schurti retired after ten hours — ironically due to a wheel falling off!

June 19 schedule

8:00 PIT OPEN
9:00~11:00 COURSE OPEN
11:00 SIGN PIT OPEN
11:15~12:00 PRACTICE
2:45~3:30 ON TO GRID
3:00 ~~LAST EVERY:MG~~
3:40 ALL WORK ON GRID STOP
3:54 ROLLING START

16:00 SUNDAY - CHAMPAGNE
?

The Mazda pit-crew showed quiet optimism with their weekend time-table (top, far left) and one car (near left, forsaking the café) survived to take 6th place in the IMSA GTX category and 14th overall. Both Stratagraph-entered Camaros also rumbled through to the 24th hour, although the second car (mid-way through a lurid spin at Tertre Rouge, left) was not classified, having spent too much of its race in the pits with major gearbox maladies. At least the Hagan team enjoyed their weekend, which is probably more than could be said for Sauber (Brun/Muller, below left, at Mulsanne) whose two cars managed just 131 laps between them. High in the weekend's list of hard luck stories must be the Belga Porsche (below, with Garretson's March) which ran strongly until near the end but was eventually unclassified as it was not running at the finish. Kremer's entry (bottom left) lasted just 25 laps but there were few worries to spoil the sleep of the younger Porsche personnel (bottom right).

practice, despite a relative lack of top speed, and for five hours it had kept with the leaders (which included its sister car). However, the Winkelhock/Neidzweidz machine had been in clutch bothers from the second hour onwards and its engine expired, too, after six hours.

Things were looking bleak for Ford, particularly as both of the neat, fast DFL powered Saubers from Germany had also fallen by the wayside — Walter Brun/Sigi Muller Jnr with starter motor failure and Hans Stuck/Dieter Quester/Jean-Louis Schlesser with engine mount breakage. The DFL vibration problem was taking a heavy toll.

As darkness shrouded the circuit of La Sarthe, only the Rondeau team carried the hopes of Ford. The first Rondeau fell by the wayside soon after midnight — this was the Jaussaud car into which

Pescarolo had moved, switching with Rondeau, the Ragnotti car having had an unproven engine installed after practice. Pescarolo was hoping to increase his lead in the Drivers' Championship. He thus hopped back into the Ragnotti car which was making up ground after early problems. All the while the Migault car was up with the leading Porsches, keeping the hopes of Ford, and of the partisan crowd, alive. But by 2.15am it was all over — the Migault car had coasted to a halt at Arnage and the Ragnotti machine had joined it there moments later, both victims of transducer ignition trigger failure.

So at the end of the day, it was only the semi-works Rondeau of Pierre Yver/Lucien Guitteny/Bruno Sotty, with a 3.3-litre DFL fitted, which kept Ford in the top 10, limping home with engine problems . . . Only one other Ford powered Group C car saw the finish — the

The Cooke Racing-BP entered Porsche 935K3 (left) of Snobeck, Servanin and Metge trails flames through the gathering dusk on its way to an eventual fifth place overall and second in the IMSA GTX class to the John Fitzpatrick Racing 935. As the survivors settle into the rhythm of the race and night falls (below) Le Mans takes on a unique and very special atmosphere.

THE BRITISH ARE COMING!

private Rondeau of Christian Bussi/Pascal Witmeur/Bernard de Dryver which had a 3.0-litre DFV in it.

Mind you, Group C unreliability wasn't confined to the Ford powered cars: the two rapid WM-Peugeots fell by the wayside, as did the two March-Chevrolets, not forgetting the Joest and Kremer cars and the unlucky Nimrod. And appalling reliability wasn't confined to Group C — the two fleet Group 6 Martini-Lancias, which on paper had a chance of outright victory, were both sitting by the side of the track within 15 minutes of the start! All of which went to underline the excellence of the cars from Stuttgart and of the men who prepared and drove them. As four time Le Mans winner Olivier Gendebien said before the race: "To win Le Mans is simple. You need a good car, fast and trustworthy. A good team. Drivers patient and mechanically sympathetic — and preferably Belgian . . . "

The massive contingent of British spectators who regularly attend the Le Mans 24-Hour race have recently had only one real hero — Derek Bell. But in 1982 there was more for them to cheer about, thanks to the return of Aston Martin to La Sarthe. It had been almost two decades since the British manufacturer had taken a serious interest in international racing, but racing had always been in the blood of the marque which won the World Sportscar Championship in 1959. The 1982 return to active competition was brought about through the enthusiasm of Aston Martin Lagonda Executive Chairman Victor Gauntlett and Aston Martin dealer Robin Hamilton.

Gauntlett is a co-founder of Pace Petroleum, an independent British company that became successful enough to buy a half share in Aston Martin Lagonda, while Hamilton is a dealer who has in the past entered production based Aston V8s for the 24-Hour classic. Between them, Gauntlett and Hamilton founded Nimrod Racing Automobiles Ltd, a long term business project involved in the manufacture, running and sale of cars and services to motor sport, and with the shorter term aim of winning Le Mans with an Aston V8 engined machine.

The 5340cc Aston V8 production engine was developed by the factory into a 580bhp racing unit, suitable for endurance races, and Nimrod was given exclusive rights to use the engine. The team commissioned Eric Broadley of Lola Cars (designer of the T70 and the current T610) to produce the monocoque tub and suspension and went into the wind tunnel to design a slippery body for good fuel economy and high top speed. 225mph was forecast but neither of the two Le Mans entries exceeded 210mph. Nevertheless, the race performances of both the works car and the private entry of Aston Martin Owners Club President Viscount Downe was most encouraging, Downe's Pace backed entry finishing seventh overall despite dire engine maladies towards the end of the event, which dropped it from a steady fourth place. Unhappily, the works car crashed due to a puncture as it was moving up through the field from a poor grid position. Overall, though, it was encouraging for a first year's performance, and Aston Martin enthusiasts could face the future with justifiable optimism.

1 Porsche 956 2649cc t/c (3708cc) GC
Porsche System
Ickx/Bell 1st, 359 laps

2 Porsche 956 2649cc t/c (3708cc) GC
Porsche System
Mass/Schuppan 2nd, 356 laps

3 Porsche 956 2649cc t/c (3708cc) GC
Porsche System
Haywood/Holbert/Barth 3rd, 340 laps

79 Porsche 935 2676cc t/c (3747cc) IGTX
John Fitzpatrick Racing
Fitzpatrick/Hobbs 4th, 329 laps

78 Porsche 935K3 2800cc t/c (3920cc) IGTX
Cooke Racing-BP
Snobeck/Servanin/Metge 5th, 325 laps

LE MANS 1982 -
THE CARS

70 Ferrari 512BB 4942cc   IGTX
Prancing Horse Farm Racing
Dieudonne/Baird/Liebert   6th, 322 laps

77 Porsche 935K3 2800cc t/c (3920cc)   IGTX
Garretson Developments
Verney/Garretson/Ratcliff   11th, 299 laps

87 Porsche 924GTR 2008cc t/c (2811cc)   IGT
BF Goodrich Co
Busby/Bundy   16th, 272 laps

32 Nimrod NRAC2-Aston Martin 5340cc   GC
Viscount Downe-Pace Petroleum
Mallock/Phillips/Salmon   7th, 317 laps

66 Lancia Beta MC 1425cc t/c (1995cc)   G5
Jean-Marie Lemerle   12th
Lemerle/Cohen-Olivar/Castellano   295 laps

81 Chevrolet Camaro 5800cc   IGT
Stratagraph Inc
Hagan/Felton   17th, 269 laps

60 Porsche 935K3 3121cc t/c (4370cc)   G5
Charles Ivey Engineering
Cooper/Smith/Bourgoignie   8th, 316 laps

90 Porsche 934 2995cc t/c (4192cc)   G4
Richard Cleare
Dron/Cleare/Jones   13th, 291 laps

61 BMW M1 3497cc   G5
Total   18th
Ennequin/Gabriel/Gasparetti   259 laps

72 Ferrari 512BB 4942cc   IGTX
North American Racing Team
Cudini/Morton/Paul Sr   9th, 306 laps

82 Mazda 254 2616cc rotary (2616cc)   IGTX
Mazdaspeed
Terada/Yorino/Moffat   14th, 282 laps

80 Chevrolet Camaro 5800cc   IGT
Stratagraph Inc   unclassified
Williams/Brooks/McGriff   141 laps

25 Rondeau M382-Ford 2998cc   GC
Primagaz
Yver/Sotty/Guitteny   10th, 306 laps

38 Rondeau M382-Ford 3299cc   GC
Christian Bussi   15th
Bussi/Witmeur/de Dryver   279 laps

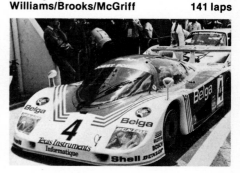

4 Porsche 936C 2516cc t/c (3523cc)   GC
Belga Team-Jöst Racing
Wollek/Martin/Martin   retd. 320 laps

50TH GRAND PRIX D'ENDURANCE, 24-HEURES DU MANS

Le Mans: 19-20 June 1982

24 hours duration over 8.47-mile circuit

RESULTS

1	Jacky Ickx/Derek Bell	Porsche 956-2.6 turbo	GC	359 laps (3044.15 miles)
2	Jochen Mass/Vern Schuppan	Porsche 956-2.6 turbo	GC	356 laps
3	Hurley Haywood/Al Holbert/Jurgen Barth	Porsche 956-2.6 turbo	GC	340 laps
4	John Fitzpatrick/David Hobbs	Porsche 935K4-2.6 turbo	IGTX	329 laps
5	Dany Snobeck/Francois Servanin/René Metge	Porsche 935K3-2.8 turbo	IGTX	325 laps
6	Pierre Dieudonne/Carson Baird/Jean-Paul Liebert	Ferrari 512BB-4.9	IGTX	322 laps
7	Ray Mallock/Mike Salmon/Simon Phillips	Nimrod NRA C2-Aston Martin 5.3	GC	317 laps
8	John Cooper/Paul Smith/Claude Bourgoignie	Porsche 935K3-2.8 turbo	G5	316 laps
9	Alain Cudini/John Morton/John Paul Sr	Ferrari 512BB-4.9	IGTX	306 laps
10	Pierre Yver/Bruno Sotty/Lucien Guitteny	Rondeau M382-Ford 3.0	GC	306 laps
11	Anny-Charlotte Verney/Bob Garretson/Ray Ratcliffe	Porsche 935K3-2.8 turbo	IGTX	299 laps
12	Jean-Marie Lemerle/Max Cohen-Olivar/Joe Castellano	Lancia Beta Monte Carlo-1.4 turbo	G5	295 laps
13	Tony Dron/Richard Cleare/Richard Jones	Porsche 934-3.3 turbo	G4	291 laps
14	Yoshiro Terada/Takashi Yorino/Allan Moffat	Mazda 254-2.7	IGTX	282 laps
15	Christian Bussi/Bernard de Dryver/Pascal Witmeur	Rondeau M382-Ford 3.0	GC	279 laps
16	Jim Busby/Doc Bundy	Porsche 924GTR-2.0 turbo	IGT	272 laps
17	Billy Hagan/Gene Felton	Chevrolet Camaro-5.7	IGT	269 laps
18	Roland Ennequin/Franco Gasparetti/Michel Gabriel	BMW M1-3.5	G5	259 laps

Dick Brooks/Herschell McGriff/Thomas Williams (Chevrolet Camaro-5.7) were running at the finish but were unclassified, having covered insufficient distance. Bob Wollek/Phillipe Martin/Jean-Michel Martin (Porsche 936C-2.5 turbo) completed 322 laps but were unclassified as they were not running at the finish. Steve O'Rourke/Nick Mason/Richard Down (BMW M1-3.5) completed 266 laps but were unclassified as they were not running at the finish.

Fastest lap: Pescarolo, 3m 36.9s (140.5mph)
Winner's average speed: 126.84mph

RETIREMENTS

Emilio de Villota/Alain de Cadenet/Desiré Wilson	Grid Plaza S1-Ford 3.9	GC	7 laps engine
Bob Akin/David Cowart/Kenper Miller	Porsche 935-2.8 turbo	IGTX	15 laps out of fuel
Ted Field/Danny Ongais/Dale Whittington	Kremer C82K5-Porsche 2.8 turbo	GC	25 laps engine
Bobby Rahal/Skeeter McKitterick/Jim Trueman	March 82G-Chevrolet 5.7	GC	28 laps split fuel tank
Brian Redman/Jim Adams/Ralph Kent-Cooke	Lola T610-Ford 3.9	GC	28 laps out of fuel
Edgar Doren/Antonio Contreras/Billy Sprowls	Porsche 935K3-3.0 turbo	G5	39 laps engine
Preston Henn/Denis Morin/Randy Lanier	Ferrari 512BB-4.9	IGTX	43 laps engine
Michel Lateste/Hubert Striebig/Jacques Heuclin	URD C81-BMW 3.5	GC	45 laps engine
Sigi Muller Jr/Walter Brun	Sauber SHS C6-Ford 3.9	GC	55 laps starter motor
Geoff Lees/Bob Evans/Tiff Needell	Nimrod NRA C2-Aston Martin 5.3	GC	55 laps accident
Mike Wilds/Ian Harrower/Francois Duret	De Cadenet Lola MM-Ford 3.0	GC	56 laps out of fuel
John Sheldon/Martin Birrane/Neil Crang	Chevron B36-Ford 2.0	G6	57 laps gearbox
Claude Ballot-Lena/Herve Regout/Jean-Claude Andruet	Ferrari 512BB-4.9	IGTX	57 laps out of fuel
Klaus Ludwig/Marc Surer/Manfred Winkelhock	Ford C100-3.9	GC	67 laps electrical problem
Manfred Winkelhock/Klaus Niedzwiedz/Klaus Ludwig	Ford C100-3.9	GC	71 laps engine
Guy Edwards/Rupert Keegan/Nick Faure	Lola T610-Ford 3.9	GC	72 laps head gasket
Hans Stuck/Jean-Louis Schlesser/Dieter Quester	Sauber SHS C6-Ford 3.9	GC	76 laps engine mount
Richard Lloyd/Andy Rouse	Porsche 924GTR-2.0 turbo	IGT	77 laps disqualified
Yves Courage/Jean-Philippe Grand/Michel Dubois	Cougar CO1-Ford 3.3	GC	78 laps driveshaft
Patrick Neve/Jeff Wood/Eje Elgh	March 82G-Chevrolet 5.7	GC	78 laps electrical problem
Chris Craft/Eliseo Salazar	Dome RC82-Ford 3.3	GC	85 laps chassis
Michele Alboreto/Teo Fabi/Rolf Stommelen	Lancia Martini-1.4 turbo	G6	92 laps engine
Tony Garcia/Fred Stiff/Albert Naon	BMW M1-3.5	IGT	104 laps engine
Jean-Pierre Jaussaud/Henri Pescarolo	Rondeau M382-Ford 3.3	GC	111 laps engine
Guy Frequelin/Robert Dorchy/Alain Couderc	WM P82-Peugeot 2.8 turbo	GC	112 laps accident
Michel Pignard/Jean-Daniel Raulet/Didier Theys	WM P82-Peugeot 2.8 turbo	GC	127 laps gearbox
Manfred Schurti/Patrick Bedard/Paul Miller	Porsche 924 GTR-2.0 turbo	IGT	128 laps lost wheel
Claude Haldi/Riccardo Teran/Francois Hesnault	Porsche 935-2.8 turbo	IGTX	141 laps differential
Jean Rondeau/Jean Ragnotti/Philippe Alliot	Rondeau M382-Ford 3.9	GC	146 laps engine
Jacky Haran/Herve Poulain/Vivian Candy	Rondeau M379C-Ford 3.0	GC	149 laps engine
Gordon Spice/Francois Migault/Xavier Lapeyre	Rondeau M382-Ford 3.9	GC	150 laps engine
Piercarlo Ghinzani/Riccardo Patrese/Hans Heyer	Lancia Martini-1.4 turbo	G6	152 laps distributor
Chuck Nicholson/Tom Walkinshaw/Peter Lovett	Mazda 254-2.7	IGTX	180 laps engine
Bernard Salem/Giulio Giudici/Thierry Perier	Lancia Beta Monte Carlo-1.4 turbo	G5	219 laps disqualified
Steve O'Rourke/Richard Down/Nick Mason	BMW M1-3.5	IGTX	266 laps engine
Bob Wollek/Philippe Martin/Jean-Michel Martin	Porsche 936C-2.5 turbo	GC	320 laps engine

THE GRID

Ickx-Bell
Porsche 956
3m 28.40s

Wollek-JM Martin-Ph Martin
Porsche 936C
3m 30.65s

Ghinzani-Patrese-Heyer
Lancia Martini
3m 31.78s

Stuck-Schlesser-Quester
Sauber SHS C6-Ford
3m 33.25s

Andretti Sr-Andretti Jr
Mirage M12-Ford
3m 37.09s

Winkelhock-Niedzwiedz-Ludwig
Ford C100
3m 38.02s

Dorchy-Frequelin-Couderc
WM P82-Peugeot
3m 39.58s

Brun-Muller-Stuck
Sauber SHS C6-Ford
3m 40.57s

de Villota-de Cadenet-Wilson
Grid Plaza S1-Ford
3m 42.77s

Doren-Contreras-Sprowls
Porsche 935 K3
3m 44.05s

Cooper-Smith-Bourgoignie
Porsche 935 K3
3m 44.92s

Mallock-Salmon-Phillips
Nimrod-Aston Martin NRA C2
3m 46.34s

Striebig-Heuclin-Lateste
URD C81-BMW
3m 47.62s

Fitzpatrick-Hobbs
Porsche 935
3m 48.50s

Courage-Grand-Dubois
Cougar C01-Ford
3m 51.62s

Akin-Cowart-Miller
Porsche 935
3m 52.31s

Hagan-Felton-Williams
Chevrolet Camaro
3m 52.59s

Yver-Guitteny-Sotty
Rondeau M379C-Ford
3m 52.69s

Cudini-Morton-Paul Sr
Ferrari 512BB
3m 54.07s

Gasparetti-Ennequin-Gabriel
BMW M1
3m 55.40s

Ballot-Lena-Andruet-Regout
Ferrari 512BB
3m 56.80s

Verney-Garretson-Ratcliff
Porsche 935 K3
3m 58.84s

Wilds-Duret-Harrower
de Cadenet LM/DRA-Ford
4m 00.29s

Cohen-Olivar-Lemerle-Castellano
Lancia Beta Monte Carlo
4m 02.58s

Birrane-Crang-Sheldon
Chevron B36-Ford
4m 04.30s

Henn-Lanier-Morin
Ferrari 512BB
4m 07.32s

Walkinshaw-Lovett-Nicholson
Mazda 254
4m 11.29s

Busby-Bundy-Schurti
Porsche 924GTR
4m 14.07s

Mass-Schuppan
Porsche 956
3m 29.32s

Alboreto-Fabi-Stommelen
Lancia Martini
3m 31.42s

Ludwig-Surer-Winkelhock
Ford C100
3m 32.50s

Field-Ongais-Whittington
Kremer Porsche C82 K5
3m 37.01s

Edwards-Keegan-Faure
Lola T610-Ford
3m 37.60s

Pignard-Raulet-Theys
WM P82-Peugeot
3m 38.06s

Holbert-Haywood-Barth
Porsche 956
3m 39.85s

Migault-Spice
Rondeau M382-Ford
3m 40.71s

Redman-Cooke-Adams
Lola T610-Ford
3m 43.06s

Craft-Salazar
Dome RC82-Ford
3m 44.12s

Rondeau-Jaussaud-Alliot
Rondeau M382-Ford
3m 46.00s

Wood-Elgh-Neve
March 82G-Chevrolet
3m 51.70s

Lees-Needell-Evans
Nimrod-Aston Martin NRA C2
3m 48.17s

Haldi-Teran-Hesnault
Porsche 935
3m 50.64s

Rahal-Trueman-McKitterick
March 82G-Chevrolet
3m 51.70s

Haran-Candy-Poulain
Rondeau M379C-Ford
3m 52.36s

Snobeck-Servanin-Metge
Porsche 935 K3
3m 52.68s

Bussi-Witmeur-de Dryver
Rondeau M382-Ford
3m 52.90s

Pescarolo-Ragnotti-Alliot
Rondeau M382-Ford
3m 54.81s

Dieudonne-Baird-Liebert
Ferrari 512BB
3m 56.52s

Miller-Bedard-Schurti
Porsche 924GTR
3m 58.65s

O'Rourke-Down-Mason
BMW M1
4m 00.23s

McGriff-Brooks-Williams
Chevrolet Camaro
4m 00.34s

Cleare-Dron
Porsche 934
4m 04.08s

Terada-Yorino-Moffat
Mazda 254
4m 04.74s

Garcia-Stiff-Naon
BMW M1
4m 10.02s .

Giudici-Salam-Perrier
Lancia Beta Monte Carlo
4m 12.79s

Raymond Touroul-Alain Gadel-Jean-Yves Gadel (Porsche 930-3.0 turbo) GB, 4m 18.81s and Richard Lloyd-Andy Rouse (Porsche 924GTR-2.0 turbo) IGT, 4m 20.81s, did not qualify. Andretti Sr-Andretti Jr (Mirage M12-Ford) were not allowed to start.

62 BMW M1 3497cc **IGTX**
EMKA Productions Ltd
O'Rourke/Down/Mason retd. 266 laps

83 Mazda 254 2616cc rotary (2616cc) **IGT**
Mazdaspeed retd.
Nicholson/Walkinshaw/Lovett 180 laps

65 Lancia Beta MC 1425cc t/c (1995cc) **G5**
Thierry Perrier disqualified
Perrier/Salam/Giudici 219 laps

50 Lancia Martini 1425cc t/c (1995cc) **G6**
Martini Racing
Patrese/Ghinzani/Heyer retd. 152 laps

11 Rondeau M382-Ford 3955cc **GC**
Jean Rondeau
Migault/Spice/Lapeyre retd. 150 laps

26 Rondeau M379C-Ford 2999cc   GC
Jacky Haran
Haran/Poulain/Candy   retd. 149 laps

10 WM P82-Peugeot 2850cc t/c (3990cc)   GC
Esso   accident
Frequelin/Dorchy/Couderc   112 laps

14 March 82G-Chevrolet 5835cc   GC
March Racing
Elgh/Wood/Neve   retd, 78 laps

12 Rondeau M382-Ford 3955cc   GC
Otis-Rondeau
Rondeau/Ragnotti/Alliot   retd. 146 laps

24 Rondeau M382-Ford 3299cc   GC
Otis-Rondeau
Jaussaud/Pescarolo   retd, 111 laps

35 Cougar C01-Ford 3299cc   GC
Yves Courage
Courage/Grand/Dubois   retd, 78 laps

75 Porsche 935 2994cc t/c (4192cc)   GG5
Jöst Racing Team
Haldi/Teran/Hesnault   retd. 141 laps

85 BMW M1 3497cc   IGT
Tony Garcia
Garcia/Stiff/Naon   retd, 104 laps

84 Porsche 924GTR 1984cc t/c (2777cc)   IGT
Canon Cameras-GTi Engineering
Lloyd/Rouse/Allam   disqual., 77 laps

86 Porsche 924GTR 2008cc t/c (2811cc)   IGT
BF Goodrich Co
Miller/Bedard/Schurti   retd. 128 laps

51 Lancia Martini 1425cc t/c (1995cc)   G6
Martini Racing
Alboreto/Fabi/Stommelen   retd, 92 laps

20 Sauber SHS C6-Ford 3955cc   GC
BASF Cassetten Team GS Sport
Stuck/Schlesser/Quester   retd, 76 laps

9 WM P82-Peugeot 2850cc t/c (3990cc)   GC
Esso
Raulet/Pignard/Theys   retd. 127 laps

36 Dome RC82-Ford 3299cc   GC
Dome Co Ltd
Craft/Salazar   retd, 85 laps

16 Lola T610-Ford 3955cc   GC
Ultramar Team Lola
Edwards/Keegan/Faure   retd, 72 laps

7 Ford C100 3955cc   **GC**
Ford   retd.
Winkelhock/Niedzwiedz/Ludwig   71 laps

31 Nimrod NRAC2-Aston Martin 5340cc GC
Nimrod Racing Automobiles Ltd
Evans/Needell/Lees   accident, 55 laps

17 Lola T610-Ford 3955cc   **GC**
Cooke Racing-Malardeau
Cooke/Redman/Adams   retd, 28 laps

6 Ford C100 3955cc   **GC**
Ford
Ludwig/Surer/Winkelhock   retd, 67 laps

19 Sauber SHS C6-Ford 3955cc   **GC**
BASF Cassetten Team GS Sport
Brun/Muller   retd, 55 laps

29 March 82G-Chevrolet 5835cc   **GC**
Garretson Developments
Rahal/McKitterick/Trueman   retd, 28 laps

71 Ferrari 512BB 4942cc   **IGTX**
Charles Pozzi-Ferrari France
Ballot-Lena/Andruet   retd, 57 laps

30 URD C81-Ford 3497cc   **GC**
Michel Lateste
Lateste/Heuclin/Striebig   retd, 45 laps

5 Kremer C82K5 2826cc t/c (3956cc) GC
Porsche Kremer Racing
Field/Ongais/Whittington   retd, 25 laps

55 Chevron B36-Ford 1975cc   **G6**
Chevron Racing Cars
Birrane/Sheldon/Crang   retd, 57 laps

73 Ferrari 512BB 4942cc   **IGTX**
North American Racing Team
Henn/Lanier/Morin   retd, 43 laps

76 Porsche 935 2800cc t/c (3920cc)   **IGTX**
Bob Akin Motor Racing
Akin/Cowart/Miller   retd, 15 laps

39 de Cadenet LM/DRA-Ford 2993cc   **GC**
Dorset Racing Associates
Wilds/Duret/Harrower   retd, 56 laps

64 Porsche 935K3 2844cc t/c (3982cc)   **G5**
Edgar Dören
Dören/Sprowls/Contreras   retd, 39 laps

37 Grid Plaza S1-Ford 3299cc   **GC**
GRID Racing
Villota/de Cadenet/Wilson   retd, 7 laps

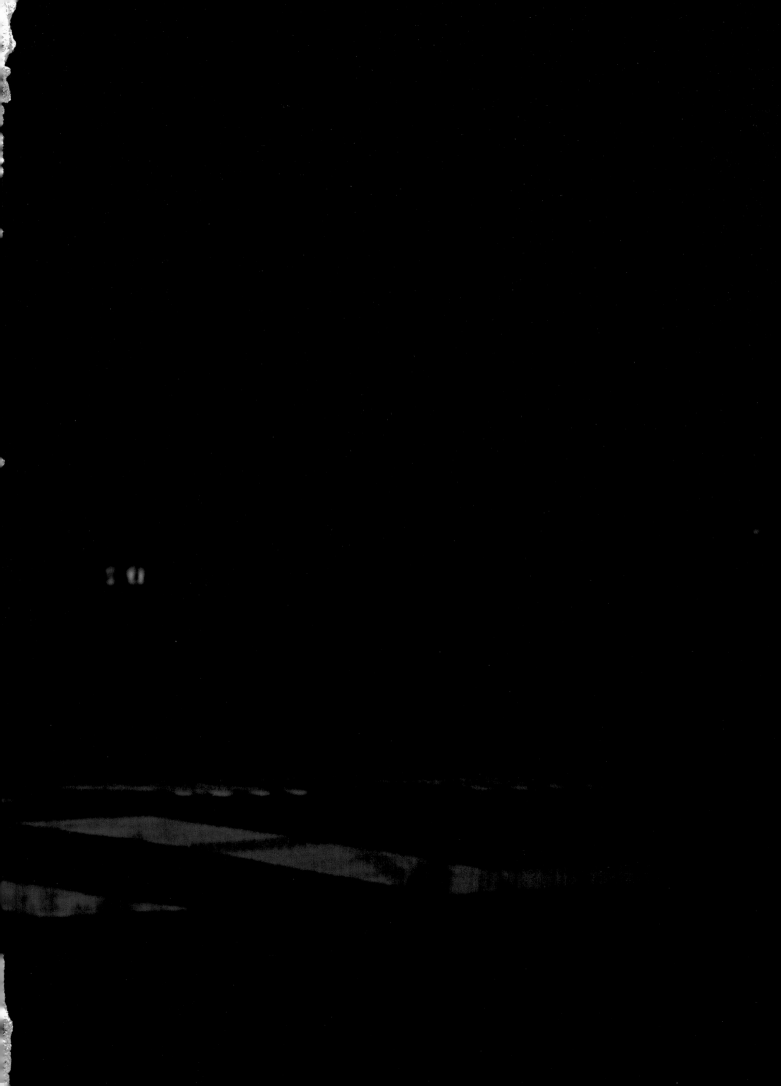

OUT OF THE DARK AGE?

The coming of Group C was widely heralded as the return of the great days in sports car racing, but although there is every possibility of a bright future, the new category had a very mixed start, as our correspondent explains.

IF the 1970s were endurance racing's dark ages, then 1982 was meant to be the start of its renaissance. Group C, the new fuel consumption formula for two-seat, fully enclosed sports cars, was designed by FISA to attract all the big names like Ford, Ferrari and Porsche back to long distance racing, using fuel economy as the carrot. The size of the fuel tank was restricted to 100 litres and the cars would only be allowed to make a certain number of stops to refuel. In six-hour or 1000km races, cars were to be allowed a maximum of five stops and in 24-hour races such as Le Mans, the limit was to be 25. Also, the rate of flow between the tank in the pits and the 100-litre tank in the car was to be restricted to 50 litres per minute, thereby ensuring that no car could refuel completely in less than two minutes. In theory. In actual fact, the rate of flow could be affected by such factors as the geography of the circuit and the gradient in the pit lane, and also depended on whether or not the car was jacked up during refuelling.

A Group C car may weigh no less than 800kg, must have two doors and two seats, and must be powered by an engine derived from a manufacturer who has already homologated a car in Group A or Group B. Its potential for ground effect is also strictly controlled, the regulations requiring a solid flat surface of specific dimensions beneath the chassis with any form of skirt system forbidden. These cars can score points in the World Endurance Championship for Manufacturers, but the ambiguous regulations also give the impression that Group B cars can score manufacturers' points as well. This led to confusion and an end-of-season dispute, but more of that later.

For 1982 only, FISA permitted cars from other groups, such as Group 5, Group 6 and IMSA, to compete in the WEC, but although these cars were required to meet the Group C fuel regulations, they were not eligible for the manufacturers' championship. However, their drivers, along with those of Group C cars, could score points in their own separate world series. This concession was made by FISA in the light of its delayed finalisation of the Group C regulations but, even so, there were so few completed cars by the end of April that races at Brands Hatch and Mugello had to be postponed until later in the season. The situation was aggravated by the difference in stature between the two world championships. Only Lancia (with its ineligible Group 6 Spyder) of the major manufacturers' was particularly interested in the drivers' championship, and most of the Group C teams aimed at Monza or Silverstone (both rounds of the manufacturers series), as occasions on which to make a début. These two features combined to make the WEC's scheduled first round on March 14 look impossibly optimistic.

The second round of the championship, the Pace Six Hours at Silverstone, then revealed perhaps the biggest flaw in the structure of the WEC. Being a *duration* event rather than a distance one, actually meant that after six hours the winning car would have covered something like 1170km. Virtually all the Group C cars were expected to have problems completing the event given their fuel consumption and the fact that all the cars were restricted to just five stops to refuel. But the problem was no more graphically illustrated than by the works Porsche 956, which made its début at Silverstone and qualified comfortably on pole position in 1m 16s. However, the amount of fuel it consumed to achieve that time revealed that a similar pace in the race would see it run out of petrol long before the six hours were up. Therefore, the 2.65-litre turbocharged engine was detuned, the boost pressure reduced and the car sent out to race, unable to lap within 10 seconds of its practice pace for fear of running out of petrol. Meanwhile, the Lancias, with their smaller, less powerful engines, fully skirted ground effects and lighter weight, ran rings round their more potent Group C rivals which were literally hamstrung by their own regulations. From the start, the "race" gradually degenerated into an economy run, boring for all concerned and especially confusing to the spectator who paid to see an event which would decide the fastest, strongest car and instead got a demonstration which only proved that Lancia travels further on 600 litres of fuel than Porsche. FISA, to its credit, has since responded positively to this problem and has announced that there will be no six-hour races in the WEC in future. Instead, the events will be of 24-hour, 12-hour or 1000km duration and the cars will not be restricted to a specific number of refuelling stops but to a more flexible maximum consumption. This at least will allow cars to stop when they want to and vary their speed if necessary between pit-stops to refuel. Needless to say, this quite substantial change to endurance racing tradition has been received in certain circles as proof positive that Porsche is manipulating the rule makers. However, as the Porsche engine, and indeed the 956 itself, is to become commercially available next season (along with a turbocharged version of the Ford DFL motor), everyone will have the opportunity to take the Germans on on equal terms.

At the end of the five round manufacturers' championship, Porsche had taken three Group C wins, at Silverstone, Le Mans and Spa-Francorchamps, with the French Rondeau *équipe* claiming first place in the other two, at Monza and the Nürburgring. Thanks to points scored by a private Rondeau at Le Mans, the Ford-powered cars went to the final round at Spa needing to finish fifth or higher in Group C to clinch the championship, *if* Porsche won the race. However, this was where the aforementioned anomaly in the regulations queered the pitch, for Porsche also claimed points scored by a Group B 911 Turbo at the Nürburgring. This brought its total to 75 points, five more than Rondeau, but as FISA claimed that Porsche had misunderstood the rules, the matter was not finally resolved until 13 October, more than a month after Spa. Then the FISA Executive Committee decided that although Porsche should be allowed to keep the 15 points in question, in future Group B cars could only score points towards their own GT championship, as had been FISA's original intention.

This was undoubtedly hard on Rondeau, all of whose points were at least scored by a Group C car, but there can be little question that the Porsche 956 was the real car of the championship. Simple, with a degree of ground effect, it was purpose-built to do the job and simply reflected the extent of Porsche's commitment to the championship. Its specification from race to race hardly altered, but at Le Mans the three race cars displayed longer, lower tail sections to increase speed on the daunting, crucial Mulsanne Straight. However, not even Porsche's season was perfect and there were problems at both Le Mans and Spa. But the fact that the German marque survived various set-backs during the 24-hour classic to emerge with a sensational one, two, three success, is what makes the marque so different from all others. Porsche was prepared for just about any mechanical eventuality and overcame misfires, fuel mixture problems and suspension bothers while most of its rivals dropped out one by one. The only thing an otherwise unmemorable 1982 Le Mans proved was that to finish first, first you have to finish.

Rondeau never wandered from the belief that the reliability of its cars, rather than sheer outright speed, was its strong point. Results tend to confirm this; at both Monza and the Nürburgring Rondeau was waiting to pick up the pieces of another team's failure. However, at the start of the season, there was every indication that the M382C design was not all that strong. At Silverstone, the car suffered two identical suspension failures and then at the Nürburgring local recruit Rolf Stommelen escaped from two more potentially lethal accidents when breakages occurred in the front suspension and the steering. Before tackling its main goal, Le Mans, the Rondeau team beefed up its cars with higher grade materials, challenging Porsche for the lead before being let down by its 3.9-litre Ford DFL engines. Finally, at Spa, Rondeau endured the loss of its quickest car which was taken off by an errant Porsche 924, to claim fourth place in Group C and, it thought, sufficient points to secure the manufacturers' championship. Then FISA decided that Porsche could count those Group B points, and Rondeau's title went down the tubes.

The M382C, an update of Rondeau's IMSA GTP chassis, was due to be superseded at Le Mans by the new ground effect 482. However, the car appeared but once, at Silverstone, where it displayed all the traditional teething problems, including a persistent tendency to overheat. It was withdrawn from Le Mans and its next appearance postponed for a year, but despite numerous test sessions it was still far from sorted by the end of the season.

The only other car to win rounds of the manufacturers' championship was Lancia's Group 6 device. Without a suitable engine to

'Hamstrung by their own regulations': at the Pace Six Hours at Silverstone, the super quick Porsche 956 (left), slowed by compliance with the fuel economy regulations, was humbled by the fleet Group 6 Lancias. The Porsches would soon come to terms with the fuel consumption regulations, but Rondeau abandoned development of their 'ground effect' 482 (above) after the Silverstone race, committing themselves to the M382C at least for this year. The Ford-powered Rondeau scored wins at Monza and the Nürburgring, but other Ford-powered cars, including the Sauber (below) and the distinctive, British, Grid Plaza, had a miserable season plagued by engine unreliability.

'Ring, Riccardo Patrese scored a famous win one day after rolling his car at Pflantzgarten!

Moral victors at the Nürburgring, Ford had a season it will probably want to forget. In Group 6 guise, the C100 made a sensational début at Brands Hatch in 1981, but when the Group C version appeared for the first time, at Monza, it was rightly attacked for its shoddy preparation. Things improved when Zakspeed was entrusted with its development and, no doubt slightly flattered by the location, it led convincingly at the Nürburgring for more than four hours. However, the fact remains that Ford failed to score a single point in the manufacturers' championship, and it was left to customers Rondeau to fly the Ford flag.

In addition to the chassis, Ford also experienced problems with its Cosworth-developed 3.9-litre DFL, which brought installation bothers to many with its heavy vibration problem and effectively cost Rondeau its shot at a second Le Mans victory. The trouble here concerned the ignition pick-up on the crankshaft damper, which failed when the latter overheated. To its credit, Cosworth was quickly onto the problem, and extensively tested revisions saw it cured by Spa-Francorchamps in September.

Third place in the manufacturers' championship was perhaps rather surprisingly taken by Nimrod Aston Martin. The British producer of high speed, luxury conveyances, sold fuel-injected versions of its 5.3-litre V8 engines to the Nimrod team, set up in 1981 by Aston dealer and enthusiast Robin Hamilton. The chassis was a direct descendant of the 1960s Lola T70, and was indeed penned by the same designer, Eric Broadley. Slightly old fashioned, the car was at least robust, if heavily overweight, but it was the engines which were to provide the bulk of the problems for Hamilton. His works team managed to blow more than a dozen motors while a second car, run privately for Viscount Downe by Richard Williams, made its solitary engine last the whole season and suffered only valve problems at Le Mans. Nevertheless, the car struggled heroically into seventh place having run as high as fourth and then, at Spa, secured enough points to demote the French WM Peugeot team to fourth place.

The WM team ventured outside Le Mans for the first time in 1982 and it was a largely unhappy season. The little turbocharged car was fast but fragile and only really performed spectacularly at Le Mans, where its renowned speed down the Mulsanne Straight was evident yet again. The German Sauber operation concluded a miserable season when entrant GS Tuning went into liquidation shortly after the last race, at Spa. Prior to that, the visually striking Sauber SHS C6, with its single-pylon delta shaped rear wing, endured endless problems with its DFL engines, whose vibrations affected the Sauber worse than most. However, the team did manage to amass a token 10 points towards the manufacturers' championship which placed it fifth overall. Also from Germany came Reinhold Joest's Porsche 936C which he ran for Belgians Jean-Michel and Phillipe Martin. For four out of the five races, they were assisted by Bob Wollek but he quickly became disenchanted with his co-drivers and he was finally left out of the line-up at Spa. That effectively relegated the 936C to the ranks of also-rans, for although it was a sound, competitive car and ran strongly amongst the first four for much of Le Mans, without Wollek the Martins couldn't maintain the same speed.

The Kremer CK5 made its début at Le Mans, but was conceived primarily as a challenger for the Deutsche Rennsport Meisterschaft. Nevertheless, it had developed into a worthy WEC contender by Spa, where it was the fastest car in a straight line. From Britain came the Lola T610 and the Grid Plaza SI. Eric Broadley's latest creation, clothed in a smooth, all-enveloping body, provoked much controversy when it first appeared at Monza where it was excluded from the race for having movable 'kick-pads', to protect the chassis said Lola, underneath the chassis. Thereafter it impressed with its straightline speed but frustrated its drivers in their efforts to bring some stability to its handling, which didn't seem to benefit from the degree of ground effect it generated. The Grid also featured venturi bodywork but was seriously affected by persistent engine failures. At Monza, Silverstone and Le Mans, encouraging performances were terminated by these abrupt and apparently unfathomable engine problems, and then Grid, already frustrated by the WEC's sparse amount of fixtures, left to contest the IMSA series in the USA.

The WEC now regards the future with optimism. There will be eight rounds of the manufacturers' championship next year, and an entirely new Group C subdivision for cars of smaller size and less powerful engines has been approved by FISA. The regulations have been slightly relaxed and the WEC's stature has been boosted by the news that a Ferrari-engined Lancia will contest the series. From Britain, there is a strong likelihood of Jaguar joining the championship at Silverstone in preparation for a concerted effort in 1984. All of which adds up to an attractive formula which has the potential to restore endurance racing's tattered reputation, while making an obvious contribution to the fuel efficiency of the ordinary motor car.

The latest, more angular, WM (above) retained its Peugeot turbo power and Esso sponsorship but it was not a very successful year for the French team, the cars' main attribute once again being their prodigious straight line speed. In taking third place in the manufacturers' championship, the Aston Martin engined Nimrod (seen below, leading the Joest Porsche 936C and conventional Rondeau at Silverstone) surprised a good many people. In spite of employing drivers of the calibre of Michele Alboreto (right, at Brands Hatch) and Riccardo Patrese, Lancia were denied the driver's title after an inspired drive by Jacky Ickx in the final round of the series.

power a pukka Group C car, Lancia decided to contest the drivers' series, using a turbocharged 2.0-litre engine which produced about 450bhp. The Lancia 5/75S featured an open cockpit with ground effects and skirts and proved easily capable of running with the Group C cars, even Porsche, and invariably set the pace. However, as one has come to expect of the Turinese products, they were let down by their reliability and the cars displayed season-long electrical problems. Le Mans was a complete disaster after a promising practice performance, as Lancia hit trouble right at the start of the race before retiring in the middle of the night. However, the cars did win at Silverstone and the Nürburgring although the latter result came by way of the Ford C100's unfortunate retirement.

It may not seem like it, but Lancia was occasionally extremely lucky to achieve the results it did. At Silverstone the winning car survived an altercation with a backmarker in the chicane and at the

ICKX'S FIRST TITLE

Remarkably, the 1982 World Endurance Championship for Drivers is Jacky Ickx's first world title and he left its winning until virtually the last lap of the last race of a season where the Group 6 Lancias gave the Group C Porsches a mighty hard time. IAN BAMSEY reports.

JACKY ICKX not only won his sixth Le Mans in 1982, he also won his first World Championship. Somewhat ironically perhaps, for the semi-retired Belgian sportscar ace did not set out to contest the World Endurance Championship for Drivers. Nor did his team, Porsche. Indeed, the only major team which began the season with the avowed intent of chasing the Drivers' Championship was the Lancia works team. But to the Italian team's chagrin, the early season rounds were either cancelled or postponed, due, by and large, to lack of support. In the end the series became an appendix to the World Endurance Championship for Makes (described earlier in these pages). Somewhat overshadowed by the Makes series, the Drivers' Championship consisted of the five rounds of the former plus three subsequent events: Mugello, Fuji and Brands Hatch.

At the conclusion of the World Endurance Championship for Makes, Lancia drivers Riccardo Patrese and Michele Alboreto could reasonably be considered favourites for the Drivers' title, simply because Porsche did not intend to contest the remaining rounds. At Mugello Henri Pescarolo, hitching a ride in the Joest Porsche 936C, was the only championship rival for the Lancia lads. He finished third, Patrese and Alboreto, sharing with Piercarlo Ghinzani, won the event. Thus, when Alboreto burst into the limelight by winning the Las Vegas Grand Prix he was already leading the World Endurance Championship for Drivers.

Generous financial incentives tempted both Porsche and Pescarolo's regular team Rondeau each to send a car to Fuji in Japan. Here Alboreto led the race but crashed, handing victory to Ickx who beat the Patrese/Fabi Lancia to the flag. Pescarolo's Rondeau looked set for third place but broke its transmission with just two laps to run. Thus, prior to the Brands Hatch finale, Ickx led the championship with 75 points to the 71 of Patrese, the 63 of Alboreto and

the 58 of Pescarolo. With 20 points for a win, Pescarolo thought it worth hitching another ride in the Joest Porsche but the decision of Porsche to send a car for Ickx meant that the real contest had to be between Stuttgart and the Italians.

The Brands Hatch showdown began in a downpour and before ten laps were up the race had been called to a halt after Winkelhock's Ford had crashed heavily and damaged the barriers. Alboreto had already gone off and lost three laps as a result of a tangle with another car and his challenge evaporated during the restarted second part of the race with engine failure. It was down to Patrese or Ickx — at the end, on the road; Fabi or Ickx. Fabi took over the leading Lancia for the final stint with a minute in hand over the Porsche. But the German machine had led the Patrese/Fabi Lancia at the termination of the first part, so that meant Ickx had to close within 6.5 seconds of Fabi to win on aggregate. He had 35 laps in which to do it — but at the time didn't know even that much. Darkness was not far off and all the competitors knew was that sometime before the scheduled culmination of the 1000km race the stewards would probably declare '10 laps to run'. When that did indeed happen an inspired piece of driving by Ickx had already drawn the Porsche to within 14.6 seconds of the Lancia. Could Jacky slash off another eight seconds in the remaining ten laps to claim the title? Patrese, watching from the pit rail, held his breath as Ickx turned the boost up . . .

Those last laps saw a mighty performance by Ickx, a performance worthy of a World Champion — a performance that poor Fabi could do nothing to withstand. And so it was that Lancia's season long struggle failed in its objective and that Porsche could boast of another major success — just days after the politicians confirmed the Stuttgart company as World Champion of Makes.

World Endurance Championship of Makes Round 1 World Endurance Championship of Drivers Round 1

Monza 1000 Kms — Monza — 18 April 1982

173 laps = 1003.40 kms (623.51 miles). Winner's average speed 112.03mph

1	H.Pescarolo/J.Rondeau/G.Francia	Rondeau M382C-Cosworth DFL	5h 33m 56.2s
2	R.Stommelen/T.Field	Porsche 935 K3-81 tc	172 laps
3	G.Ciuti/M.Benusiglio/G.Piazzi	Osella PA7-BMW	167 laps
4	V.Merl/D.Schornstein	Porsche 935	167 laps
5	M.Casoni/J.Castellano/M.Thatcher	Lancia Montecarlo tc	163 laps
6	G.Frequelin/R.Dorchy/J.-D.Raulet	WM-Peugeot P82 tc	162 laps

Fastest lap: Riccardo Patrese (Lancia Martini tc), 1m 44.3s (124.40mph)
Class winners: Group C: Pescarolo/Rondeau/Francia
Group 5: Stommelen/Field
Group 6: Ciuti/Benusiglio/Piazzi

IMSA: de Buono/Govoni	Ferrari 512BB	150 laps
Group 4: Dron/Cleare	Porsche 934 tc	150 laps

World Endurance Championship of Makes Round 2 World Endurance Championship of Drivers Round 2

Pace Petroleum 6 Hours — Silverstone — 16 May 1982

240 laps = 1132.56 kms (703.68 miles). Winner's average speed 117.20mph

1	R.Patrese/M.Alboreto	Lancia Martini tc	240 laps
2	J.Ickx/D.Bell	Porsche 956 tc	237 laps
3	J.-M.Martin/P.M./B.Wollek	Porsche 936C tc	231 laps
4	G.Francia/D.Truffo	Osella PA9-BMW	228 laps
5	H.Pescarolo/G.Spice	Rondeau M382-Cosworth DFL	227 laps
6	R.Mallock/M.Salmon	Nimrod Aston Martin NRA/C2	227 laps

Fastest lap: Patrese/Alboreto, 1m 21.18s (130.02mph)
Class winners: Group C: Ickx/Bell
Group 6: Patrese/Alboreto

Group 5: Lassig/Doren	Porsche 935 K3 tc	223 laps
IMSA: Moretti/Baldi	Porsche 935 78-81 tc	223 laps
Group 4: J.Winther/L.Viggo-Jensen	BMW M1	204 laps

World Endurance Championship of Makes Round 3 World Endurance Championship of Drivers Round 3

Nürburgring 1000 kms — Nürburgring — 30 May 1982

44 laps = 1004.74 kms (624.32 miles). Winner's average speed 105.77mph

1	R.Patrese/M.Alboreto	Lancia Martini tc	5h 54m 10.83s
2	H.Pescarolo/R.Stommelen	Rondeau 382C-Cosworth DFL	43 laps
3	H.Kelleners/U.Grano/E.Calderari	BMW M1	41 laps
4	M.Ketterer/T.Fischaber/E.Schimpf	BMW 320i	39 laps
5	R.Lloyd/T.Dron/H.Volker	Porsche Carrera GTR tc	39 laps
6	A.Hahne/H.Becker	Mazda RX-7	39 laps

Fastest lap: Manfred Winkelhock (Ford C100-Cosworth DFL), 7m 23.97s (115.06mph)
Class winners: Group C: Pescarolo/Stommelen
Group 6: Patrese/Alboreto
Group 5: Kelleners/Grano/Calderari
IMSA: Lloyd/Dron/Volker

Group 4: J.Winther/L.Viggo-Jensen	BMW M1	38 laps

World Endurance Championship of Makes Round 5 World Endurance Championship of Drivers Round 5

Spa 1000 kms — Spa Francorchamps — 5 September 1982

144 laps = 1004.54 kms (624.19 miles). Winner's average speed 102.317mph

1	J.Ickx/J.Mass	Porsche 956 tc	6h 6m 4.14s
2	D.Bell/V.Schuppan	Porsche 956 tc	141 laps
3	R.Patrese/T.Fabi	Lancia Martini tc	140 laps
4	J.-M.Martin/P.Martin	Porsche 936C tc	134 laps
5	F.Migault/G.Spice	Rondeau M382C-Cosworth DFL	133 laps
6	G.Francia/L.Moreschi	Osella PA9-BMW	132 laps

Fastest lap: Ickx, 2m 22.15s (109.78mph)
Class winners: Group C: Ickx/Mass

Group 5: G.Moretti/M.Baldi	Porsche 935/78-82	132 laps

Group 6: Riccardo Patrese/Teo Fabi

IMSA: R.Lloyd/J.Palmer	Porsche 924 Carrera GTR	123 laps
Group 4: J.Winther/L.Viggo-Jensen	BMW M1	124 laps
Group B: G.Memminger/F.Muller	Porsche 911 tc	108 laps

World Endurance Championship of Drivers Round 6

Trofeo Banca Toscana — Mugello — 19 September 1982

191 laps = 1001.80 kms (622.49 miles). Winner's average speed 98.63mph

1	M.Alboreto/P.Ghinzani	Lancia Martini tc	6h 18m 40.05s
2	C.Fabi/A.Nannini	Lancia Martini tc	6h 20m 12.21s
3	B.Wollek/H.Heyer/H.Pescarolo	Porsche 936C tc	184 laps
4	G.Francia/L.Moreschi	Osella PA9-BMW	175 laps
5	W.Brun/S.Muller Jnr	Sauber SHS C6-Ford	175 laps
6	D.Schornstein/V.Merl/B.Wollek	Porsche 935	175 laps

Fastest lap: Teo Fabi (Lancia Martini tc) and Piercarlo Ghinzani, 1m 47.88s (108.76mph)
Class winners: Group C: Wollek/Heyer/Pescarolo
Group 6: Alboreto/Ghinzani
Group 5: Schornstein/Merl/Wollek

IMSA: D.Truffo/F.Violati	Ferrari 512BB	148 laps
Group 4: E.Kofel/P.Zbinden/M.Vanoli	Porsche 924 GTR	147 laps
Group B: F.Muller/G.Memminger	Porsche 911	143 laps

World Endurance Championship of Drivers Round 7

Round 7 — Mount Fuji 6 Hours — Fuji — 3 October 1982

260 laps = 1118.00 kms (694.72 miles). Winner's average speed 117.02mph

1	J.Ickx/J.Mass	Porsche 956 tc	6h 0m 41.05s
2	R.Patrese/T.Fabi	Lancia Martini tc	258 laps
3	M.Nakamura/K.Misaki	March 75S-Toyota	243 laps
4	N.Nagasaka/F.Sato	BMW M1	238 laps
5	K.Hoshino/N.Tachi/A.Suzuki	Toyota Celica C	234 laps
6	T.Walkinshaw/T.Yorino/M.Sekiya	Mazda 254i	228 laps

Fastest lap: not given
Class winners: Group C: Ickx/Mass
Group 6: Patrese/Fabi
Group 5: Nagasaka/Satu
IMSA: Walkinshaw/Takashi/Sekiya

World Endurance Championship of Drivers Round 8

Shell Oils 1000 — Brands Hatch — 17 October 1982

211 laps = 887.50 kms (551.47 miles). Winner's average speed 98.76mph

1	J.Ickx/D.Bell	Porsche 956 tc	5h 35m 01.6s
2	R.Patrese/T.Fabi	Lancia Martini tc	5h 35m 06.3s
3	D.Hobbs/J.Fitzpatrick/B.Wollek	Porsche 935 tc	202 laps
4	J.Palmer/D.Wilson	Ford C100-Cosworth DFL	201 laps
5	M.Surer/K.Ludwig/M.Winkelhock	Ford C100-Cosworth DFL	200 laps
6	J.Paul Jnr/F.Jelinski	Kremer Porsche CK5 tc	198 laps

Fastest lap: not given
Class winners: Group C: Ickx/Bell
Group 6: Patrese/Fabi

Group 5: J.Cooper/P.Smith	Porsche 935	184 laps
IMSA: Hobbs/Fitzpatrick/Wollek		
Group 4: T.Dron/R.Cleare	Porsche 934 tc	180 laps

FINAL POSITIONS

	World Endurance Championship for Drivers			World Endurance Championship for Makes	
1	J.Ickx	95	1	Porsche	75
2	R.Patrese	89	2	Rondeau-Cosworth	62
3	D.Bell	70	3	Nimrod-Aston Martin	24
4	T.Fabi	66	4	WM-Peugeot	21
5	M.Alboreto	63	5	Sauber-Cosworth	10
6	H.Pescarolo	61	6	Ford-Cosworth	10
7	J.Mass	55	7	Lola-Cosworth	3
8	G.Francia	49			
9 =	R.Stommelen	30			
9 =	V.Schuppan	30			

* Round 4 of both Championships was Le Mans; see pp140/141 for results

LIKE FATHER, LIKE SON

The very liberal rule book which governs the International Motor Sports Association's Camel GT series encourages a terrific variety of top quality endurance machinery to contest the American championship, and this year the winning team was almost entirely home grown.

BRINGING to fruition the promise he demonstrated over the past two seasons, John Paul Jr ran away with the International Motor Sports Association's Camel GT series. And with his father, twice winner of the World Endurance Drivers Championship, as a co-driver, young Paul added the Camel Endurance title to his collection as well.

1981 had been a tough year for the JLP Racing team. They didn't win a race until late fall. Then, at Pocono, everything fell into place. A win there, and a last lap triumph over series champion Brian Redman in the Daytona finale, provided a warmup for the '82 season. Their year-old, tube frame, Atlanta built Porsche 935 ran faster, further and longer than its rivals in the early season Florida long distance classics at Daytona and Sebring, and in the 500 kilometer event at Charlotte, North Carolina.

Paul Jr drove it to a solo victory in the Road Atlanta sprint season opener, but then switched to a Chevrolet-Lola T600 for sprint races on the tight, twisty Laguna Seca, Mid-Ohio and Lime Rock circuits, winning the first, and finishing fourth and second in the other events.

JLP's new 935-based machine, from the pen of Lee Dykstra, America's foremost designer of road racing machinery, was also built in Atlanta. The only Porsche parts on the JLP-4 model are the

'greenhouse' and the engine/transmission unit. The suspension utilises a pure racing layout rather than the traditional production based 935 type.

Developed to take advantage of the liberal rules governing the construction of production based cars — IMSA has chosen to go with their own rulebook rather than to adopt the new FISA formulae — the new machine made its début mid-season at Brainerd, where the youngster won with it. He added another sprint win at Portland, Oregon before the new car was sent back to the shops for development as an endurance racer.

The father and son team took the Mosport 1000km race with the old car and then finished second at Road America. They planned to bring the new machine back for the fall Road Atlanta endurance test, but Paul Sr crashed the car heavily in practice, and it was with the old 935 that they won their hometown race, and Junior clinched the GT title.

At Pocono, the anniversary of the beginning of the JLP streak, they finished second, and Junior clinched the Camel Endurance Championship.

Driving a modified Kremer K4, former IMSA champion John Fitzpatrick ran up four wins, including sprint victories at Mid-Ohio and Lime Rock, and, with David Hobbs sharing the cockpit, long distance races again in Ohio and at Road America.

A spate of early season mechanical failures kept the California based Englishman from finishing near the top of the points chart. Paul's closest competition for Redman's crown came from Ted Field and Danny Ongais.

The Interscope team started the season with three Kremer built Porsche 935s, a pair of K3s and a K4. When Ongais had recovered sufficiently from his terrible injuries at Indianapolis the year before, he set about shaking down the pair of Chevrolet-Lolas that had been delivered to the team's California headquarters the previous summer.

With Ongais off racing an Indycar, Field and Bill Whittington won the six-hour race at Riverside in April. Then Field and Ongais won the late night 250 miler at Daytona in July and the 500 miler at Pocono two months later. But except for these highlights, the Interscope team's fortunes were as black as their cars.

The Ford factory effort was confined to five races this season. Indy racing star Rick Mears was paid a substantial sum to drive the Mustang bodied Zakspeed car, and with a thorough aerodynamic development program the Ford proved to be almost as quick down the straight as the big 800 horsepower Porsches, despite the handicap of its tiny, 1.7-litre turbo powerplant.

Unfortunately Mears didn't complete a race, and only a sterling performance by Klaus Ludwig in the backup car at Sears Point saved the Dearborn team from a season of absolute frustration. Ludwig's California victory was their sole bright spot in the season.

Bob Akin hired Derek Bell as co-driver for his Porsche team, which fielded entries only in the endurance races. Akin's Kremer K3 was replaced mid-way through the season by a monocoque chassised 935 with a Lola T600 nose. Very fast in a straight line, the L1 Porsche proved difficult to sort and the team's best result was a second place in the first race of the season.

A late season entry was the V12 powered Jaguar XJR5, a GTP car from Bob Tullius's Group 44 team. Designed by Dykstra, the striking coupé didn't make its first racing appearance until Road America, but Tullius and co-driver, Canadian Bill Adam, finished third.

A crash in practice at Mid-Ohio meant that the car only appeared again for the last two races, but the car is a potential winner in long distance races despite the handicap of an engine that is 100 horsepower down on a Chevy and nearly 300 down from a 935.

Bob Garretson's March programme ran out of steam early in the season after the factory's US representative, David Wilson, suffered a sudden but terminal illness. Toward the end of the season some international colour was lent the Camel series by the addition of Emilio de Villota's Cosworth-GRID (with Desiré Wilson sharing the seat) and the Charles Ivey Porsche 935 of John Cooper and Paul Smith.

IMSA's GTO category, which is loosely based on the old FISA Group 4, was highlighted by a battle between Don Devendorf's Datsun 280ZX Turbo, and the Chevrolet Corvette and Ford Mustang of René Rodriguez and Tico Almeida's Miami based T&R Racing team. Devendorf only ran half of the races, but he won six of them, while the T&R cars proved unreliable. The Porsche 934 of Chet Vincentz and Wayne Baker performed well, winning a pair of races, but they only entered the season ending endurance tests, and finished well back in the points.

Logan Blackburn's normally aspirated Datsun 280ZX won five times in GTU, but the likeable former club racer skipped too many races to hope to capture the title in the very competitive junior Camel category. Mazda drivers Jim Downing and Roger Mandeville duelled all season long in the RX7s, with the title going right down to the last race.

Dave Kent, whose cars won the GTU championship for Mazda in 1981, embarked on an ambitious campaign for Toyota in '82. The task of simultaneously developing the old Celicas he'd inherited from George Follmer and building a pair of new cars proved too great, and the Toyota effort came to naught.

Mazda was also successful in the Champion Spark Plug Challenge, a series for Group 1½ style cars on radial ply street tyres. New rules for '82 encouraged entrants to build front-wheel-drive cars, but in the end the championship came down to a three-way shootout at Daytona among conventional rear drive cars driven by Chuck Ulinski, Dave Lemon (Mazda RX-3) and Irv Pearce (AMC Spirit).

New rules in the Kelly-American Challenge for saloon cars gave an advantage to V6 engines, and for the first time the championship wasn't won by a V8 powered machine. Camaro driver Craig Carter won over half of the 11 races in the series with six-cylinder power, while four time former champ Gene Felton scored late in the season at Pocono in a V6 Camaro constructed by legendary oval builder Ray Dillon.

For the first time IMSA sanctioned a Renault Cup series. Six races were held, in conjunction with east coast Camel dates, with as many as sixty cars showing up for each event. James Reeve won the title from Don Knowles and Dennis Shaw.

IMSA CAMEL GT AND

IMSA Camel GT Championship Round 1, Endurance Championship Round 1
21st 24 Hour Pepsi Challenge — Daytona 30/31 January 1982
719 laps = 2760.96 miles. Winner's average speed 114.794mph

1	J.Paul Jnr/J.Paul Snr/R.Stommelen	Porsche 935	24h 03m 05.301s
2	B.Akin/D.Bell/C.Sieber	Porsche 935	708 laps
3	M.de Narvaez/J.Wood/B.Garretson	Porsche 935	683 laps
4	Y.Katayama/Y.Terada/T.Yorino	Mazda RX7	644 laps
5	T.Almeida/R.Rodriguez/E.Soto	Porsche Carrera RSR	642 laps
6	L.Mueller/K.Rude/A.Moffat	Mazda RX7	640 laps

Fastest lap: H.Haywood (Porsche 935), 1m 49.80s (125.902mph)
Class winners: GTX: Paul Jnr/Paul Snr/Stommelen. GTO: Almeida/Rodriguez/Soto. GTU: Katayama/Terada/Yorino.

IMSA Camel GT Championship Round 2, Endurance Championship Round 2
Coca Cola 12 Hours — Sebring — 20 March 1982
244 laps = 1268.80 miles. Winner's average speed 105.401mph

1	J.Paul Jnr/J.Paul Snr	Porsche 935	12h 02m 16.072s
2	B.Rahal/M.de Narvaez/J.Trueman	March 82G-Chevrolet	244 laps
3	M.L.Speer/T.Wolters/C.Mendez	Porsche 935	237 laps
4	D.Febles/P.Ferrer/C.Soldevila	Porsche Carrera	235 laps
5	B.Leven/H.Haywood/A.Holbert	Porsche 935	231 laps
6	R.Manderville/A.Johnson/J.Kline	Mazda RX7	224 laps

Fastest lap: J.Fitzpatrick (Porsche 935), 2m 34.49s (121.173mph)
Class winners: GTX: Paul Jnr/Paul Snr. GTO: Febles/Ferrer/Soldevila. GTU: Manderville/Johnson/Kline.

Danny Ongais (above), recovered from his 1981 Indy injuries, was the main challenger to John Paul (preceding page).

IMSA Camel GT Championship Round 3
Road Atlanta — 4 April 1982
60 laps = 150 miles. Winner's average speed 107.378mph

1	John Paul Jnr	Porsche 935	1h 24m 29.219s
2	Danny Ongais	Porsche 935 K3	1h 25m 43.697s
3	Kevin Cogan	Ford Mustang Turbo	59 laps
4	Ted Field	Lola T600-Chevrolet	59 laps
5	Dennis Aase	BMW M1	58 laps
6	John Fitzpatrick	Porsche 935 K3	56 laps

Fastest lap: Paul Jnr, 1m 19.88s (113.570mph)
Class winners: GTX: Paul Jnr. GTO: Aase. GTU: Logan Blackburn (Datsun ZX) 30 laps.

IMSA Camel GT Championship Round 4, Endurance Championship Round 3
LA Times/Toyota 6 Hours — Riverside — 25 April 1982
192 laps = 633.60 miles. Winner's average speed 103.765mph

1	T.Field/B.Whittington	Lola T600-Chevrolet	6h 00m 48.937s
2	A.Holbert/H.Grohs	Porsche 935	190 laps
3	M.L.Speer/T.Wolters	Porsche 935	183 laps
4	B.Akin/C.Siebert/D.Bell	Porsche 935	183 laps
5	R.Ratcliff/G.Clay	Porsche 935	182 laps
6	D.Cowart/K.Miller	March 82G-BMW	175 laps

Fastest lap: Grohs, 1m 42.14s (114.549mph)
Class winners: GTX: Field/Whittington. GTO: T.Almeida/E.Soto (Porsche Carrera) 172 laps. GTU: J.Cook/J.Mullen (Mazda RX7) 174 laps.

IMSA Camel GT Championship Round 5
Laguna Seca — 2 May 1982
53 laps = 100.7 miles. Winner's average speed 106.65mph

1	John Paul Jnr	Lola T600-Chevrolet	56m 39.123s
2	Danny Ongais	Lola T600-Chevrolet	57m 00.647s
3	Johnny Fitzpatrick	Porsche 935 K4	52 laps
4	Ted Field	Lola T600-Chevrolet	52 laps
5	David Hobbs	Porsche 935 K3	52 laps
6	Don Devendorf	Datsun ZX Turbo	49 laps

Fastest lap: Ongais, 1m 02.04s (110.251mph)
Class winners: GTX: Paul Jnr. GTO: Devendorf.

IMSA Camel GT Championship Round 6, Endurance Championship Round 4
Camel 500 — Charlotte — 16 May 1982
138 laps = 310 miles. Winner's average speed 100.806mph

1	J.Paul Snr/J.Paul Jnr	Porsche 935	3h 4m 615s
2	D.Cowart/K.Miller	March 82G-BMW	137 laps
3	B.Akin/C.Siebert	Porsche 935	133 laps
4	G.Clay/R.Ratcliff	Porsche 935	132 laps
5	M.L.Speer/T.Wolters	Porsche 935	130 laps
6	B.Hagan/G.Felton	Chevrolet Camaro	30 laps

Fastest lap: Paul Jnr, 1m 09.95s (115.797mph).
Class winners: GTX: Paul Snr/Paul Jnr. GTO: Hagan/Felton. GTU: L.Blackburn/G.Alderman (Datsun 280ZX) 129 laps.

IMSA Camel GT Championship Round 7
Mid-Ohio — 23 May 1982
42 laps = 101.36 miles. Winner's average speed 96.079mph

1	John Fitzpatrick	Porsche 935 K4	1h 2m 56.876s
2	Danny Ongais	Lola T600-Chevrolet	1h 3m 11.929s
3	Ted Field	Lola T600-Chevrolet	42 laps
4	John Paul Jnr	Lola T600-Chevrolet	40 laps
5	Don Devendorf	Datsun ZX Turbo	39 laps
6	René Rodriguez	Chevrolet Corvette	39 laps

Fastest lap: Ongais, 1m 27.14s (99.151mph).
Class winners: GTX: Fitzpatrick. GTO: Devendorf. GTU: J.Crevier (BMW M1) 39 laps.

IMSA Camel GT Championship Round 8
Lime Rock — 31 May 1982
69 laps = 105.57 miles. Winner's average speed 105.33mph

1	John Fitzpatrick	Porsche 935 K4	1h 00m 9.319s
2	John Paul Jnr	Lola T600-Chevrolet	1h 00m 41.224s
3	Ted Field	Lola T600-Chevrolet	68 laps
4	Danny Ongais	Lola T600-Chevrolet	66 laps
5	John Paul Snr	Porsche 935	65 laps
6	Del Russo Taylor	Chevron-Buick	63 laps

Fastest lap: Fitzpatrick, 49.54s (111.183mph) — record.
Class winners: GTX: Fitzpatrick. GTU: Joe Varde (Mazda RX7) 40 laps.

IMSA Camel GT Championship Round 9
Paul Revere 250 — Daytona — 3/4 July 1982
65 laps = 249.6 miles. Winner's average speed 116.609mph

1	T.Field/D.Ongais	Lola T600-Chevrolet	2h 8m 5.781s
2	M.L.Speer/T.Wolters	Porsche 935	63 laps
3	H.Montoia/A.Naon	BMW M1	63 laps
4	P.Henn/B.Henn/R.Lanier	Porsche 935	61 laps
5	Logan Blackburn	Datsun 280ZX Turbo	61 laps
6	Jim Downing	Mazda RX7	61 laps

Fastest lap: John Paul Jnr (Porsche 935), 1m 50.62s (124.968mph).
Class winners: GTX: Field/Ongais, GTO: Montoia/Naon. GTU: Blackburn.

IMSA Camel GT Championship Round 10
Brainerd — 11 July 1982
42 laps = 126 miles. Winner's average speed 113.258mph

1	John Paul Jnr	Porsche 935	1h 6m 45.020s
2	Danny Ongais	Lola T600-Chevrolet	1h 7m 2.490s
3	Ted Field	Lola T600-Chevrolet	42 laps
4	Bill Koll	Rondeau M382C-Chevrolet	41 laps
5	Del Russo Taylor	Chevron-Buick	38 laps
6	Logan Blackburn	Datsun 280ZX Turbo	38 laps

Fastest lap: Paul Jnr, 1m 31.56s (117.955mph).
Class winners: GTX: Paul Jnr. GTO: Tico Almeida (Ford Mustang) 37 laps. GTU: Blackburn.

IMSA Camel GT Championship Round 11
Sears Point — 25 July 1982
42 laps = 100 miles. Winner's average speed 92.03mph

1	Klaus Ludwig	Ford Mustang Turbo	1h 5m 47.418s
2	Danny Ongais	Lola T600-Chevrolet	40 laps
3	Skeeter McKitterick	Rondeau Chevrolet	40 laps
4	John Fitzpatrick	Porsche Kremer 935 K4	39 laps
5	John Devendorf	Datsun ZX Turbo	37 laps
6	Rich Sloma	Chevrolet Corvette 427	36 laps

Fastest lap: Ongais, 1m 33.52s (97.121mph) — record.
Class winners: GTX: Ludwig. GTO: Devendorf. GTU: Joe Varde (Mazda RX7) 30 laps.

IMSA Camel GT Championship Round 12
Portland — 1 August 1982
53 laps = 101.495 miles. Winner's average speed 101.014mph

1	John Paul Jnr	Porsche 935	1h 00m 17.138s
2	Ted Field	Lola T600-Chevrolet	1h 00m 54.572s
3	Don Devendorf	Datsun 280ZX Turbo	50 laps
4	Pat Usher	Chevrolet Corvette	49 laps
5	Chuck Kendall	BMW M1	38 laps
6	Rich Sloma	Chevrolet Corvette	48 laps

Fastest lap: John Fitzpatrick (Porsche 935 K4), 1m 4.86s (106.290mph) — record.
Class winners: GTX: Paul Jnr. GTO: Devendorf. GTU: Roger Manderville (Mazda RX7) 24 laps

IMSA Camel GT Championship Round 13, Endurance Championship Round 5
Labatt's 50 Camel GT — Mosport Park — 15 August 1982
227 laps = 558.19 miles. Winner's average speed 92.918mph

1	J.Paul Jnr/J.Paul Snr	Porsche 935	6h 26m 464s
2	C.Cord/J.Adams	Lola T600-Chevrolet	222 laps
3	M.Hinze/R.Lanier	March 82G-Chevrolet	221 laps
4	B.Akin/D.Bell	Porsche 935	220 laps
5	M.L.Speer/T.Wolters	Porsche 935	210 laps
6	J.Cooper/P.Smith	Porsche 935	209 laps

Fastest lap: Danny Ongais (Lola T600-Chevrolet), 1m 19.89s (110.807mph).
Class winners: GTX: Paul Jnr/Paul Snr. GTO: Wayne Baker/Tony Vincenze (Porsche 934 Carrera) 208 laps. GTU: Roger Manderville/Amos Johnson (Mazda RX7) 208 laps.

IMSA Camel GT Championship Round 14, Endurance Championship Round 6
Pabst 500 — Road America — 22 August 1982
125 laps = 500 miles. Winner's average speed 105.922mph

1	J.Fitzpatrick/D.Hobbs	Porsche 935 K4	4h 43m 13.700s
2	J.Paul Jnr/M.de Narvaez	Porsche 935 JLP-3	124 laps
3	B.Tullius/B.Adams	Jaguar XJR-5	123 laps
4	C.Cord/J.Adams	Lola T600-Chevrolet	122 laps
5	D.Cowart/K.Miller	March 82G-BMW	119 laps
6	M.Hinze/R.Lanier	March 82G-Chevrolet	119 laps

Fastest lap: Ted Field (Lola T600-Chevrolet), 2m 08.85s (111.758mph).
Class winners: GTX: Fitzpatrick/Hobbs. GTO: Rob Raub/Chris Gleason (Pontiac Firebird) 112 laps. GTU: Joe Varde/Jeff Kline (Mazda RX7) 111 laps.

IMSA Camel GT Championship Round 15, Endurance Championship Round 7
Lumbermens 6 Hours — Mid-Ohio — 5 September 1982
231 laps = 554.40 miles. Winner's average speed 92.133mph

1	J.Fitzpatrick/D.Hobbs	Porsche 935	6h 1m 2.561s
2	C.Cord/J.Adams	Lola T600-Chevrolet	229 laps
3	M.Hinze/R.Lanier	Porsche 935	227 laps
4	B.Akin/H.Haywood	Porsche 935	226 laps
5	J.Cooper/P.Smith	Porsche 935	219 laps
6	D.Devendorf/T.Adamowicz	Datsun ZX Turbo	218 laps

Fastest lap: Ted Field (Lola T600-Chevrolet), 1m 28.44s (97.693mph).
Class winners: GTX: Fitzpatrick/Hobbs. GTO: Devendorf/Adamowicz. GTU: George Alderman/Logan Blackburn (Datsun ZX) 218 laps.

IMSA Camel GT Championship Round 16, Endurance Championship Round 8
Sprite 500 — Road Atlanta — 12 September 1982
124 laps = 312.48 miles. Winner's average speed 100.544mph

1	J.Paul Jnr/J.Paul Snr	Porsche 935	3h 6m 28.365s
2	P.Henn/D.Bundy	Porsche 935	123 laps
3	D.Cowart/K.Miller	March 82G-BMW	123 laps
4	M.L.Speer/T.Wolters	Porsche 935	119 laps
5	R.Rodriguez/J.Greenwood	Chevrolet Corvette	119 laps
6	R.Manderville/A.Johnson	Mazda RX7	116 laps

Fastest lap: Paul Jnr, 1m 20.58s (112.584mph).
Class winners: GTX: Paul Jnr/Paul Snr. GTO: Rodriguez/Greenwood. GTU: Manderville/Johnson.

IMSA Camel GT Championship Round 17, Endurance Championship Round 9
Camel GT 500 — Pocono — 26 September 1982
170 laps = 500 miles. Winner's average speed 109.833mph

1	T.Field/D.Ongais	Lola T600-Chevrolet	4h 33m 47.775s
2	J.Paul Jnr/J.Paul Snr	Porsche 935	178 laps
3	C.Vincenz/W.Baker	Porsche 934	166 laps
4	B.Koll/S.McKitterick	Rondeau M382C-Chevrolet	166 laps
5	T.Garcia/A.Montoia/G.Ullom	BMW M1	165 laps
6	W.Frank/R.Bartling	Porsche 934	163 laps

Fastest lap: Ongais, 1m 26.19s (116.95mph) — record.
Class winners: GTX: Field/Ongais. GTO: Vincenz/Baker. GTU: J.Downing/J.Maffucci (Mazda RX7) 160 laps.

IMSA Camel GT Championship Round 18, Endurance Championship Round 10
Daytona — 28 November 1982
84 laps = 322.56 miles. Winner's average speed 106.673mph

1	D.Ongais/T.Field	Lola T600-Chevrolet	3h 1m 25.684s
2	J.Fitzpatrick/B.Wollek	Porsche 935	84 laps
3	D.Bell/R.Lanier	Porsche 935	83 laps
4	A.Holbert/P.Henn/D.Bundy	Porsche 935	83 laps
5	B.Hagan/G.Felton	Chevrolet Camaro	82 laps
6	D.Devendorf/T.Adamowicz	Datsun ZX Turbo	82 laps

Fastest lap: Ongais, 1m 45.36s (131.207mph) — record.
Class winners: GTX: Ongais/Field. GTO: Hagan/Felton. GTU: J.Downing/J.Maffucci (Mazda RX7), 79 laps.

FINAL POSITIONS
IMSA Camel GT Championship 1982

1	John Paul Jnr	235
2	Ted Field	167
3	Danny Ongais	138
4	John Paul Snr	137
5	John Fitzpatrick	125
6	Terry Wolters	84

COULD DO BETTER...

In a school report, Ford's first full season with the much vaunted C100 would probably be described as 'character building'. Plagued by unreliability and lack of outright speed, the car developed painfully slowly, but, as our WEC correspondent reports, things can only get better.

THE Ford C100 made its race début at Brands Hatch in 1981, in the Flying Tiger 1000km. Designed by Len Bailey and in Group Six specification, the car had completed only 400 miles of frequently interrupted testing, but performed faultlessly at Brands, where it secured pole position. The car was neat and obviously generated a lot of grip, but in the race retired two laps after its first fuel stop with gearbox failure.

After this promising maiden outing, Ford might have seen itself on the verge of repeating its 1960s successes. Then, the GT40 had won the Le Mans 24-Hour race four years in a row, from 1966 to 1969, including Jacky Ickx's sensational defeat of Hans Hermann's Porsche 908 in the last year, the closest ever 'genuine' finish. But when Ford set out to cultivate its racey image with the Group C C100 in 1982, it cannot have bargained on acquiring the appearance of a somewhat second rate, backyard special.

Eberhardt Braun's revised design first appeared at Paul Ricard in February, where ATS Grand Prix driver Manfred Winkelhock and Zakspeed contractee Klaus Ludwig, gave the car its preliminary shake down tests. Only weeks before, the Group 6 WEC contender from Lancia lapped the Ricard short circuit in 1m 09s, but the best the Ford could achieve was a disappointing 1m 13s. Compounding the embarrassment, the world's motoring press captured for posterity pictures of the C100 lifting its inside front wheel as it rounded the French circuit's tighter turns.

After the first day's running, the car underwent extensive suspension changes overnight. While retaining the same geometry as the car which appeared at Brands Hatch, Ford experimented with various spring rates, shock absorbers and roll bars, the situation aggravated by the Schmidtthelm spring maker's delay in supplying the desired parts.

The C100's WEC race début had been posted as 14 March, first round of the World Endurance Championship at Brands Hatch, but the Ricard problems forced Ford to postpone it. Instead, Ford announced the revised car would run competitively for the first time at Zolder, Belgium, on 21 March, in the Deutsche Rennsport Meisterschaft opener. "The results of that first test required Ford to re-think completely the C100's suspension geometry and spring rates", said Peter Ashcroft, Director of Ford Motorsport (Europe),

"the car has more downforce than we anticipated and our estimate of the spring rates required was very wrong".

Unfortunately, Zolder hardly transpired to be the up-turn in fortunes Ford had envisaged and the C100 was even humbled by its Zakspeed turbo Capri stablemate! Ludwig qualified his Jagermeister liveried car fourth fastest after problems balancing the brakes and selecting fourth gear. The revised front suspension however, did improve the handling, enabling Ludwig to run fourth in the race behind Klaus Niedzwiedz's Capri and the Porsche 936s of Bob Wollek and Rolf Stommelen. Then the C100 tangled with the latter, and damaged the suspension putting Ludwig out of the race.

Another DRM round followed and then the C100 made its WEC début in the Monza 1000km in April. The new chassis arrived late for practice and only participated in the second session. Frankly the car was a mess and Ford was rightly criticised by the racing press for its shabby preparation. The car's performance was hardly any better, with the engine down on power and the chassis giving the drivers an exciting ride through Monza's fast corners. In the race, it ran as high as third before a ruptured water pipe cooked the engine.

Frustrated and probably under pressure from sponsors, Ford revealed soon after Monza that it had withdrawn the C100 from the DRM. Disappointed with the car's form, Ford decided to take the C100 away from the critical gaze of the German press and announced that it would not reappear in the DRM until the Norisring "Money Race" on 27 June. Ford also moved its preparation away from the Cologne factory to Erich Zakowski's Zakspeed premises at Niedersizzen. While it was there, it was also mooted that the C100 would receive the 1.7-litre turbo engine from the Capri. This at least would allow blistering performance if only for a short while with the turbo's boost pressure turned up!

Such a car never appeared unfortunately, but at Silverstone, the second round of the WEC, a completely new C100 arrived. The car had been revamped from stem to stern, saving 70kg in weight and retaining only the suspension uprights from the original model. Tony Southgate, former BRM, Shadow and Lotus Grand Prix designer, was responsible for the revisions, which had kept Zakspeed so busy that it had still not found the time to build a second car. However, as Ford pointed out, until the C100's specification was finalised, there was no point in producing a replica.

This time, Ford appeared to have got it right. For the first time ever a C100 managed to lap the short Nürburgring, on race rubber, faster than the Group 5 Capri on qualifiers. Winkelhock qualified it fourth fastest for the Pace Six Hours at Silverstone, and in the race he and Ludwig had the C100 in a worthy third position before the almost inevitable problems set in. A blocked fuel filter disrupted the car's practice but it was a fuel pump, on the left-hand tank, which gave trouble in the race. Already delayed by a puncture, the C100 had to refuel earlier than normal because the pump would not deliver the remaining 20 litres of fuel in the tank. The car pressed on but first a split water radiator and then a failing clutch dropped it down in the field.

Disappointed but now primed with optimism, Zakspeed arrived at the Nürburgring expecting to do well. With the 1000km race so close to Le Mans in the calendar, many teams, including Porsche, chose not to participate, and the C100 grabbed the opportunity to shine. The fuel pumps had been relocated and remounted on rubber in the side pods to prevent a repetition of the Silverstone problem. The nose cone was also reprofiled to give greater downforce and the suspension slightly softened. Winkelhock and Ludwig, with years of Nürburgring experience behind them, had no trouble putting the car on pole position. It was the highlight of the C100's season.

There were more fuel pressure problems in the race, the gauge

The C100 was announced in 1981 (left) and made its first appearance in Group 6 trim at the wet Flying Tiger 1000 at Brands Hatch in September, (above right) qualifying on pole but succumbing to gearbox bothers. By mid-1982 the car had been completely revamped by Southgate and Zakspeed, emerging first at Silverstone and rejoining the DRM fray with this Ludwig-driven entry (right) at Norisring. As if the general development problems were not enough, Winkelhock's car for the last round of the season, at Brands Hatch, (below right) was damaged by a fire during practice.

indicating that there wasn't any above 8000rpm, but the car took the lead from the green light and held it for four hours. Then Ludwig staggered into the pits where the mechanics worked feverishly on the left-hand side of the transmission. The C100 tried to rejoin the race after makeshift repairs but the differential finally seized completely just a few yards down the pit lane.

At last, the second C100 was ready for Le Mans in June and, from this point onwards, Ford continued to run two cars for Ludwig/Marc Surer and Winkelhock/Niedzwiedz. A third entry had been made for this race as Ford had been expected to field two brand new cars and the original chassis. However, it did not materialise and Ludwig was entrusted with the care of the new car, Winkelhock taking over the old one. Although the cars handled well, there was a distinct lack of straightline speed and, to make matters worse, Winkelhock's practice engine was suspected of being down on power. The C100s qualified sixth and eleventh but success at the Sarthe was thwarted by the other weak link in Ford's chain, the Cosworth developed 3.9-litre DFL.

Winkelhock was in the lead when he had to stop to rectify a clutch problem but, finally, the engine blew up after six hours. By this time, the Surer/Ludwig car was already stationary at the end of the Mulsanne Straight, stranded by electrical failure. Similar problems later stopped the remaining Rondeau M382s, both using 3.9 DFL engines. Was there a connection? To Cosworth's chagrin there was.

The 3.3 DFL was increased in capacity by means of a longer stroke and further changes to the engine included revised fuel pump belt drive, new air intake trumpets, new cylinder liners and the adoption of a damper for the crankshaft. In this form the DFL develops 540 bhp at 9500rpm with a wide spread of power between 5000 and 9500rpm. However, that damper on the crankshaft is an indication of where the DFL's biggest problem lies: vibration. Virtually all the engine's users complained about the problem which, in severe cases, could quite literally lead to the destruction of several ancillary parts. But at Le Mans, it was the *damper* itself which proved to be the catalyst of disaster. Heat caused the rubber bush to expand and cut the wires of the ignition pick-up, which is mounted adjacent to the damper.

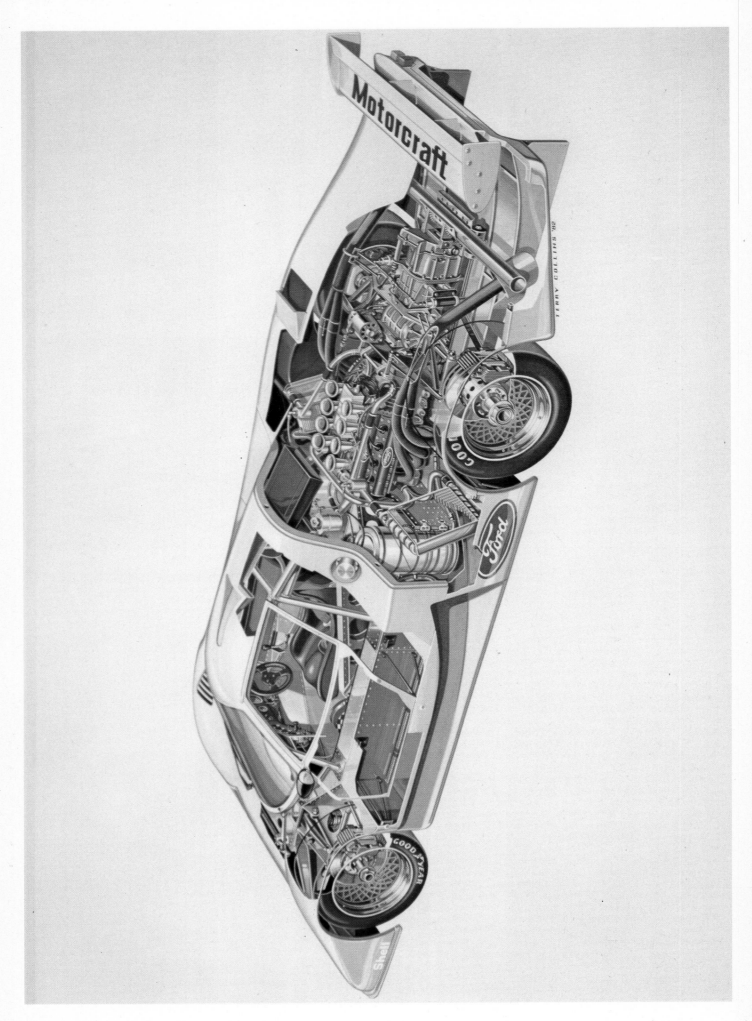

156

The C100 in 1982 guise, developed and prepared in the Zakspeed works to Tony Southgate's specifications, looked outwardly near identical to the original car, but under the skin (left) there were many changes. For much of the year, development was hampered by unreliability but in the final race, at Brands Hatch in October, Surer and Winkelhock (right) were running together in the lead of the streaming wet event before taking each other off.

This was quickly pin-pointed by Cosworth who used the 11 week gap between Le Mans and the Spa-Francorchamps 1000km to solve the problem. It produced new crankshaft dampers which it tested extensively on the C100 and the Rondeau. Although the conditions of Le Mans were never suitably simulated at Silverstone or the Nürburgring, there were no subsequent failures on either of the revised DFLs and, by Spa, all Cosworth's customers had at least one engine to the latest specification.

For Ford, the Belgian event, final round of the WEC for Manufacturers, was much like the preceding four. Once again its relative sloth down the straights was a big problem on the fast Ardennes road circuit and both cars suffered a variety of problems, including broken exhaust primaries. On a partly damp track, the Surer/Ludwig car held second place briefly, using intermediate tyres but as the surface dried, it slipped back to share its sister's tale of woe. Ford bowed out of the Manufacturers' series, having failed to score a single point, by finishing 18th and 23rd.

Amid rumours that Ford is considering a smaller Group C programme in 1983, three C100s were entered for the first time, at Brands Hatch, final round of the WEC for Drivers. The weekend began badly when two of them burst into flames during a preceding test session, fuel leaking from a faulty seal on the metering unit and igniting in the engine bay. The cars, Winkelhock's, and Ludwig's DRM machine (crewed by Jonathan Palmer and lady driver Desiré Wilson), were fortunately not badly damaged. The C100's career began at Brands and 12 months later it repeated its 1981 feat by taking pole position again, this time with Surer at the wheel. To complete a grand day for Ford, Winkelhock shared the front row with his Swiss team mate.

As so often in the past though, it all turned sour in the race. The Shell Oils 1000 began in a torrential downpour and the two C100s made the most of the spray-free air in front of them — *at once*. For

four laps, Winkelhock and Surer bounced off each other's bodywork as they circulated *side by side* in the rain. Finally, this immature exhibition came to an end when Surer lost control on a puddle and punted his team mate off into the barriers! The Swiss continued but Manfred stepped from his shattered wreck and returned to the pits in time to see the race stopped! The German was then transferred to Surer's undamaged machine which eventually finished in fifth position after fuel mixture and suspension bothers, one place and one lap behind Palmer and Wilson. In contrast to their team mates, this crew never indulged in any heroics and treated the race with a mature respect which might stand them in good stead with Ford, when it comes to choosing next year's drivers . . . But for a late puncture, they might even have finished third!

Looking back on 1982, Peter Ashcroft summed up the C100's career so far. "It has taken Ford longer to learn the Group C ropes than some people. However, I don't find that surprising as it is our first serious endurance venture since the GT40. I am aware of the rumours of our withdrawal but there are no plans yet and Ford will make an announcement in a couple of months time."

However, it is clear that Ford's poor season is not simply the result of being educationally backward. The C100 was not a good car to start with and Tony Southgate's efforts only rounded off the rough edges. As for the drivers, one can't help but question their suitability for endurance racing: Ludwig and Winkelhock were constantly trying to prove their superiority over one another, with wretched effect on the machinery.

Next year Ford will be back, but in what form? Southgate has designed a new car, which monocoque construction specialist John Thompson is presently putting together. The new car will almost certainly feature the DFL turbo, which tested briefly in England in August, but which Cosworth is keeping very close to its chest.

But one thing is certain; for Ford it can only get better.

FADED JEWEL

The SCCA's Can-Am Championship was once one of the most prestigious racing series in the world, with powerful factory teams and a host of top class drivers chasing the gold. The series still attracts overseas drivers and some interesting cars, but Can-Am is struggling. STEVE POTTER reports.

AL Unser Jr stopped off on his way to Indianapolis and won the 1982 Can-Am championship. Nowadays, much of the lustre is gone from the Can-Am, which was once the crown jewel of American road racing, and the 1982 season will be mostly remembered for the precocious performances of the 20-year-old son of a three time Indy winner.

The year before, his first in road racing after a sterling teenage career in the fearsome sprint cars, young Unser won the Robert Bosch SuperVee title in a Ralt owned by Arizona car dealer Rick Galles. Indy car competition has always been the team's long term goal, but the Can-Am was deemed a good halfway step up from SuperVee.

Front line competition was even thinner in '82 than the year before, but Unser's performance would have stood him in good stead at the Can-Am's zenith. He was near the Riverside track record the first afternoon that he sat in the car, and usually the quickest man on the track.

Galles bought the Lola-based Frissbee project from Brad Frisselle, and hired Trevor Harris, designer of the 1981 series winning VDS 001, as well as the original Frissbee. Partway through the year

the Galles team introduced its own car, the GR3, the next step in the progression of Harris's Frissbee and VDS designs.

Unser wasn't most people's preseason pick. That role belonged to Patrick Tambay, who had quit Formula One in disgust after the South African Grand Prix and signed to drive in the Can-Am for VDS. The Frenchman, twice the series champion, led the rain soaked Road Atlanta opener until the mid-point when he tried to pass a backmarker in a corner instead of waiting for the next straight. The collision knocked Tambay out of the race and gave the lead, and ultimately the race, to Unser.

After Tambay got the call to take Villeneuve's place at Ferrari, the favourite's mantle descended on the tall youngster's shoulders. His chief competition came from Tambay's replacement at VDS, Al Holbert, and from Danny Sullivan, the sole driver at Newman Racing. Amongst them they divided victories in the nine race schedule. Unser and Holbert had four each, while Sullivan repeated his '81 Caesars Palace win.

The 40 point difference in their tallies at season's end was the result of three runner up finishes for Unser against one runner up and two thirds for Holbert, who was also hurt by not participating in

The Unser family has turned up another winner in Al Jr (left) who took the title through consistent front running performances. Danny Sullivan scored only one win, at Caesars Palace, but put the Newman Racing/Budweiser March (above) into third place overall, two ahead of Jim Crawford's converted F1 Ensign (below).

the first race.

John Morton, John Kalagian, Randy Lewis and Rex Ramsey all stood backup, but none had the financial resources necessary to mount a challenge to the top triumvirate.

Nor did Bertil Roos, who didn't even have a five-litre car. Driving a four-year-old, two-litre car the expatriot Swede, head of his own driving school at Pocono, Roos gave free lessons to most of the Can-Am's drivers. Second overall at Road Atlanta, third at Mosport and Road America and fifth at Caesars left him fourth in the overall standings, and winner by a wide margin in the two-litre category.

Jim Crawford brought his fendered Ensign to North America at mid-season after winning the British F1 series, and despite running just four races (in which he finished second, third, fourth and fifth) he finished fifth in the final standings.

Officials of the Sports Car Club of America, the group that sanctions the Can-Am, had realized that their series was in trouble even before the season started. In an attempt to generate interest in the series they opened it up to FISA Group C specification cars — to the loud protest of most of their present contestants, who feared that without the constraint of fuel consumption regulations the new coupés would quickly dominate the races.

There were rumours that Porsche's US distributor had committed several 956s to the series, but ultimately the SCCA decided that it would enforce the FISA fuel regulations on the Group C cars, and in that way control their speed. In the end there were no Porsches. The only Group C car to appear was Ralph Kent Cooke's Cosworth DFL powered Lola T610, which appeared at Road America with the talented Jim Adams in the cockpit, but was far from competitive.

The future of the series is cloudy. The top three teams from 1982, Galles, VDS and Newman, are all going to Indy car racing in '83, although Newman's sponsor, Budweiser beer, confirms that they will continue series sponsorship for another two years. Some of the races were well attended, and at season's end the SCCA announced a preliminary six race schedule, with at least two more dates expected.

There has been speculation that the rulemakers might reduce the displacement and horsepower output of the single seat open cockpit cars, in order to stimulate Group C entries. With IMSA failing to adopt the FISA rules there is currently no place in North America other than the Can-Am for the Group C cars to race.

SCCA CAN-AM CHAMPIONSHIP:RESULTS

Round 1 — Road Atlanta — 23 May 1982
59 laps = 148.68 miles. Winner's average speed 99.711mph
1	Al Unser Jnr	Frissbee-Chevrolet	1h 29m 27.0s
2	Bertil Roos	Marguey-Hart	1h 29m 43.0s
3	Danny Sullivan	March 827-Chevrolet	58 laps
4	Rex Ramsey	Lola-Chevrolet	58 laps
5	William Blackledge	Ralt RT2-Honda	55 laps
6	Frank Joyce	CAC 2-Chevrolet	55 laps

Fastest lap: Unser Jnr. 1m 15.510s (120.143mph)

Round 2 — Mosport Park — 6 June 1982
51 laps = 125.41 miles. Winner's average speed 110.35mph
1	Al Unser Jnr	Frissbee-Chevrolet	1h 08m 11.367s
2	Danny Sullivan	March 827-Chevrolet	1h 08m 48.522s
3	Bertil Roos	Marguey-Hart	49 laps
4	Jacques Villeneuve	Lola T296 Ford	48 laps
5	Rex Ramsey	Lola T530-Chevrolet	48 laps
6	Jim Trueman	Cicale Ralt RT1-Hart	48 laps

Fastest lap: Sullivan, 1m 14.540s (118.76mph)

Round 3 — Mid-Ohio — 27 June 1982
63 laps = 151.2 miles. Winner's average speed 102.23mph
1	Al Holbert	VDS001-Chevrolet	1h 28m 44.705s
2	Al Unser Jnr	Frissbee-Chevrolet	1h 29m 50.493s
3	John Morton	Frissbee-Chevrolet	61 laps
4	Randy Lewis	CAC 1-Chevrolet	61 laps
5	John Kalagian	Frissbee-Chevrolet	60 laps
6	Frank Joyce	CAC 2-Chevrolet	59 laps

Fastest lap: Holbert, 1m 22.22s (105.08mph) — record

Round 4 — Elkhart Lake — 25 July 1982
40 laps = 160 miles. Winner's average speed 114.819mph
1	Al Holbert	VDS001-Chevrolet	1h 23m 36.61s
2	Danny Sullivan	March 827-Chevrolet	1h 23m 57.03s
3	Bertil Roos	Marguey CA82-Hart	39 laps
4	John Morton	Frissbee-Chevrolet	38 laps
5	Randy Lewis	CAC 1-Chevrolet	38 laps
6	Frank Joyce	CAC 2-Chevrolet	37 laps

Fastest lap: Holbert, 2m 01.354s (118.661mph)

Round 5 — Trois Rivieres — 5 September 1982
60 laps = 126.0 miles. Winner's average speed 82.728mph
1	Al Holbert	VDS001-Chevrolet	1h 31m 23.3s
2	Jim Crawford	Ensign N180-Cosworth	59 laps
3	Danny Sullivan	March 827-Chevrolet	59 laps
4	John Morton	Frissbee-Chevrolet	58 laps
5	Jim Trueman	March 822-Hart	58 laps
6	John Kalagian	Frissbee-Chevrolet	58 laps

Fastest lap: not given

Round 6 — Mosport — 12 September 1982
60 laps = 147.48 miles. Winner's average speed 116.658mph
1	Al Unser Jnr	Frissbee GR3-Chevrolet	1h 15m 53.009s
2	Danny Sullivan	March 827-Chevrolet	1h 16m 15.658s
3	Al Holbert	VDS001-Chevrolet	1h 16m 27.082s
4	John Morton	Frissbee-Chevrolet	57 laps
5	Jim Crawford	Ensign N180-Cosworth	57 laps
6	John Kalagian	Frissbee-Chevrolet	57 laps

Fastest lap: Unser Jnr, 1m 11.873s (123.167mph) — record

Round 7 — Caesars Palace — 26 September 1982
66 laps = 149.9 miles. Winner's average speed 91.2mph
1	Danny Sullivan	March 827-Chevrolet	1h 38m 29.366s
2	Al Unser Jnr	Frissbee GR3-Chevrolet	1h 39m 18.0s
3	Al Holbert	VDS001 Chevrolet	1h 39m 44.0s
4	Jim Crawford	Ensign N180B-Cosworth	65 laps
5	Bertil Roos	Marguey-Hart	63 laps
6	John Kalagian	Frissbee-Chevrolet	63 laps

Fastest lap: Sullivan, 1m 27.106s (93.734mph)

Round 8 — Riverside — 3 October 1982
60 laps = 152.40 miles. Winner's average speed 120.472mph
1	Al Holbert	VDS001-Chevrolet	1h 15m 54.058s
2	Al Unser Jnr	Galles GR3-Chevrolet	1h 16m 39.900s
3	Danny Sullivan	March 827-Chevrolet	59 laps
4	Geoff Brabham	Galles GR3-Chevrolet	59 laps
5	John Morton	Frissbee-Chevrolet	59 laps
6	Randy Lewis	CAC 1-Chevrolet	58 laps

Fastest lap: not given

Round 9 — Laguna Seca — 10 October 1982
60 laps = 114 miles. Winner's average speed 114.151mph
1	Al Unser Jnr	Galles GR3-Chevrolet	59m 55.250s
2	Al Holbert	VDS001-Chevrolet	59 laps
3	Jim Crawford	Ensign N180B-Cosworth	58 laps
4	John Kalagian	Frissbee-Chevrolet	56 laps
5	Horst Kwek	Toleman TG280-Hart 420R	56 laps
6	Jacques Villeneuve	Osella PA8-BMW	56 laps

Fastest lap: Unser Jnr, 56.810s (120.401mph)

FINAL POINTS

1	A.Unser Jnr	540	6	J.Morton	129
2	A.Holbert	500	7	J.Kalagian	122
3	D.Sullivan	390	8	R.Lewis	71
4	B.Roos	173	9	R.Ramsey	68
5	J.Crawford	150	10	F.Joyce; J.Trueman	54

TOMORROW, THE WORLD

In recent years, Formula 2 hasn't always lived up to its role as a Grand Prix nursery, but the three drivers who took this year's title fight down to the wire did much to re-establish the Formula's credibility. IAN PHILLIPS, Racing News Editor of *Autosport*, London, reports.

PURELY and simply 1982 was a vintage year for Formula 2. A three cornered fight to the final flag in the European Championship, involving three exciting new talents, was just what the Formula needed. After two successive years with paid professionals taking the title, 21-year old Corrado Fabi took the honours in the works Roloil March-BMW and emerged as one of racing's brightest stars.

The focal point of the series was the battle between the two Honda supported teams, Ralt and Spirit, and the main BMW attack, from March and Maurer. The final score in terms of races won was 10-3 in favour of the BMW-powered teams, which was a complete reversal of pre-season form.

The BMW success was almost entirely the doing of the works March team, who won eight races on their way to their sixth European Championship title. Simplicity and reliability were the keynotes of their approach and they paid handsome dividends. Ralph Bellamy's 822 chassis was perfectly matched to the Michelin radials and proved to be a superior combination to the more powerful Honda-engined cars on Bridgestone tyres.

An exhaustive winter test programme by March might have delayed the final specification of the 822 but by the third of the 13 races the team was showing its strength. Fabi should have won the Thruxton round, in April, by a lap, but when Corrado's engine broke, his team mate Johnny Cecotto staged a brilliant comeback drive

A major part of the attraction of Formula 2 is the type of circuit which the championship visits; real street circuits like Pau are nowadays lost to Grand Prix racing and will soon be lost to Formula Two. Championship runners up Cecotto (left) and Boutsen (leading from the start, above) finished first and second here in May.

after a pit stop to take the honours. From that point on the March machine almost steam-rolled the championship, with either one or the other of their two drivers finishing in the first three in all the remaining races.

Fabi scored wins at Mugello, Vallelunga, Hockenheim, Donington and Misano while the former motorcycle World Champion proved his ever increasing four wheel ability with wins at Thruxton, Pau and Mantorp Park and furthermore he scored points in 10 of the 13 rounds. The main championship challenge to the March team came in the form of Thierry Boutsen in the Marlboro Spirit-Honda. Formed by former March men John Wickham and Gordon Coppuck, Spirit's programme was based around the 1981 championship winning Honda engines and Bridgestone tyres. With drivers Boutsen and Stefan Johansson it was a powerful line-up. Johansson took five pole positions in the first eight races but suffered endless misfortunes which kept him out of the results. By contrast, Boutsen finished in 12 races, 10 times in the points. He added a mean streak to his already skilful driving and took three excellent wins, at Nürburgring, Spa and Enna. The team had a couple of bad races in the middle of the year, which the March boys took full advantage of, and so entering the final race, Fabi, Boutsen and Cecotto could all take the title.

Cecotto had the upper hand in that either of his rivals had to win to overhaul his total, but if he finished second that would be good enough whatever the others did. Fabi was in rare form, taking pole position by 0.3s but a further special ingredient in the form of rain an hour before the start spiced up the battle even further. With the track very wet but the skies clearing, Fabi and Cecotto started on slicks, Boutsen on wets. The Spirit-Honda built up a colossal lead

*A sensation during the early part of the season was F2 débutant Stefan Bellof, winning the first two rounds in his works Maurer with conspicuously strong BMW power (top). Some silly mistakes apart, steadiness kept Kenny Acheson in the top ten (above), although the Ralt was a late developer and its Bridgestone tyres inconsistent. Michelin runners invariably enjoyed an advantage, as shown prominently on the works March-BMWs, and with flashes of inspiration by AGS' capable Philippe Streiff (top, right). "Look out, it's **behind** you!" Two substantial accidents, a stretched budget, and an ageing Toleman precluded Thierry Tassin from the results he deserved.*

in the opening stages and had time to change to slicks and still emerge in the lead. But by this time Fabi was in his beautiful flowing stride, having survived the crisis laps, and inevitably he took the lead. The only Bridgestone dries compatible with the wet tyre settings were only good for 20 laps and so Boutsen's efforts were in vain in this win or bust situation. Despite the Belgian's heroic efforts justice was done in that the title went to the best all round combination. Poor Cecotto was not even able to defend his position as he was pushed off on the first lap, although that still left him with a good second place overall in the series. German Stefan Bellof was the early season sensation with the works Maurer which had the advantage of Michelin tyres and the very powerful Heidegger BMW engines. The double German Formula Ford champion set a record by winning his first two F2 races, but thereafter, despite setting five fastest laps, he never really looked like winning again — although his driving of the neat little Maurer chassis was extremely spectacular and very reminiscent of Keke Rosberg in his early days. The Maurer was probably the best car — controversial skirts system apart — but sadly internal politics wrecked any serious attempt on the championship by Bellof or his more experienced team mate Beppe Gabbiani, who returned to the F2 scene after an abortive F1 year with Osella.

Tall Frenchman Philippe Streiff had a good début year in the AGS and emerged as a strong runner in the second half of the year. By complete contrast former Toleman team mates Kenny Acheson and Stefan Johansson had frustrating seasons in their respective Honda powered Ralt and Spirit chassis. The Ulsterman gave the championship-defending Ralt team their best result of the season with second place at Thruxton and he also took fastest lap at Pau, but for the team generally it was a disappointing year. As already mentioned, Johansson had appalling luck, but when he was running well he was still the most spectacular, explosive and aggressive driver the Formula could boast.

Jonathan Palmer came into F2 with the Ralt team amid great fanfare and publicity following his British F3 success and notable F1 test sessions. His year began and ended with accidents but out of it all he emerged as a very good driver. Luck was rarely on his side but he drove especially well at Nürburgring, Mugello and Donington and must be one of next season's favourites for the title.

Alessandro Nannini, a 21-year-old Italian with barely a season's racing experience, looked to be a very fine prospect with the Minardi team, while Mike Thackwell, still just 21, only did half the races with a private March on a shoestring budget. The New Zealander remains one of racing's brightest prospects and his surefire talent carried his little team to two excellent third places at Pau and Spa.

The championship as a whole was noteworthy not only for the tense battle between three fine young drivers and the Honda-BMW confrontation but for its general high standard of technical excellence. March ultimately deserved the title because their hardware combination was a superior engineering exercise to those of the opposition who may have had the upper hand in one or other of the departments but not all round.

As a Formula, Formula Two goes from strength to strength. All the season's grids were full and the variety of circuits provided a mean challenge to drivers and constructors while at the same time retaining the essential ambiance of sport. Long may it continue.

EUROPEAN F2 CHAMPIONSHIP

Round 1 — Silverstone — 21 March 1982
47 laps = 137.80 miles. Winner's average speed 115.07mph

1	Stefan Bellof	Maurer MM82-BMW	1h 11m 51.38s
2	Satoru Nakajima	March 812-Honda	1h 12m 12.64s
3	Beppe Gabbiani	Maurer MM82-BMW	1h 12m 12.76s
4	Roberto del Castello	Toleman T850-BMW	1h 12m 19.06s
5	Alessandro Nannini	Minardi FLY281B-BMW	1h 12m 22.86s
6	Jo Gartner	March 822-BMW	1h 12m 58.08s

Fastest lap: Christian Danner (March 822-BMW), 1m 29.35s (118.13mph)

Round 2 — Hockenheim — 4 April 1982
30 laps = 126.570 miles. Winner's average speed 120.57mph

1	Stefan Bellof	Maurer MM82-BMW	1h 3m 3.44s
2	Thierry Boutsen	Spirit 201-Honda	1h 3m 8.23s
3	Corrado Fabi	March 822-BMW	1h 3m 16.34s
4	Johnny Cecotto	March 822-BMW	1h 3m 16.60s
5	Beppe Gabbiani	Maurer MM82-BMW	1h 3m 28.13s
6	Thierry Tassin	Toleman DS1-Hart	1h 3m 35.79s

Fastest lap: Bellof, 2m 4.21s (122.42mph)

Round 3 — Thruxton — 12 April 1982
55 laps = 129.58 miles. Winner's average speed 121.82mph

1	Johnny Cecotto	March 822-BMW	1h 3m 49.22s
2	Kenny Acheson	Ralt RH6/82H-Honda	1h 4m 1.00s
3	Thierry Boutsen	Spirit 201-Honda	1h 4m 5.09s
4	Beppe Gabbiani	Maurer MM82-BMW	1h 4m 17.21s
5	Phillipe Streiff	AGS JH19-BMW	1h 20m 26s
6	Richard Dallest	March 822-BMW	1h 4m 28.37s

Fastest lap: Cecotto, 1m 7.37s (125.90mph) — record

Round 4 — Nurburgring — 25 April 1982
9 laps = 127.70 miles. Winner's average speed 117.84mph

1	Thierry Boutsen	Spirit 201-Honda	1h 5m 1.37s
2	Corrado Fabi	March 822-BMW	1h 5m 1.54s
3	Johnny Cecotto	March 822-BMW	1h 5m 59.35s
4	Kenny Acheson	Ralt RH6/82H-Honda	1h 6m 2.15s
5	Stefan Bellof	Maurer MM82-BMW	1h 6m 10.75s
6	Stefan Johansson	Spirit 201-Honda	1h 6m 13.77s

Fastest lap: Bellof, 9m 6.51s (119.89mph)

Round 5 — Mugello — 9 May 1982
42 laps = 136.88 miles. Winner's average speed 110.171mph

1	Corrado Fabi	March 822-BMW	1h 14m 32.79s
2	Johnny Cecotto	March 822-BMW	1h 14m 36.92s
3	Stefan Johansson	Spirit 201-Honda	1h 14m 42.87s
4	Thierry Boutsen	Spirit 201-Honda	1h 14m 44.05s
5	Jonathan Palmer	Ralt RH6/82H-Honda	1h 14m 56.67s
6	Kenny Acheson	Ralt RH6/82H-Honda	1h 15m 30.82s

Fastest lap: Fabi, 1m 44.21s (112.684mph)

Round 6 — Vallelunga — 16 May 1982
65 laps = 129.24 miles. Winner's average speed 102.36mph

1	Corrado Fabi	March 822-BMW	1h 15m 45.40s
2	Phillipe Streiff	AGS JH19-BMW	1h 15m 56.23s
3	Pascal Fabre	AGS JH18-BMW	1h 16m 36.31s
4	Stefan Johansson	Spirit 201-Honda	64 laps
5	Jonathan Palmer	Ralt RH6/82H-Honda	64 laps
6	Thierry Boutsen	Spirit 201-Honda	64 laps

Fastest lap: Stefan Bellof (Maurer MM82-BMW), 1m 8.63s (104.30mph)

Round 7 — Pau — 31 May 1982
73 laps = 125.15 miles. Winner's average speed 82.55mph

1	Johnny Cecotto	March 822-BMW	1h 31m 00.03s
2	Thierry Boutsen	Spirit 201-Honda	1h 31m 15.93s
3	Mike Thackwell	March 822-BMW	1h 32m 17.02s
4	Frank Jelinski	Maurer MM82-BMW	72 laps
5	Kenny Acheson	Ralt RH6/82H-Honda	72 laps
6	Jonathan Palmer	Ralt RH6/82H-Honda	72 laps

Fastest lap: Acheson, 1m 12.37s (85.31mph)

Round 8 — Spa Francorchamps — 13 June 1982
23 laps = 99.705 miles. Winner's average speed 102.57mph

1	Thierry Boutsen	Spirit 201-Honda	58m 17.47s
2	Johnny Cecotto	March 822-BMW	58m 40.06s
3	Mike Thackwell	March 822-BMW	59m 05.44s
4	Phillipe Streiff	AGS JH19-BMW	59m 11.00s
5	Corrado Fabi	March 822-BMW	59m 14.17s
6	Jonathan Palmer	Ralt RH6/82H-Honda	1h 00m 07.55s

Fastest lap: Thackwell, 2m 29.48s (104.40mph)

Round 9 — Hockenheim — 20 June 1982
30 laps = 126.70 miles. Winner's average speed 120.53mph

1	Corrado Fabi	March 822-BMW	1h 3m 4.32s
2	Beppe Gabbiani	Maurer MM82-BMW	1h 3m 6.92s
3	Stefan Bellof	Maurer MM82-BMW	1h 3m 8.52s
4	Stefan Johansson	Spirit 201-Honda	1h 3m 46.63s
5	Frank Jelinski	Maurer MM82-BMW	1h 3m 49.83s
6	Johnny Cecotto	March 822-BMW	1h 3m 51.26s

Fastest lap: Fabi, 2m 4.28s (122.34mph)

Round 10 — The Howitt Trophy Race — Donington — 4 July 1982
70 laps = 137.01 miles. Winner's average speed 108.59mph

1	Corrado Fabi	March 822-BMW	1h 15m 42.11s
2	Johnny Cecotto	March 822-BMW	1h 15m 42.7s
3	Jonathan Palmer	Ralt RH6/82-Honda	1h 15m 57.70s
4	Beppe Gabbiani	Maurer MM82-MBW	1h 16m 08.49s
5	Phillipe Streiff	AGS JH19-BMW	1h 16m 12.60s
6	Stefan Bellof	Maurer MM82-BMW	1h 16m 15.95s

Fastest lap: Fabi, 1m 03.82s (110.41mph) — record

Round 11 — Mantorp Park — 18 July 1982
62 laps = 126.22 miles. Winner's average speed 96.50mph

1	Johnny Cecotto	March 822-BMW	1h 18m 28.4s
2	Phillipe Streiff	AGS JH19-BMW	1h 18m 53.8s
3	Beppe Gabbiani	Maurer MM82-BMW	1h 18m 58.1s
4	Thierry Boutsen	Spirit 201-Honda	1h 19m 29.11s
5	Christian Danner	March 822-BMW	1h 19m 31.8s
6	Pascal Fabre	AGS JH19-BMW	64 laps

No official fastest lap issued by organisers

Round 12 — Enna — 1 August 1982
45 laps = 138.41 miles. Winner's average speed 119.72mph

1	Thierry Boutsen	Spirit 201-Honda	1h 9m 22.15s
2	Stefan Bellof	Maurer MM82-BMW	1h 9m 26.42s
3	Johnny Cecotto	March 822-BMW	1h 10m 32.23sd
4	Phillipe Streiff	AGS JH19-BMW	1h 10m 43.61s
5	Frank Jelinksi	Maurer MM82-BMW	1h 10m 45.07s
6	Christian Danner	March 822-BMW	44 laps

Fastest lap: Bellof, 1m 30.75s (122.01mph) — record

Round 13 — Misano Adriatico — 7 August 1982
60 laps = 130.04 miles. Winner's average speed 99.50mph

1	Corrado Fabi	March 822-BMW	1h 18m 25.19s
2	Alessandro Nannini	Minardi FLY2818-BMW	1h 18m 35.58s
3	Beppe Gabbiani	Maurer MM82-BMW	1h 18m 40.28s
4	Christian Danner	March 822-BMW	1h 18m 55.21s
5	Stefan Bellof	Maurer MM82-BMW	1h 18m 56.33s
6	Thierry Boutsen	Spirit 201-Honda	1h 19m 10.60s

Fastest lap: Bellof, 1m 10.89s (110.06mph) — record

FINAL POSITIONS

1	Corrado Fabi	57	6	Philippe Streiff	22
2	Johnny Cecotto	56	7	Kenny Acheson	12
3	Thierry Boutsen	50	8	Stefan Johansson	11
4	Stefan Bellof	33	9	Jonathan Palmer	10
5	Beppe Gabbiani	26	10	Alessandro Nannini	8

FABI - SIMPLY THE BEST

As the European Formula Two Championship went right down to the wet final round, Corrado Fabi, younger of the two racing brothers, emerged not only as a worthy champion but also, as IAN PHILLIPS explains, as a star of the future.

IT was an honour to be at Italy's Autodromo Santamonica on the Adriatic coast during the first weekend of August 1982, for anybody who saw the final round of the European Formula 2 Championship also saw the final emergence of a superstar — Corrado Fabi.

Although Fabi had scored more wins with his works March-BMW than either of his two remaining rivals for the European title, he was still nine points, or one win, adrift in the championship. He *had* to win that race. Throughout the weekend he had been quickest in every practice session and so was starting from pole position. Then, as if the ingredients were not already exciting enough, it rained an hour before the start. If there was a flaw in Fabi's make-up it was his reputation for not being interested in driving in the wet. But this wasn't just plain wet — it was wet, sure, but under a clear sky and drying quite quickly. Undoubtedly the trickiest conditions imaginable in racing. There was really no option but to start on slicks unless you wanted to risk a pit stop. For Fabi here was the supreme test and he passed it with flying colours, to win both race and title.

That Santamonica victory gave him a total of five wins for the year, and the championship by just one point. But mere statistics do not go beyond proving that Fabi won more races than anybody else. He was, quite simply, the best. He should certainly have won seven of the year's 13 races and given a slice of luck might have won nine. His performances throughout the year were, undoubtedly, of 24 carat perfection. What makes Fabi's future so exciting is that he is still only 21 years old and, up to the end of September 1982, his career had spanned just 47 races!

Corrado was born on 12 April 1961, the second son to parents whose talcum powder mining interests ensured that their offspring had the opportunity to exploit their sporting interests from an early age. Elder son Teo was a proficient skier and it was a visit to the exclusive resort in the mountains behind their Milanese home that spawned the family motor sport interest. Aged just nine, Corrado spotted a fair ground Go-kart track and the first chapter opened. His father bought him a kart and for the next seven years nothing else interested him. Big brother Teo decided it was fun too and before long the Fabi brothers made up 50% of the Italian national team. But there was a snag, Corrado was only 14 in the year the

team won the European Championship and although they counted his points from the early races he was barred from the second part because he was too young!

Corrado 'retired' from karting when he was 17 and waited for a year until he was able to take up real motor racing. Brother Teo had already graduated and, as soon as he was old enough, Corrado raced his brother's well-used Formula 3 March in the final six races of the 1979 Italian Championship. A third place in the final race of the year earned him an invitation to join Paul Pavenello's works March F3 team for the European Championship the following year, alongside Michele Alboreto. A three cornered championship fight went to the final round, with Alboreto finally taking the title and Fabi finishing in third slot. But for a puncture in the final round, he might well have captured second from Thierry Boutsen.

While Teo had been leading the works March Formula 2 team, March boss Robin Herd had also kept an eye on the younger Fabi brother and, in fact, signed him up well before the F3 season was over, to replace Teo as he progressed to Formula 1. So, not yet 20 years old, Corrado found himself leading the works March-BMW Formula 2 team but he didn't let anybody down. Typically, for a young man who has taken every bold step with a nothing-but-charming self-confidence, he had no worries about the responsibilities or the prospects: "I think it was Robin who took the risk. He had no experienced drivers". Herd's faith in Corrado and Thierry Boutsen paid off with three wins, one of them to Fabi who was retained to lead the seemingly impossible offensive against the Honda-powered teams in 1982.

For one so young, Corrado certainly knows what he wants and it would be uncharitable to say he has always had it. But after certain communications problems internally with the team in 1981, he made sure that Robin Herd was contracted to attend over half of the 1982 races. There was a suspicion in 1981 that Corrado needed motivating before he gave of his best (something he disagrees with, plausibly claiming mechanical problems) but it was certainly noticeable that Herd's presence brought new purpose to Corrado's efforts.

At such a tender age and having had a relatively easy entry into international motor racing, perhaps it wasn't surprising that a little boost to the motivation was required. But about one thing there is no doubt, Corrado has an uncanny natural ability, the like of which is rare. He has the knack of making it all look so easy. His style is

In capturing the European Formula Two crown, Fabi (above) won five hard fought races and might have won several more, although he had to give best to Thierry Boutsen at the 'Ring (left). Fabi's driving is relaxed as well as quick. At Pau (right and below) as else-where he drove superbly but was eventually sidelined by broken wheel studs while challenging for the lead.

relaxed and inch perfect. Where other drivers tend to look untidy and hurried when trying really hard, Corrado remains smooth and unruffled. Mechanically he is sympathetic and intelligent. If there is time to work at improvement on the car he will use it to its maximum — witness all his pole positions being taken in the final five minutes of practice.

As a person, Corrado is much more outgoing than his elder brother but he has the same correct manners and charm. He bubbles schoolboy enthusiasm off the track and his team love him. He makes a point of saying "Good morning" and "Bi-Bi" to everyone at the start and end of the day and it's little things like breaking away from the 'management' victory dinner at Mugello to search out the restaurant where the mechanics were and thank them all personally that go a long way to making him a complete racing driver.

Every decade throws up one, maybe two drivers who are head and shoulders above the rest. Currently the void is gaping but Corrado Fabi has both the ability and the personality to fill it perfectly.

FORMULA RALT?

There's no escaping the truth of the old saw 'horses for courses', although even the best horse needs a good stable. RUSSELL BULGIN watched the breeding of the omnipotent Ralt RT3 and and the craft of Murray Taylor Racing combine to give Tommy Byrne the tools to finish the job.

If, in 1982, Formula 3 became Formula Ralt, then crucial competitive parameters shifted. Top teams still sought a chassis which could offer consistent wins — after all, in the technologically complex 'eighties, such is still the very essence of the sport — but now that deceptive goal was attained through evaluating millimetric ride height adjustments and affixing slivers of aerodynamically-subtle polyurethane; details meant everything. No longer did exploiting alternative design concepts developed by manufacturers other than Ralt make racing sense to serious teams.

So team structure — those vital working relationships woven tight or irreparably snagged during a 20 race season — took on a new importance. Superficially, the basic economic pattern of Formula 3 seemed stable; save that, worldwide, justifying £100,000 for a season of racing which rates as minor league stuff in the major media became even tougher.

Drivers with the ever-ready readies therefore made huge efforts to seek out the best possible driver-engineer liaison; when chassis are ostensibly out-of-the-box equal, then competitiveness is purely determined by the joint intellect displayed in a pitlane debrief.

And, as with a lot of contemporary Formula 3-think, it was 1981 Marlboro British Formula 3 champion Jonathan Palmer who shaped this trend. In his championship year he bought not only the single best chassis of 1980 — Stefan Johansson's Ralt RT3 — but also the car's development engineer, Dick Bennetts.

That canny appreciation of the often misunderstood engineer-driver-chassis interplay separated Palmer's approach from that of the rest of the 1981 runners; or, as they became, the also-rans. Pre-season testing not only honed the Ralt to a fresh level of race-wise competence, but also forged the Bennetts-Palmer link to an almost telepathic pitch.

Formula 3 insiders now tend to categorise teams according to the engineering flair and racing feel displayed by the team chief. Thus Dick Bennetts' low-profile but technically sound approach scores highly, while the glittering, money-talks, Murray Taylor Racing gameplan ranks less well. Because, capable as the ex-journalist is, he has to rely on his staff to initiate the latest tweak-of-the-week; which puts him at the mercies of a fickle labour market.

But it was a mutual confidence between Murray Taylor, his engineering sidekick Paul Thompson and driver Tommy Byrne which gave the offhand Irishman a Palmer-clone season start; that, and a 1981 Ralt chassis without the difficult-to-sort underskin changes of the superficially similar newer model. That was one approach, founded on logic and hard graft.

In the year's unlikeliest combination, discreet Englishman James Weaver — Formula 3's answer to Derek Bell — pooled his abilities with the streetwise blarney-bluster of Irishman Eddie Jordan to achieve a string of second-best placings. Dave Scott began his second Formula 3 year with the much-respected, ex-Mario Andretti Grand Prix wrench Glenn Waters in control of a compact show.

Whereupon Scott and his crew showed an area of collective weakness which, while casting an unflattering light on his often

'I HAD TO WIN...'

Tommy Byrne is used to doing things the hard way and not always taking the most obvious route. This year he combined winning the British F3 Championship with his first tentative steps into F1, but next year, as JEREMY SHAW, Features Editor of *Autosport*, London, explains, holds several possibilities.

TOMMY Byrne has achieved a tremendous amount during the last 12 months. In 1981, he was racing a Formula Ford 2000 Van Diemen — very successfully but on a budget so limited that he hardly knew, from week to week, whether he would be able to take part in the next championship race or not. He got through all that, with the help of a few friends, and won both the British and European Championships to boot. He then decided to take a step backwards by competing in the end-of-season Marlboro Formula Ford Festival at Brands Hatch.

It was a very brave move. Tommy had already won a pair of Formula Ford championships the previous season, so he had nothing to prove and much to lose. Surely, he was just putting his reputation on the line. If he had not won, he would have lost credibility, especially as he was known to be driving the most fancied car — the Van Diemen RF81 with which Ayrton da Silva had already swept the board during the season.

The Irishman's victory on that November weekend has been well-chronicled. So has his impressive Formula 3 debut the following weekend, which came about as his prize for winning the Festival. His superb second place was televised nationally on BBC television and Byrne's performance so impressed F3 team manager Murray Taylor that the Irishman was immediately signed up for the 1982 season, with a proviso that he could raise sufficient sponsorship over the winter. As it happened, Tommy never did manage to find anything like a full budget, but it's amazing how far some people can get with cheek and determination alone . . .

It all started for Byrne back in 1976 when a friend suggested to car-mad Tommy that he should take a trip down to the Mondello Park Racing School. "It was fantastic," he recalls, "I just fell in love with the racing car!"

Prior to that day, the young man from Blackrock, Dundalk, had no particular interest in motor racing. That changed over-night and he was soon saving as hard as he could to buy his own car. Byrne made his first real impression, co-incidentally, at Brands Hatch in 1977 when Mondello's John Murphy brought him over to compete in the Formula Ford Festival. Tommy caused quite an upset by qualifying easily for his semi-final but then throwing away any opportunity of making the final by spinning — an occurrence that had already frequently punctuated his short racing career. "I must admit, I did tend to be a bit hairy!"

Byrne was spurred on by his early promise, however, and soon realised that his best chance of moving on was to gain a works FF1600 drive, which he achieved in 1979. At the age of 21, Tommy proved fast in the new PRS car but had still not curbed his enthusiasm and failed to notch the results that had been expected from him. He parted company with the Holman brothers shortly before the end of that year but determination is certainly not lacking in Tommy, who quickly bounced back in a Royale lent to him by some friends.

This in turn led to him being offered a seat with the works Van Diemen team in 1980, and with them Byrne won the RAC and BARC Championships before moving on into FF2000, again with Ralph Firman's successful cars, to win another pair of championships.

Then came his move backwards into FF1600 for the Festival: "Ralph said that he had no driver and offered it to me as a joke. He said I would have nothing to gain but I said, 'Sure, I'll do it. No problem.'"

As he now says, "that's when it all started happening".

His Festival victory was rewarded by the F3 drive at Thruxton, where Byrne ran close with Dave Scott's Ralt for a few laps before dropping back to what he modestly describes as "a bad second place".

"But I could have won it", he claims. "I went over a kerb early in the race and damaged a skirt. If it hadn't been for that I reckon I could have won".

Tommy said at the time that he had found the car very easy to drive — "much nicer than I thought it would be" — but he had to wait another four months before having the chance to expand on that confident statement.

"Murray rang me up six days before the first race of the season and said that I was racing". This was just before the first Silverstone F3 round of the 1982 season. Taylor had been unable to secure a driver who could, first, be capable of winning the championship for him (his drivers had finished a close second and third in each of the previous two seasons) and, second, could bring some sponsorship with them. But the New Zealander prides himself on his intention of running "the best driver available" rather than simply taking someone for a bag of sponsorship money. He therefore turned to Tommy.

Shell Oils and Lucas supported the team from the start and Byrne repaid that confidence in him with a fine victory in that opening race, despite a minimum of pre-season testing. "The car was very good," explains Tommy, "there was no real problem. You must remember though that I *had* to win that race. If I hadn't, I'd have been out on my ear".

And it didn't stop there. He won four of the next five races, too, and could have taken the other one had it not been for a spin at Woodcote while comfortably leading the International Trophy meeting event at Silverstone.

Something of a lean patch followed over the next month, Tommy not happy with the car but unable to find out what was wrong. Eventually, it was found that the chassis had been flexing and some strengthening in time for the British GP meeting at Brands Hatch led to Byrne romping away to another clear victory. This one led to an offer from the Theodore Formula 1 team to contest the final five Grands Prix of the season, with support from Rizla.

It was an opportunity too good to miss. The gritty Irishman could not qualify for his first Grand Prix, at Hockenheim, but he did make the field at both the Österreichring and Las Vegas, filling the last slot on the grid at each. How does he look back on the experience? "It was very good for me to find out what Formula 1 was like," he says, "and I'm very grateful to Theodore for that. But I found out that I don't want to be in Formula 1 if I'm only going to be at the back of the field".

The end of the Grand Prix season allowed Tommy to return, perhaps with some relief, to the Formula 3 fray, where his clear championship lead had gradually been whittled away by Enrique Mansilla. These two protagonists enjoyed some close battles over the final few races ... MORE TO FOLLOW

Byrne returned with a win at Silverstone on 3 October, and fastest lap into the bargain, while Mansilla could only manage third, a couple of seconds adrift. Mansilla took another third place in the penultimate round, at Brands Hatch a week later, but here Byrne was only fourth and Mansilla also took fastest lap. That put the pair dead level on points, leaving the title to be decided at the final round, at Thruxton.

With everything to play for, both drivers gave everything in the wet finale. Neither of them actually led the race, that going to Martin Brundle, and apart from scrabbling briefly alongside at the chicane on the first lap, Mansilla never led Byrne — eventually falling back with tyre problems to finish third and runner-up in the championship.

To Byrne, it was a satisfying ending to a busy and occasionally difficult season. As part of his reward for winning the Marlboro championship, Tommy tested the Marlboro McLaren F1 car, impressing more with his obvious speed in the car than with his over cocky attitude afterwards. Perhaps he was already resigned to not being able to step straight back into F1 for 1983.

But where does that leave the talented Irishman for 1983? "I certainly wouldn't want to go back into F1 with an uncompetitive team", he vows, "but I think I might go to do Formula Atlantic in America. I already have some good contacts in the States, and there are a lot of Irish-Americans over there who might be in a position to get me either back into F1 or into Indy-cars. We'll just have to wait and see".

One thing is certain. We haven't heard the last of Tommy Byrne, although it remains to be seen whether he can achieve as much in the next 12 months as he did in 1982.

'A STEP INTO F1...'

Juan Manuel Fangio's talented protegé Oscar 'Poppy' Larrauri took the Marlboro Euroracing 101 to a convincing European F3 Championship and, with a little help from the five-times World Champion, secured a testing contract with Ferrari. TIM TYLER looks back on his winning season

WHEN James Weaver and Eddie Jordan's band of happy-go-lucky Paddies struck a deal with Yokohama Tyre's European distributor, Pacemaker, suddenly new life was pumped into a dying series. Together they proved the lackadaisical Michelin engineers could be beaten, that Paolo Pavanello's Marlboro Euroracing hard charger Oscar 'Poppy' Larrauri — the worthy champion — was not invincible and that the Martini equipe did not always win at home, on tight Mickey Mouse tracks.

The decision by March Engineering to stop production of F3 cars opened the door for Euroracing to develop their own chassis. "I had no option," commented Pavanello, "so we set about improving the March 813s I already had. The monocoque is narrower, the front track wider and has better aerodynamics, altogether the car is 15kph quicker". After just two days of testing, the Marlboro Euroracing 101s dominated the opening race with a devastating 1-2 result. Baldi's old March and Michelin were cleaning up again . . .

So what were Poppy Larrauri's thoughts of the car and his season? "Very easy to balance and sensitive to the slightest adjustment. Fantastic on fast tracks like Monza, Mugello and Zeltweg, but it could be better on small tracks, we have a 'turn in' problem . . . like last year."

"I learnt French to gain the most from the Michelin technicians, but we only did two days testing for the season's production tyres. I was disappointed. For sure our biggest advantage was all the Michelin tyres were designed around our car!"

To endorse this theme further, Poppy's closest challenger was team mate Emanuele Pirro who, in his own words, had "a very disappointing year, I expected more". Between them Pavanello's duo scooped 10 victories.

For a second attack on the Euro F3 series Alain Ferté joined Philippe Alliot in the all new ground effects works Marlboro Martini Mk37's. (Alliot remained in the team on the promise of a F2 drive in '83). However, like fellow driver Didier Theys, these two found something fundamentally wrong as they struggled to record competitive times. Dire under/oversteer, coupled with a basic lack of traction demoralised the teams, although Theys shone in the opening races, before major modifications restored the works cars as an occasional threat to Poppy and Pirro.

Once again, Lady Luck moved in mysterious ways at Monaco, for out of the blue Alliot and Ferté held the front row. Alliot led for all but the final half lap until Ferté rudely punted him sideways at Station hairpin and went on to win (and become the only man to win this F3 Grand Prix twice). "I was faster than Philippe but could not pass. The hairpin was the safest place to push someone out of the way. I had no option!" said Ferté afterwards.

Automobiles Martini's only real success came in the inevitable water fights held after practice and racing, something that got out of hand at Monza, where spectators and police also became involved and as a result of which there is no Euro F3 qualifier at Monza in 1983!

James Weaver only contested four rounds of the series, yet scored three impressive victories and a second place. Suddenly the Briton and Yokohama tyres were the greatest thing since sliced bread, everyone forgot that Weaver found it impossible to win a race in the Marlboro series or that Yokohams were terrible at Zelt-weg and Zandvoort. Gentleman Jim's major stumbling block in England was keeping 16 sponsors happy and this was the main reason why both Jordan and Weaver forgot to sign on in time at Monaco. In Europe he could concentrate on just racing.

Other drivers of note included Claudio Langes who started the year as Trivellato's pay driver in the Dallara. The car, on Pirelli tyres, was a disaster and Langes, through Pirelli, came to an arrangement with Gary Anderson for a works Anson drive, alongside the fast talking but slow driving Gero Zamagana. Immediately Langes became a front runner, to prove the effectiveness of both the Anson chassis and Pirelli tyres.

Roberto Ravaglia plugged along with dogged determination, picking up a handful of fifth and sixth placings with the Dallara. Mid-season modifications saw the wide nose section go in favour of some Ralt RT3 look-alike treatment, except that it still refused to go around corners!

John Nielsen, having won three straight European FSV championships, returned to F3 with backing from VW in the inevitable Ralt, his sixth example to date. He drove with great determination, enough to win the German F3 championship, but had little luck in Europe.

Nielsen's works John Judd Brabham VW unit was a singleton entry in ths series and proved to be on equal terms with Alfa or Toyota. Next year with a vast injection of cash from VW the Dane will contest the entire championship, on Goodyear tyres.

Again Alfa Romeo dominated the championship on the engine front and it is nice to record that through racing they have been able to incorporate modifications on their road engines. Alfa, in conjunction with electrical wizards Magneti Marelli, ran an electronic brain pack for the Kugelfischer mechanical fuel injection system. Apart from that there was no development work from Novamotors on the Alfa or Toyota units in the Euro series, but Guido Cappellotto ran new flat topped Mahle aluminium pistons in his Alfa for Novamotors in the Italian series.

Michelin's run away success made the company complacent; just two days work went into their evaluation of what was required for the season. It was not enough. The combination of Yokohama and, initially, James Weaver brought success and sales. By the final race half the grid used Yokohama instead of Avon or M&H, and the company proved with Swiss privateers Jo Zeller and Jakob Bordoli that just about anyone could bolt on Yokohamas and run

THE TOP SIX

1	Oscar Larrauri	91
2	Emanuele Pirro	62
3	Alain Ferté	42
4	James Weaver	33
5	Didier Theys	30
6	Philippe Alliot	25

'Poppy' (above) won the Euro F3 title in commanding style and can now ponder a future in Formula One, beginning with a testing contract with Ferrari. In May, Alain Ferté (left) became the first driver to win the prestigious Monaco F3 race for a second time but the rest of his season was very low key. James Weaver's brief sortie into Europe with the Eddie Jordan entry (below) netted three wins and a second place in four outings and begged a few questions of both the British and Euro series.

competitively against Michelin. But Michelin could always dig deep into their stocks for Euroracing and find something 'special'. Watch out in '83! Pirelli works driver Claudio Langes and ocasionally the arrogant Paolo Giangrossi proved quick in practice, but usually Michelin or Yokohama held the upper hand in the race.

The problems of transporting racing teams across many different countries were made blatantly obvious on two occasions. After Monaco, as Pino Trivellato's Dallara team headed back home the truck driver unfortunately fell asleep behind the wheel and crashed heavily into a bus, killing two people. The cars were destroyed and Pino Trivellato was eventually forced to stop racing at the end of the season. Anson too had a disaster en route to Jarama when their truck veered off the road and fell on its side . . . damage to the cars was confined to one broken wing mirror, but more of a miracle was that some of Eddie Jordan's mechanics in the sleeping compartment scrambled out unhurt. Talk about the luck of the Irish!

Embarrassing moments? Poppy certainly had a few! the conflict between Argentina and Britain brought police protection at Donington, "Everyone was sympathetic, the British are very gentle people, they only cared about the sport. The biggest problem was journalists! Marlboro thought it best if I did not go to Silverstone in case something happened to me!"

So what does the future hold for Poppy? "Thanks to Juan Manuel Fangio I have a testing contract with Ferrari, it's a step into F1, but I'd rather race. I have kept in touch with ATS but they might only run one car. It's hard but I'll find a way, I believe in myself and my abilities."

**ALL AMERICAN
RACING**

STILL NO CHANGE OF LUCK

For the best part of four years now, through Formula One and Indy racing, Mario Andretti has been suffering a lean spell. Last year he lost Indy in the appeal court, this year he didn't even make the start. American Editor STEVE POTTER reports on Andretti's troubled season.

IF Mario Andretti thought that switching from Formula One to Indy car racing was going to change his recent run of bad racing luck, he was mistaken. The former Indy 500 winner hadn't scored a Grand Prix victory since winning the world drivers championship in 1978, and when Pat Patrick, Andretti's part-time employer the year before, offered him a drive for the full 1982 CART season, Andretti took it, despite memories of the awful business at Indianapolis the year before.

In 1981 Andretti took the flag a few seconds behind Bobby Unser, his former Penske team mate, and then awakened the next morning to find himself declared the winner after Unser was assessed a one lap penalty for an improper pass. Appeals went on for months before Unser was finally declared the winner, and Andretti knocked back down to the runner up position.

It must have seemed like a bad dream to Andretti, but the outcome at Indianapolis in 1981 was much better than that of a year later.

On joining the team full time, Andretti assumed the role of test and development driver for Patrick Racing, a task that team mate Gordon Johncock never cared for. Andretti threw himself into the testing programme with the enthusiasm and skill that has always characterized his performance in this area. Even before the season started Andretti had established the Gordon Kimball designed Wildcat Mk8B as the chief challenger to the supremacy of Geoff Ferris' new Penske PC10.

The season opener at Phoenix was encouraging. Johncock qualified next to pole-sitter Rick Mears, while Andretti was back in the third row. But it was Andretti who split the Penske drivers at the finish, just four seconds back from Mears after 150 miles. A blown engine ended Andretti's race after a first row start at Atlanta.

It was Andretti's fine feel for chassis set-up that found the little extra speed for the Patrick Wildcats during the final practice session before race day at Indianapolis, and though he and Johncock were starting from the second row behind the Penskes of Mears and Kevin Cogan and A.J.Foyt's March, Patrick's men now had the speed to run with anyone.

Sad to say, Andretti didn't get a chance to use it. Coming down for the start Cogan apparently got caught out when his Cosworth came onto the boost, bumped off Foyt's car and into the path of Andretti. The Wildcat nosed into the side of the Penske, and Andretti's race was run before the green flag ever came out.

Off course it was Andretti's team mate, Johncock, who benefitted from the new set-up. As Andretti watched from the pits, fuming

about Cogan's inexperience in Indy cars, Johncock held off Mears for the last couple of laps and added a full length Indy win to his rain shortened triumph almost a decade earlier.

A couple of weeks later Johncock won again at Milwaukee's flat mile oval, while Andretti, the third fastest qualifier, ran out of fuel.

In the meantime, Andretti went to Le Mans to contest the 24-Hour race with his son Michael as co-driver in Harley Cluxton's Mirage. And the French officals refused to let the car even start the race after a confused last minute charade over the placement of an oil cooler in the chassis!

If poor Mario thought things couldn't get much worse, he was right. In fact, they got better. He took a pair of second places in the next two Indy car races, behind Bobby Rahal at the Cleveland airport circuit, and behind team mate Johncock at Michigan. Third place when the PPG series returned to Milwaukee in August was followed by DNFs at Pocono, Riverside and Road America.

Andretti took pole on the high banked, two-mile Michigan oval, but lost the race to Johncock by half a lap at the finish. He led the race at Pocono before his gearbox failed, led convincingly at Riverside until the ignition cut out, and again at Elkhart Lake's Road America until his transmission let him down again. Second behind Rahal when the circus returned to Michigan was little balm for Andretti.

He finished third in the finale at Phoenix, but by that time he'd written off his involvement with Pat Patrick's team, and signed up to race in 1983 with a new team being formed by Lola's North American distributor, Carl Haas, and Paul Newman. The two Patrick cars ran as separate teams, but it was always clear that Patrick preferred Johncock, his driver for over a decade. He sometimes said that when Johncock retired he would close down his team.

Andretti is scheduled to begin applying his testing and development skills to the new Lola T700 in January. He'll be the only driver on the team, although rumours persist that eventually there will be a second car for young Michael Andretti, the winner of the '82 Bosch SuperVee championship. In any case Lola won't even sell customer cars until the new car is fully developed.

Andretti turned down the offers to return to Formula One after his brilliant pole winning effort for Ferrari at Monza in September. Perhaps next year his luck will change.

Andretti running outside of Pete Halsmer and team mate Johncock just before the last two collided (above) at the season finale at Phoenix. Andretti survived to finish third behind Sneva and Mears.

A CLOSE RUN THING

The Indy 500 could never really be accused of lacking drama and spectacle, but this year was definitely one for the history books. After a remarkable startline accident, the restarted race provided the closest finish ever seen at the Brickyard, as STEVE POTTER reports.

THERE is really no way adequately to describe the Indy 500. The roar that wells up at the start of the race from the mouths of a third of a million people is so great that it almost drowns out the sound of the 33 racing engines.

Each year's race is a classic, but of course some are artistically better than others. This year's had it all. qualifying speeds that would do an airplane proud, a crash at the start that brought out the red flag, a barnburner of a race for first place throughout the last third of the race, and finally the closest finish in Indianapolis history. The 66th running of the Indianapolis 500 Mile Sweepstakes had it all.

The number of entries, 109 at $1000 each, that the Speedway received prior to April was a record and, although many of these represented backup cars, 73 drivers were nominated for the field of 33.

The real record breaking started on the second day of practice when Rick Mears started pressing harder with his right foot on the loud pedal of his new Penske PC-10. He clicked off a lap of 203mph in the latest Geoff Ferris design, flirting with the absolute track record.

In practice leading up to the first weekend of qualifying, nine drivers broke 200. Mears was the fastest of them, cutting one 2.5-mile lap of the rectangular course in his Gould Charge at just 43.12 seconds — good for a 208.7mph average. His new team mate, Kevin Cogan, who replaced '81 winner Bobby Unser in the Norton Spirit, pressed Mears all week, and wound up second fastest in practice.

The new Penskes were really in a class by themselves, carving neat and tidy lines through the corners, glueing themselves to the track as though they were on rails. Patrick Racing had a pair of new Wildcat 8Bs for Gordon Johncock and Mario Andretti and, while they were just a couple of ticks of the watch behind the new Penskes, their drivers appeared to be on the ragged edge trying to match the pace.

Also on the ragged edge in practice, though a good ten miles off the quickest speeds, was Texan Gordon Smiley's 81C, one of 26 of the Bicester built chassis entered.

On the pole qualifying day, first Cogan (204.082), and then Mears (207.004) cracked the Indy qualifying mark. Barely an hour later, Smiley, a veteran of the Aurora F1 series, got a little loose as he came around to take the green flag. He overcorrected a little, and at that moment the March found traction and drove itself almost head on into the wall. It was the most violent crash in Indianapolis history — the car was broken to bits — and Smiley, crushed by the impact with the wall, became the first driver to perish in an Indycar in almost a decade.

Four time winner A.J.Foyt captured the outside of the front row with a new March that showed remarkable straight-line speed. Andretti and Johncock were joined in the second row by former Le Mans winner Bill Whittington, who was also March mounted. When qualifying was completed over half the field was comprised of

Throughout the last couple of laps of the 1982 500, the two leaders, Gordon Johncock and Rick Mears, battled nose to tail and even side by side (left) towards the closest finish Indy has ever seen. At the flag, the veteran Johncock in Pàt Patrick's Cosworth-powered Wildcat Mk8B held off Mears' Penske by just 16/100 of a second. Tom Sneva fought hard for much of the race to maintain fourth place at the end after his engine failed with just three laps to run. Until then, Sneva (below) had challenged for the lead with the Texaco Star entered March 82C.

Marches.

Chip Ganassi, a Formula Ford and Super Vee graduate, was the quickest of the nine rookies, a crop that included Bobby Rahal, Danny Sullivan, and Hector Rebaque.

Josele Garza, who wowed the local media representatives a year ago as a rookie, hired Bobby Unser as a team manager for 1982. The young Mexican barely made the race, the slowest qualifier at 194.500mph.

Out of luck was Dan Gurney's All American Racers. The team was out of the Indy field for the first time since its inception nearly two decades ago. AAR was running a turbocharged version of the Chevy V8, and development problems plagued them all month. Five of the stock block powered customer Eagles did qualify, including Pete Halsmer's turbo version, but only rookie Herm Johnson's was in the top half of the field.

Come race day, the first attempt at a start ended in a wild melée that eliminated two of the top contenders. As the field rolled down to take the green flag Cogan's Penske suddenly veered to the right, caromned off Foyt's March, and into the path of Andretti's Wildcat. Andretti T-boned Cogan, and both were eliminated from the race, as were the cars of rookies Roger Mears (Rick's older brother) and Dale Whittington (sibling of Bill and Don).

Foyt's car suffered only minor damage, and on the restart he grabbed the lead, then held it for the first 40 laps of the race. He yielded finally to Mears and Johncock, before retiring with a jammed transmission.

The middle portion of the race featured a close duel among Mears, Johncock, and March men Tom Sneva and Pancho Carter. Rahal was the leading rookie, running at times in the top five until his engine failed with 26 laps remaining. Rookie of the Year honours ultimately went to Jim Hickman, a Datsun dealer from Atlanta with Formula Ford and SuperVee experience, who guided his March to a steady seventh place finish.

Eventually, badly timed pit stops and weakening engines dropped Sneva and Carter out of contention, and left the run to the checker to Johncock and Mears. Carter would eventually finish third, ahead of Sneva, whose Cosworth DFX expired with three laps to go.

A precisely matched set of Goodyear tyres helped bring the STP Wildcat's handling in perfectly with 150 miles to go, and Johncock, the winner of the rain shortened '73 race, held the upper hand. At least until he made a last stop for fuel and tyres 14 laps from the end. The last rubber wasn't as well matched and the car began to understeer, scrubbing off precious speed through the corners.

Mears quickly gobbled up Johncock's 12 second margin, but found that when he was directly behind the Wildcat the turbulence upset his own car's handling. On the penultimate lap he pulled the Penske level as they flew down the front straight at 210mph, but Johncock gritted his teeth, didn't back down, and dived into the first turn still ahead. Mears tried again as they came down for the flag, but fell short by a car length, the narrowest margin in the 71-year history of the race.

INDIANAPOLIS 500
Indianapolis: 30 May 1982
200 laps of 2.5-mile circuit = 500 miles

RESULTS

1	Gordon Johncock	Wildcat MK8B-Cosworth DFX	3hrs 5m 09.14s
2	Rick Mears	Penske PC10-Cosworth DFX	3hrs 5m 09.30s
3	Pancho Carter	March 82C-Cosworth DFX	199 laps
4	Tom Sneva	March 82C-Cosworth DFX	197 laps*
5	Al Unser	Longhorn LRO3-Cosworth DFX	197 laps
6	Don Whittington	March 81C-Cosworth DFX	195 laps
7	Jim Hickman	March 81C-Cosworth DFX	189 laps
8	Johnny Rutherford	Chaparral 2K-Cosworth DFX	187 laps*
9	Herm Johnson	Eagle-Chevrolet	186 laps
10	Howdy Holmes	March 82C-Cosworth	186 laps

* DNF

Fastest lap: Mears, 44.88s (200.535mph) — record
Winner's average speed: 162.026mph

RETIREMENTS

Sneva, 197 laps, engine; Rutherford, 187 laps, water leak; Bobby Rahal, March 82C-Cosworth DFX, 174 laps, engine; Gary Bettenhausen, Lightning-Cosworth DFX, 158 laps, engine; Hector Rebaque, March 82C-Cosworth DFX, 150 laps, pit fire; Danny Sullivan, March 82C-Cosworth DFX, 148 laps, accident; Chip Ganassi, Wildcat Mk8-Cosworth DFX, 147 laps, engine; Bill Whittington, March 81C-Cosworth DFX, 121 laps, engine; Mike Chandler, Eagle-Chevrolet, 96 laps, engine; Tom Bigelow, Eagle-Chevrolet, 96 laps, engine; A.J.Foyt, March 82C-Cosworth DFX, 95 laps, gearbox; Johnny Parsons, March 82C-Cosworth DFX, 87 laps, engine; Danny Ongais, Interscope 003-Cosworth DFX, 62 laps, accident; Jerry Sneva, March 81C-Cosworth DFX, 61 laps, accident; Chet Fillip, Eagle-Cosworth DFX, 60 laps, accident; Pete Halsmer, Eagle-Chevrolet tc, 38 laps, transmission; Tony Bettenhausen, March 82C-Cosworth DFX, 37 laps, gearbox/accident; Dennis Firestone, Eagle-Chevrolet, 37 laps, transmission; Josele Garza, March 82C-Cosworth DFX, 1 lap, engine; Kevin Cogan, Penske PC10-Cosworth DFX, 0 laps, accident; Mario Andretti, Wildcat Mk8D-Cosworth DFX, 0 laps, accident; Roger Mears, Penske PC9B-Cosworth DFX, 0 laps, accident; Dale Whittington, March 82C-Cosworth DFX, 0 laps, accident.

THE GRID

Mears 207.004mph	Cogan 204.082	Foyt 203.332
Andretti 203.172	Johncock 201.884	Whittington (Bill) 201.658
Sneva (Tom) 201.027	Whittington (Don) 200.725	Ongais 199.148
Carter 198.950	Ganassi 197.704	Rutherford 197.066
Sullivan 196.292	Johnson 195.929	Rebaque 195.684
Unser 195.567	Rahal 194.700	Holmes 194.468
Mears 194.154	Brabham 198.906	Firestone 197.217
Chandler 198.042	Whittington (Dale) 197.694	Hickman 196.217
Parsons 195.929	Snider 195.493	Bettenhausen (Tony) 195.429
Sneva (Jerry) 195.270	Fillip 194.879	Bettenhausen (Gary) 195.673
Bigelow 194.784	Halsmer 194.595	Garza 194.500

MEARS: TAKING OVER

Even in Indy car racing, where the top drivers seem to go on forever, a new generation is on the move and the old guard is looking to its laurels. From Sprint Buggies, through road racing and off-road racing, Rick Mears has become a three-time Indy car champion. STEVE POTTER reports on CART's new look.

IF A.J.Foyt, now 47 and in the twilight of a three decade career, has a successor in Indycar racing, that man is probably Rick Mears. In 1982 the former off-road racer won his third CART driving title in four years. Mears clinched the PPG Indy Car World Series with two races still remaining on the schedule.

The winner of four of the first nine races, and a top five finisher in three others, Mears easily outdistanced his competitors for the crown. He led twice as many laps as Gordon Johncock, the next strongest runner throughout the season, and almost as many as Johncock and the rest of the CART runners put together.

Mears first sat in an Indy Car in 1976, and his seven seasons make an interesting comparison with Foyt's almost a quarter of a century earlier. With almost the same number of starts (Mears 71 — Foyt 76), each won three titles (Foyt's under the aegis of USAC, of course), 17 races and finished second 11 times.

The tricky Phoenix mile was the site of the season opener, and Mears ran away with that race from the pole, a feat he repeated at the high speed Atlanta oval, deep in the heart of stock car country. He won the pole at Indy, too, and then finished second to Gordon Johncock in an epic race. But Indy is still sanctioned by USAC, and it won't carry points for the PPG series until 1983.

Mears' season hit a lull near the midpoint. The Gould Charge finished third at the June Milwaukee race, and fourth at the Cleveland 500 road race, before dropping out of the rich Michigan 500 at

Roger Penske's steeply banked two-mile oval and the August Milwaukee 200 miler.

He then bounced back with wins in the 500 miler at Pocono and the 500 kilometer road race in the late summer desert heat at Riverside. Fifth place at Road America in Wisconsin clinched the title.

The PC-10, designed by Geoff Ferris and built in the Penske shops in England, represented a sharp departure from the successful PC-9 and PC-9B designs from the past two seasons. A very slim monocoque permitted Ferris to include wider ground effect ducts on the new car, which also proved much easier to set up for the range of tracks on which CART competes.

In stark contrast to the success that Mears enjoyed with his PC-10 was the ill fortune that dogged his new team mate, Kevin Cogan, the replacement for Bobby Unser in Penske's Norton Spirit. Tub twisting crashes in practice sessions and races were punctuated with mechanical failures.

Cogan qualified on the pole at the Riverside road race, and led most of the event before his engine broke. Second place behind Mears at Pocono was the best that the Formula Atlantic graduate could do after finishing a promising third in the Phoenix opener.

For the first half of the season the main pressure on Mears came from veteran Gordon Johncock. In addition to his Indy win, and second place at Atlanta, Johncock posted victories at the June Milwaukee 150 miler and the Michigan 500 and for a time led Mears in

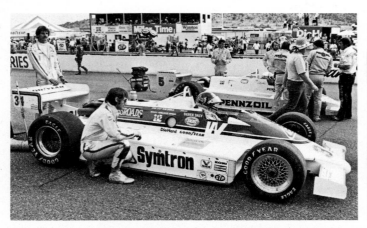

the point standings. A string of transmission failures and other mechanical difficulties during the second half of the season dropped Johncock from contention. His team mate, Mario Andretti, finished second four times, but was unable to break into the win column with only the Phoenix race remaining on the schedule.

It was Bobby Rahal, a rookie in Indy Cars, but wealthy in road racing experience, who provided most of the competition for Mears in the second half of the season. Running with a team that was also new to the circuit, Jim Trueman's Red Roof Inns équipe with Steve Horne as crew chief, Rahal took a few races to get his bearings. The ovals appeared to baffle him until he got to Indy. After starting from the second half of the field, he ran in the top five until his engine expired.

At Cleveland, a punishing 500 kilometer road race run on an airport circuit on the shores of Lake Erie, Rahal ran a heady race and came home the victor. Some said it was a matter of the right horse for the course, but then Rahal finished no lower than third in the next three oval races, run at the high banked Michigan oval, the tricornered Pocono circuit, and the tricky flat Milwaukee State Fair mile saucer.

Topping that he returned to Michigan and won the fall 150-mile sprint. Bobby Rahal, who spent many years nosing around the fringes of Formula One, has found his niche close to home. Twenty-nine is a tender age for Indy Car drivers and Rahal can expect a

Rick Mears and Mario Andretti (facing page) were at opposite ends of the CART success scale in 1982. Mears, a 31-year-old from Bakersfield, California, came to Indy car racing via sprint buggies, SuperVee and F5000, moving into Championship racing in 1976. This year he won his third CART title in four years and failed, by the smallest margin ever, to win his second Indy 500. Andretti, another former Indy winner and Grand Prix World Champion, didn't even make the start at Indy after falling foul of Mears' erratic team mate Kevin Cogan — and he fared no better in the majority of the CART sanctioned events, his best results being a couple of early season second places. Having left the Williams Grand Prix team at the end of a difficult season, Derek Daly turned to CART racing at Phoenix in November (top left). Although his début with the Wysard Racing March lasted only two laps, he impressed many people and will be back for more in 1983. The only driver to give Mears anything like a run for the title was Indy winner Gordon Johncock, but Gordy faded somewhat in the second half of the season and ended the Phoenix race in the wall (top right), after mixing with Pete Halsmer. Rookie Bobby Rahal (above) took over from Johncock as Mears' principal challenger and looks to have a very promising future in CART, again based on a road racing background. Tom Sneva led Mears and Andretti home at the season finale (following page), but generally had a poor year with George Bignotti's leading March.

long career in them.

George Bignotti, for years Indy's master mechanic, didn't enjoy a fruitful second year with his own team. Running a pair of Marches for two-time national champion Tom Sneva and reigning Can-Am titlist Geoff Brabham brought scant results. Sneva did win the first Milwaukee race and the season's finale at Phoenix, and finished second at Riverside, but Brabham's year was disappointing. He finished fourth at Pocono and third at the Michigan fall sprint.

Also enduring disappointing years were A.J.Foyt himself, Johnny Rutherford and Al Unser Sr, who have 10 Indy 500 victories between them. And no race victories at all in 1982.

Foyt planned a full season of CART racing after recovering from the serious injuries he suffered at Michigan in 1981. But except for second place at the Milwaukee 150 Foyt was unable to crack the top 20 coming into the last race of the year. He had another bad crash at Michigan, this time after tangling with Cogan, and he was fortunate to escape injury.

Rutherford found that his Chaparral was simply outdated in its fourth season, and halfway through the season Jim Hall bought a March. Rutherford well and truly crashed the new yellow car at Pocono but then finished fourth in the Michigan sprint.

Al Unser Sr had two new Longhorn cars in '82, but neither of them performed up to expectations, and only sheer persistence brought him a string of top five finishes. A fine road racer, Unser almost won the Road America race at Elkhart Lake, Wisconsin, but ran through his fuel allotment, turning the win over to former Brabham F1 driver Hector Rebaque.

Bill Alsup, second in the PPG series in '81, had the worst season of his career in '82. He had no more success with the potentially quick, but very tricky, ex-works PC-9B than anyone else, and midway through the season he lost chief mechanic Laurie Gerrish, who had worked with Bobby Unser during his tenure with Penske. Jerry Eisert came along to replace Gerrish, and Alsup's performances immediately improved.

Two promising youngsters made their first Indy Car appearances. Al Unser Jr took time off from his run to the Can-Am crown to look around at the CART scene. Driving the Forsythe March at Riverside he qualified tenth and quickly passed his father's Longhorn on the way to second place. Fuel mixture problems caused him to run dry before the end of the race, but he was very impressive.

So was John Paul Jr, the IMSA Camel GT champ, who made a guest appearance in the Wysard March at Road America. He charged up to third before a piston burned.

CART had three road races in 1982, but they have more in the works for '83 including events at Mid-Ohio and Laguna Seca. Rumours that the Indy Cars would return to Europe seemed unfounded, but it seems likely that the circuit will come to be evenly split among short oval, superspeedway and road circuits. And there's a good chance that they will be asked to sanction the Indy 500, the one event that USAC retains.

CART/PPG INDY CAR WORLD SERIES : RESULTS

Round 1 — Kraco Stereo 150 — Phoenix — 28 March 1982
150 laps = 150 miles. Winner's average speed 118.727mph
1	Rick Mears	Penske PC10-Cosworth DFX	1h 15m 48.231s
2	Mario Andretti	Wildcat Mk8B-Cosworth DFX	1h 15m 52.4s
3	Kevin Cogan	Penske PC10-Cosworth DFX	149 laps
4	Johnny Rutherford	Chaparral 2K-Cosworth DFX	149 laps
5	Gordon Johncock	Wildcat Mk8B-Cosworth DFX	149 laps
6	Pancho Carter	March 82C-Cosworth DFX	147 laps

Round 2 — Stroh's 200 — Atlanta — 1 May 1982
132 laps = 200 miles. Winner's average speed 164.750mph
1	Rick Mears	Penske PC10-Cosworth DFX	132 laps
2	Gordon Johncock	Wildcat Mk8B-Cosworth DFX	132 laps
3	Danny Sullivan	March 82C-Cosworth DFX	125 laps
4	Roger Mears	Penske PC7-Cosworth DFX	125 laps
5	Bill Alsup	Penske PC9C-Cosworth DFX	121 laps
6	Herm Johnson	Eagle-Chevrolet	115 laps

Round 3 — Gould/Rex Mays 150 — Milwaukee — 13 June 1982
150 laps = 150 miles. Winner's average speed 126.987mph
1	Gordon Johncock	Wildcat Mk8B-Cosworth DFX	1h 10m 52.69s
2	AJ Foyt	March 82C-Cosworth DFX	1h 11m 04.49s
3	Rick Mears	Penske PC10-Cosworth DFX	149 laps
4	Tom Sneva	March 82C-Cosworth DFX	149 laps
5	Kevin Cogan	Penske PC10-Cosworth DFX	146 laps
6	Johnny Parsons	March 82C-Cosworth DFX	146 laps

Round 4 — Budweiser Cleveland 500 — Cleveland — 4 July 1982
125 laps = 500 miles. Winner's average speed 101.234mph
1	Bobby Rahal	March 82C-Cosworth DFX	3h 3m 44.0s
2	Mario Andretti	Wildcat Mk8B-Cosworth DFX	3h 4m 05.0s
3	Al Unser	Longhorn LRO3-Cosworth DFX	125 laps
4	Rick Mears	Penske PC10-Cosworth DFX	124 laps
5	Gordon Johncock	Wildcat Mk8B-Cosworth DFX	124 laps
6	Geoff Brabham	March 82C-Cosworth DFX	123 laps

Round 5 — Norton Michigan 500 — Michigan — 18 July 1982
250 laps = 500 miles. Winner's average speed 153.925mph
1	Gordon Johncock	Wildcat Mk8B-Cosworth DFX	3h 14m 54s
2	Mario Andretti	Wildcat Mk8B-Cosworth DFX	250 laps
3	Bobby Rahal	March 82C-Cosworth DFX	245 laps
4	Al Unser	Longhorn LRO3B-Cosworth DFX	245 laps
5	Tom Bigelow	Eagle Gurney-Chevrolet	245 laps
6	Gary Bettenhausen	Penske PC7-Cosworth DFX	241 laps

Round 6 — Tony Bettenhausen 200 — Milwaukee — 1 August 1982
200 laps = 200 miles. Winner's average speed 109.132mph
1	Tom Sneva	March 82C-Cosworth DFX	1h 49m 57.545s
2	Bobby Rahal	March 82C-Cosworth DFX	199 laps
3	Mario Andretti	Wildcat Mk8B-Cosworth DFX	199 laps
4	Howdy Holmes	March 82C-Cosworth DFX	197 laps
5	Kevin Cogan	Penske PC10-Cosworth DFX	197 laps
6	Pancho Carter	March 82C-Cosworth DFX	196 laps

Round 7 — Dominos Pizza/Pocono 500 — Pocono — 15 August 1982
200 laps = 500 miles. Winner's average speed 145.879mph
1	Rick Mears	Penske PC10-Cosworth DFX	3h 25m 39.0s
2	Kevin Cogan	Penske PC10-Cosworth DFX	3h 25m 41.0s
3	Bobby Rahal	March 82C-Cosworth DFX	197 laps
4	Geoff Brabham	March 82C-Cosworth DFX	197 laps
5	Tony Bettenhausen	March 82C-Cosworth DFX	195 laps
6	Gordon Johncock	Wildcat Mk8B-Cosworth DFX	193 laps

Round 8 — Air Cal 500 — Riverside — 29 August 1982
95 laps. Winner's average speed 115.944mph
1	Rick Mears	Penske PC10-Cosworth DFX	2h 42m 14.0s
2	Tom Sneva	March 82C-Cosworth DFX	2h 43m 20.0s
3	Johnny Rutherford	March 82C-Cosworth DFX	93 laps
4	Roger Mears	Penske PC7-Cosworth DFX	90 laps
No other finishers			

Round 9 — Road America 200 — Elkhart Lake — 19 September 1982
50 laps = 200 miles. Winner's average speed 109.156mph
1	Hector Rebaque	March 82C-Cosworth DFX	1h 49m 56.09s
2	Al Unser	Longhorn LRO3C-Cosworth DFX	49 laps (DNF)
3	Bobby Rahal	March 82C-Cosworth DFX	49 laps
4	Josele Garza	Penske PC9-Cosworth DFX	49 laps
5	Rick Mears	Penske PC10-Cosworth DFX	48 laps
6	Phil Kruger	Kingfish-Chevrolet	45 laps

Round 10 — Detroit News Grand Prix 150 — Michigan — 26 September 1982
75 laps = 150 miles. Winner's average speed 140.515mph
1	Bobby Rahal	March 82C-Cosworth DFX	1h 4m 3.0s
2	Mario Andretti	Wildcat Mk8B-Cosworth DFX	1h 4m 16.0s
3	Geoff Brabham	March 82C-Cosworth DFX	74 laps
4	Tony Bettenhausen	March 82C-Cosworth DFX	74 laps
5	Howdy Holmes	March 82C-Cosworth DFX	74 laps
6	Bill Alsup	Penske PC9B-Cosworth DFX	74 laps

Round 11 — Miller High Life/Bobby Ball 150 — Phoenix — 6 November 1982
150 laps = 150 miles. Winner's average speed 110.997mph
1	Tom Sneva	March 82C-Cosworth DFX	1h 21m 5.0s
2	Rick Mears	Penske PC10-Cosworth DFX	1h 21m 11.2s
3	Mario Andretti	Wildcat Mk8B-Cosworth DFX	150 laps
4	Kevin Cogan	Penske PC10-Cosworth DFX	148 laps
5	Bobby Rahal	March 82C-Cosworth DFX	148 laps
6	Tony Bettenhausen	March 82C-Cosworth DFX	147 laps

FINAL POINTS

1	R.Mears	294	4	G.Johncock	186
2	B.Rahal	242	5	T.Sneva	144
3	M.Andretti	188	6	K.Cogan	136

DECLINE AND FALL

Tradition in the States doesn't always stretch back quite so far as tradition in Europe, but the rapid demise of the once all powerful sanctioning body, USAC, still caused serious rifts in the fabric of American racing — extending even to USAC's holy of holies, Indianapolis.

THE United States Auto Club was once the most powerful sanctioning body in America. Formed on an almost *ad hoc* basis in 1956 after the American Automobile Association closed down its contest board and pulled out of racing in the wake of the Le Mans disaster, USAC derived its power by virtue of sanctioning the Indianapolis 500.

To this day Indianapolis stands alone among American motorsports events as a national spectacle. Indeed, for years it billed itself as the "greatest spectacle in racing". In the late 50s, when all road racing was by its very nature amateur, and stock car racing was something done on weekends by hillbillys after a long night of drinking and partying, USAC had the only game in town. It wasn't by accident that USAC located its headquarters just down the road from the monolithic old Speedway on the west side of Indianapolis.

The beginning of USAC's downfall could be traced as far as 1963, when Colin Chapman brought his F1 inspired Lotuses to the old brickyard and Jim Clark very nearly won the race. It was just never the same after that. The technical innovation that Chapman's cars inspired brought new teams and drivers into Indy car racing.

A lot of the new car owners were men like Dan Gurney, who had himself driven in Europe, Roger Penske, a former road racer whose considerable driving skill was overshadowed by his business acumen, and Pat Patrick, an oil man who wanted to run his racing team as efficiently as he did his oil wells.

This new breed of car owner differed from the old sportsmen who dominated the sport a generation earlier, and they came into conflict with the hobbyist officials and administrators who dominated the scene at USAC. The new car owners wanted to treat racing as a business, and they were particularly incensed when men who ran chemist shops or radio stations during the week got together evenings and wantonly drafted new technical regulations that threatened to make millions of dollars worth of racing equipment obsolete overnight.

USAC could be said to have died in April of 1978, when an aircraft carrying the better part of the sanctioning body's staff crashed during a thunderstorm. With most of the competent officials gone from USAC it took the car owners, headed by Penske and Patrick, only a few months to organize the Championship Auto Racing Teams, Inc.

CART and USAC negotiated during the fall of 1978, but it soon became clear that the old timers from the Speedway had no intention of sharing any of their power. Both groups scheduled their own series of races, with most of the top teams lining up with CART. USAC retained dates at Pocono, as well as Indy. In fact, USAC came to be seen as a puppet of the Speedway officials, and they attempted to bar the rebellious teams from participating in the Memorial Day classic.

It took a federal court order to get the CART teams into the track, but from that time onward it was clear that USAC had lost the battle. In 1980 USAC compromised with CART and a jointly sanctioned season was scheduled. That lasted only until the Speedway's president, John Cooper, realized that USAC had ceded most of the power to the car owner's group. He pulled the plug on it by threatening to replace USAC at the Speedway.

Cooper suddenly left his post at the Speedway the day before practice began for the 1982 race, and his replacement took several opportunities thereafter to let everyone know that he had not made up his mind which group would be asked to conduct the '83 running of the race. USAC sanctioned no other Indy car races this season, and its sprint car and midget series were reduced to regional status.

Even if the Speedway does sign a sanction agreement with USAC for 1983, the writing is on the wall. The shift of power in Indy car racing has already taken place. CART runs the show.

DOWN TO THE WIRE

As the NASCAR Winston Cup Grand National Championship went all the way to the last round to find a winner, the series continued to provide some of the most exciting racing to be found anywhere in the world and, as American Editor STEVE POTTER reports, 1982 saw the emergence of some new stars.

WITH 30 races on the schedule it's remarkable, but NASCAR's Winston Cup championship has come down to the last race of the season in each of the last four years. In some ways 1982 was a carbon copy of '81. The stock car racing circus rolled into Riverside, California, far from its base in the Southeast, to decide the title on the only road course on the schedule.

Once again Bobby Allison was pursuing Darrell Waltrip in the points chase. Between them they had dominated the season, together winning a total of two-thirds of the races.

In '81 Allison won at Riverside, but Waltrip stroked home sixth, gathering enough points to take home the Winston Cup. This year in the end Waltrip prevailed, by virtue of a third place finish at Riverside, compared with Allison, who won the race but finished the year with 4417 points to Waltrip's 4489.

Coming into that last race Waltrip had won a dozen events, compared with eight for Allison. Waltrip ran up most of his victories on the short tracks, less than a mile in length, while all but one of Allison's wins came on superspeedways.

Allison has been competing on the Grand National circuit for nearly two decades, but he has never won the Winston Cup. He quit Kentucky coal miner Harry Ranier's team at the end of '81 over differences of opinion concerning racing strategy. Ranier's men wanted to run conservatively after Allison had run up a big point lead in the early part of the season.

Allison boiled as he watched Waltrip gnaw away at the margin that separated them through most of '81. This year Allison signed up with Digard Racing, the team that provided an unhappy home for Waltrip for several seasons before stock car racing's most outspoken driver hitched on with the legendary Junior Johnson before the '81 season.

The match was better for Allison, who won the season opening

Daytona 500 going away. A year earlier he had dominated the race in Ranier's car until an error in the pits dropped him behind Richard Petty, who went on to win the premier stock car race for the seventh time. This year the Digard crew didn't make a single error and Allison's Gatorade Buick led most of the last half of the race after Waltrip's Mountain Dew Buick dropped out with engine failure.

Allison didn't find his way to victory lane again until Dover, Delaware, when the season was better than a third over. By that time Waltrip had run up five victories, on the short tracks at Bristol, North Wilkesboro and Nashville, and the Atlanta and Talledega superspeedways.

Neither driver had the point lead though. That was held for the first half of the season by Terry Labonte, a Texan who didn't win a race all season. Credit NASCAR's peculiar scoring system, which is designed to encourage, yea force, all contenders for the season championship to enter every last one of the races.

The winner of a Grand National receives 180 points, and can get five more points if he leads the most laps. Any driver who leads a lap gets five points, too. Second gets 170, but is also eligible for the five point bonus for leading the most laps. Dropping out at the half-way point usually results in the award of over 100 points, so even a DNF doesn't necessarily hurt a driver too badly.

After a string of mechanical problems during the early part of the season, following his Daytona 500 win, Allison ran up a string of superspeedway wins in the middle third of the season, notching victories at Dover, Pocono (twice), again at Daytona and at Michigan. That string of wins gave him the lead in Winston Cup standings over Labonte. Waltrip repeated his Talledega, Bristol and Nashville wins, and posted other high finishes as he also moved past Labonte in the points. The triumph in the Talladega 500 made him the first repeat winner of that event in its 12-year history.

With continuing backing from Winston, the NASCAR Grand National series can rely on fields of quality and quantity, strong intermake rivalry and big crowds (facing page and top right). In the end, Buicks took the top four slots with Richard Petty's Pontiac and Dave Marcis's Chevy completing the top six. The younger Petty, Kyle, was also Pontiac mounted and backed by STP, but neither he nor Ford runner Bill Elliott (top left) really lived up to their true potentials during the 30-race championship. By finishing third in the final race, Darrell Waltrip scraped home ahead of Bobby Allison for his second consecutive Winston Cup. At the National 500, at Charlotte in October, Waltrip's car was heavily damaged in a seven car pile up and, although his pit crew kept the Buick running (above), Waltrip was for once out of the top six when the flag fell. Bobby Allison (left) was Waltrip's main challenger throughout the year, and a regular winner on the superspeedways, but once again the Winston Cup escaped the leader of the 'Alabama Gang', although he won the Daytona 500 as he pleased (left).

In the final third of the season Allison won a short track event at Richmond and the penultimate round on the high banked, 1.5-mile Atlanta oval. But Waltrip's wins at the Dover and Rockingham miles and on the short tracks at North Wilkesboro and Martinsville, moved him slightly ahead of Allison going into Riverside.

Cale Yarborough, who won the Winston Cup three times as Waltrip's predecessor in Junior Johnson's car, now runs a reduced schedule. He still managed to win three times, at Rockingham, Michigan and Darlington. Harry Gant, who racked up runner-up finishes all over the place in '81, had more than one '82 season victory going into the last race. He scored his first ever Grand National win in the spring at Martinsville, and followed that up with his first superspeedway win at the fall Charlotte race.

Singleton winners included independent driver Dave Marcis, who won in the spring at Richmond, Dale Earnhardt, who scored his and Ford's first win in ever so long, and Neil Bonnett, who added another Ford win in the World 600 at Charlotte in May. Tim Richmond scored his first big league racing win on the road course at Riverside in June.

Richmond, a former Indy 500 Rookie of the Year, seems to have found a home in NASCAR. His career in Indy cars was meteoric. Spectacular, but brief. The rest of the 1980 season, after he captured the fancy of the once a year racing media in Indiana, was punctuated by violent crashes into concrete walls, and by the end of the season he was without a ride. In '81 Valvoline bought his way into a car that was qualified by George Snider after Richmond failed to make the field in his own car.

But the young Ohioan has done well in NASCAR. He seems more at home in the closed cars, and his driving has shown more maturity than it did a couple of years ago. He joins the likes of Terry Labonte, Morgan Shepherd, Jody Ridley, Kyle Petty, Ricky Rudd and Bill Elliott as potential stars over the next decade of stock car racing.

And of course there's Geoff Bodine, the winner of the Champion Spark Plug Rookie of the Year title. This award is determined by a point system that is fully as complicated as the one for the Winston Cup, and there are rules for eligibility as well.

A rookie contender must register his intention with the sanctioning body, and veterans of other forms of big time racing, or drivers who have competed in more than five Winston Cup events in a year, are ineligible.

Bodine, several times a champion in NASCAR's short track modified division, had a one-shot ride for the Daytona 500. He was the first car out of that race, and didn't pick up a full time ride and register with NASCAR until the season was a quarter over. It took him a few races to get dialled in, but in the second half of the season he was a consistent top ten finisher — placing as high as third at Riverside — and he won the rookie title handily from Mark Martin, a young short track champion with the American Speed Association.

Bodine and Martin are legitimately labelled potential superstars in NASCAR, and it is significant that they are from New England and the Midwest respectively, because NASCAR is making a determined effort to shed its status as a regional series. Richard Petty went through the season without a win, and he and the drivers of his generation are nearing retirement. In five years NASCAR will probably be dominated by a new group of drivers, many of whom have yet to post their first wins in the series.

FINAL POINTS

1	Darrell Waltrip	4489	4	Harry Gant	3877
2	Bobby Allison	4417	5	Richard Petty	3814
3	Terry Labonte	4211	6	Dave Marcis	3666

NASCAR WINSTON CUP

Round 1 — Daytona 500 — Daytona — 14 February 1982
200 laps = 500 miles. Winner's average speed 153.991mph

1	Bobby Allison	Buick Regal	3h 14m 49.0s
2	Cale Yarborough	Buick Regal	3h 15m 11.87s
3	Joe Ruttman	Buick Regal	200 laps
4	Terry Labonte	Buick Regal	199 laps
5	Bill Elliott	Ford Thunderbird	198 laps
6	Ron Bouchard	Buick Regal	198 laps

Round 2 — Richmond 400 — Richmond — 21 February 1982
250 laps = 135.5 miles. Winner's average speed 72.914mph

1	Dave Marcis	Chevrolet Malibu	1h 51m 30s
2	Richard Petty	Pontiac Grand Prix	250 laps
3	Benny Parsons	Pontiac Grand Le Mans	250 laps
4	Dale Earnhardt	Ford Thunderbird	250 laps
5	Terry Labonte	Chevrolet Monte Carlo	249 laps
6	Joe Millikan	Pontiac Grand Prix	249 laps

Round 3 — Valleydale 500 — Bristol — 14 March 1982
500 laps = 266.5 miles. Winner's average speed 94.225mph

1	Darrell Waltrip	Buick Regal	2h 49m 52s
2	Dale Earnhardt	Ford Thunderbird	500 laps
3	Morgan Shepherd	Buick Regal	500 laps
4	Terry Labonte	Chevrolet Monte Carlo	499 laps
5	Bobby Allison	Chevrolet Monte Carlo	498 laps
6	Harry Gant	Buick Regal	498 laps

Round 4 — Coca Cola 500 — Atlanta — 21 March 1982
287 laps = 436.81 miles. Winner's average speed 124.824mph

1	Darrell Waltrip	Buick Regal	3h 29m 58s
2	Richard Petty	Pontiac Grand Prix	287 laps
3	Cale Yarborough	Buick Regal	287 laps
4	Benny Parsons	Pontiac Grand Le Mans	287 laps
5	Harry Gant	Buick Regal	286 laps
6	Morgan Shepherd	Buick Regal	286 laps

Round 5 — Carolina 500 — 27 March 1982
492 laps = 500 miles. Winner's average speed 108.992mph

1	Cale Yarborough	Buick Regal	4h 35m 27s
2	Terry Labonte	Chevrolet Malibu	491 laps
3	Benny Parsons	Pontiac Grand Le Mans	491 laps
4	Bobby Allison	Chevrolet Malibu	491 laps
5	Morgan Shepherd	Buick Regal	489 laps
6	Joe Millikan	Pontiac Grand Prix	489 laps

Round 6 — Rebel 500 — Darlington — 4 April 1982
367 laps = 500 miles. Winner's average speed 123.544mph

1	Dale Earnhardt	Ford Thunderbird	4h 03m 27s
2	Cale Yarborough	Buick Regal	367 laps
3	Bill Elliott	Ford Thunderbird	367 laps
4	Benny Parsons	Pontiac Grand Le Mans	367 laps
5	Tim Richmond	Buick Regal	366 laps
6	Terry Labonte	Buick Regal	366 laps

Round 7 — Northwestern Bank 400 — North Wilkesboro — 18 April 1982
400 laps = 250 miles. Winner's average speed 97.646mph

1	Darrell Waltrip	Buick Regal	2h 33m 37s
2	Dale Earnhardt	Ford Thunderbird	400 laps
3	Benny Parsons	Pontiac Grand Le Mans	400 laps
4	Terry Labonte	Buick Regal	400 laps
5	Richard Petty	Pontiac Grand Prix	399 laps
6	Harry Gant	Buick Regal	399 laps

Round 8 — Virginia 500 — Martinsville — 25 April 1982
500 laps = 262.5 miles. Winner's average speed 75.073mph

1	Harry Gant	Buick Regal	3h 30m 01s
2	Butch Lindley	Buick Regal	499 laps
3	Neil Bonnett	Ford Thunderbird	497 laps
4	Ricky Rudd	Buick Regal	496 laps
5	Darrell Waltrip	Buick Regal	496 laps
6	Dave Marcis	Chevrolet Caprice	496 laps

Round 9 — Winston 500 — Talledega — 2 May 1982
188 laps = 500 miles. Winner's average speed 156.697mph

1	Darrell Waltrip	Buick Regal	3h 11m 19s
2	Terry Labonte	Buick Regal	188 laps
3	Benny Parsons	Pontiac Grand Le Mans	188 laps
4	Kyle Petty	Pontiac Grand Prix	188 laps
5	Morgan Shepherd	Buick Regal	188 laps
6	Donnie Allison	Buick Regal	188 laps

Round 10 — Music City 420 — Nashville — 8 May 1982
420 laps = 250 miles. Winner's average speed 83.502mph

1	Darrell Waltrip	Buick Regal	2h 59m 52s
2	Terry Labonte	Buick Regal	419 laps
3	Ron Bouchard	Buick Regal	418 laps
4	Joe Ruttman	Buick Regal	417 laps
5	Neil Bonnett	Buick Regal	417 laps
6	Bobby Allison	Buick Regal	416 laps

Round 11 — Mason Dixon 500 — Dover Downs — 16 May 1982
500 laps = 500 miles. Winner's average speed 120.136mph

1	Bobby Allison	Buick Regal	4h 09m 43s
2	Dave Marcis	Buick Regal	497 laps
3	Dale Ernhardt	Ford Thunderbird	497 laps
4	Terry Labonte	Buick Regal	496 laps
5	Mark Martin	Buick Regal	496 laps
6	Ron Bouchard	Buick Regal	494 laps

Round 12 — World 600 — Charlotte — 30 May 1982
400 laps = 600 miles. Winner's average speed 130.058mph

1	Neil Bonnett	Ford Thunderbird	4h 36m 48s
2	Bill Elliott	Ford Thunderbird	400 laps
3	Bobby Allison	Buick Regal	399 laps
4	Cale Yarborough	Buick Regal	398 laps
5	Buddy Baker	Buick Regal	398 laps
6	Jody Ridley	Ford Thunderbird	398 laps

Round 13 — Van Scoy Diamond Mines 500 — Pocono — 6 June 1982
200 laps = 500 miles. Winner's average speed 113.572mph

1	Bobby Allison	Buick Regal	4h 24m 06s
2	Tim Richmond	Buick Regal	200 laps
3	Benny Parsons	Pontiac Grand Le Mans	199 laps
4	Harry Gant	Buick Regal	199 laps
5	Terry Labonte	Chevrolet Monte Carlo	199 laps
6	Ricky Rudd	Pontiac Grand Prix	199 laps

Round 14 — Budweiser 400 — Riverside — 13 June 1982
95 laps = 400 miles. Winner's average speed 103.816mph

1	Tim Richmond	Buick Regal	2h 23m 51s
2	Terry Labonte	Buick Regal	95 laps
3	Geoff Bodine	Pontiac Grand Prix	95 laps
4	Dale Ernhardt	Ford Thunderbird	95 laps
5	Neil Bonnett	Ford Thunderbird	95 laps
6	Roy Smith	Buick Regal	94 laps

Round 15 — Gabriel 400 — Michigan — 20 June 1982
200 laps = 400 miles. Winner's average speed 118.101mph

1	Cale Yarborough	Buick Regal	3h 23.13s
2	Darrell Waltrip	Buick Regal	200 laps
3	Bill Elliott	Ford Thunderbird	200 laps
4	Bobby Allison	Buick Regal	200 laps
5	Ricky Rudd	Buick Regal	200 laps
6	Kyle Petty	Pontiac Grand Prix	200 laps

Round 16 — Firecracker 400 — Daytona — 4 July 1982
160 laps = 400 miles. Winner's average speed 163.099mph

1	Bobby Allison	Buick Regal	2h 27.09s
2	Bill Elliott	Ford Thunderbird	160 laps
3	Ron Bouchard	Buick Regal	160 laps
4	Morgan Shepherd	Buick Regal	160 laps
5	David Pearson	Buick Regal	160 laps
6	Geoff Bodine	Pontiac Grand Prix	160 laps

Round 17 — Busch 420 — Nashville — 10 July 1982
420 laps = 250 miles. Winner's average speed 86.524mph

1	Darrell Waltrip	Buick Regal	2h 53m 35s
2	Terry Labonte	Chevrolet Monte Carlo	419 laps
3	Harry Gant	Buick Regal	419 laps
4	Ricky Rudd	Pontiac Grand Prix	419 laps
5	Tim Richmond	Buick Regal	419 laps
6	Geoff Bodine	Pontiac Grand Prix	418 laps

Round 18 — Pocono 500 — Pocono — 25 July 1982
200 laps = 500 miles. Winner's average speed 115.496mph

1	Bobby Allison	Buick Regal	4h 19m 45s
2	Richard Petty	Pontiac Grand Prix	200 laps
3	Terry Labonte	Buick Regal	200 laps
4	Ron Bouchard	Buick Regal	200 laps
5	Buddy Baker	Pontiac Le Mans	200 laps
6	Darrell Waltrip	Buick Regal	199 laps

Round 19 — Talladega 500 — Talladega — 1 August 1982
188 laps = 500 miles. Winner's average speed 168.157mph

1	Darrell Waltrip	Buick Regal	2h 58m 26s
2	Buddy Baker	Buick Regal	188 laps
3	Richard Petty	Pontiac Grand Prix	188 laps
4	Cale Yarborough	Buick Regal	188 laps
5	Terry Labonte	Buick Regal	188 laps
6	Bill Elliott	Ford Thunderbird	188 laps

Round 20 — Champion Spark Plug 400 — Michigan — 22 August 1982
200 laps = 400 miles. Winner's average speed 136.454mph

1	Bobby Allison	Buick Regal	2h 45m 53s
2	Richard Petty	Pontiac Grand Prix	200 laps
3	Harry Gant	Buick Regal	200 laps
4	Geoff Bodine	Pontiac Grand Prix	200 laps
5	Benny Parsons	Buick Regal	200 laps
6	Buddy Arrington	Chrysler Imperial	199 laps

Round 21 — Busch 500 — Bristol — 29 August 1982
500 laps = 266.5 miles. Winner's average speed 94.38mph

1	Darrell Waltrip	Buick Regal	2h 49m 32s
2	Bobby Allison	Buick Regal	500 laps
3	Harry Gant	Buick Regal	500 laps
4	Terry Labonte	Buick Regal	499 laps
5	Morgan Shepherd	Buick Regal	499 laps
6	Dale Ernhardt	Ford Thunderbird	499 laps

Round 22 — Southern 500 — Darlington — 6 September 1982
367 laps = 500 miles. Winner's average speed 115.224mph

1	Cale Yarborough	Buick Regal	?h 21m 00.0s
2	Richard Petty	Pontiac Grand Prix	367 laps
3	Dale Ernhardt	Ford Thunderbird	367 laps
4	Bill Elliott	Ford Thunderbird	367 laps
5	Buddy Baker	Pontiac Grand Prix	365 laps
6	Lake Speed	Buick Regal	365 laps

Round 23 — Wrangler 400 — Richmond — 12 September 1982
400 laps = 216.8 miles. Winner's average speed 82.8mph

1	Bobby Allison	Chevrolet	2h 37m 06s
2	Tim Richmond	Buick Regal	400 laps
3	Darrell Waltrip	Buick Regal	399 laps
4	Ricky Rudd	Pontiac Grand Prix	399 laps
5	Neil Bonnett	Ford Thunderbird	398 laps
6	Terry Labonte	Buick Regal	398 laps

Round 24 — CRC Chemicals 500 — Dover Downs — 19 September 1982
500 laps = 500 miles. Winner's average speed 107.642mph

1	Darrell Waltrip	Buick Regal	4h 38m 42.5s
2	Kyle Petty	Pontiac Grand Prix	500 laps
3	Bill Elliott	Ford Thunderbird	500 laps
4	Geoff Bodine	Pontiac Grand Prix	500 laps
5	Benny Parsons	Buick Regal	496 laps
6	Dave Marcis	Chevrolet	495 laps

Round 25 — Holly Farms 400 — North Wilkesboro — 3 October 1982
400 laps = 250 miles. Winner's average speed 98.071mph

1	Darrell Waltrip	Buick Regal	2h 32m 57s
2	Harry Gant	Buick Regal	2h 33m 11s
3	Terry Labonte	Chevrolet Monte Carlo	399 laps
4	Richard Petty	Pontiac Grand Prix	399 laps
5	Geoff Bodine	Pontiac Grand Prix	399 laps
6	Joe Ruttman	Pontiac Grand Prix	398 laps

Round 26 — National 500 — Charlotte — 10 October 1982
334 laps = 500 miles. Winner's average speed 137.208mph

1	Harry Gant	Buick Regal	3h 38m 38.78s
2	Bill Elliott	Ford Thunderbird	3h 38m 41.31s
3	David Pearson	Buick Regal	333 laps
4	Joe Ruttman	Buick Regal	331 laps
5	Benny Parsons	Buick Regal	331 laps
6	Buddy Baker	Pontiac Grand Le Mans	331 laps

Round 27 — Old Dominion 500 — Martinsville — 17 October 1982
500 laps = 262.5 miles. Winner's average speed 71.315mph

1	Darrell Waltrip	Buick Regal	3h 41m 5.0s
2	Ricky Rudd	Pontiac Grand Prix	3h 41m 7.2s
3	Richard Petty	Pontiac Grand Prix	500 laps
4	Terry Labonte	Buick Regal	498 laps
5	Joe Ruttman	Buick Regal	498 laps
6	Buddy Baker	Pontiac Grand Le Mans	498 laps

Round 28 — American 500 — Rockingham — 31 October 1982
492 laps = 500 miles. Winner's average speed 115.122mph

1	Darrell Waltrip	Buick Regal	492 laps
2	Bobby Allison	Chevrolet Monte Carlo	492 laps
3	Neil Bonnett	Ford Thunderbird	492 laps
4	Terry Labonte	Buick Regal	491 laps
5	Morgan Shepherd	Buick Regal	491 laps
6	Richard Petty	Pontiac Grand Prix	491 laps

Round 29 — Atlanta Journal 500 — Atlanta — 7 November 1982
328 laps = 500 miles. Winner's average speed 130.885mph

1	Bobby Allison	Chevrolet Monte Carlo	328 laps
2	Harry Gant	Buick Regal	328 laps
3	Darrell Waltrip	Buick Regal	328 laps
4	Tim Richmond	Buick Regal	328 laps
5	Joe Ruttman	Buick Regal	327 laps
6	Dave Marcis	Buick Regal	327 laps

Round 30 — Winston Western 500 — Riverside — 21 November 1982
119 laps = 500km. Winner's average speed 99.823mph

1	Tim Richmond	Buick Regal	3h 7m 0.24s
2	Ricky Rudd	Pontiac Grand Prix	3h 7m 8.09s
3	Darrell Waltrip	Buick Regal	119 laps
4	Neil Bonnett	Ford Thunderbird	119 laps
5	Mark Martin	Buick Regal	118 laps
6	Ron Bouchard	Oldsmobile Cutlass	117 laps

LOOKING GOOD

Traditionally, all forms of road racing have had a fairly shaky existence in the USA, but with well subscribed grids, colourful and identifiable cars and competitive racing for a reasonable budget it seems Trans-Am has found success. STEVE POTTER reports on the championship.

THE Sports Car Club of America appears to be backing a loser with its Can-Am series, and the notion of saving it by making it a refuge for the Group C cars that IMSA won't accept seems an unlikely one. Instead the club ought to get behind the Trans-Am, which once appeared even deader than the Can-Am does now. Thoughtful rule making, aimed at making a wide variety of cars competitive, and lots of hard work by the administrators involved has brought the once moribund sedan series back to robust health.

Elliot Forbes-Robinson, a former SuperVee champion who went on to drive in the Can-Am for Paul Newman, started the season as a part time competitor in NASCAR's Winston Cup stock car series, and finished up as champion in the CRC Chemicals sponsored Trans-Am series of 100 mile sprint races.

Joe Huffaker didn't have Forbes-Robinson's Pontiac Trans-Am finished in time for the season opener at Road Atlanta in May, but after a pair of second places, behind Porsche 924 Turbo driver Doc Bundy at Sears Point and Portland, Forbes-Robinson notched up

consecutive victories at Laguna Seca, Seattle and Mid-Ohio. He also won at Riverside in September and, with the exception of Road America, where he dropped out with engine trouble, the title winner finished in the top five in every race he entered.

America's all time club racer, Jerry Hansen, entered just three races with his Corvette, but he won two of them, at Road Atlanta and Elkhart Lake. Paul Newman made just one appearance, at Brainerd, but on a damp track he drove his turbocharged Datsun to victory.

The Trans-Am rules limit all cars to ten inch wide wheels at all four corners, and weights are assigned in an attempt to keep power to weight ratios constant for a wide variety of sedans. The rules permit full tube frames, which are cheap to build, but require that body work be kept stock so that the cars present easily identifiable shapes to the paying customers. Although the crowds still don't compare with those for the rival Camel GT series, the entries at each of the ten events were strong — generally forty or more, and the prospects for the series are rosy.

Harry 'Doc' Bundy was an early season winner with the handsome, Escort-backed Porsche Carrera Turbo (left) until the Pontiacs began to find their stride. Elliot Forbes-Robinson (above) took over at the front and went on to give Pontiac their first ever Trans-Am title with the Mecham Racing MSE Trans-Am, prepared by Joe Huffaker. The cleverly contrived Trans-Am rules allow a wide variety of reasonably inexpensive and readily identifiable cars into the series — which is just what the paying customer likes to see. American cars, such as Phil Currin's Greenwood-style Corvette, can compete on pretty well level terms with the likes of Bruce Leven's Carrera (below) and Frank Leary's Datsun Turbo 280ZX, Tom Gloy's Mustang and Bob Bergstrom's Carrera show typical variety at Laguna Seca's 'Corkscrew' (right).

LADY IN DRAG

Last year, Shirley Muldowney gave best to Jeb Allen in the NHRA World Championships, but this season the sport's leading lady put the Pioneer sponsored Top Fuel dragster back on top for an unprecedented third title. Our American correspondent reports on the drag racing scene.

TWO years ago Shirley Muldowney became the first multiple winner of the National Hot Rod Association's World Championship. With financial backing from Pioneer Stereo and Valvoline, Muldowney won her third World title in 1982.

Muldowney's hot pink charger was challenged in the Top Fuel class in the early part of the NHRA 12 racemeet National series by an innovative ground effect dragster, piloted by another female racer, rookie Lucille Lee.

Frank Hawley, a 25-year-old Canadian, drove the Chi Town Hustler to the Funny Car title, breaking the stranglehold on the "flopper" class that Don Prudhomme and Raymond Beadle have held since 1974. Meanwhile Lee Shepherd's Reher & Morrison Camaro dominated the Pro Stock ranks, despite changes in the rules that should have equalized the competition.

Much of the credit for Muldowney's third Top Fuel championship must go to her crew chief Rahn Tobler, and her son John Muldowney, who assisted Tobler with the preparation of the Swindahl chassis and the 2000 horsepower supercharged Keith Black Plymouth replica engines. Muldowney estimated that her driving contributed only 10% towards the success of the team. That may be overly modest, but it's true that without the money to replace the used up engine and driveline pieces, and the mechanical skills to set the car up right, no team stands a chance in the Top Fuel arena.

Muldowney won four of the dozen National events, and made it to the final in another three.

It might have been five wins, but her engine stalled at the starting line as she lined up for the final run against Dick LaHaie in the first meet of the year, the Winternationals. She came back to win the Gatornationals in Florida, beating two of the sport's legendary performers in the process, former crew chief/boy friend Connie Kalitta in the semi-final and, in the final round, Don Garlits, who mostly

confines his activity these days to match racing at backwater tracks.

She beat Kalitta again in the first round of the Springnationals in Ohio, and in the finals knocked off Lucille Lee, who had earlier in the season won her first National meet. Muldowney added the Northstar race at Brainerd and, for a crowning triumph, she captured her first US National at Indianapolis.

Muldowney's closest competition came from Mark Oswald, who campaigned the deep blue Candies & Hughes car. Oswald beat Muldowney in the finals of the Cajun meet in his team's home town, Baton Rouge, Louisiana, and later in the season added the Summernationals classic at Englishtown, New Jersey.

Kalitta finished third in the points with victories in the Molson meet at Sanair in Quebec and the Golden Gate Nationals outside San Francisco. Dwight Salisbury and Jim Barnard each won single meets.

The Chi Town Hustler team is a legend among America's drag racing fans, but this is the first year that the team campaigned the NHRA's National circuit. A lot of famous teams don't. The problem is that it's the NHRA that keeps most of the money from its championship series. The purses aren't nearly high enough to cover the expenses involved in running a professional car.

The National series is heavily covered by the drag racing media, most of which is a captive of the NHRA, and the sponsorship money that the media attention generates for the top teams helps make up what the purses lack.

But what pays the bills for the most top teams is the countless nights of exhibition runs and match races at little drag strips out in the sticks. A promoter will pay top dollars to a big name and, since they seldom have tough competition, they can back off the nitromethane in the fuel mix, and save their engines.

Shirley Muldowney (top left) is a great deal more than a pretty face, as NHRA's male Top Fuel competitors will readily admit. As 43-year-old Shirley, from Mount Clemens, Michigan, captured her third World title, her only concession to being a lady was the pink colour scheme of her Pioneer and Valvoline backed, Keith Black engined dragster (left). Shirley is not the only female front runner on the NHRA Championship trail, as Lucille Lee (top right) won her first National with the innovative Jolly Rancher fueller. In the end though, the main opposition again came from the men, with Mark Oswald (right) finishing the season as runner up, with two National wins for the Candies & Hughes team, and the evergreen Connie Kalitta taking two more with 'Bounty Hunter', to take third slot.

In the first year in which Frank Hawley campaigned the superb Chi Town Hustler funny car (previous page) on the NHRA National trail, the team cleaned up the series, breaking the eight year run of success by Don Prudhomme and Ray Beadle. Billy Meyer even beat Prudhomme and Beadle for the 1982 runner up slot with the Burt Reynolds/Hal Needham Racing Pontiac (left). Beadle (below) had a mixed year with a couple of wins followed by two very large accidents with the Blue Max Ford EXP. At the Winternationals, where Beadle qualified first, a fuel line broke heading for the traps, starting a fire which caused a rear tyre to blow and sent the car cartwheeling off the end of the strip from over 200mph, without injury to the driver! Lee Shepherd's neat Camaro (bottom) was runaway winner of the National Pro Stock class although by the end of the season Warren Johnson's Oldsmobile was beginning to give the Chevy driver a hard time.

After the Chi Town car scored good results in the first few races of the National season, the Minick-Coil-Farkonas team decided to go the distance, and young Frank Hawley and his crew used the knowledge they'd gathered through running for years on tricky, beat-up drag strips around the country to put together a season of remarkable consistency. Beadle was strong during the first part of the year, but then lost the combination. It took Kenny Bernstein until the last few races to get his own act together and by that time Hawley had an unassailable lead in the Funny Car category.

At season's end Hawley had three wins, to two each for point runner-up Billy Meyer, Prudhomme and Beadle. Bernstein, Tripp Shumake and Al Segrini each won one meet.

Liberalization of the rules for Pro Stock should have made for close competition in the NHRA professional class, for cars that most closely resemble real street machines. It didn't. Lee Shepherd's Camaro made it to the finals in all but one of the National events. He won half a dozen of them, finishing as runner-up in another five. He scored 50% more points than his nearest competitor, Frank Iaconio.

Iaconio's Camaro bested Shepherd's in the finals twice, while the Oldsmobile of third place finisher Warren Johnson came on strong in the second half of the season, beating Shepherd in the finals at three of the last five events. Former class champion Bob Glidden won one race with his Ford EXP.

In the Carolina Bobtail 250 for 10-wheel trucks, Charlie Baker (below) showed them the way home with his V12 Cummings-powered Kenworth. These are no ordinary trucks; Baker turned a fastest qualifying lap at almost 108mph and averaged 81.8mph on his way to the $11,000 first prize. The first ten rows of the bleachers aren't empty because truck racing isn't popular, they're empty because 100mph trucks might take a lot of stopping.

RALLYING
INTERNATIONAL

QUATTRO v THE REST

When the Audi Quattro burst spectacularly onto the rallying scene, many observers predicted that that was the beginning of the end for 'conventional' rally cars. In spite of the Quattro's remarkable success, it is not yet quite all-conquering, as our rallies correspondent reminds us.

THE biggest single factor influencing global rallying in 1982 has been the Audi Quattro. This revolutionary, four-wheel-drive, turbo-charged car has dominated virtually wherever it has gone, except in the most prestigious of all championships — the World Rally Championship.

In the hands of National status drivers, the car has clinched titles on two continents and in three countries. The car has shown its promised supremacy in all conditions except on asphalt and that exception has basically been through sheer bad luck anyway.

Stig Blomqvist was the first to take a title this year. He steam-rollered his way through the Swedish Championship behind the wheel of a Sweden Dealer Team Audi Quattro. The second title went to Harald Demuth, with his German Dealer car taking that country's series without a hitch. A trip across the Atlantic sees John Buffum incontestably setting the seal on the SCCA Championship in the USA, again driving an Audi Quattro.

The presitigious British Open title bid failed, despite Hannu Mikkola behind the wheel of an Audi UK Quattro, as did Michele Cinnotto's challenge for the Italian Championship in another Quattro. In other countries the car was banned before it could appear: that happened in Finland and Belgium, but, that apart, the Quattro has announced itself with a roar.

The concept of founding national teams has also brought success, yet the Audi base at Ingoldstadt in Germany houses team management that is still reluctant to let Quattros fall into private hands, such is the technical complexity of the car.

When the Quattro was announced, it sent team managers rushing back to the drawing boards, eagerly ready to change their new car plans, but convention still rules the roost. The Opel Ascona 400, a conventional, front-engined, rear-wheel-drive car, has shown its forte in the World Championship with past World Champion, Walter Röhrl, at the wheel, while a similar car took Jimmy McRae to his second consecutive British Open title. Another Ascona 400, this time Italian, took 'Tony' Fassina to victory in the complex European Rally Championship, with McRae a close second in his British Ascona.

Convention too has won through in most other major championships around the world. The hotly contested Irish Tarmac Championship fell to the Talbot Sunbeam of John Coyne. In Finland, Hamaleinen took his Nation's series in a Ford Escort RS, whilst New Zealand's closely fought championship went this year to Tony Teesdale, again in an Escort. The French Championship, meanwhile, was won by Jean Luc Therier driving a Renault 5 Turbo, but it was back to a Ford Escort for the South American series, where Domingo DeVitta won through in the end. In Belgium, the young Marc Duez took his national title in a Porsche 911.

Whether these conventional cars will win again in 1983 must remain a ponderable question now that specialist Group B cars become more commonplace. Indeed the idea of convention itself may have changed by this time next year. Most manufacturers are deeply involved with projects to produce new specification rally cars in accordance with the new vehicle regulations implemented by FISA. Most will have turbocharged engines and some are bound to follow the example set by Audi and turn to four-wheel drive. This could well have been the final year of the conventional car winning championships — if so let's savour the memory well.

Impressive though the Quattro was in the British Open Championship, driven by Hannu Mikkola (above), in Britain at least it had to give best to convention, in the guise of Jimmy McRae's Opel Ascona 400 (right).

TACTICAL VICTORY

On paper, there seemed little to stop the Audi Quattro from dominating the World Rally Championship and nothing to stop Hannu Mikkola from dominating the Quattro line-up, but in the end Walter Röhrl boxed clever to repeat his 1980 championship win and Mikkola was upstaged by that French lady . . .

THIS year's championship was one to confound the pundits' right from the word go. Everyone expected the Audi Quattro to devastate the opposition, just as everyone expected Hannu Mikkola to produce better results for the team than Michele Mouton would. How wrong they all were. It was Walter Röhrl who dominated the scene in his Rothmans Opel Ascona 400, while Mouton proved to be the safer bet for Audi.

Röhrl last won the World Championship in 1980 when he drove for the Fiat team. Then, he drove aggressively to win. For 1982, he set about proving he could win again using tactics in place of outright speed. He never had the intention of beating the Audi Quattro through sheer pace alone; he realised that that would be folly. Instead he was content to finish events as the highest placed 'conventional' car driver, except in Brazil, where he was out to show the world his speed. He failed; he just couldn't beat the relentless onslaught of a Quattro attack — perhaps then the world realised that his 1982 tactics were, after all, the best.

Audi answered his tactical approach to the championship by fielding massive teams in both the Acropolis Rally (four cars) and San Remo Rally (six cars). In Greece the tactics failed when only one car finished, albeit the winning car, while in San Remo they worked, pushing Opel down the finishing order and starving it of both manufacturers' and drivers' points. Both teams made errors this year — Audi completely missed the Safari, while Röhrl missed the 1000 Lakes, either of which could have given the respective teams good chances of scoring points.

The year was remarkable in many ways. It saw Team Toyota Europe return to rallying with a debut 1-2 win in the New Zealand Motogard Rally and it saw the small Renault team win in Corsica. It witnessed the first Group B car (the Lancia Rally) involved in both the spectacle of impressive performances and of dramatic accidents; and it saw one man, Hannu Mikkola, lift himself from the ashes of defeat to finish the year respectably. It was also a year when the form book was thrown out of the window. One can only hope that more manufacturers will contest the 1983 series as the lack of teams in 1982 was the only real dissappointment in a hard fought World Rally Championship.

As night falls, Walter Röhrl is heading for a safe second place on the Acropolis (below) with the Rothmans backed Ascona 400, behind Michele Mouton.

MONTE CARLO RALLY

WALTER Röhrl was to start his season with a début win for his new team. it was all part of his plan not only to drive his way through to the World Champion's crown for a second time, but to think his way through as well. His win in the French Alps did, however, come as a surprise.

This 1982 Monte Carlo was a strange one: it lacked snow and ice. The temperature was low enough, but warm weather prior to the event thawed the traditional ice covered roads leaving good, clean (and dry) tarmac. It was as if Monte Carlo had turned into Corsica. The familiar Monte Carlo Rally ice note crews still carried out their tasks, but more often than not they reported back with news of clear stages.

Saby's fifth-placed Renault 5 Turbo

Walter Röhrl was joined in the Rothmans Opel Rally Team by Jochen Kleint, a driver who had proved himself on the Monte before. There was a duel between the Ascona 400s, but a more important fight soon developed between Röhrl and the Audi Quattros.

Hannu Mikkola, Michele Mouton and Röhrl represented the only serious contenders in this year's Championship. Mikkola was Audi's main hope, while Mouton was there to attract publicity. She certainly did that in Monte Carlo. The unfortunate French Miss managed to hurl her Quattro full bore over the only un-noted patch of ice in her rally. The result was disastrous. Her Audi slammed head-on into the corner of a house; her car was wrecked. She and co-driver, Fabrizia Pons, were lucky to escape without injury.

Mikkola continued alone for Audi, chasing Walter Röhrl's lead hard. The battle went well into the final night before the Finn gave in to Röhrl's supremacy. The German driver had his way, and round one fell to the ex-World Champion.

SWEDISH RALLY

STRANGE weather wasn't restricted to the Cote D'Azur early in '82, Sweden had its troubles too. A warm spell had almost succeeded in robbing this Drivers-only round of its magic: snow. The forest roads

Blomqvist found some of the elusive Swedish snow

were clearing of the stuff, but enough lined the roads to provide banks for the Scandinavian drivers to bounce off. Most stages were covered in solid ice or slush, in sufficient quantity to give the Audi Quattros a definite advantage, while Walter Röhrl was further handicapped — this being his first trip to Sweden.

Three Quattros lined up for the Audi team: Hannu Mikkola and Michele Mouton had their regular cars and were helped by Stig Blomqvist driving the same Swedish Dealer Team Quattro which he used for his home championship. Any advantage Blomqvist had was thrown away on the rally's opening stages when his car developed a fuel feed problem, dropping him down the leader board.

Instead, the lead was in Mikkola's hands but he was being challenged by both Ari Vatanen in his Escort RS and Ola Stromberg driving a Saab 99EMS, with Röhrl taking things steady and maintaining a middle order position. Then Stromberg retired after a bank clouting episode filled his car's radiator grill with snow and caused the Saab's head gasket to blow.

It then seemed certain to be an Audi Quattro 1-2-3 in Sweden, but disaster struck the team on the final night section. First Mikkola left the road, putting his car off through a snow bank. Blomqvist drove past whilst Mikkola tried to regain the road. His car was half way back on the track, when a charging Mouton arrived on the scene and promptly punted him back off. Both drivers lost time, Mikkola dropping from the lead to 16th place, while Mouton sank to fifth.

Meanwhile, Blomqvist took the win, Vatanen finished second and Walter Röhrl drove safely to third place, a little annoyed at being beaten by an Escort, but consoled by it being only his first attempt at this peculiar event. He had after all strengthened his lead in the championship.

RALLY OF PORTUGAL

FOR 1982, the route had changed. Instead of the popular tarmac stages being run late in the rally, they were run as the pipe opener. Henri Toivonen lapped them up, building himself a useful lead, as team mate to Röhrl in the Rothmans Opels. Then, as the rally reverted to its usual gravel tests, the young Finn broke two Ascona axles, relegating himself to an also-ran's position until a clutch failure retired him from his misery.

Pond was knocked from second place by gearbox failure

Mikkola was there to snap up the lead, with Röhrl second, but that too was short lived. Mikkola rolled his Quattro out of the event in thick fog during a road section. The reason was a mis-heard note from co-driver, Arne Hertz. Walter Röhrl was out too. His Opel suffered a steering breakage causing it to roll heavily down an embankment; nobody was hurt but there were no points for the series leader in Portugal.

Michele Mouton went on to win. It was her second World Championship victory at the wheel of the Quattro and it set her up as a threat to Röhrl's hopes in 1982. Both Tony Pond and Per Eklund had their share of second place. Eklund carried it through to the end in his Toyota Celica, while Pond retired in spectacular fashion when the Datsun prop-shaft tore a gaping hole in the car's floor after its gearbox seized.

The Austrian, Franz Wittman, finished in an incredible third place, while Timo Salonen wrecked Datsun's chances of a score after a brainless attack at one particular stage ripped his car's suspension clean off.

WORLD RALLY CHAMPIONSHIP

SAFARI RALLY

THE Safari again proved to be a local benefit, with Shekhar Mehta taking his fifth rally victory behind the wheel of a Datsun. The car-bumping battle which he and Rauno Aaltonen had had in 1981 was nearly repeated, although the Finn was driving a Rothmans Opel on this occasion.

The two battled on against the clock, with Aaltonen obviously the quicker of the two, then the Opel engine broke, leaving Mehta to assert himself once again.

Kirkland's Datsun Silvia took third place

Behind those two drivers, Tony Pond was impressing the regulars with his efforts. The Datsun driver achieved a magnificent fourth place despite losing a host of time with his car stuck in a mud hole. Pond's car, along with the other Datsuns, soon became the talking point of the event when it was learned that the Datsun mechanics were able to perform axle changes in an astounding nine minutes.

Walter Röhrl's championship chase was strengthened yet again with a second place finish, given greater importance by Audi missing the event completely.

TOUR OF CORSICA

THE tiny Mediterranean island of Corsica played host to both Röhrl and Mouton, providing the stage for their impressive acts. Mikkola was also entered but retired after his Quattro's wheels had barely turned in anger on the first stage. His car's transmission had failed, but he was lucky even to start the event. His original car had been wrecked by a mechanic just hours before the start and a practice car was hurriedly prepared as a replacement.

Röhrl, in typically Corsican setting, heading for fourth

Röhrl had the better of Mouton during the whole rally, but could only manage fourth place behind the winning Renault 5 Turbo of Jean Ragnotti, Andruet's Ferrari 308 GTB and the Porsche 911 of Bernard Beguin.

Soon after the start, Andruet and Ragnotti were locked in battle, with Bettega intervening briefly in his Lancia Rally — the first World Championship Rally for this new Group B car. His run finished in an accident which put him out of rallying for the rest of the year with two badly broken legs.

Markku Alén was driving a second Lancia but his lot was to suffer steering problems, finally returning a ninth place finish. While drama struck the mid-field runners, Ragnotti and Andruet continued their fight at the front. Then a freak rain storm caught many drivers on unsuitable tyres and Ragnotti, who had chosen rain tyres, stormed away into an unassailable lead.

Andruet closed the gap during the final day but not before succumbing to clutch trouble, resigning himself to second place overall. Michele Mouton drove a good rally but was rewarded with a low scoring seventh place at the finish as Röhrl extended his lead still further.

ACROPOLIS RALLY

THIS Greek round saw a massive Audi attack from four cars: Mikkola, Mouton, Cinotto and Wittman. Opel replied with three cars for Röhrl, Toivonen and Britain's Jimmy McRae (having his first taste of foreign World Championship rallying).

The event was to be its usual long and hard self: ideal conditions for the Quattros. Mikkola took an immediate lead, then retired shortly after with suspension failure. Markku Alén took over the lead in his Lancia Rally, but lost it to Mouton when his car's gearbox gave trouble (a problem that had plagued the car in development).

Toivonen was second of the three Opels, third overall

Michele Mouton retained the lead through the following four days to the finish, while Röhrl, her ever present shadow, again drove steadily to finish second. The young Henri Toivonen brought his Opel home in third place; a position once held by McRae before electrical troubles relegated him to sixth.

Datsun's three official entries dwindled to just one at the finish — that of Mehta. Tony Pond's car went off the road following suspension damage, while Salonen retired when his Datsun differential failed.

Mouton had gained another five points over Röhrl's score, notching up her second win of the year and setting an all time record for the Acropolis Rally — she had finished the event devoid of road time penalties.

MOTOGARD RALLY

THE action moved to New Zealand for the next round, the islands having been omitted from the series for 1981. The two Audi Quattros were there for Mikkola and Mouton, the French lady by then showing herself to be carrying the flag for her team. Röhrl too was there as a single entry from Opel. It was therefore no surprise that he should take no chances, finishing an eventual third.

Mikkola shot into the rally lead straight away, then fuel injection problems slowed him, giving Mouton her share of the spotlight as rally leader. Chasing the lady hard was Björn Waldegard, marking

Fifth-placed Millen was first of the locals and won Group 2

the occasion of Toyota's return to rallying with an impressive début for the Celica. Röhrl was third, as a determined Tony Pond struggled on in sixth place, fighting his badly understeering Datsun all the way.

Mikkola came back into the fight just as Mouton retired her Quattro with a broken oil pipe, but it was Waldegard leading, while the number two Toyota, driven by Per Eklund, slipped through in front of Röhrl's Opel. Mikkola was soon up to second place and ready to pounce, but his attempt was thwarted by a broken steering arm — Mikkola retired again!

Waldegard went on to maintain first place, giving Toyota Team Europe a début win for the lightweight Celica. As if to put the icing on the team's celebratory cake, Per Eklund brought the other Celica home in second place, while Röhrl managed a predictable third, ahead of Timo Salonen's Datsun.

RALLY OF BRAZIL

DUE to take place before this rally was the Codasur Rally in Argentina, but doubts had surrounded the event ever since the South Atlantic crisis flared up into a fully fledged war and sure enough, the rally was cancelled. The Codasur would have been a round of both the drivers' and manufacturers' championships, while Brazil, scheduled for a month later was to count only for drivers' points. A FISA meeting then decided to bestow the honour of full championship status to Brazil and that decision was enough to make both Opel and Audi send cars.

Brazil was Michele Mouton's third win of the year

Audi had two Quattros for its usual team, Mikkola and Mouton, while Rothmans Opel, just as in the previous round, sent just one car, to be driven by the championship leader, Walter Röhrl. Apart from an entry for Shekhar and Yvonne Mehta (in a Datsun Silvia) and Domingo DeVitta in his Escort RS2000, that was about it.

It seemed the Brazilian organisers had gone to a great deal of trouble arranging a four-day rally for such a small number of top crews, although the organisation had its own troubles to contend with. With but a handful of days to go before the start, the Clerk of the Course was sacked, amid some confusion, and the rally naturally suffered as a consequence.

That was of little concern to Mikkola though, for again bad luck struck down his chances; he put his Quattro off the road on a muddy bend and was out of time when he eventually regained the road. His team mate, Mouton, took the rally lead, but she too lost time (with a damaged transmission) leaving Röhrl to take the premier place.

Röhrl kept that lead for the next two and a half days, while Mouton fought tooth and nail to win it back. That she did during the rally's closing stages; leaving Röhrl to wonder if he could ever beat the Quattro. Shekhar Mehta retired almost within sight of the rally finish, with a con-rod through his Datsun engine block, which left DeVitta to take third place, thereby earning himself FISA 'A' grading.

RALLY OF THE 1000 LAKES

AS usual, the Finns spent most of the event run-up period deeply involved in trying to out-psych each other: this was, after all, their home event — the event each and every Finn *had* to win!

It featured one of the strongest fields of 1982 but Röhrl was conspicuous by his absence. The rally was too specialised for his — and Opel's — liking, so, instead, full team status was bestowed on Henri Toivonen. Audi were in quite the opposite position, with three

Airikkala brought Mitsubishi back with third place

Quattros: Mikkola and Mouton were there and so was Stig Blomqvist. Markku Alén gave the Lancia Rally evolution car its first taste of World Championship rallying, while Ari Vatanen had entered an Escort RS. The top Finnish drivers were rounded off by Timo Salonen, driving a Datsun Silvia Turbo.

The rally was compressed into a day and a half, and soon turned out to be a battle between Mikkola and Blomqvist. Mouton rolled her Quattro out of the running; Vatanen's Escort engine seized; Alén's Lancia engine broke and Toivonen crashed after a strong challenge for the lead. One of two Mitsubishi Lancer Turbos entered (marking the return of the Japanese team to rallying) retired while in Anders Kullang's hands, and the other, Pentti Airikkala's, went on to finish third.

That drama all took place behind the two Quattros; the Swedish Rally adversaries were again locked in battle but that soon ended. In stepped the team manager to issue orders before the rally's final leg. That order was to finish in their then present positions — which they did and Mikkola won.

MONTE CARLO
January 16-23

1	W.Rohrl/C.Geistdorfer	Opel Ascona 400	G4	8h 20m 33s
2	H.Mikkola/A.Hertz	Audi Quattro	G4	8h 24m 22s
3	J-L.Therier/M.Vial	Porche 911SC	G4	8h 32m 38s
4	G.Frequelin/J-F.Fauchille	Porsche 911SC	G4	8h 37m 40s
5	B.Saby/F.Sappey	Renault 5T	G4	8h 43m 34s
6	D.Snobeck/D.Emanuelli	Renault 5T	G4	8h 50m 28s
7	J.Kleint/G.Wanger	Opel Ascona 400	G4	8h 59m 40s
8	P.Touren/J-L.Alric	Renault 5T	G4	9h 06m 34s
9	J-P.Ballet/'Tilber'	Porsche 911SC	GB	9h 09m 00s
10	J.Barth/R.Kussmaul	Porsche 924	GB	9h 09m 46s

Walter Röhrl   *World Champion 1982*

SWEDEN
February 12-14 (Drivers only)

1	S.Blomqvist/B.Cederberg	Audi Quattro	G4	3h 40m 15s
2	A.Vatanen/T.Harryman	Ford Escort	G4	3h 42m 51s
3	W.Rohrl/C.Geistdorfer	Opel Ascona 400	G4	3h 44m 29s
4	P.Eklund/R.Spjuth	Saab 99T	GA	3h 45m 20s
5	M.Mouton/F.Pons	Audi Quattro	G4	3h 46m 08s
6	L.Lampi/P.Kuukkala	Ford Escort	G4	3h 46m 14s
7	S.Nilsson/A.Olsson	Datsun 160J GT	G4	3h 48m 41s
8	K.Grundel/R.Melleroth	VW Golf GTi	GA	3h 50m 30s
9	B.Thorsell/J-O.Bohlin	Ford Escort	G4	3h 51m 09s
10	M.Ericsson/J.Sandstrom	Audi 80 Coupé	GA	3h 52m 48s

PORTUGAL
March 2-6

1	M.Mouton/F.Pons	Audi Quattro	G4	7h 39m 36s
2	P.Eklund/R.Spjuth	Toyota Celica	G4	7h 52m 43s
3	F.Wittman/P.Diekman	Audi Quattro	G4	8h 07m 25s
4	C.Torres/F.Lopes	Ford Escort	G4	8h 30m 58s
5	A.Coppier/J.Laloz	Citroen Visa	GB	8h 54m 11s
6	M.Silva/R.Bevilacqua	Ford Escort	G4	9h 01m 12s
7	A.F.Cunha/C.Resende	Opel Ascona	G2	9h 29m 09s
8	C.Dorsche/P.Trivero	Citroen Visa	GB	9h 35m 39s
9	O.Tabatoni/M.Cadier	Citroen Visa	GB	9h 40m 36s
10	J.Fleck/S.Klein	Opel Kadett GT/E	G2	9h 40m 55s

SAFARI
April 8-12

1	S.Mehta/M.Doughty	Datsun Violet	G4	4h 26m
2	W.Rohrl/C.Geistdorfer	Opel Ascona 400	G4	5h 07m
3	M.Kirkland/A.Lavitan	Datsun Silvia	G4	6h 16m
4	T.Pond/T.Harryman	Datsun Silvia	G4	7h 00m
5	J.Shal/A.Khan	Datsun Violet	G2	8h 15m
6	R.Collinge/M.Fraser	Range Rover	G2	8h 54m
7	Y.Takshashi/M.Gohil	Subaru	G2	12h 20m
8	F.Tundo/O.Thompson	Mitsubishi	G2	12h 53m
9	J.Alam/A.Khan	Subaru	G2	13h 51m
10	R.Khoda/J.Matharu	Subaru	G2	15h 35m

TOUR OF CORSICA
May 6-8

1	J.Ragnotti/J-M.Andrie	Renault 5T	G4	14h 11m 19s
2	J-C.Andruet/'Biche'	Ferrari GTB	G4	14h 16m 57s
3	B.Beguin/J.Lenne	Porsche 911	G4	14h 20m 11s
4	W.Rohrl/C.Geistdorfer	Opel Ascona 400	G4	14h 20m 41s
5	B.Saby/F.Sappey	Renault 5T	G4	14h 27m 31s
6	G.Frequelin/J-M.Fauchille	Porsche 911SC	G4	14h 35m 16s
7	M.Mouton/F.Pons	Audi Quattro	G4	14h 43m 48s
8	F.Vincent/F.Calvier	Porsche 911SC	G4	14h 43m 55s
9	M.Alen/I.Kivimaki	Lancia Rally	GB	14h 53m 18s
10	R.Simonetti/J-M.Simonetti	Renault 5T	G4	15h 35m 43s

ACROPOLIS
May 31-June 3

1	M.Mouton/F.Pons	Audi Quattro	G4	12h 54m 44s
2	W.Rohrl/C.Geistdorfer	Opel Ascona 400	G4	13h 08m 23s
3	H.Toivonen/F.Gallagher	Opel Ascona 400	G4	13h 17m 21s
4	S.Mehta/Y.Mehta	Nissan Violet GT	G4	13h 27m 28s
5	G.Moschous/ A.Constandakatos	Nissan Violet	G4	13h 36m 44s
6	J.McRae/I.Grindrod	Opel Ascona 400	G4	13h 40m 16s
7	P.Mouschoutis/'Silef'	Fiat 131 Abarth	G4	14h 21m 48s
8	A.Maniatopoulos/S.Kokkinis	Renault 5T	G4	14h 37m 28s
9	Y.Iwashita/Y.Nakashara	Nissan Silvia	G2	14h 53m 10s
10	F.Heisler/W.Blieberger	Ford Escort	G2	16h 10m 40s

MOTOGARD
June 26-29

1	B.Waldegard/H.Thorszelius	Toyota Celica	G4	10h 28m 08s
2	P.Eklund/R.Spjuth	Toyota Celica	G4	10h 31m 21s
3	W.Rohrl/C.Geistdorfer	Opel Ascona 400	G4	10h 33m 37s
4	T.Salonen/S.Harjanne	Nissan Silvia	G4	10h 41m 25s
5	R.Millen/J.Belfleur	Mazda RX7	G2	10h 54m 55s
6	T.Teesdale/G.Smith	Ford Escort	G4	11h 30m 17s
7	J-L.Leyraud/E.Johnston	Ford Escort	G4	11h 37m 22s
8	M.Stewart/D.Parkhill	Ford Escort	G2	11h 51m 26s
9	P.Adams/J.Scott	Toyota Starlet	G2	11h 55m 06s
10	R.Cook/W.Jones	Nissan Bluebird	G2	11h 56m 54s

BRAZIL
August 10-15

1	M.Mouton/F.Pons	Audi Quattro	G4	8h 16m 24s
2	W.Rohrl/C.Geistdorfer	Opel Ascona 400	G4	8h 51m 49s
3	D.Devitta/D.Muzio	Ford Escort	G2	10h 15m 30s
4	A.Rodrigues/J.Mattos	VW Passat	G2	11h 41m 08s

There were only four classified finishers. R.Costa and V.A.Vierra (VW Passat) finished in fifth place on 12h 7m 32s but were not eligible for World Championship points as their car was alcohol fuelled.

RALLY OF THE 1000 LAKES
August 27-29

1	H.Mikkola/A.Hertz	Audi Quattro	G4	4h 19m 05s
2	S.Blomqvist/B.Cederberg	Audi Quattro	G4	4h 19m 33s
3	P.Airikkala/J.Piironen	Mitsubishi Turbo	G4	4h 23m 22s
4	T.Salonen/S.Harjanne	Nissan Silvia T	G2	4h 25m 02s
5	A.Laine/R.Virtanen	Talbot Sunbeam	G2	4h 31m 04s
6	R.Brookes/R.Morgan	Vauxhall Chevette	G4	4h 37m 10s
7	H.Uotila/T.Leino	Ford Escort	G2	4h 48m 10s
8	J.Kinnunen/J.Nieminen	Ford Escort	G2	4h 51m 03s
9	S.Mustonen/E.Pakkanen	Ford Escort	G2	4h 53m 47s
10	H.Palmroos/I.Riipinen	Ford Escort	G2	4h 55m 55s

SUPERCARS

The advent of new regulations is always a time for rapid development and the latest Group A, B and N categories have unwittingly 'opened the floodgates' for manufacturers' purpose-built rally cars. The supercar, however, was part of the scene long before this year's changes.

THE tip of a gigantic iceberg has been seen in 1982: the advent of the supercar in rallying. It has been made possible by a new set of vehicle regulations implemented by the governing body, FISA. Cars complying with the new Groups A, B and N have only been seen this year; until now, cars have been categorised into Groups 1 to 4, and even before that, in Groups 1 to 6. The decision to take a major step forward by changing the vehicle regulations was made in the light of an ever increasing trend of professionalism within rallying. These new rules were seen as a way of stopping supercars developing, but instead, they have opened the flood gates for the motor manufacturers to design and produce purpose-built rally cars.

Since the first manufacturer entered a 'works' car in an international motor rally, there has been a need to control vehicle eligibility. Without control, it wouldn't be long before a manufacturer would realise that in order to win, and so increase company prestige, a small car with a massive engine would be ideal. The ideal is usually also the impracticable, and since motor manufacturers sell practical cars as a general rule, these 'ideal' cars wouldn't bear any resemblance to a showroom model.

So, in 1957 a set of vehicle regulations was laid down by the sport's government, the FIA based in Paris. It set up a commission, the Commission Sportive International (CSI), to make the rules, and those rules later became known as 'Appendix J', so called because that was the heading under which they came in the FIA Yearbook.

Groups 1 and 3 cars were, respectively, Series Production Saloon cars with a minimum annual production figure of 5000, and Series Production GT (Sports) cars with a minimum figure of 1000. Generally speaking they were the most popular cars to be found in European rallies. Then, according to the rules laid down in 'Appendix J', when these cars were modified or tuned, Group 1 cars became Group 2 with a minimum production requirement of 1000 per year and Group 3 became Group 4 with a 500 production figure.

As time passed by, manufacturers were recognising more and more the prestige to be gained from beating a rival manufacturer in rallies. Proper "Competition Departments" were launched and heavily financed by their parent companies. By the early 1960s BMC had a thriving workshop at Abingdon, turning out unbeatable Mini Coopers and Healey 3000s and at Coventry there was the Rootes team with its Rapiers. Already, their biggest rivals were the French and Germans, although Ford was by then taking an interest as well.

The Mini Cooper gave way to the Cooper 'S' in Group 2 trim and it proved almost unbeatable. The age of the purpose-built competition car was dawning. The French realised it and were not slow to make inroads into the idea themselves, but in the meantime these French teams joined French organisers in launching a vindictive campaign against British cars.

British teams had earned themselves a reputation for manipula-

Early exponents of the purpose built rally car were Renault, through their Alpine competition department. This is Bernard Darniche's car on its way to winning the 1973 Austrian Alpine Rally.

ting the rules and driving cars right through any loopholes they found. Soon, personalities who were adept at rule bending came to the fore but, it must be said, not all rule benders were from British teams, they were simply answering the audacious behaviour of others.

Following the Mini Cooper 'S' came the Ford Escort Twin Cam, a car aimed right at the competition field. It still competed in Group 2, against the Saab V4s, and the BMW 2002s, while Group 4 cars were tending to snatch outright victories, with cars like the Lancia Fulvia HF and Fiat 124 Spider. Group 5 and 6 cars were around but, as they were classed as prototype cars, they could only exist to provide spectacle. These cars were further modified Group 2 and 4 cars operating within much freer guidelines and no minimum production figure was attached to the category.

These prototypes were rarely seen in the regular international rallies; they were restricted to the Marathon rallies of the day. None but the biggest manufacturers could afford to invest, if that's the word for it, in prototype machinery anyway, so the groups were basically only seen on Europe's racing circuits.

The first hint of a need to tighten up vehicle regulations came in 1968. The French company, Renault, had developed a purpose-built competition car, the Alpine-Renault 1300, later fitted with a 1600cc engine. It was a massive step forward and one that prompted Europe's manufacturers to re-think their plans.

The car was way ahead of its rivals at the time. It had a glassfibre bodyshell, the interior was barely a two seater and its engine was slung behind the rear wheels giving superb traction on loose surfaces. It weighed in at just 650kg with a power output from its 1600cc engine in Group 4 trim of 155bhp. It was of little wonder the car featured regularly in the winner's circle; its competition, typically, came from Group 2 Escorts (162bhp and 785kg), Fiat 124 Spiders in Group 3 (150bhp and 895kg) and Lancia Fulvia HFs also in Group 3 (155bhp and 780kg).

That diminutive, steel-blue demon had started the ball rolling. Ford's answer was the unfortunate GT70, a prototype car with a low slung glassfibre body housing a V-engine, midships and driving through a transaxle. The car did actually see the light of day in competition, but was scrapped later when a policy decision dictated further Escort development.

It was becoming obvious that to win rallies, cars would have to be in the competitive Group 4 category, which meant two seater 'sports' cars. Then, with the rally world still reeling from the shock of the Alpine-Renault and the prospect of a GT70, Lancia stopped everyone dead in their tracks.

In 1972 an answer to the Renault was wheeled out of Lancia's workshops in Turin: the Stratos had been born. It was the result of high technology development, a complete departure from traditional lines and backed by a massive budget. Lancia came straight in with a Group 4 car, producing (or providing proof of producing) 200 cars within 12 consecutive months — the vehicle regulations had been amended by the early 1970s: Group 4 cars now needed a minimum production of 400 in two consecutive years, while Group 2 needed 1000 similarly produced.

Lancia had managed to beat the rules that were originally laid down to prevent such a thing happening in the first place. From that moment, all manner of cars were being conceived in workshops around Europe, but none appeared. Instead, the team manipulators managed to push traditional Group 2 cars into Group 4, cars like the Escort and Fiat 131. The teams claimed that so popular were their cars in competition, that there must have been more than 400 two seater examples in existence around the world. They were rarely challenged.

By the late 1970s manufacturers were turning out some pretty strange cars; 'homologation specials' became a term on many people's tongues. There was the Group 1 Chrysler Avenger fitted with a 2-litre engine — it used a cylinder block exported to the South American market — which soon became unbeatable in its class. Export parts lists found themselves under close scrutiny by competition managers in search of that extra tweek to give them the edge. The Vauxhall Chevette HS appeared, as did a 16-valve Toyota. It was all a far cry from the days when vehicle regulations were introduced to restrict tuning modifications. The need for a change was obvious, before the situation became uncontrollable.

That change has now come about. 1982 was the first year to see the new groups in use, but ironically, instead of forcing manufacturers back to the days of 'production' car rallying, it has seen the Lancia Stratos syndrome repeated.

The new regulations are again related to production figures: Group A cars require a 5000 minimum figure, Group B cars, two seaters, 200 minimum, whilst Group N requires 5000. Unlike under the old regulations, limits on modifications to basic models are extremely stringent. So much so, that the only way of producing a competition car from a base that's suitable to sell to the public is to make the changes through what is called 'evolution'. This is a process of modifying 10% of the original minimum production figure

— for Group B that would mean 20 'rally' cars. This evolution is the real key to what the new cars are all about.

Audi proved it can make an ideal competition car and sell the unlikely machines to the public as well — the Quattro is living proof. Renault thought the same, hence the 5 Turbo. Although they are both Group 4 cars, they were developed for the new regulations. So perhaps the possibility of selling 200 special models wasn't out of the question after all, but at a price.

The inevitable soon happened and it was due to Lancia again. The Lancia Rally was launched: a worthy successor to the Stratos with its space frame, lightweight body (970kg) and its boosted mid-engine power (300bhp). It will soon be followed by a purpose designed Ford: again boosted and with a special bodyshell.

These two manufacturers are just the tip of the iceberg, swelled in proportions by the growing interest of Japanese manufacturers in producing competitive rally cars.

It is no real wonder these new regulations have deteriorated to a set of construction plans for, basically, prototype cars, cars the man in the street would never dream of buying. They have been thought up by the manufacturers themselves. Just as the old CSI was advised by the manufacturers' organisation, the BPICA, so is the new FISA commission advised. The manufacturers decide the rules themselves, then make recommendations to FISA; predictably, the technological intellect weighs heavily in BPICA's favour.

With those rules agreed, the BPICA then has the task of vetting homologation proposals from fellow manufacturers — the logic being one of 'setting a thief to catch a thief'! However unlikely it seems, the system is working well.

As with any change in rules, there has been a changeover period where cars from Groups A and B have competed with cars of the old Groups 2 and 4. In 1982, the Group 4 cars were far more competitive than those in Group B. The changeover period will end in December 1983, by which time Group B should be well established.

Lancia has produced the first Group B car aimed at outright vic-

With the Escort's success, Ford had little incentive to pursue the troublesome GT70 theme (left). The car was conceived in January 1970, unveiled exactly a year later and shelved almost immediately. Had it been a success and come face to face with cars like the Alpine and Lancia's Stratos (below left) how different would rallying have looked today? Lancia's successor to the Stratos, the mid-engined, spaceframed Rally (right) is perhaps more akin to a racing car than to the traditional rally car and, well-built though it is, its inherent frailty worries some. Meanwhile, the Quattro (below) remains 'state of the art' in the purpose built rally car league — but for how long?

tory, whilst as a contradiction, the only other purpose built Group B car is the Citroen Visa Trophy, based on the workaday Visa. It is the 'clubman's' Group B car — cheap, easy to maintain and competitive within its 1300cc class. It heralds a movement amongst the less traditional rally car manufacturers to become involved.

Citroen has set a classic example of how to produce a Group B car economically. It is the epitome of what the new rule changes were originally aimed at — more economical rallying, in cars more akin to ordinary commuter machines.

Manufacturers have, however, turned to Group A with thoughts of cars for the clubman. That group will be a virtual replacement for Group 1, the category that has long been the reserve of the up-and-coming factory driver or 'serious' amateur. Most have developed a car for such uses alongside more exotic machinery and certainly for 1983, there will be fierce rivalry between factories in Group A championships. That group is also seen to be the domain of the Japanese manufacturers, as they have both the annual production figures and range of models to turn out a competitive car, maybe even producing a Group A car to challenge Group B cars just as Talbot did when the Group 2 Sunbeam took the manufacturers' World Championship Title from a Group 4 Ford Escort in 1981.

Group N is the forgotten category in Britain. Home manufacturers are not interested in homologating cars and, in this group, cars can only be driven by Nationals of the country of homologation. The same cannot be said for Europe though. There, Group N cars are seen regularly on numerous events, but that may possibly be due to the nature of the rallies (mostly tarmac) which particularly suits these near standard production cars.

The advent of these new cars, particularly the Group B supercars does pose a question of safety. In 1982 the Lancia Rally had already acquired a bad reputation, one driver broke both of his legs in an accident during the Tour of Corsica, while another narrowly missed serious injury when he was catapulted through the roof of his car during an Italian event.

Manufacturers are encouraged to make weight sacrifices and that inevitably leads to flimsier bodyshells, while engines produce ever more power. That ball was set in motion by Audi, its Quattro producing over 320bhp. It is not unusual for modern rally cars to produce around 270bhp, but the new breed must be looking to over 300bhp to stay competitive. The new Ford Escort is reputed to produce around 320bhp, while Audi is rumoured to be investigating an engine rated at over 400bhp.

These power figures are produced by boosting the engine, either by turbocharging or supercharging. This method has been popularised by restrictions in the new vehicle regulations with regard to modifications allowed to a car's induction system. With boosting, it is a simple matter to increase boost pressure for a docile standard engine to almost double for a competition unit.

This dramatic increase in power will take its toll of cars in two ways: tyres and safety. Tyres particularly are being developed along the lines of Formula One technology to cope with the demands of high power outputs. For tarmac rallies we should soon see tyres bolted to the rims, as in Formula 1, while for loose surface events the tyres will not only have to give the best traction but they will also have to withstand potentially higher wear rates.

Safety is an even greater problem now that speeds have increased so much over the past few years — and without the new breed of supercars even being seen. Accidents do happen, witness Ari Vatanen's accidents during his year of chasing the World Champion's title, Henri Toivonen's accident in the 1000 Lakes Rally and Jimmy McRae's accident in Wales. They were all accidents in the true meaning of the word. If they had been in Group B cars, who is to say they wouldn't have been fatal.

Spectators too will be in greater danger, so we may also see a change in the type of rally taking place. Faster stages could be dropped in favour of those with more bends and slower averages. The possibilities are immense — it looks like we're back to that iceberg we began with.

LUCKY JIM!

This year the prestigious British Open Championship attracted six works teams, the very best of the Scandinavian drivers and the dreaded Audi Quattro, but in the end — the very end — Scotsman Jimmy McRae hung on to his title. Our rallies correspondent describes the highly competitive series.

JIMMY McRae was lucky to retain his British Open Champion's title this year. He never once led the five-rally series, but played second fiddle to two Finnish drivers — his own team mate Henri Toivonen, and Hannu Mikkola, the latter a past holder of the title himself. It was only on the last handful of tests on the very last rally that the Scotsman won through.

McRae, the reigning British Champion, was picked at the beginning of the season to drive in the prestigious Rothmans Opel Rally Team alongside the electrifying young Finn, Henri Toivonen. Their cars were to be Opel Ascona 400s, the model that took McRae to victory the year before. They were prepared in Opel's German base at Russelsheim, in the same workshop as the World Championship cars and by the same personnel. This combination of highly competitive cars and drivers would ordinarily be enough to frighten off any opposition, but for 1982 the British Championship was to benefit from five other factory supported teams, with equally competitive pilots.

The biggest threat came from Audi. A small team had been built in Britain under the Audi Sport UK banner, with David Sutton Motorsport preparing a Quattro and Hannu Mikkola driving it.

The Quattro had dominated many rallies in 1981, including Britain's RAC Rally, which Mikkola won by an impressive margin. When the team's intention to contest the Open Championship was announced, there were many worried team managers, insistent

that the car's unfair advantage would ruin their own chances.

Ford provided an Escort RS for the reigning World Champion, Ari Vatanen, to be prepared by MCD Services of Widnes, with an engine supplied by David Wild from Essex. Despite the model's age and lack of recent development, Vatanen had taken the World title with a similar car the year before.

Toyota GB were represented by the Swedish driver, Per Eklund, driving a 1981 model Celica on the first round, after which it was replaced with a newer shaped specimen and one which was lighter and slightly more powerful. Toyota was to be the only Japanese manufacturer with an interest in the 1982 series.

Dealer Team Vauxhall had taken the 1981 Manufacturer's title with its Chevette HSR, with Tony Pond behind the wheel. For 1982, the team changed its name to GM Dealer Sport, to encompass the Opel marque as well, but the team personnel were still the same. Two cars were fielded, both Chevette HSRs, one for Russell Brookes, in Andrews Heat for Hire colours and the other, an unsponsored car, for Terry Kaby. Both were experienced British forest drivers, but neither held out much hope, pitched against the fast Scandinavian crews.

The last of the factory teams was Peugeot/Talbot, but it was programmed to contest only the three later rounds, its driver, Stig Blomqvist, having a prior committment to his native Swedish National Championship, where he was driving an Audi Quattro.

There were, of course, a few other serious contenders from Britain, but they were private entrants and would only tackle a few rallies. The most successful of these was a young Derbyshire man, Ian Tilke, who, in his Escort RS, featured strongly amongst the top finishers. Chris Lord also challenged strongly in his Sunbeam, upholding Talbot honour until the factory team took over.

The month of February traditionally opens the Championship, when the Mintex International Rally takes place. The event was a compact affair lasting just over 24 hours and centred on York, it made excellent use of the popular Yorkshire forests and Hannu

McRae fought off the Quattro challenge with his German prepared, Rothmans backed Ascona 400. He won two rounds but was second to Mikkola in his native Scotland (left). Ford's hopes rested on Ari Vatanen (above, on the Manx) but his best result was third on the Mintex, won by Mikkola (below). Russell Brookes scored a couple of second places, including the Manx (bottom).

Mikkola and the Audi Quattro took to those forests like a duck to water. The team romped to victory, leaving British rallying stunned in its wake. Mikkola was followed home by fellow Finns Toivonen and Vatanen, with Britain's Champion, McRae, a lowly fourth.

At the finish, Jimmy McRae lost his normal cheery expression. It had been replaced by one of worry, but a worry that he had expected since hearing who his rivals would be.

His concern was shared by Russell Brookes and Terry Kaby, for they too were eager to impress with their performances. But they were all outdriven by the Finns.

Ari Vatanen had taken his Escort RS to third place after a thrilling drive and a tremendous battle with another Escort making a rare appearance in the series. That was Pentti Airikkala's car and the past British Champion made Vatanen, and Toivonen, work hard. Airikkala's rally ended two thirds of the way into the event with steering failure, but not before he bettered both of them and even challenged Mikkola at one point. Airikkala had lost none of his magic and it was sad that he couldn't be a regular competitor.

Henri Toivonen's drive to second place and his last minute tussle with Ari Vatanen made him a firm favourite with British fans. The young man had talent and flair, maybe he was a little impetuous too, but above all he exuded excitement and that's everything rallying should be.

The home drivers had been beaten fair and square, but the next round was over the unpractised tarmac roads of Ireland, where Brookes, McRae and Kaby have all found success in the past. The future looked bright, but they still had to overcome nearly five whole days of driving in the toughest rally of the series, the Circuit of Ireland.

It all started on Good Friday, with a string of tests in Ulster, and the Audi Quattro was soon in trouble. Mikkola's car had broken a driveshaft, a prelude to a rally dogged with transmission troubles for the four-wheel-drive machine. The Opels shot to the fore, with Ari Vatanen for close company, while both Brookes and Kaby were hovering in the wings. The second day's rallying started early and it was Henri Toivonen's turn for trouble. His Opel careered into a stout bank damaging its steering. The accident also damaged Toivonen's hand and the tenacious youngster drove for the following three days with a blood stained bandage wrapped around it. At times the pain was unbearable, but it served to strengthen both the following he had from the fans and the admiration he commanded from the other drivers.

Meanwhile, McRae and Vatanen battled on, vying for fastest special stage times for two long days. Then, on the third, during the final leg back to the rally's base in Belfast, Vatanen went off. His Escort RS was badly damaged, he was penalised for receiving illegal assistance, but he carried on to finish seventh. It was then Russell Brookes who challenged McRae, but the Scot had opened up too much of a lead and stormed home nearly five minutes ahead of the Chevette driver.

McRae had upheld his Irish speed and remained the hero of the Irish spectators. Toivonen drove magnificently to third place and maintained his Championship lead over McRae, while John Coyne pipped Billy Coleman to fourth place and the honour of being first home driver in the 1982 Circuit.

The forest roads of mid-Wales and the tarmac of the Epynt Ranges were to play host to the third round, the Welsh International. The event had been surrounded by doubts since the start of the season. Did it have enough finances? Would the Army deny the use of its Ranges because of the Falklands War? Fram Filters stepped in to support the rally and the Army gave its sanction, but there were still problems.

The compact overnight rally suffered from weak organisation, reducing itself to a shambles. It did, however, provide the Audi Quattro with a victory, but not in Mikkola's hands. The Finn was away, competing in Corsica, so his place was taken by the past World Champion, Bjorn Waldegard. It was Waldegard's first ever rally in a Quattro but he soon found his feet and started to shake off the opposition.

Both McRae and Vatanen fell by the wayside: McRae after a mighty accident on the tarmac of Epynt and Vatanen after being excluded for a route infringement. That left Henri Toivonen to snatch second place and strengthen his series lead, while Stig Blomqvist, in his first Talbot drive of the year, returned a lacklustre performance to finish third.

Eyes turned north for the penultimate round, the Scottish International. It provided four days of hard slog through both lowland and highland forests and provided the Quattro with its third win of the year.

Hannu Mikkola was back behind the wheel, but after a first test steering breakage, victory looked remote. The Audi limped through that opening special stage, collected a massive time penalty and lay in last position. Mikkola was faced with the daunting task of bettering everyone else by more than one second per kilometer of special stage to regain lost time.

McRae took new heart and set about challenging hard, but it was Ari Vatanen and Stig Blomqvist setting the pace. It continued well into the third day, then in the space of just two special stages, the lead changed three times. Vatanen retired his Escort RS with a broken transmission, handing the lead to Blomqvist. Then on the next test, the Swede's Sunbeam lost its oil pressure, damaged engine bearing and retired, handing the number one position to Jimmy McRae, but Mikkola had fought his way back to second place and was closing the gap quickly.

As McRae led the field down Scotland's Great Glen on the final night, it was only a matter of time before Mikkola would steal his

McRae's closest challenger was his own team mate, Henri Toivonen (above), while Stig Blomqvist (below) could manage only ninth.

lead. McRae fought to the bitter end, but all in vain: with a handful of tests remaining, he was powerless in holding back the Quattro; a Quattro that had a very determined Mikkola at its wheel.

So, Mikkola had another victory under his belt, while Henri Toivonen had his hands full fending off a challenging Russell Brookes to finish third. McRae's second place meant he was still in touch with the title race, as the Open Championship entered its final round, the Rothmans Manx International.

This was the second tarmac rally of the series but, unlike the Circuit of Ireland, crews were allowed to practice the stages and make their pace notes. The tarmac tests served to give McRae an advantage, slim though it was, as everyone had that opportunity to reconnoitre the special stages.

A hard, three-day rally faced the drivers, three days that were sure to spell mechanical troubles for their cars, such is the blistering pace set on the island's roads. Mikkola's Quattro was the first to expire, the car's engine was at fault this time, but not before transmission troubles, again, plagued it. Henri Toivonen held the lead for the first day, with both Vatanen and McRae breathing down his neck. Then, early in the second day, a tyre on Toivonen's car punctured, handing the premier place to Vatanen. Then, as had happened in Scotland, the lead changed again. Vatanen retired his Escort RS after rolling it sideways, crumpling the bodyshell: Toivonen retook the lead.

As the second day drew to a close, Henri Toivonen looked certain to be the new Open Champion. His lead was strong and he was driving the tests faster than second place McRae. But just as nothing in sport is ever certain until the finishing line is crossed, disaster struck the flying Finn on the final day's first special stage.

In thick fog, Toivonen drove his Opel off the road and out of the running, McRae took the rally lead and with it the title. Russell Brookes was still close behind McRae, so close that a puncture could have spelled disaster for the Scot, but that was not to be. So, on a cool September evening in the Isle of Man, Jimmy McRae wheeled his Rothmans Opel Ascona 400 up the finishing ramp and secured his second consecutive British Open title, dispelling all of his earlier fears and injecting new life into the aspirations of other British drivers. The fans' favourite had won again.

ROTHMANS RAC OPEN RALLY CHAMPIONSHIP

MINTEX INTERNATIONAL
February 26/27

1	H.Mikkola/A.Hertz	Audi Quattro	2h 32m 02s
2	H.Toivonen/F.Gallagher	Opel Ascona 400	2h 35m 45s
3	A.Vatanen/N.Wilson	Ford Escort RS	2h 36m 02s
4	J.McRae/I.Grindrod	Opel Ascona 400	2h 39m 04s
5	T.Kaby/M.Nicholson	Chevette HSR	2h 39m 26s
6	R.Brookes/M.Broad	Chevette HSR	2h 44m 00s
7	B.Dobie/D.Rogers	Ford Escort RS	2h 44m 54s
8	I.Cathcart/D.West	Opel Ascona 400	2h 47m 05s
9	C.Lord/B.Harris	Talbot Sunbeam	2h 48m 33s
10	S.Bannister/J.Robinson	Ford Escort RS	2h 50m 42s

CIRCUIT OF IRELAND
April 9-13

1	J.McRae/I.Grindrod	Opel Ascona 400	7h 19m 19s
2	R.Brookes/M.Broad	Chevette HSR	7h 24m 15s
3	H.Toivonen/F.Gallagher	Opel Ascona 400	7h 27m 09s
4	J.Coyne/C.Farrell	Talbot Sunbeam	7h 28m 53s
5	B.Coleman/B.Neville	Ford Escort RS	7h 29m 22s
6	H.Mikkola/A.Hertz	Audi Quattro	7h 37m 32s
7	A.Vatanen/N.Wilson	Ford Escort RS	7h 44m 53s
8	G.Buckley/J.Caplice	Opel Ascona 400	7h 46m 36s
9	W.Henry/R.McNamee	Ford Escort RS	7h 50m 03s
10	J.Price/H.Wyllie	Renault 5 Turbo	8h 01m 42s

WELSH INTERNATIONAL
May 7/8

1	B.Waldegard/P.Short	Audi Quattro	2h 56m 01s
2	H.Toivonen/F.Gallagher	Opel Ascona 400	2h 57m 59s
3	S.Blomqvist/B.Cederberg	Talbot Sunbeam	3h 05m 17s
4	P.Collins/J.Savage	Ford Escort RS	3h 07m 46s
5	F.Tuthill/R.Jones	Ford Escort RS	3h 09m 22s
6	J.Churchill/R.Evans	Ford Escort RS	3h 11m 49s
7	C.Lord/B.Rainbow	Talbot Sunbeam	3h 12m 54s
8	I.Tilke/T.McMahon	Ford Escort RS	3h 13m 44s
9	B.Danielson/D.Booth	Ford Escort RS	3h 15m 07s
10	B.Fowden/D.Jenkins	Triumph TR8	3h 15m 53s

SCOTTISH INTERNATIONAL
June 12-15

1	H.Mikkola/A.Hertz	Audi Quattro	5h 10m 46s
2	J.McRae/I.Grindrod	Opel Ascona 400	5h 11m 16s
3	H.Toivonen/F.Gallagher	Opel Ascona 400	5h 14m 33s
4	R.Brookes/M.Broad	Chevette HSR	5h 14m 53s
5	M.Wilson/P.Short	Ford Escort RS	5h 16m 27s
6	T.Kaby/M.Nicholson	Chevette HSR	5h 23m 03s
7	P.Eklund/D.Whittock	Toyota Celica	5h 25m 46s
8	K.Wood/P.Brown	Triumph TR8	5h 30m 22s
9	R.Lyons/I.MacFarland	Talbot Sunbeam	5h 49m 25s
10	J.Weatherley/R.Smith	Citroen Visa	5h 51m 31s

MANX INTERNATIONAL
September 16-18

1	J.McRae/I.Grindrod	Opel Ascona 400	5h 00m 25s
2	R.Brookes/M.Broad	Chevette HSR	5h 02m 54s
3	B.Fisher/A.Frazer	Ford Escort RS	5h 12m 23s
4	M.Patrick/P.Short	Opel Ascona 400	5h 13m 46s
5	I.Tilke/T.McMahon	Ford Escort RS	5h 25m 30s
6	J.Price/D.Davies	Renault 5 Turbo	5h 33m 03s
7	R.Farrington/M.Wasley	Ford Escort RS	5h 35m 01s
8	T.Bengry/P.Watkins	Opel Ascona 400	5h 38m 04s
9	M.Freestone/J.Gittins	Ford Escort RS2000	5h 39m 07s
10	M.Hutchinson/N.Harris	Ford Escort RS	5h 39m 16s

FINAL POSITIONS

DRIVERS

1	Jimmy McRae	47	6	Ari Vatanen	12
2	Henri Toivonen	36	7	Terry Kaby	11
3	Hannu Mikkola	35	8	Ian Tilke	9
4	Russell Brookes	32	9	Stig Blomqvist	8
5	Bjorn Waldegard	15	10	Bertie Fisher	8

MANUFACTURERS

1	Opel	60	6	Toyota	22
2	Audi	51	7	BL	20
3	Vauxhall	37	8	Renault	19
4	Ford	29	9	Lada	8
5	Talbot	29	10	Porsche	7

'TONY' ON TOP

Italy's 'Tony' Fassina clinched the complicated European Championship with a steady run to victory in the Rothmans Cyprus Rally (above) with his Opel Ascona 400. The pressure was taken off Fassina when his closest challenger, British Open Champion Jimmy McRae (also Ascona mounted) went out of the Cyprus round with suspension damage and third placed Andrea Zanussi (below right, winning the Rally du RACE) did not appear. Marc Duez was another regular front runner with his Belga sponsored Porsche seen (right) on the way to winning the Criterium Lucien Bianchi in Belgium.

FINAL POSITIONS
European Rally Championship

1.	Tony Fassina	446 points
2.	Jimmy McRae	368 points
3.	Andrea Zanussi	264 points
4.	Guy Colsoul	176 points
5.	Marc Duez	172 points
6.	Stig Blomqvist	160 points
7.	Eugenio Ortiz	160 points
8.	Massimo Biasion	152 points
9.	Jean Luc Therier	150 points
10.	Antonio Zanini	147 points

MOTORSPORTS
WORLDWIDE

JAGUAR, DÉJÀ-VU

1982 hasn't been just another jubilee year for Jaguar, celebrating its 60 years since Bill Lyons started making his sporty Swallow sidecars commercially. ANDREW WHYTE tells how the Jaguar marque returned to the winner's circle on both sides of the Atlantic, and cites the situation 25 years ago as a parallel.

Tom Walkinshaw has been in the forefront of the Jaguar racing revival in Europe, turning the XJ-S into a winner during 1982, although at Donington (above) the car retired from the lead, with a holed radiator.

AS a works team, the Jaguar company of Coventry hasn't raced since 1957. Racing and to some degree rallying had even then established Jaguar as a World Car, and record exports followed — to America especially.

Through the late 'fifties and early 'sixties, Jaguar continued to provide competition services and encouragement both to private individuals and to teams — in particular to Briggs Cunningham in the USA and David Murray in the UK. Jaguar also prepared racing engines for Lister and for saloon cars used in such specialist events as the *Tour de France*.

Jaguar's last great competition season in Europe was 1963. True, the 'lightweight' version of the E-type used then was a bit of a disappointment; it could beat the fabulous Ferrari GTO, sometimes, in sprint races and if a topnotcher like Graham Hill was at the wheel, but that car never quite made it as a winner over long distances. The Mark Two saloon was another matter. Its performances in the *Tour de France* and the Alpine high-speed rallies were outstanding but its weight and lack of 'twitchability' made it quite unsuitable for stage rallies, which were rapidly becoming the norm.

In racing, the disappearance of the saloon Jaguar came suddenly. Here, it was a simple case of Ford arriving on the scene, with Galaxies and Mustangs, Cortina GTs and Lotuses, and hotted-up Anglias in club racing.

The European Touring Car Championship (or "Challenge" as it was originally called) did not begin until 1963. At that time Jaguar's young German importer, Peter Lindner, was doing a fine job in the land of the Mercedes and the BMW. His friend Peter Noecker, driving works-prepared, Lindner-developed 3.8-litre Jaguars, was declared the first European touring champion, winning every round he entered.

It was the last important competition success for Jaguar east of the Atlantic — until 1982!

Back in the 'fifties, David Murray was regarded as a canny tactician and his *Ecurie Ecosse* Jaguars were always beautifully turned out. Sir William Lyons and his colleagues admired the Edinburgh-based team for these two factors and, of course, because it often turned up trumps, as on the classic occasion of Le Mans in 1956. Then, the factory D-types "blew" the race early on but a "Scottish" Jaguar defeated the Astons and the Ferraris to save the day.

Now it is another shrewd Scot who's bringing the Jaguar name back to the circuits. Tom Walkinshaw began his racing with a Sprite, and continued with a Lotus. He knew he was good, but not a World Champion in the making; so he channelled his skills towards saloon cars. His performances in Capris and BMWs in the 'seventies were always competent, often memorable. Ironically, perhaps, Walkinshaw's determined driving of the Alpina-BMW in winning the 1977 TT led then Jaguar driver Andy Rouse to overdo things. Rouse spun out of the race and hit the bank hard with the BL-Broadspeed XJ12C and Jaguar were soon again out of motor sport. In fairness to Tom, it should be said that BL had already taken the decision to withdraw their 'Big Cats' from racing with hardly a finish to their name.

Walkinshaw won the TT again in 1981, this time sharing a customer's — Chuck Nicholson's — Mazda RX7. "The best way to win a race is in the longest possible time". That was one of David Murray's maxims and Murray would have been proud of Walkinshaw that day. Having rapidly reeled-in the leading BMW on a damp circuit, the little Mazda promptly slowed, maintaining a tantalisingly small lead to the flag.

Although much of his flourishing business relates to BMW sales, service and tuning equipment (he represents Alpina in Britain), Tom Walkinshaw is totally independent and TWR, or Tom Walkinshaw Racing, itself is described as "motor engineers and consultants" in one industrial directory. When he was looking at the new Group A European touring car race regulations, Walkinshaw had no hesitation in talking to some of his Jaguar friends of long-standing, after all, 1981 was the first full year of revival for Jaguar Cars Ltd as an individual company within BL. Soon he was talking to new Jaguar boss, John Egan, and it did not take long for agreement to be reached. TWR would prepare first one XJ-S, and later a second one, to race in Europe in 1982; Motul oil would provide most of the sponsorship. Jaguar would provide technical advice and assistance but, with the wariness (and commonsense) of experience, not involve itself directly.

The results of the first season's racing — considered *as* a first season — were gratifying, to say the least. There *was* bad luck, like the car being pushed out of the lead at Monza, and having to retire (again after leading) when the radiator was holed at Donington. Then there was the worst moment of all, when both cars were racing together for the first time, at Spa-Francorchamps, and, strategically, just about everything that could go wrong did. Basically, the tyres and the weather conspired to pull Jaguar down from the lead into the ruck within a lap! The final disaster in this 24-hour event came when, during the night, the two Jaguars had to retire after separate, unnecessary accidents.

But the season's good news outweighed the bad, by far. Championship results began at Vallelunga in April with a third place; then came the first victory, on the long and fast Brno road circuit in Czechoslovakia.

Wiper trouble kept Walkinshaw and Nicholson in second place for the Österreichring round in June but a week later, on 4 July, came the sweetest victory so far. As Peter Lindner and Peter Noecker had done in 1961, 1962 and 1963, with the 3.8 Jaguar Mark Two, Tom Walkinshaw and Chuck Nicholson won Germany's gruelling six hours of Nürburgring. It was an historic win. Czechoslovakia had been important, but somehow this meant much more: to win in Germany, a major export market, where two of Jaguar's biggest commercial rivals are made.

The Spa race came after this, and brought the team down to

earth in time for Silverstone, Jaguar's home circuit and now home of the world's longest-established motor race, the RAC Tourist Trophy.

It's fascinating that, nowadays, fuel consumption is such a big factor in racing — especially as the early TT races placed emphasis on weight in relation to use of fuel and, of course, the cars were *touring* cars, in the grand manner. The first TT winner, in 1905, was an Arrol-Johnston. Those early races were on the Isle of Man. From 1928 to 1936 the TT was held on the Ards circuit, SE of Belfast, but a bad accident in the latter year took the race to Donington for a couple of years before war intervened.

Afterwards, the TT returned to the closed roads of Northern Ireland, this time at Dundrod on the other side of the Ulster "capital". It was here that Stirling Moss won for Jaguar in 1950 and 1951. Another accident put an end to car racing at Dundrod after 1955 and the race moved to Goodwood, then to Oulton Park where it lost its way as a touring car race by opening its grids to Group 6 cars.

Since moving to Silverstone in 1970, the TT has regained much of its stature. Usually it has been for Group 2, and usually it has been a BMW field day, so to win the TT with Jaguar meant everything to Tom Walkinshaw. There had been a kind of patriotic fervour in 1976 and 1977, when BL's "cats" failed to dispose of the BMWs, and there was the same support this year.

The quiet way in which TWR had tackled the season, and Jaguar's own low-key marketing approach, almost seemed to work against both parties on 12 September, when a relatively small crowd came to Silverstone. Moreover, the daily press corps was at Monza for the Italian Grand Prix, so there was little to be seen in Monday's papers, which could have reported a one-two victory for Jaguar for the first time since 1963.

The 500km race was a convincing win for Tom Walkinshaw and Chuck Nicholson, with the second TWR XJ-S driven, as at Spa, by Peter Lovett and Pierre Dieudonne, a worthy runner-up. The Jaguar's main rival, Patrick Motors' V8 Rover, retired when lying third and not far behind, so 1982 champions, Helmut Kelleners and Umberto Grano, brought their BMW home third.

Although there was one race to go, at Zolder, where Walkinshaw had won a national race in the XJ-S early in the season, the TT effectively confirmed the team's future and the co-operation between TWR and Jaguar was already assured for 1983, even before Walkinshaw and Nicholson won that final, Zolder round, with Dieudonne and Jeff Allam second.

Throughout the dark days of the late '70s, Jaguar's engineering — under Bob Knight, successor to Bill Heynes — had remained as aloof as it could from the centralising forces of BL. This policy gave Jaguar as a whole the strength to be re-identified when BL's Sir Michael Edwardes appointed John Egan in 1980 to run Jaguar as a unit on its own, or very nearly on its own. Knight retired that year, and Jim Randle became head of Jaguar product engineering.

Jim Randle and his colleagues — Trevor Crisp, Tom Jones, Malcolm Oliver, and many more — are in direct contact with the people throughout the world who are racing Jaguars seriously. This

In 1951, Stirling Moss (below) won the Tourist Trophy, at Dundrod, with the XK120C — the first Jaguar designed specifically for racing. It was a spectacularly successful car, winning at Le Mans in 1951 on its European debut and taking another debut win on the other side of the Atlantic in the Sheldon Cup race at Elkhart Lake in September 1952, driven by future World Champion, Phil Hill. In 1982, Jaguar scored their third win in the TT.

Bob Tullius's handsome XJR5, destined for IMSA GTP and FIA Group C racing, was announced in January 1982 and first ran in June after typically thorough Group 44 development. It scored third place in its race début in August.

includes TWR, of course, and the Goss XJ-S in Australia. There is much admiration, too, for the professional, if shoestring, operation of Gran Turismo Jaguar in Ohio. Their ancient E-type is piloted brilliantly, and has been for many seasons, in SCCA events by the English driver Fred Baker.

It was not to Ohio, but to Wisconsin, however, that Jim Randle made his way, late in July 1982. Jaguar may not be racing as a company, but its interest in the sport has been rekindled.

Last year we reported how Bob Tullius's tubular-framed XJ-S came second in the 1981 SCCA Trans Am series, winning three races in a season which for him had started late simply because 'Group 44' had very nearly shut its doors on motor-racing during the previous winter.

Robert Tullius is famous for the meticulous preparation of his cars, and for his own "bright-as-a-new-pin-*and*-as-sharp" image. He is highly professional. He is also very single minded — the only surprising thing about Bob as a racing driver, perhaps, his age. Suffice it to say that he was racing the oval dirt tracks with a 1937 Ford V8 coupé more than thirty years ago, before taking to drag-racing and scrambling. He sold copiers for Remington Rand until 1957, when he was head-hunted by Eastman Kodak. In 1963 his racing activity was taking up so much of his time that he left, an action prompted by the offer of a job *and* preparation space for his TR4 by the Washington Triumph agent, Walter Hutcherson — the man whom Tullius reckons did more than anyone to help him make a career of racing.

In the 'sixties he gained good victories with his Ford Cortina-Lotus and a Dodge Dart, but as time went on, and BL was formed, he moved closer to the British firm, taking championship after championship, year in, year out.

Tullius's first season with Jaguar was 1974, when he won his regional title with a V12 E-type prepared by his Group 44 team in Virginia. In 1975, he took the national crown, winning the run-off at Road Atlanta at the season's end, by which time the "E" was obsolete, and about to be replaced by the very different XJ-S. 1977 and 1978 saw Tullius become the first man to make a racer of the XJ-S; he won the drivers' Trans Am championship both years, with Jaguar being named champion manufacturer in 1978. Tullius's experience has naturally provided TWR with a shortcut or two. After concentrating on Triumph cars again for a while, it looked to Tullius as though he must close the racing shop. Then, early in 1981, it all clicked again, with sufficient sponsorship and encouragement to keep on racing. Quickly, so quickly, he got a new team together, under his faithful crew-chief of ten years' standing, Lawton 'Lanky' Foushee. A new-look XJ-S was built for the equally new-look Trans Am and, hey presto, three trips to the winners' circle!

As 1981 progressed, another dream was taking shape. Jaguar in Britain and America approved it, and in January 1982 it was announced — the glorious Jaguar V12-engined FIA Group C/IMSA GTP mid-engined coupé designated "XJR5".

It is not surprising, knowing Tullius's thoroughness, that this handsome and beautifully-executed beastie did not appear until it was good and ready, in August. The Lee Dykstra-designed, semi-monocoque construction prototype first ran at Summit Point in June and was tested further over two days at Road Atlanta, before arriving at Road America where Jim Randle first saw it on 30 July.

Randle and Dykstra both move and think quietly, and the rapport was immediate. "They're a great bunch together", says Randle, referring to Tullius, Dykstra, Foushee, and all who have created the XJR5. "We love working with them. They're so adaptable and so very competent, and a credit to the name of Jaguar; to reach such a standard, this quick, really is an achievement". Jim Randle came home impressed by the simulated race that had been run by Bob Tullius and his Canadian co-driver Bill Adam, neither of whom could report a major fault.

Late in August the team returned to Road America, to be joined this time by John Egan. In its first-ever race, the XJR5 finished a worthy third. "Who could ask for more?" said Egan delightedly.

Shortly afterwards, practising at Mid-Ohio, Bob Tullius made a rare (very rare) mistake and punted the XJR5 into the scenery, hard. Fortunately Tullius was unruffled by the accident — experience again: "1982 is a planned development year for the XJR5", he stressed as the car was coming together again in late September, incorporating several modifications and lighter body panels. "Everything we do with the car right up through Daytona's three-hour finale is calculated to make us 100% ready for 1983. That's when you'll really see us in the hunt for IMSA's endurance crown".

On the specific question of Le Mans, everyone is justifiably reticent. Jaguar's five victories between 1951 and 1957 helped to make the company what it is today. To go back there and not win *could* be argued against; no-one, nowadays, expects to win Le Mans first time out; on the other hand, to go back and seek to finish honourably *could* be just as high an ideal.

Meantime John Egan, Jim Randle, and their colleagues in Coventry are delighted with the potential shown by Tom Walkinshaw and Bob Tullius and their respective teams. They've won no championships in this revival year for Jaguar, but they've won respect from the racing fraternity and from enthusiasts around the world who see the situation almost as a Second Coming, after a quarter of a century! In 1957, Jaguar gave up racing in Europe, but provided support for David Murray's private *Ecurie Ecosse* team which gave the Coventry firm its fifth victory at Le Mans. Tom Walkinshaw is 1982's David Murray.

In 1957, too, Briggs Cunningham's team of Momo-prepared D-types was representing Jaguar in the USA, and winning more often than not, through the superb driving of Walter Hansgen, the national sports-car champion. Robert Tullius's Group 44 might be seen as today's Cunningham/Momo/Hansgen trio all rolled into one. The Jaguar revival certainly has an element of déjà-vu from the heady days of the late 'fifties.

A HEALTHY SPECTRUM

All around the world there are championships for single seaters, saloons, sports cars and virtually anything on wheels. JEREMY SHAW, Features Editor of *Autosport*, London, looks at some of them and discovers that worldwide motorsport is alive and well and producing tomorrow's stars.

THE broad spectrum of European motor racing seems fairly healthy at the present time with a strong base of FIA-supported championships for a variety of different formulae plus a much wider selection of national championships.

England apart, the main interest is to be found in France, Germany and Italy, with Spain and the Scandinavian countries also running competitive series, while the Eastern Bloc also have their own thriving but little-publicised motor sporting centres.

The three main countries have all adopted Formula 3 as their major single-seater series and although locally built cars, such as Martini and Dallara have shown strongly in recent seasons, Ron Tauranac's Ralt cars have taken over in much the same way as they have in Britain and, indeed, most other countries of the world.

Each of the major countries has produced some exciting new drivers, among them Pierre Petit and Michel Ferté (younger brother of Alain, who is the only man to have twice won the Monaco F3 race) from France; Bernard Santal from Switzerland; Stefano Livio, Luigi Giannini and Ivan Capelli from Italy; and Austrian Gerhard Berger. The future of F3 on the continent seems secure.

Several of these drivers have developed from their own country's

Around the world there is still tremendous variety in the racing calendar, from the almost universal star breeding ground of FF1600 (above right) to series such as the European Renault 5 Championship (above).

junior formulae or from the field of karting, which seems to have produced so many of the current breed of top Formula 1 drivers. Italy seems particularly strong in this respect, drivers such as Riccardo Patrese, Elio de Angelis, Andrea de Cesaris and Teo Fabi having all started with impressive karting successes, although the country also has a 'grading' system that includes FF2000 and Formula Italia as well as a whole host of sports and saloon car series, prime among which is probably the Alfa Romeo GTV series.

France, similarly, has its own proving-ground category in Formule Renault Turbo, this being a new series brought in at the beginning of this year to replace the old Formule Renault and Super Renault. The single seater cars utilise the Renault 5 Gordini Turbo engine, thereby giving the drivers a taste of the "new generation" turbo engines early in their careers and there is no reason to suppose that the fledgling championship, backed by the might of Elf and the 'Régie' will not continue to produce talent of the likes of Didier Pironi, René Arnoux and Alain Prost.

The German and Austrian training ground is based, much like Britain's, on Formula Ford 1600, which has a very strong following. FF2000 has also been introduced successfully by European Formula Drivers Association supremo Daniel Partel, the slightly more powerful cars proving very popular in their first full season.

The Scandinavian and Benelux countries follow similar lines, all

these countries having well-established FF1600 championships which enjoy both full grids and competitive racing. EFDA also oversee full European Championships for both FF1600 and FF2000, although the former has taken on a new format this year with the establishment of regional series in Scandinavia, Benelux and Germany/Austria. The top runners from each region were then invited to take part in a European Final at Zandvoort, where 20-year old German Volker Weidler emerged victorious, although it must be said that the series lacked some of its past lustre in that there was virtually no British representation. Hopefully, that situation will be improved next season.

The FF2000 series was run on conventional lines with a 9-race series proving rather more popular. Ayrton da Silva finally emerged victorious over England's Calvin Fish, although Dutchman Cor Euser, the previous year's FF1600 Euro-champion, also showed well and did enough to clinch both the Dutch and German 'Golden Lion' titles.

Formula Super Vee has remained fairly strong in Europe, or at least in Germany where most of the 'European Championship' rounds take place, although the withdrawal next year of official support from VW, who for years have backed the series in association with Castrol, is likely to sound its death-knell unless the competitors themselves can find a viable solution.

The Sports 2000 division receives good support both in Scandinavia and the Benelux countries, where thriving championships are run, the best of these plus the British championship supposedly combining to form another of Partel's EFDA Euro-series Championships, although, like the FF1600 series, this has not been as well-subscribed as in recent seasons.

The European Renault 5 Championship, which has been running successfully for a number of seasons, has utilised the R5 Turbo model for the past couple of years and has provided some very good racing, this having taken over from the successful BMW M1 Procar series of 1979/80. The cars, of course, are nothing like as exciting as the M1s, but at least they provide some extremely close racing and have provided worthy supporting races at several European Grands Prix.

Another interesting saloon car series is run in France. This is very similar to the British RAC series, except that, for 1982, it has been run for Group A cars and has produced some thrilling dices between a closely-matched selection of BMWs, Rovers, Chevrolet Camaros, Alfa Romeos and Peugeots. If next year's Tricentrol British series is as good then we should be in for some exciting racing.

FRENCH motor racing has been undergoing a period of change in recent seasons. The mid-1970s saw a concerted effort by, primarily, Elf and Renault — two of the very largest companies in France — to promote young drivers and establish a 'stepping stone' series of categories that would help to develop their talents. Thus, *Formule Renault* and *Formule Renault Europe,* using 1300cc and 1600cc engines respectively, were intended to be the French equivalent of the British Formula Ford and Formula 3 championships.

Furthermore, Elf and Renault not only offered good incentives to drivers taking part in the championships but were also prepared to take the successful ones further, into teams which they themselves supported in Formulae 1 and 2. Jacques Laffite, Didier Pironi and Alain Prost are just three drivers who profited in this manner and all are now, of course, fully established within Grand Prix racing.

The intention was for the Renault Europe series either to take over from or run alongside Formula 3 in a full European championship, although this plan never really reached fruition and was eventually abandoned. For 1982, however, a new tack has been employed. Gone are the two Renault and Renault Europe series, their places taken by an all-new *Formule Renault Turbo* division, which purports to give young drivers a chance to handle turbo engines at an early stage in their careers. The engines are virtually standard Renault 5 Turbo units, upon which very little work can be carried out, and they fit snugly into the back of single-seater chassis. The Magny-Cours-based Martini factory continues to produce the vast majority of these cars, just as they did with the old categories and this at least serves to ensure that a high level of competitiveness is retained.

The logical graduation from the Renault category is to Formula 3 and this has at last become an integral part of the French scene. In the late 1970s, Renault produced a very competitive Formula 3 engine, taken from the Renault 20 and used to great effect by Alain Prost in 1979, but the company never took any great interest in supplying engines to other teams and have since backed out of the formula completely. But with the failure of Renault Europe to establish itself on the international calendar, F3 has now become more accepted in France and a steadily-more competitive national series has evolved during the past couple of seasons.

Pierre Petit has dominated this year's championship with a Dave Price Racing-tended Ralt RT3, latterly powered by a Volkswagen engine, although it must be said that the Crédit Agricole-supported driver enjoyed a distinct chassis advantage for much of the year. Most of his rivals opted for the latest 'ground-effect' Martini MK37 chassis and were sadly disappointed. Only the works-tended car of Michel Ferté (brother of double Monaco F3 race winner Alain) and the Serge Saulnier-run MK37 of Patrick Gonin came close to challenging Petit's RT3, although late-season races saw the emergence of Swiss Bernard Santal (a product of the very successful La Châtre Racing School) and Francois Hesnault as serious challengers, both of them having switched from Martini to ... you guessed it ... Ralt!

France also boasts a most popular saloon car championship and indeed this, which runs to regulations peculiar only to France, has become established as the country's premier racing championship. The 15-round series takes in all the top French circuits, including the marvellous Rouen and Clermont Ferrand (Charade) tracks, and in 1982 it proved to be a very open affair with a whole assortment of BMWs, Alfa Romeo GTVs, Rovers, Peugeots, Renault Fuegos, Audis, Chevrolet Camaros and even a Volvo 242 Turbo regularly challenging for the leading positions. The participation of such well-known names as Jean-Pierre Beltoise, Guy Frequelin, Alain Cudini and Jean-Louis Schlesser assured good support from both competitors and spectators, although in the end it was long time BL exponent René Metge who claimed the honours in his Marlboro-Rover V8, winning from the previous year's champion Jean-Pierre Malcher. A few years ago, several British Group 1 contenders, notably Stuart Graham, used to make regular trips to compete in the French series, although the French series' slightly specialised rule changes from the generally accepted 'norm' in other parts of Europe have meant that the championship has become rather insular over the past couple of seasons. Maybe that will change next year ...

GREAT BRITAIN

Saloon car racing, with its obvious attraction of machinery with which the spectator can readily identify, continues to be immensely popular around the world. In the French domestic championship (with its own rather individualistic rules) René Metge gave the Marlboro backed British Rover a well-earned victory (left), while in Britain the Rovers battled season long with the Capris of Andy Rouse, Gordon Spice (below) et al leaving the overall title to Win Percy's indecently quick Toyota. The well supported Formula Ford 2000 ranks and vastly oversubscribed Ford 1600 category continue to bring out potential stars of the future, one of the brightest prospects to emerge from the British Pace 2000 championship and the European 2000 championship being Brazilian Ayrton Senna da Silva (right). da Silva won both championships in fine style and threatens to do great things in Formula 3 in 1983. In the junior Ford category, another South American, Brazilian Mauricio Gugelmin, was the man to beat with his Van Diemen (below right), although home grown talent such as Julian Bailey and Rick Morris made Gugelmin work hard for his championship and Bailey won the prestigious Formula Ford Festival at Brands Hatch.

THERE is no country in the world that can rival the variety of competitive forms of motor racing to be found in Great Britain. Over 60 major championships are contested each season, ranging from the Formula 1 and Formula 3 categories at the top end of the scale right down to series for humble 850cc Minis; and there is tough competition to be found all the way through.

The Formula 3 championship is certainly the most prestigious single-seater racing category currently to be found in England, and is covered in depth elsewhere in this publication, but this is certainly not the only division which attracts international drivers.

The British Formula 1 Championship, which was revived this year after a 12-month sabbatical, failed to attract competitors in any significant numbers, due mainly to the high cost of competing and the sad lack of incentives offered. Promised television deals failed to materialise, financial rewards were minimal and only five of the intended nine rounds actually took place. It was therefore hardly surprising that rarely were there even as many as half a dozen starters, although it was interesting to note that two of the top four points scorers came from overseas.

This international flavour has been prevalent in British motorsport for many years, particularly in Formula Ford racing, which, in England, has become widely acclaimed as the first stepping stone for young drivers on their way to Formula 1.

"The University of Motor Racing," was how one young American driver described the British scene a few years ago, and that description still fits.

Formula Ford 2000 was introduced seven years ago in order to relieve some of the pressure from FF1600, which at that time was almost saturated with over-subscribed entries at each race, and the larger-engined division has really taken off over the past couple of seasons. Irishman Tommy Byrne topped the scales in 1981 by winning both British and European crowns in his works-run Van Diemen car, despite plenty of tough opposition, while the season just passed has seen even larger and more competitive fields and some superb racing.

A new star has emerged in the form of Brazilian Ayrton Senna da

Silva, a former kartist who also shone in the 1981 FF1600 season, although fellow former kart driver Calvin Fish has kept the home flag flying with some sterling performances in a self-run car. This pair finished first and second, respectively, in both the Pace British and European championships and this south America versus England theme has been mirrored in FF1600 circles, where 19-year Mauricio Gugelmin has led a strong Latin challenge against the likes of Julian Bailey and the experienced Rick Morris.

This cosmopolitan nature of the 'junior' single-seater formulae ensures world-wide publicity and prestige, and thus secures a positive future for motor racing at this level. Any lack of these critical ingredients would soon spell disaster, as it has in the case of both Formula Atlantic and Formula SuperVee.

These two formulae thrive in other parts of the world but have become starved in England, simply because the ever-increasing cost of competing is not reflected in the returns to the driver, be they measured in prize money or, more importantly, public acclaim. Formula SuperVee has died completely in England, a series that ran for ten years being dropped at the beginning of 1982, while Atlantic has only continued thanks to the enthusiasm of a small band of competitors, led by Irishman Alo Lawler. Without proper support from the promoters, it is difficult to see how much longer the formula can be kept going, although its loss would be a sad one, for the cars look and sound good and, in the past, have provided some excellent entertainment for spectators.

Some of the best entertainment value to be seen at the moment, however, is provided by the RAC British Saloon Car Championship, which has recently completed its 25th year of competition. The four engine capacity classes, which, perhaps unfortunately, are governed by a ceiling of 3500cc, thus excluding the American V8s which proved spectacular but expensive in the mid-1970s, attract a wide variety of cars and the sensible restriction of the amount of modifications mean that the cars still closely resemble those which Mr Spectator can readily see in day-to-day use. He likes that.

The battles for the lead at this year's races between Rovers and Ford Capris have provided some tremendous action, even though it

was once again a driver dominating one of the smaller classes who took the championship honours. It is interesting to note that 1973 was the last year in which the overall champion came from the largest class, Frank Gardner taking the spoils then with his amazing SCA Freight Camaro. Nevertheless, by winning again this season, Win Percy has equalled Bill McGovern's achievement of winning three consecutive British Saloon car titles.

The RAC series represents the pinnacle of saloon car racing in this country but there are a huge selection of other series, ranging from those catering for heavily modified Special Saloons — which have been brought in with the intention of providing lower cost racing — to the 'everyday' Production Saloons. For some reason, however, this latter divison has seen rather sporadic interest this season, although the 'one-make' championships, of which there are series for American V8s (ASCAR), Ford Fiestas, Mini Metros, Mini 1000s. Mini 850s and Renault 5s, all receive excellent support and the nature of their regulations, which heavily restrict the amount of work that can be done on a car, are highly conducive to very competitive racing at modest cost.

The same sort of hierarchy exists for those wishing to race a massive variety of sports cars, including a relatively new form of 'GT' racing. This has evolved over the last couple of seasons, primarily at the instigation of the Donington Park race organisers,

whereby powerful engines are installed in some unlikely-sounding chassis, although a close inspection under the skin of these cars reveals that virtually all are based upon older single-seater racing cars. Some good examples of competitors' ingenuity include a BMW M1 fitted with a 3.4 litre Essex GAA V6 engine, a Renault 5 with BMW F2 power and a 7-litre Chevrolet-motivated Skoda . . . the racing proves as exciting and popular as it sounds.

A group of more specialised forms of racing include Clubmans Sports, which grew from the basic early Lotus 7 days to a relatively sophisticated level today where cars tend to be almost as fast as pukka Formula 3 cars. The difference is that a Clubmans car can be run on a fraction of the budget . . .

The 750 Motor Club take this low-cost notion further by specifically promoting and encouraging a variety of championships, most of which ban any form of sponsorship, while historic car categories are also run regularly by a separate band of clubs, all with excellent support.

It all adds up to a comprehensive package of motor sport, which sees hundreds of drivers competing each and every weekend. It also encompasses a thriving industry of manufacturers and suppliers who not only have a ready market at home but are also able to spread their wings overseas. Without doubt, Britain is still the centre of the motor sporting world.

TEETHING TROUBLE

As Group C took over the limelight on the international sports car racing scene, the German Racing Championship went through a year of change. There were inevitably problems and thin grids, but as JEREMY SHAW reports, the championship still looks to have a healthy future.

THE first year of a new concept is always the most difficult one. The DRM (Deutsche Rennsportmeisterschaft, or German Racing Championship) has seen the typical symptoms of a transitional year. Apart from the last four rounds, the series had to struggle with not particularly good entries, although it might be said that even IMSA wasn't that much better this year.

If one looks at the final DRM points table, it's remarkable that the first three places are occupied by old Group 5 and Group 6 cars. Of the 10 races held, only four were won by Group C cars but, as a measure of the progress made by the series towards the end of the year, the last four races were all won by Group C cars, with Groups 5 and 6 no longer candidates for outright wins.

After twice taking the runner-up-position and after no less than seven years in the series, Strasbourg-based Bob Wollek finally took the title. Bob, always a quiet and modest person, could invariably count on the reliability of his well-proven Joest-Porsche 936/80, equipped with a 4-valve, 2.1-litre engine. He finished in each race, won three and was never lower than fourth. For the last two races he switched to the 936C and with his second place in the penultimate round secured the title.

The Kremer-team started the season with a brand new replica of a 936, called the 936/82, this one with 2-valve engine. Kremer driver Rolf Stommelen was a strong challenger to Wollek before the Kremer team was excluded from the Salzburgring race, after they had tried to work on an engine which had been sealed by the scrutineers after the final practice. When they checked the engine again after the warm-up they found the markings "unofficially" changed and Kremer's licence was suspended later in the year. Stommelen made a come-back at Wunstorf and he won from Wollek in the closest race of the year, held in very hot weather conditions. It was his last race with the 936, and for the last four rounds Rolf drove the superb CK5, winning the penultimate round on the short Hockenheim circuit.

The spectacular Zakspeed Capris of Niedzweidz and Ludwig (above) proved to be Ford's strongest weapon in the DRM as the C100 faltered. There is a place for virtually everything in the web of British racing and at the Willhire 24-hour race at Snetterton the Morgan +8 shared by Mary Lindsay (left) provided competitive variety.

The old faithful Capri turbo had a marvellous start to the season in the hands of Klaus Niedzwiedz. The blond Klaus dominated the opening Zolder round and won the only race held on the full Nürburgring circuit; after three rounds he led the series with 52 points from Wollek's 45. Thereafter, he didn't finish in the next three races and had to give up his hopes. The highlight of Niedzwied's season was probably the prestigious Norisring race where he finished fourth after having started from the last place on the grid.

The only 'works' Group C car on the grid at Zolder in March was the Ford C100, driven by Klaus Ludwig. It soon became apparent that the factory prepared car wasn't competitive, mainly because of unsatisfactory handling, a problem in fact due to basic faults in the monocoque design. After a second bad performance at Hockenheim, Ford retired the C100 with the announcement that they would make a comeback at Norisring in June. In the meantime Klaus Ludwig drove his last year's DRM-winning Capri and earned 27 points with it.

The C100 did indeed come back at Norisring and nearly won the race (Winkelhock was beaten by less than a second by the works Porsche 956 of Jochen Mass, running on its last few drops of fuel). Then the Ford did win two races in the wet (Hockenheim GP and Supersprint, Nürburgring), both in the hands of Ludwig. Zakspeed's treatment on the C100 was successful; the troublesome car can at least win 100-mile races now.

Other Group C entries came from Sauber (their highest position was Heyer's fourth at Hockenheim) but the car has serious chassis problems besides the bad vibration problem of the Cosworth DFL. Of the other domestic entries, the URDs, with BMW engines, were not very successful and were run on a low budget, while Karl-Heinz Becker entered a Lola T 600 with 1.6-litre BMW turbo for the penultimate round and finished fifth in the final Supersprint race.

Occasional entries from abroad were Gianpiero Moretti in his Moby-Dick 935 (fourth at Salzburg), Ian Dawson's Grid (fifth at Hockenheim), and John Cooper (fifth in the April Hockenheim race).

The best sprint race for Groups 5, 6 and C cars in Europe was again at the Norisring, with 26 starters, among them 12 Group C, eight Group 5 and three Group 6 cars. Three BMW M1s completed the Norisring grid and the race started in front of 80,000 spectators in the former Nazi stadium, so the state of the German Championship is still pretty healthy in spite of the changes!

GERMANY

GERMANY has two permanent circuits, Hockenheim and Nürburgring, and the DRM (Deutsche Rennsportmeisterschaft, German Racing Championship) is the highest class of motor racing in Germany. Alongside the World Endurance Championship, the German Sprint races, held over 100 miles, are the only other races realistically open to the expensive Group C car; one can therefore generally expect to see a strong entry from foreign Group C teams next year, following on from this season's start.

Below the DRM there are various other national series, beginning with Formula (single-seater) racing. There is both a national Formula 3 series and a national SuperVee-championship. The German F3 isn't as important as the British series, although the number of entries is even higher than in the Marlboro series.

As in Britain, Ralts are the cars to beat. This year's champion was Denmark's John Nielsen, in the Ralt RT3-VW, from Swiss Bruno Eichmann's Toyota-powered Ralt.

Austrian Walter Lechner won both the European and the national SuperVee championships. FSV, however, has seen its last year and VW will now concentrate on building F3 engines. In the last few years, the grids in SuperVee steadily became smaller. One should remember, however, that Keke Rosberg among others started his career in one of the VW-powered 1600cc cars and FSV was a great success in its day.

There is also a FF1600 championship and this was won by the promising Volker Weidler, who was also winner of the European series.

As for production cars, there are two national championships, one for hillclimb-racing (run in a division south and a division north, with one final race) and the other one for circuit racing. There are various classes and categories (divided according to capacity), and Germany also has a Renault 5 turbo Cup and a VW Golf Cup. Of these, the Renaults are more popular and the organisation is much better. There have been a lot of protests among the Golfs in the past and also the entries are weaker.

Finally there is the Rallye-Championship, won in superb style by Harald Demuth in his Audi Quattro, while Toyota runs a Starlet-Cup and Opel a Cup for Opel Kadett-cars, completing Germany's varied sporting scene.

AUSTRIA

AUSTRIA may well have Niki Lauda but motor racing isn't particularly popular in the country of Mozart. The national "Staatsmeisterschaft", for instance, has really confusing regulations with Formula 2, Formula SV and FF running together in the same race! The Renault 5 Cup is generally contested by very old examples of the breed, so the only series of relatively high quality seems to be the inevitable FF1600, which is always well supported.

The Rallye-Staatsmeister title seems to be heading the way of Gerhard Kalnay (Ascona 400) from the well-known Franz Wittmann in the Quattro, Kalnay leading with 87 points from Wittmann's 32 with three events still to come at the time of writing, although one has to mention that Wittman hasn't competed in the full series.

Probably the most popular kind of motor racing in Austria is Rallycross, mainly thanks to some strong results on the international scene by Franz Wurz, former European-champion and still one of the front runners in this year's European series in his Audi Quattro, disputing the 1982 title right to the end with Martin Schanche. Also in a similar four-wheel-drive car is Wurz's arch rival Walter Maier and the national championship is a contest between these two. Austria has a permanent rallycross circuit, the Leruring near Vienna, and it also has the two high speed road racing circuits of Zeltweg and Salzburg, the precarious financial position of the last named being at least partly a result of poor spectator attendances and a sad comment on the state of Austrian motor sport.

SWITZERLAND

AFTER the 1955 Le Mans disaster, motor racing on closed circuits was strictly forbidden by the Swiss government. That situation has changed not an inch up to now and there are no indications that the situation *will* change. So, the Swiss racers have to organize their races on circuits abroad, preferably, of course, not too far from the border. The circuits most used are Hockenheim and Dijon, although occasionally Zeltweg, Monza and even Misano host Swiss races. The championship consists of 11 rounds, held on circuits and hills on a 50-50 basis. To make preparation easier, all the road race rounds take place first, then the hillclimb 'season' starts. There is a Group N for normal road cars (in various capacity classes), then a class for Groups A and B — this year's champion in the latter category being Georg Eggenberger in a Group A Opel Kadett. Further there is a "Group C" class, run in fact with old Group 5 and 6 cars: the winner of that poorly supported class was Ruedi Caprez (Osella).

In single seaters, Formula 3 is well established and this year's Champ is European Series regular Jo Zeller in the Ex-Schindler Ralt RT3-Toyota. FF1600 has good entries and, towards the end of the year, the championship had still to be decided between the two drivers René Togg and Benoit Morand.

Sports 2000 cars have had their first year's competition in the alpine country; there were not more than 6 or seven starters in the first round, but now there are at least 10, and usually more, per race. Beat Blatter, former F3-driver, won the Sports 2000 class.

Switzerland also has three one-marque-cups — for Mazda 323GTs, Renault 5s, both turbo and normally aspirated, and a Golf GLS Cup (1.5-litre, 70hp cars).

Rallies are run mainly in the French speaking part of Switzerland, because the landscape there is better suited to the sport and this year the series was won by Jean-Pierre Balmer and Fabio Cavalli in an Opel Ascona 400.

ITALY

OF all countries in the world, Italy probably boasts the motor racing scene which bears most resemblance to that in Britain. The Italians have a comparable number of International status events to Britain's, although they are fortunate in hosting not one but two Grands Prix (including that of San Marino). They have also evolved a similar hierarchy of single-seater championships in order to assist their young drivers aspiring towards Formula 1.

In Italy, as in Britain, the premier national single-seater championship caters for Formula 3 cars. This series has in recent seasons become almost as prestigious as our own and is certainly no less closely fought. In 1982, veteran campaigner Enzo Coloni emerged as champion and it was interesting to note that he soon saw fit to switch from the trusty March-Alfa which he ran at the beginning of the season to one of the almost ubiquitous Ralt RT3s.

Past seasons have seen March, Martini and the locally-built Dallara cars proving fairly evenly matched, although this past season has seen a definite swing towards the Weybridge-built Ralts. Coloni apart, the equally experienced Guido Cappellotto led the series until mid-way through the year in his RT3, run by former F3 champion Luciano Pavesi, while up-and-coming youngsters Pier-Luigi Martini, Ivan Capelli and Ruggero Melgrati all ran similar cars before the season's end. Happily though, the neat Dallara cars still proved very competitive on the tighter, twistier tracks, with Stefano Livio, Luigi Giannini and Fernando Cazzaniga all winning.

Moving down the scale, the Italians have their own parallel to Formula Ford, called Formula Fiat Abarth, and this has brought to prominence a whole string of talented drivers. This, together with a thriving karting scene that appears far more closely related to actual motor racing than is the case in England, ensures a good flow of young talent.

Current Formula 1 drivers Riccardo Patrese, Elio de Angelis, Michele Alboreto and Andrea de Cesaris all made their way through karting, Formula 3 and Formula 2, while some other drivers who seem to be going in the same direction, having displayed their talents in karting and/or Formula Fiat, include 1982 European F3 front-runner Emanuele Pirro (Formula Fiat champion in 1980), impressive new F2 runner Alessandro Nannini (1981 Formula Fiat champion) and F3 Anson driver Claudio Langes (fourth in the 1981 Formula Fiat series). There is no doubting that the Italian 'grooming' system works.

Italy also boasts a strong 'club' racing scene with a variety of championships catering for all sorts of cars. Two of the best known series are for Renault 5 cars, in which 1982 Arrows F1 driver Mauro Baldi began his career, and the new Alitalia-backed Alfasud championship, which has witnessed some very hairy races in several European countries, although it started, of course, in Italy.

THE major road and oval racing circuits — whose results are reported in the US daily press — represent only the tip of the iceberg in North American motorsports. So large, and diverse, is the sum of motorsports activity in America that its size has never been accurately gauged.

The first level below the major series consists of the support series staged by the major road racing and oval track sanctioning bodies, and below that stands a group of primarily oval track series. This third tier is somewhat loosely organized, but its members keep point records and book dates at different tracks. Some of these, such as the World of Outlaws, travel all over the continent, while most of them confine their activities to one region within the US.

But, in terms of sheer numbers, the vast majority of American racing machines are weekend specials that are campaigned at one of the drag strips, dirt, or paved oval short tracks that dot the countryside in every region of the nation. So numerous are these little racing plants that there is a fat volume, *The National Speedway Directory*, that simply lists the names, descriptions and locations of hundreds of them. And the authors admit that there are many tracks they haven't found yet.

This giant body of racers, many thousands in number, supports a healthy speed parts industry that caters to their needs. It's a market whose size and importance is just being comprehended in England. Said Cosworth's Jack Field, "If we could just sell $5.00 worth of equipment to each one of them we would double the size of our business".

Cosworth hasn't come close to that yet, but their share of the piston market has increased, and their BD series of engines is now finding its way into Midget racing.

Of course, for North American drivers with ambitions of running at Indianapolis or in Europe, midgets and sprint cars are no longer the suitable training ground. The young lions today are racing SuperVees.

Last year it was a young Unser, Al Jr, who won the Bosch SuperVee series, this year a young Andretti, Michael, winning in style with an Indy car lookalike Ralt RT5 (below). Also Ralt mounted, in an RT4, was Atlantic runner-up Norm Hunter (bottom).

SUPER VEES

Michael Andretti succeeded Al Unser Jr as champion in the Bosch sponsored SuperVee series, winning six of the 11 events. Young Andretti, fresh from a year of Formula Ford competition, drove an Arciero Ralt RT-5 that was painted to resemble his father's Wildcat Indy car, and even shared STP as a sponsor.

Ralts dominated the series almost totally, with the exception of Peter Moodie's Anson victory at Road America. Ed Pimm, another young Ford grad, but without a famous surname, found modest sponsorship from Jim Trueman's Red Roof Inn motel chain, finished second in the final point standings and won once. In fact no driver other than Andretti won more than one event. Jerrill Rice won the Detroit Grand Prix preliminary, while former drag racer Mike Miller took the oval event at Michigan International.

But the best find of the season was probably a youngster from Upstate New York, Davy Jones, who didn't turn 18, the minimum age for SCCA racing, until just before the Detroit race. A veteran of Ford racing in Canada, Jones pressed the leaders at Detroit in his ageing RT-5 until he spun. He was always a factor in the remaining races, although he didn't win until Laguna Seca, near the end of the season. Jones found time to do three British F3 races during breaks in the SuperVee season, and is headed for a full season there in '83.

NORTH AMERICAN FORMULA ATLANTIC

Whitney Ganz was the only driver to win more than one of the nine CASC sanctioned North American Formula Atlantic races, but he only finished third in the point standings. The title went to 35-year-old Dave McMillan, a New Zealander with long experience in North America.

McMillan, who skipped the first two events, won a race, but second place finisher Norm Hunter didn't. That probably cost him the championship because the rules only allow a competitor to count his best eight results, and Hunter had to discard some of his points. Other race winners included Geoff Brabham, who only entered the season opener at Long Beach, Rogelio Rodriguez, who only started twice, Tim CoConis, John David Briggs, Tommy Phillips, and Roberto Moreno, the Brazilian star who competed in just the last two races.

The Atlantic series has lost much of its lustre since the likes of Gilles Villeneuve, Keke Rosberg, Bobby Rahal and Bertil Roos were regular competitors, and the current participants seem dead set against the adoption of Formula Mondiale, to which the CASC is firmly committed. SuperVee has already eclipsed the Atlantic series as a stepping stone in North America (and in the price of admission to a driver's seat as well) and the future of Atlantic racing is cloudy.

BILSTEIN RABBITS

Think of them as Group 3/4th Golfs. The Bilstein Rabbits run on Goodyear NCT street tyres, and engine modifications beyond blue-printing are forbidden. Some alterations to the suspension, including the installation of Bilstein shocks, are required. The little sedans run on road courses and ovals as preliminary events to SCCA and CART pro events.

Gary Benson won the championship for the fourth time in the five seasons that it has been contested. Paul Hacker, who last year became the only man to snap Benson's winning string, finished third behind his brother Karl, while Wally Dallenbach Jr, son of the former Indy car star, finished fourth.

Not that the racing wasn't close. The biggest margin of victory in the nine race series was just over three seconds, and the average was just over a second. Benson won five races, while Karl Hacker won three. Paul Hacker won the remaining race.

SCCA CLUB RACING

While the SCCA's professional series grab the headlines the vast majority of the club's 3000 licensed drivers compete in regional and national amateur events. There is a staggering number of classes, over 20 in all, and the competition, which is run during the season in geographical divisions, climaxes with the Champion Spark Plug Road Racing Classic at Road Atlanta. Participation in club events has been hurt slightly by the economic recession, but is still healthy.

Flying Rabbit! The Bilstein Cup action isn't always as spectacular as this performance by Jim Clinkenbeard but the production based VWs almost always provide incredibly close racing right down to the flag, and low costs ensure plenty of entries. Star attraction in the prestigious Bathurst 1000 was Australian farmer (and former World Champion) Alan Jones (above right). His uncompetitive Mazda retired with gearbox failure but elsewhere, with a Porsche 935, he was virtually untouchable.

SHORT TRACK RACING

Many of the local oval tracks have found the going tougher. A newsletter that goes out to race promoters throughout the country has been filled with advice about how to cope with short fields. But these cars don't go out of date quickly, and as soon as the economy perks up their owners will wheel them out of their garages again.

One factor that may speed their return is the increasing adoption of "9:1" engine rules. That refers to a maximum permitted compression ratio. It's easily checked with a P&G meter, and without high compression the big V8s that dominate American short track racing don't make the last 10% of their potential horsepower — 10% which also means short engine life.

The big growth has been in regional and national touring circuits. The World of Outlaws runs over 50 dates per year for its winged open wheel sprint cars. They race only on dirt tracks, with a nucleus of a dozen full time racers, and at each event a score or more part timers who compete regionally. As usual the action has been dominated by the likes of Doug Wolfgang, Sammy Swindell and Steve Kinser.

Kinser's older cousin Sheldon, a long time Indy driver, captured USAC's sprint car title. That series has shrunk from its former national prominence to become a Midwestern regional attraction. Kevin Olson captured USAC's Midget series. On the West Coast the CRA in Southern California and the NARC near San Francisco are the sprint racing organizations. Brent Kaeding won the NARC title handily, while Dean Thompson and Bubby Jones battled for the CRA championship down to the wire.

Dave Kelly won the URC sprint title on the East Coast, where fans tend to prefer a heavier roofed open wheel car called a Modified. DIRT, which runs modified races on, appropriately enough, dirt tracks, crowned Jack Johnson as its champion, while NASCAR's Northeast paved modified title went once again to Richie Evans.

Fendered oval machinery, generically labled "Stock cars" or more properly, Late Model Sportsman, are increasing in popularity throughout the country. Pavement is the preferred surface everywhere but the South, where it shares popularity with dirt tracks.

In the Midwest the strongest organization is the ASA, whose champion in '82 was Mike Eddy. In the South, NASCAR dominates local short track racing, but there is an Alabama based touring pavement racing group called All Pro, which shares a rule book with ASA. Randy Couch is the All Pro champ, while Ronnie Sanders and Sam Ard were the NASCAR regional Late Model titlists. On the West Coast, Doug Williams won NASCAR's Winston West title.

THE old Tasman series of races, which traditionally attracted a number of top European drivers to Australia and New Zealand during the winter months for an "off season" championship, subsided during the 1970s. There were a number of reasons for this, although two of the most important were an unwillingness (or inability) of top Grand Prix drivers to take part and the ever-increasing costs of running the F1/F5000-type cars.

The collapse of this series led to something of a slump in the region's motor sport action as overseas publicity and interest fell to a negligible level, although there has been a considerable upsurge again in recent years as the new 'Formula Pacific' cars (the same as F Atlantic but re-named for geographic reasons!) have become established.

This rationalisation of regulations within the region as a whole and adoption of F Pacific cars as the premier single-seater category is now beginning to pay dividends as the reasonable cost levels and increased spectator interest led to a distinct strengthening of the national championships run in both Australia and New Zealand. This has also been aided by the re-acceptance of a serious January series of races in New Zealand and also the determination of the Australian GP organisers to attract several top-line GP drivers to their annual Calder Raceway date in November.

In 1981-82, for the first time, FISA lent their support to a Pacific Basin Championship for these cars, including two races apiece in Australia and New Zealand plus one each in Macau and Selangor.

The series attracted good support, not only from the 'local' countries but also from further afield. Young Brazilian Roberto Moreno set the standard in his Ralt RT4 — Ron Tauranac's cars have dominated in the region for the last couple of seasons — although he failed to score, due to a practice accident, in the most prestigious race of all, the Macau Grand Prix.

Each year, a fine entry is drawn to the tiny island near Hong Kong during early November in order to race round a magnificent 3.8-mile street circuit. Local businessman (and Formula 1 entrant) Teddy Yip ensures that the weekend is a great success.

There is another well-established single-seater championship in the Far East. In Japan, to be exact. Formula 2 cars compete in a 6-round All-Japan series, to which the organisers always import at least a couple of leading European contenders in order to keep the locals on their toes. However, the specialised local knowledge, particularly with regard to tyres, which play an important role in the races as Dunlop, Bridgestone and Yokohama fight for supremacy, usually results in a Japanese victory. That's good for morale!

Japan also has a Formula 3 series of its own, from which some talented drivers have been sent to Britain on a 'scholarship' deal, among them Satoru Nakajima, Toshio Suzuki and Shoruko Sasaki.

A flourishing 2-litre sports car category has also been run there for some years now and this led to the Mount Fuji circuit hosting Japan's first ever round of the WEC in October.

Sports and GT cars also contest a worthwhile championship in Australia, the series having gained tremendously in popularity and significance this season with the appearances of former World Champion Alan Jones. Not surprisingly, he proved totally untouchable in his Porsche Australia-entered 935.

One of the biggest races on the Australian calendar, however, is the Hardie 1000km Touring Car race held each October at the magnificent Mount Panorama track at Bathurst. This event always attracts a huge entry, pulling from the already strong national touring car series and also attracting strong overseas representation.

The touring car scene has proved popular with spectators and now has strength in depth. Together with the F Pacific cars, they form the backbone of motor sport in the Australasian region.

The 47th Australian Grand Prix, held at Calder circuit near Melbourne, attracted several Grand Prix drivers to compete with the regular runners in the Australian Gold Star Championship. Jacques Laffite (wearing a helmet borrowed from Alan Jones) had a stirring battle with local front runner Alfredo Costanzo (above) for some 30 laps of the 100 lap race. Laffite eventually finished second in his Ralt RT4, some 15 seconds behind his compatriot Alain Prost, also RT4 mounted. In fact, Costanzo was the only non-Ralt driver in the race and by taking his Tiga FA81 to fifth place, behind the two French Grand Prix drivers, last year's winner Roberto Moreno and New Zealander Dave McMillan, he clinched the Formula Pacific Australian Gold Star Championship. Pacific, Ralt dominated, provides some excellent racing and Costanzo (below, chasing the Ralts of John Smith and Richard Davison) had to work hard for his title.

FORMULA Atlantic has developed a strong following over the last couple of years and now provides the mainstay of South African motor racing. It has thus filled a void that appeared after the collapse through ever-increasing costs of the Formula 1 series in the mid-1970s and then the subsequent failure of a rather vague F2/Atlantic/Libre series that followed. The current Atlantic Championship, however, differs from the category in other parts of the world in that it utilises the 2.3-litre equivalent Mazda rotary engine. To begin with, this was used alongside the more commonplace Ford Cosworth BDA unit but, for the past couple of seasons, it has been used exclusively.

This change in the regulations has proved popular among competitors as the engines are readily available in South Africa, are easily tuned and relatively cheap to run. Trevor van Rooyen, one of the leading Atlantic competitors and a former Formula Ford champion in England, said earlier this year: "You can pick up an old engine in a scrap yard for a couple of hundred pounds at the most and then spend the same on it again and have a really competitive motor."

Not only are the engines cheap, but they are also very fast, the class lap record time at Kyalami being not far short of a back-of-the-grid Formula 1 time and, on most other circuits that the championship visits, times are already better than the old F1 records.

The adoption of the Mazda engine together with excellent support from Sigma, who have just finished their second year of sponsoring a 12-round series, has lent a new stability which is now beginning to pay dividends in terms of increased competitor support, and, as a result, more spectator interest.

The 1982 Sigma Championship was not decided until the final

In spite of being promoted to the forefront of the South African domestic racing scene by cash shortages in the once popular F1 championship, Formula Atlantic, South African style, has rapidly established a reputation for fast, close racing and good quality fields. There is also a degree of variety amongst the Mazda rotary powered racers with such interesting entries as Tony Martin's ex-works Maurer (above).

round at Kyalami, where van Rooyen, who had led the series since the very first round back in February, crashed on some oil dropped by a slower car and allowed Graham Duxbury, who British enthusiasts may remember competing in the British FF2000 championships a couple of years ago, to come through, win the race and also claim the championship crown by just four points.

Up until this year, old March cars have tended to dominate the races, but the art of 'ground-effects' was introduced this year by van Rooyen's Ralt RT4 and the ex-works Maurer chassis of former champion Tony Martin, leading to a 'revolution' of new Ralts appearing as well as Duxbury's new March 822.

Formula Ford 1600, which, of course, launched the meteoric career of South Africa's only World Champion, Jody Scheckter, and also, through the 'Driver to Europe' Sunshine Series, produced drivers of the calibre of Kenny Gray, Desiré Wilson and Mike White, is not quite so popular now as it was in the mid-70s, since when some of the lap records still stand, although the formula still provides some exciting racing for club competitors.

WINNING PARADOX

Even if nostalgia isn't what it used to be, historic racing seems never to have had it so good. MARK HUGHES, Editor of *Autosport*, London, reports on the continuing popularity of Britain's best known historic championship and the emergence of a successful and exciting new series.

IN a time of recession which seems to have hit all forms of motor racing except its Formula 1 pinnacle, the paradox of historic racing continues. Although the cars are valuable investment assets and expensive to run, the number of devotees of historic racing is on the increase, and the number of championships catering for them is proliferating. The nostalgia value also attracts spectators — classic meetings like Silverstone's St John Horsfall now draw bigger gates then ever — and promoters have cashed in on the benefits by staging more and more historic races.

For many years, Britain's premier category of historic racing has been the championship presently sponsored by Lloyds & Scottish (previously backed by JCB), and while this series has continued to be highly prestigious — competitor interest is so high that entries have to be by invitation only — there are new championships emer-

ging to claim some of the limelight. The best of these in 1982 was the Atlantic Computers Historic GT Championship, which jumped on a bandwagon created by the David Piper and Mike Knight inspired Super Sports series in the previous season. With spectacular sports cars built as recently as 1970 eligible for the Atlantic trail, spectators were able to see evocative cars far more immediate in their memories, and the championship's success in its first year suggests that their imaginations were captured.

Nowadays, historic racing offers both spectacle and variety, be it in the now oversubscribed Lloyds and Scottish series (above) or the excellent new Atlantic Computers Historic GT Championship, catering for spectacular big bangers like Ian Scott/Richard Berry's Lola T222, driven at the British Grand Prix by Gerry Marshall (right).

AN extra fixture brought the number of rounds up to six for 1982, and Mike Salmon won his class (sports cars, post-war to 1957) every time out with Viscount Downe's beautiful Aston Martin DBR1, to win the title with a 100 per cent record, just as Michael Bowler had done the previous year. The class was not the most competitive one, but, to be fair, Salmon drove superbly all season to add this accolade to his seventh place in the Pace Petroleum Nimrod Aston Martin at Le Mans. His nearest rivals — Chris Drake, John Pearson (Jaguar D Types) and Ken Rogers (Cooper-Jaguar) — were a long way behind in the points, but consistent in their finishing.

The other sports car class, for Lister-Jaguars and cars built between 1958 and 1960, has always been well-supported in the past, but this year there were fewer Listers about, and one of them, that of David Ham, sprung the major surprise of the series by beating 1981 Champion Bowler. Ham's 'knobblie' Lister (so-named because of its contrast with the smoother, Mike Costin-bodied version run by Bowler) won the class four times, while Bowler and Stephen Langton took one win apiece.

The most popular of the five classes, however, has always been the most recent single-seater category (for cars built between 1958 and 1960) from which the leading cars come. The withdrawal of JCB meant that their long-time ace, Willie Green (Champion in 1979 and 1980), had to seek another ride this year, but he found an equally competitive mount in Ken Moore's Cooper-Climax, with which he won two rounds. He led three of the other four races, and would have taken the class at the end of the year but for a spin at the third Brands Hatch round and defeat by Albert Obrist's Ferrari 246 Dino after a furious dice at the St John Horsfall meeting. Such was the

Mike Salmon kept a 100% winning record with Viscount Downe's beautiful Aston Martin DBR1 (top). Salmon's ex-works 1957 car was driven to victory in the Nürburgring 1000km in 1959, by Stirling Moss and Jack Fairman. Variety is the spice in the Lloyds and Scottish series, with cars such as Sid Hoole's Cooper-Climax and the very different Listers of David Ham and Stephen Langton (right), Ham's 'knobblie' version being a surprise class winner. Willie Green's Cooper might have had the edge on Bruce Halford's Lotus and John Harper's Connaught at the Brands Hatch start (below, right) but Halford won the class, in spite of Green's spectacular efforts (bottom). Fittingly, series sponsor John Foulston (far right) won the big class of the immensely successful Atlantic Computers series with his McLaren M8D.

rear-engined car's speed that championship organiser Bert Young has suggested that only front-engined cars will be eligible in 1983.

The deserved winner of the class, with five points more than Green, was former Grand Prix driver Bruce Halford, who drives the Lotus 16 which he raced in World Championship events more than 20 years ago. Bruce has always proved threatening with this car, but this year his previous problems with unreliability receded to give him three class victories, including a sensational overall win at the first round despite starting from the back of the grid. He missed the final race because of a gearbox problem, but finished second in his other two events, a fine record in such a competitive class. The other winner was Obrist, a rapidly improving driver who silenced his critics with a fine win in front of the Grand Prix crowd at Brands Hatch. Richard Attwood sadly made only one appearance, at the first round, in a BRM P25, but made an impact by finishing second.

A marvellous drive at the last Brands Hatch round, and two other class wins, gave John Harper a narrow advantage in the 1953-57 single-seater class over the Maserati 250Fs of Bobby Bell and the Hon Amschel Rothschild. Bell will be particularly remembered for his magnificent drive from the back of the grid to win the class at the Grand Prix meeting. A change for 1982 saw this class contain the indecently quick 2-litre ERAs (even though they were built, of course, before the war), the most exciting of which was the Hon Patrick Lindsay's 'Remus'. Unfortunately this car did only one race before its exuberant pilot damaged it . . .

The 1.5-litre ERAs stayed in the 1931-52 single-seater category, but Nick Mason's and Patrick Marsh's cars were squarely beaten by class winner Richard Pilkington's Talbot-Lago, Alan Cottam's Cooper-Bristol and Gerry Walton's Connaught.

The championship will continue for 1983, but under what name no-one knows. Lloyds & Scottish, a finance house, have merged with Bowmaker, and the new identity has yet to be decided. What does seem likely, however, is that the series will gain an international flavour with a couple of rounds in the United States, the first stage, perhaps, in a plan which will see championship rounds supporting several European Grands Prix. Such is the popularity of historic racing . . .

THIS was the growth area in 1982. Taking over from the Willhire Championship of years gone by, sponsorship from John Foulston's Atlantic Computer Leasing raised the status of this sports car category by several notches. Big bangers are definitely back.

This championship also had a class structure, but to add to the confusion of spectators the three classes defined at the beginning of the year became four at the second of the ten rounds! The three classes *were* for pre-1971 cars of under 5-litres, pre-1971 cars of under 2-litres, and pre-1969 cars. It turned out that there was so much interest in this last group that the under 2-litre cars were given their own division, and from here the Champion came.

Six class wins gave Richard Thwaites the title in the oldest surviving Chevron B6 (chassis number 03), while Richard Budge finished second in class to win the Bellini Models Championship for the 2-litre cars, an honour that was denied Thwaites because the rules did not allow him to be recognised as both class and overall champion. While these two were locked in combat all year, Ray Bellm, Bob Linwood (B8s) and Simon Hadfield (Lotus 47) made sure that this was the most competitive class.

The larger classes, meanwhile, provided the battles at the front. Thanks to wins in the two opening rounds, series sponsor Foulston led the pre-1971 class throughout the season with his former Can-Am McLaren M8D, which was the quickest car in the championship, thanks largely to the best possible engines from Chaparral (Jim Hall's concern which runs Johnny Rutherford in Indy Car racing) that are reputed to develop 575bhp. Ray Mallock also won three races in the Marsh Plant Lola T70 to finish second in the class despite doing only half a season, while Gerry Marshall's Noel Gibbs owned Lola T222, Ted Williams's March 707 and Mike Wheatley's BRM P154 proved to be worthy opposition.

The pre-1969 big bangers were led home by Foulston's McLaren M1C-mounted number two driver, John Brindley, in five of the ten races. Although he also had the benefit of Chaparral's powerful Chevrolet V8s, Brindley is such a good driver that the class ought to have been his anyway, nearest rivals Wheatley (in the Lola T70 which he ran until the final round) and Nigel Hulme (Lola T70 Spyder) achieving their second and third slots in the final placings through admirable consistency. Charles Agg, a man to watch in 1983, also took a class win at one round in his McLaren M1C.

The last class, for cars up to 2-litres built before 1969, went to Vin Malkie in the Plygrange backed Chevron B19, easily the best in the class until Rick Whyman's appearance at the end of the season in a similar B19 owned by Paul Howarth. Tony Charnell won a couple of rounds before being forced to withdraw after an engine blow-up at mid-season, while Nick Mason and Ian Giles were consistent points scoring opponents.

This first season under Atlantic's sponsorship was an unqualified success, although behind the scenes some of the competitors were not entirely happy with the way the series was run. Regardless of that, it should go from strength to strength in 1983 with the addition, it is rumoured as *Automobile Sport* went to press, of two new classes for prototypes and cars up to 1600cc.

A NOBLE EFFORT

Confounding many critics, Richard Noble overcame all obstacles to take Thrust 2 back to the USA and another attempt to bring the official Land Speed Record back to Britain. Before the team's efforts were again washed out, Noble came closer to his goal than many believed possible.

Richard Noble completes final checks, with the air starter line still attached, before a run at Black Rock (above). Black Rock was selected as an alternative site after Bonneville flooded in October, with enough water for Noble to take a dip, watched by designer John Ackroyd (left). Thrust 2, on tyreless aluminium wheels (below) achieved a best average of 590.866mph, compared with Gary Gabelich's kilometre record of 630.388mph. Noble believes that with favourable weather conditions and fewer engine problems the record is in reach in 1983.

The European Rallycross Championship provided spectacular entertainment for a growing number of enthusiasts throughout the year, with the title finally going, for the third time and after a three-year absence, to Austrian Franz Wurz in the works supported Audi Quattro (above). Part of the attraction of European rallycross is in the variety of often exotic machinery which contests the series; Joss Fassbender's immaculate Alpine A310, with Renault V6 power (above left), is typical of the unlikely cars to be found raising the dust and slinging the mud. In December, Brands Hatch hosted the first ever British Rallycross Grand Prix, attracting most of the top Europeans including Lars Nyström and Matti Alamaki (above) who fought out second and third places behind Wurz in the last heat before Wurz was excluded from the meeting for some over exuberant pushing and shoving. Martin Schanche, one of Wurz's principal rivals with his Zakspeed Escort, has his own flamboyant way of celebrating victory (left) as at Valkenswaard in Holland in August where he began a hat trick of wins.

GROUP C TAKES OFF

Unsullied by the political wranglings of the real thing, motor racing in miniature continues to thrive as the bumper crop of quality models keeps on coming. This season, as JUSTIN DANIELS reports, tastes have shifted a little from Formula 1 to the attractions of Group C.

FOUR themes have dominated the thinking of manufacturers in the sporting model car field during 1982. Formula One, Le Mans past and present, rallying and the ever-growing historic racing scene not only in the UK but in the USA and mainland Europe.

The worldwide economic recession has also left its mark in that during this year it was no longer viable for manufacturers to make "marginal" interest subjects that only usually sell well during "boom" times. Thus we've had a plethora of Ferraris of all shapes and sizes during 1982 because Ferrari enthusiasts are so thick on the ground; so the modelmakers' thinking goes: that you can always make money if you release a Ferrari! Were any Prancing Horse enthusiast to have bought everything offered him this year he could well have had to give up eating or consider divorce in order to keep up with the demands made on his pocket!

Hi Fi's splendid 1/43 Renault RE30 turbo

Model manufacturers who create miniatures of F1 cars almost invariably lag about a year behind the full-size objects. Most new issues in 1982 have therefore been of the leading 1981 cars. But another factor has come into play this year and that is the general apathy among the model buying public for F1 models. It appears from talking to some of the formerly avid supporters that they are jaundiced about the whole scene and beginning instead to follow Group C and sports-car developments in general.

Western Models, the leading UK makers of F1 miniatures, released two fine versions of the McLaren MP4, first as it appeared in America in '81 and then as it won the British Grand Prix. To satisfy all levels of fanaticism the company included with the model waterslide decals to represent the car as it raced in Britain — ie without "Marlboro" advertising, and with an extra set of decals for the ciggie sponsored car as it practised.

It's worth noting by the way that all F1 constructors insist that no models of their cars should be made without a licence being obtained, this licence giving the model maker access to the car and its plans in the interests of making accurate representations. There's a fee of course, about 50p per model. Western Models pay it and make accurate models, most continental manufacturers, if not all, do not pay, do not have access to the cars or plans and therefore have to rely on their own researches. The result is that most mainland European F1 modelmakers make silly mistakes which are aggravating to say the least, but, as they often make cars that Western do not, the avid collector has little alternative but to buy the "pirate" productions.

Tenariv in France is one such "pirate" who makes acceptable

replicas and few errors. One of his best this year was the Talbot Ligier JS17, their "Ragno" Arrows A3 left a little to be desired in the decal area and their '81 World Championship winner — the Brabham BT49C from Las Vegas in '81 was very good indeed. The same company also put out a good Ferrari 126C but without too much detail, a fair Saudia Williams FW07C and a good Renault RE30.

Other good F1 models in 1/43 scale (the scale that we're generally covering because not much is happening in any other!) included a brilliantly conceived '82 Ferrari 126C from new Italian maker Hi-Fi who proved his skill was no fluke with an equally well-detailed and thought out '82 Renault Turbo. Fellow Italian Francisco de Stasio who manufactures under the name "FDS" came up with a tail-end of the grid filler with Tambay's old Theodore TY01 and a "superkit" of this year's Ferrari 126C Monaco car with lift-off body, full engine, chassis and cockpit detail and all for £11.75 in Britain which is generally considered a bargain price for that type of detail in this scale.

One highlight of many F1 fans' year was the discovery in Japan of a small quantity of the old Tamiya 1/12 scale Lotus 49 Gold Leaf Graham Hill winged car kits and of the earlier Lotus 49 of Jim Clark. Both were imported with photocopy instructions but snapped up eagerly by those who thought their only chance would have been to have found one of these "gold age" plastic kits at a premium — yes — that is beginning to happen with obsolete but desirable unbuilt kits both metal and plastic.

There were a couple of new 1/12 scale plastic F1 kits released during the year — Protar in Italy came up with a very complicated version of the Renault RE23, and Heller of France with a fairly good Ligier gave us quite a lot to think about because their instructions are not so easy to follow!

One welcome release in 1/43 scale F1 was from Meri in Italy who released four versions of the Lotus 49, enabling the cars of Hill, Siffert and Clark (2) to be made. Unfortunately, although the kits were technically accurate, several vital decals were omitted by the makers and we're now hoping that they'll print a supplementary sheet to put matters right. Nevertheless we've waited years for good small scale models of the various 49 types and at last someone has part filled the gap, now all we need is a good Repco Brabham and . . .

Two generations of Le Mans cars, Tron's 'Crockfords' Ferrari (below) and Classic Car Kits' 1968 and 1969 winning Gulf Ford GT40s.

Le Mans has always featured large in the modelling field and 1982 proved to be no exception. Even in January, Tron of Italy were releasing Ferrari BB512s liveried as "Crockfords" and "European University" and by October there had been no let up in the flow from many diverse makers. Highlights of the Le Mans and sports-racing year in modelling were provided by the superb Team Gulf Le Mans winning GT40s of 1968 and 1969 from Grand Prix Models, by Tenariv's fine Cobra Daytona of '65 and by the same company's Guy Edwards Lola T600 from LM '81 which, despite having decal errors, still built up into a fine replica of that startling vehicle.

Ford's C100 naturally came in for some attention with the "mule" '81 Brands Hatch car being made by Mini Racing of France and the '82 Monza car by Tenariv. As we write, Grand Prix Models are making the '82 Le Mans C100 with active help from Ford and enjoying co-operation and encouragement from Porsche and Rothmans with their urgent efforts to be first with a model of the 956 1982 winner. It should be available around Christmas time if all goes well.

The International rally scene was at one time one of the most neglected in modelling, but former "Triple C" Editor Brian Harvey got his Grand Prix Models company well involved with a fine series of Grp 4 Escorts, Chevettes, Saab Turbos, TR7 V8s and this year

Western Models' magnificent W125 is available as a kit or built.

The historic car scene in modelling has never been so fruitful as in 1982. Western Models released a beautiful Mercedes W125 GP in 1/24 and Casadio in Italy came up with what should have been a beautiful series in 1/20 based on the Auto Union C-Types. These Casadio models look good when built but are a nightmare to put together for few parts fit correctly and the castings are very poor for the high price asked. There's good news on the horizon, however, for Western are about to release a Ferrari 250GTO in 1/24 based on Nick Mason's example — the former Ecurie Francorchamps Le Mans and Tour de France car — so we'll have a gem to work on for Christmas.

On the small scale historic scene the activity has been hectic. Makers of ready-made die casts, Brumm have deluged us throughout the year with models like a Lancia Ferrari D50, 4½-litre Lago Talbot and Alfa Romeo 2900 Mille Miglia, all of good quality, low price and accurate. They've also perpetrated some monstrosities like their Boyle Special Maserati 8CTF which is about 9mm too long and looks like a mobile sausage. French makers Eligor came out with what is probably the finest small scale Bugatti T35 ever made and, on the kit scene, there have been at least half a dozen historic gems to choose from each month. If we had to pick one or two to

Grand Prix Models' metal Quattro kit, in RAC winning livery.

with a beautiful Audi Quattro, representing Mikkola's car as it won the RAC, plus Ford's prototype RS1700 Turbo — modelled even before it rallied. But GPM were not to have it all their own way. Continental eyes had noticed that rallying was "go" and several makers quickly jumped on the bandwagon. Record Models brought out a superb Opel Ascona 400 in "Rothmans" livery and a fine Monte Carlo Rally Ferrari 308GTB in "Pioneer" livery. From Italy came the Toyota Celica Acropolis 1980 car from Hi-Fi and from Record/Solido and Top 43 a whole raft of Renault 5 Turbos liveried for just about every event that one ran on. Best for our money was Bruno Saby's attractive RAC car — dubbed the "yumping frog" by marshalls on many stages as its too soft suspension tried to cope with the surfaces of Keilder and other nightmares (to a Frenchman anyway!).

Grand Prix were quick off the mark with the RS1700 turbo prototype.

Built-up metal Bugatti T35B from Eligor — one of the best ever.

suggest you look at, they'd include Grand Prix Models' superb "Essex Wire" Ford GT40 Le Mans, the same company's incredibly detailed Ferrari 512 "S" (another model based on a Nick Mason owned car), Scale Racing Cars' superb 1971 Ferrari 312P and Record's beautiful Porsche 904 GTS from Le Mans 1964.

We're indebted to Grand Prix Models (167 Watling Street, Radlett, Herts, UK) for their help in the compilation of this annual survey. For anyone interested in a further insight into this miniature world of automobile sport, Grand Prix Models publish a monthly magazine "Four Small Wheels" of which they will send sample copies to any yearbook reader (anywhere) for just £1. It contains an in depth survey of what's new each month and could well be worth a look. Until 1983 — good modelling.

More Motoring Titles

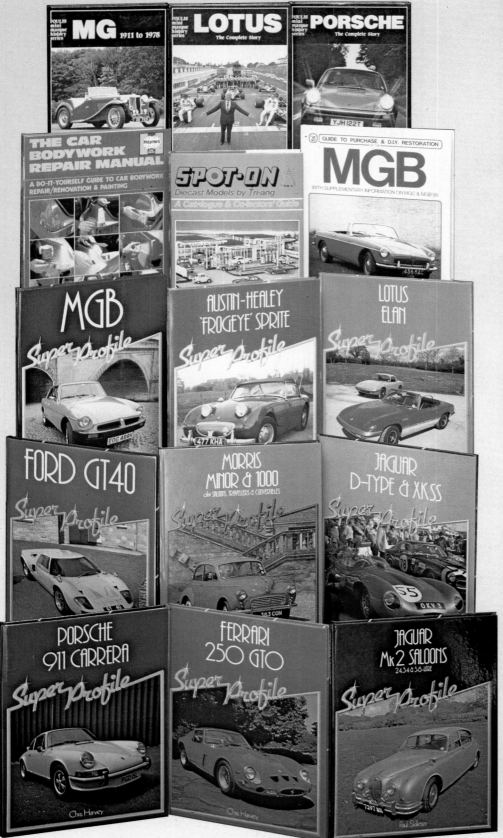

Super Profiles

Each title takes a single model of particular interest to enthusiasts and gives an incredibly detailed profile by means of sections on history, evolution, specification, contemporary road tests, owners views, buying, clubs, specialists and books. Then there is a photo gallery of the subject model showing its evolution from prototype to, where applicable, the end of its production. Of the ninety photographs in this section, twenty are in colour!

Titles available:
Ford GT40, Austin Healey "Frogeye" Sprite, Jaguar D Type and XKSS, Morris Minor, Lotus Elan, Porsche 911 Carrera, MGB, Jaguar MK2 Saloons, Ferrari 250 GTO.

£5.95 each (inc. p&p).

MGB. A Guide to Purchase and Restoration
by Lindsay Porter

This book gives the reader a basic history of the MGB, tells the prospective buyer how to find a good example and how to raise the cash. Next comes several sections dealing with the nuts and bolts of restoration, from the wheels upwards. 200 pages, 655 photographs and 25 line illustrations.

£9.95 (inc. p&p).

Spot-On Diecast Models by Tri-ang
by Graham Thompson

Since production ended in the mid-sixties, Spot-On models have been sought by collectors because they accurately mirror contemporary motoring of the fifties and sixties.

Graham Thompson's comprehensive work details, and pictures, every model produced by the Company and gives dates of manufacture, special features and colour schemes. 160 pages. Over 200 monochrome photographs/45 colour plates. **£7.95** (inc. p&p).

Foulis Mini Marques

A compact yet concise history and development of the particular model covered. Immensely readable and packed with black and white photos and illustrations including many of historical interest to the enthusiast.

Titles available to date include Ferrari, AC, Alfa Romeo, MG, Lotus, Rolls Royce, Jaguar and Porsche.

£6.95 (inc. p&p).

The Car Bodywork Repair Manual

This large, heavily illustrated volume really is a complete guide to practical do-it-yourself car bodywork repair/renovation and refinishing.

No matter whether the user wishes to touch in a scratch, remove a car park dent or fit a new wing this book will provide practical guidance which should enable the average owner to produce a professional finish. 234 pages, over 500 monochrome illustrations plus 16 pages of full colour. **£8.95** (inc. p&p).

Grand Prix Volumes One and Two
by Mike Lang

Formula 1 World Championship Motor Racing. Volume One covers the years from 1950 to 1965, Volume Two 1966 to 1973. Also in preparation Volume Three 1974 to 1980.

Average 240 pages, 239 illustrations and photos.

Volume One **£10.95** (inc. p&p).
Volume Two **£12.95** (inc. p&p).

Porsche 911
by Chris Harvey

This book offers a wealth of technical detail along with history, anecdotes, practical advice and compulsive armchair reading in the form of contemporary road testers' reports and comparisons with contemporary rivals. 215 pages, hundreds of photos, many in colour. **£18.95** (inc. p&p).

Rally Navigation
by Martin Holmes

This is a new revised edition of one of our most popular books. Packed with vital information for the rally navigator and of equal value to the experienced and novice competitor. **£8.95** (inc. p&p).

For Your Enjoyment.

INDEX

ACKNOWLEDGMENTS

The following photographers contributed to AUTOMOBILE SPORT 82 83:

Autosport
Ian Bamsey
Hugh Bishop
Jeff Bloxham
Cockpit Photo
Trevor B.Collins
Hal Crocker
Justin Daniels
DPPI
First Line International
Art Flores
Ford Motor Company
Geoffrey Goddard
Mike Harding
Martin Holmes
Jeff Hutchinson (IPA)
Indianapolis Motor Speedway
International Speedway Corporation
Charles B.Knight

Bill Mantovani
W.H.Murenbeeld
Lisa Newsome
Robert Newsome
John Overton
Steve Perry
Eric Sawyer
Jad Sherif (IPA)
Mike Slade
W.J.Staat
Brian Stenzel
Keith Sutton
Talbot-Gitanes
Thrust Cars Ltd
John Townsend
R.Whitby
Andrew Whyte
Colin Windell
Tim Wren

Helmet and circuit drawings by Marcel Ashby

A DECADE AGO

WORLD CHAMPION DRIVER 1972
Emmerson Fittipaldi
Lotus 72-Ford